Dare Me!

Dare Me!

The Life and Work of Gerald Glaskin

John Burbidge

MONASH University Publishing

Monash University Publishing
Building 4, Monash University
Clayton, Victoria 3800, Australia
www.publishing.monash.edu

Monash University Publishing brings to the world publications which advance the best traditions of humane and enlightened thought.

Monash University Publishing titles pass through a rigorous process of independent peer review.

www.publishing.monash.edu/books/dm-9781921867743.html

Series: Biography

Design: Les Thomas

Cover image: George Britnell

The author and publisher thank copyright holders for granting permission to reproduce illustrative material. Every effort has been made to trace the original source of copyright material contained in this book. The publisher would be pleased to hear from copyright holders to rectify any errors or omissions.

National Library of Australia Cataloguing-in-Publication entry:

Author:	Burbidge, John, author.
Title:	Dare me! : the life and work of Gerald Glaskin / John Burbidge
ISBN:	9781921867743 (pbk.)
Notes:	Includes bibliographical references and index.
Subjects:	Glaskin, G. M. (Gerald Marcus), 1923-2000.
	Authors, Australian--Biography
	Homosexuality and literature--Australia--History.
Dewey Number:	A823.3

Printed in Australia by Griffin Press an Accredited ISO AS/NZS 14001:2004 Environmental Management System printer.

The paper this book is printed on is certified against the Forest Stewardship Council ® Standards. Griffin Press holds FSC chain of custody certification SGS-COC-005088. FSC promotes environmentally responsible, socially beneficial and economically viable management of the world's forests.

For Leo

About the Author

Australian-born John Burbidge has lived and worked in Belgium, Canada, India and the United States. For many years, he was Communications Director for the Institute of Cultural Affairs, an international NGO engaged in community and organisational development, before becoming an independent writer/editor. His articles on a variety of subjects have appeared in magazines, newspapers, periodicals and books in several countries. He has edited volumes of civil society, rural development and a memoir. His autobiographical account of coming out as a gay man in India and an anthology of travel-inspired stories are in progress. *Dare Me!* is his first biography.

Contents

Preface

Some years ago, a friend told me about a book he had seen in a Seattle bookstore that he thought might interest me. It turned out to be an anthology of Australian gay and lesbian writing edited by Robert Dessaix. I bought it and set about devouring its contents. About two-thirds the way through the introduction I was stopped short by Dessaix's reference to the novel *No End to the Way* by Neville Jackson. What caught my attention was Dessaix's assertion that the book was 'in a real sense … the first Australian gay novel', coupled with qualifiers like 'astounding' and 'remarkable'. But what really hooked me was his allusion to the fact that the book was set in 1960s Perth, and the implication that its author presumably hailed from that city around that time as well.

I had grown up in 1960s Perth, was reasonably well read and acquainted with the work of a number of local writers, but I had never heard of either Neville Jackson or this ostensibly groundbreaking novel of his. Furthermore, as a gay man myself surely I would have caught a whiff of this Jackson and his writing. But this was not the case. How could that be? I was intrigued and perplexed. Who was this man who dared to write about such a verboten topic and set his story in the very time and place in which I grew up? What drove him to do this? What kind of person was he? What else had he written? How could I obtain a copy of the book and find out if Dessaix's enthusiastic endorsement of Jackson's work was merited?

Initial searches drew a blank. In desperation, I wrote to Dessaix and he kindly alerted me to where I could obtain a copy of the book. Eventually I did and although it did not have the ring of great literature, the book exuded an openness and honesty about the world of male-to-male relationships that I found refreshing and compelling. What is more, the fact that the story took place in Perth during the period when I was struggling to define myself sexually was terribly important to me. If it had been Adelaide, Brisbane or Hobart, not to mention the much larger metropolises of Melbourne or Sydney, it would not have had nearly the same impact on me as it did. Here was someone writing about the place I knew best in the world and about experiences and emotions with which I could readily identify. Novels by other Western Australian writers like Randolph Stow and Kenneth (Seaforth) Mackenzie had gone part way down this road but this one went much farther. Although I didn't know it at the time, I was not alone in being deeply affected by this book. Its liberating message and unusual writing style had left its imprint on many other young men in Australia and abroad, and continued to do so long after its initial publication.

Having read *No End to the Way* I was even more tantalised to discover who this Jackson was and what made him tick. Repeated attempts to track him down proved futile until I discovered that Neville Jackson was a pseudonym for Gerald Marcus Glaskin. I checked all the Glaskins in the Perth telephone directory and found one G. M. I suspected this was my man but I wouldn't know for sure until I contacted him. Since I was living about as far from Perth as one can, I decided to wait until my next visit there to arrange a meeting. What I wanted to achieve from such a meeting was ill defined, but I intuited it would reveal itself once we met. However, my next visit to Perth was preoccupied with family matters so I postponed making contact until I returned the following year. One Sunday morning I finally dialled Glaskin's number. Someone with a marked European accent answered. As I explained who I was and the purpose of my call, I was subjected to a series of questions that gave me the distinct impression I was being screened by a most determined private secretary. That wasn't far from the truth. The longer we talked, the more the trust level between us seemed to grow. The polite but emphatic voice on the other end of the line identified himself as Leo van de Pas, Glaskin's long-time partner. He regretted to inform me that Glaskin had died six months before.

My procrastination had caused me to miss the boat. If only I had called Glaskin on my previous trip to Perth we might have made contact. Then again, I would have been faced with a seriously ill 76-year-old man confined to hospital for the last several months of his life. I am not sure it would have been pleasant or fruitful for either of us to have met then. I would have encountered Glaskin probably at the lowest point in his colourful and turbulent life, although undoubtedly I would have grasped something of his unbounded spirit and aggressive response to any challenge. Instead, I took the next option that presented itself. Van de Pas invited me over for a chat about Glaskin, which I gratefully accepted. Six hours later I left van de Pas's flat, my head spinning with stories about this remarkable person. I didn't know what to do with it all. Clearly, there was more to this man than I had bargained for. Saturated yet inspired, I returned to the United States and pondered this Pandora's box I had opened.

My first inclination was to write an article or two about the man and his work, but this didn't seem adequate. Nothing less than a biography, I felt, would do him justice. But as soon as I resolved to write his biography I was besieged by questions. Many were of a practical nature, concerning the funding, research, writing and publication of such a book. As challenging as these were, they were overshadowed by one that drove me to take up the task in the first place and to pursue it against substantial odds: Why, in spite of having 20 books published in a variety of genres and subjects – some quite successfully – was Glaskin so ignored in his home country, state and city? What made Europeans buy his books, while his fellow Australians by and large passed them up? I tried to refrain from premature speculation about answers to this question. As I began scouring written records and contacting those who knew Glaskin, I expected answers would reveal themselves, or at least clues that might lead me to answers. Such clues often came in form of further questions. Was his lack of recognition in Australia due to his audacious and at times overbearing personality? Was it due to his un-apologetic embracing of his homosexuality? Was he a victim of Australia's legendary 'tall poppy syndrome'? Was it the fact that he was from distant Western Australia and not the power centres of Australia's eastern seaboard? Was he just a third-rate writer who had an early flash-in-the-pan success he could not sustain?

In seeking answers to these questions I discovered two things. First, I encountered a writer who was as bold in his choice of subject matter as he was experimental in writing style. He enjoyed playing with structure, voice and point of view, and blurring the lines between fiction and non-fiction. He worked in many genres and a variety of forms, and rarely followed up one book with a similar one, much to the chagrin of his agents and pub-lishers. Driven to push the boundaries of acceptability, as well as to test his own writing skills, Glaskin produced a substantial body of work, albeit one difficult to categorise and of variable literary quality. But however one assesses his writing, there is little doubt that Glaskin deserves recognition as an important, groundbreaking writer for his time and place.

I also discovered a person much grander than I ever imagined – more utterly charming and stunningly beautiful, more highly articulate and creatively gifted, more hilariously funny and naturally dramatic, more deeply sensitive and personally caring, and more bitterly angry and stoically tenacious. In the process, I learned about some of the values, attitudes and prejudices of the Australian literary and cultural establishment of his day and the wider society of which he was a part, which both nurtured him and, he felt, oppressed him, so that he fought against them at times as if his very life depended on it.

Foreword

How is it possible? How can it be that the Australian author of no fewer than 20 books, many critically acclaimed both at home here and overseas, with sales many Australian writers today could only envy; a man who not only rubbed shoulders with those in the literary limelight across the globe but counted some of them amongst his close friends and admirers, has now been almost totally forgotten? Even his widely read novel *No End to the Way*, a work that changed thousands of men's lives in many countries through its outspoken approach to the taboo subject of homosexuality, is almost unknown today. It is as if Gerald Glaskin lived out his tumultuous and prolific life as a writer on the far side of the moon. How can this have happened?

As John Burbidge explains in his illuminating biography, it is at least in part for reasons that a younger generation of Australians might find difficult to understand. Today Perth, where Glaskin was born and lived for much of his life, is the wealthy capital of a state riding high on the mining boom, a vibrant cultural as well as commercial hub. Wherever you are in the rest of the country or in Asia, you can be in Perth in a matter of just a few hours. Homosexuality is no longer illegal there and in most circles no longer a source of shame. Yet when Glaskin was growing up before the Second World War, and even for several decades after the war, to live in Perth meant to live on the far-flung fringes of the most isolated continent on earth. Western Australia was the quintessence of everything that cultivated, sensitive and especially homosexual Australians detested about their country and often fled. As Burbidge points out, as late as 1964 Xavier Herbert could call Perth 'a mean and ugly city', with 'colourless' streets and 'an air of poverty ... a place that has been made out of nothing – by a lot of people without much talent'. Although a handful of Western Australian writers, including Dorothy Hewett, Elizabeth Jolley, Randolph Stow and Herbert himself did gain recognition, it was all too easy to be overlooked by the rest of the country and the rest of the world. A gay writer who was audacious enough to write unapologetically about homosexuality was all the more likely to find himself passed over.

It is a mark of John Burbidge's talent as a biographer that he has succeeded not only in bringing Gerald Glaskin – the *enfant terrible* of Western Australian letters, the master of both charm and vitriol – brilliantly to life in all his pugnacious and provocative flamboyance, but also in bringing to life the society he lived in. As Burbidge has discovered through meticulous research, Glaskin himself was, in a sense, one of a kind, richly and combatively unlike anyone else in our literary history. Yet, paradoxically, he also emerges as the very distillation of what it has meant until quite recently to be an artist in Australian society, or perhaps an Australian of any sensitivity at all. Indeed, some might say that the frustrations Glaskin faced in his desire to live a civilised life in the country of his birth in the 1950s, the 1960s and even later in the century have not completely disappeared even today. Modern communications notwithstanding, the sense of living in exile from the true wellsprings of culture and civilised values somewhere 'over there' (usually in Europe or North America, but increasingly in Asia) still haunts many educated Australians; our writers and artists still hunger for acclaim from abroad; the public arena still has little space for creative endeavour compared to sport, war, fashion and what Glaskin called 'the cult of the moron'; while attitudes to Asia and Asians have changed markedly for the better since the late 20th century, the lives of Aboriginal Australians (in whom Glaskin was vitally interested) have not; and although people are less likely to talk unashamedly about 'bloody poofters' than they were in Glaskin's day, and gay Australians can now easily find safe zones to live, work and socialise in, precisely the same prejudices that made homosexuals' lives a misery in Glaskin's younger days are alive and taking their toll in cities and towns across Australia today.

The country of large families, chooks in the backyard, pianolas in the living room and days spent lying in the sun or sitting on the front verandah listening to the cricket on the radio may have vanished. But Burbidge leaves us wondering if, in its heart and (to use an old-fashioned word) in its soul, Australia has changed as much as we might have thought. In other words, although *Dare Me!* is the biography of a very singular man, it is also the portrait of a nation. It will, I am sure, lead many readers to reflect in fruitful ways on what it is about Australia that makes them feel, as Glaskin did, so deeply attached to it, yet at the same time strangely beached there, one eye perpetually on the lookout for sails billowing on the horizon, promising rescue or at least treasures from the wider world.

John Burbidge has written a biography that not only journeys into another's consciousness, revealing what has until now been hidden, but one that invites us to journey afresh into our own consciousness, unearthing and confronting what has been hidden there. It leaves us feeling bigger than when we began it. All good biographies should do this, but few do with quite the verve and lightness of spirit of *Dare Me!*

— *Robert Dessaix*

Acknowledgements

In researching Glaskin's life and work, I was continually amazed how receptive people were to my overtures, as well as most grateful for their contributions. Many who had never heard of Gerald Glaskin went to great lengths to answer my questions, verify a story or check facts. Those who did know him – family members, friends and acquaintances – generously shared their memories and opinions about the man and his work, and opened doors for me that otherwise would have remained closed. With apologies to any whom I have inadvertently omitted, I would like to thank the following persons for their contributions to this book:

Alfred Anangwe, Paul Barron, David Bell (National Archives of Australia), Tracey Bennett (*The West Australian* archives), David Bolt, Sally Bolt, Marion Boughton, (*The Sunday Times* archives) Vera Vaughan Bowden, Andrew Bowman (Carnamah Historical Society), David Buchanan, Val Buchanan (Department of Justice, WA), Ethel Webb Bundell, Allan Burbidge, Loris Carberry, John L. Carr (Public Records Office, UK), Yan Christensen (Graham Greene Birthplace Trust), Jan Clifford, Andrew Clinton, Alex Cohen, Leon Comber, Max Connor, Gail Cork (Literature Board, Australia Council), Kevin Cotter, Rob Cover, Jessica Christie (*The West Australian* archives), Jill Crommelin, Jo Darbyshire ("The Gay Museum" exhibition, Western Australian Museum), Donald Darroch, Frank Davey, Geoffrey Davis, Bob Dawson, Ila Dellar, Hope Dellon (St. Martin's Press), Bill de Meyrick, Wibbine de Ruig (ECI, the Netherlands), Myree Denny, Nevill Drury (Unity Press), Ray Duffy, Wilgha Edwards (Australian Defence Force Academy library), Ainslie Evans (Katanning Historical Society), Nicola Evans (Literature Board, Australia Council), Jeremy Fisher, James Glance, Audrey Glaskin, Llew Glaskin, Roland Glaskin,

Hens Gottmer, Diane Grljusich, Bill Grono, Han Suyin (aka Dr Elizabeth Comber), Hameedah Ibrahim (National Library Board, Singapore), David Harrop, Nicholas Hasluck, Hilary Heath, Elisabeth Hebdige, Carol Hetherington (AustLit), Kevin Hewison, Elaine Hill (Gower Publishing Limited), Tricia Hille (Cottesloe-Peppermint Grove-Mosman Park Library), David Hough, Steven Howell (J. S. Battye Library of West Australian History), Tom Hungerford, Peter Hurford, Victoria Hutchinson (Booktrust, UK), Wendy Jenkins, J. C. Johnson (Howard Gottlieb Archival Research Center, Boston University), Rae Kean, David Kelly, Ivan King, Charles Kissane, Menno Kohn (Internationaal Literatuur Bureau, the Netherlands), Trisha Kotai-Ewers (Fellowship of Australian Writers, WA), Alexey Kuzmin, Gabriel Ladikos (Gordon & Gotch Australia), Margot Lang, Paul Lee, Frederike Leffelaar (De Boekerij), Beverley Lewis, Andrew Liardet, Anne Loader (Léonie Press), Bryant & Tedye McDiven, Alistair McIntosh, Jane McKenzie (Rottnest Island Authority), Ian Manhire (Corgi/ Transworld Books), Murray Mason, Roger Mauldon, Patsy Millett, Rod Moran (*The West Australian*), Christine Nagel, Mason Nelson, Clive Newman (Fremantle Press), Colin Nicholas, Noridah Jamaluddin (National Archives of Singapore), Jason Oliphant (*The West Australian* archives), Ong Eng Chuan (National Library Board of Singapore), Thomas Otness (Kalamunda Public Library), Jacqueline Parkhurst, Maria Pasich (Hollywood Private Hospital), Jean Paton, Kevin Pearce, Helen Pecheniuk (National Library of Australia), Glen Phillips, Graeme Powell (National Library of Australia), Reece Plunkett (Gay and Lesbian Archives of Western Australia), Michael Redhill, Sebastian Ritscher (Mohrbooks AG), Alan Roberts (HMS – HMAS *Kanimbla* Association), Jean Rose (Random House Group Archive & Library), Jan Rutherford (Special Collections, Murdoch University, Perth), Vincent Ruthnaswamy, Donna Sadka, Rupert Schieder, Kevin Scully, Hanspeter Schlieper, Alan Seymour, Jodie Smith (Carnamah Historical Society), Carole Stabb (Perth Modern School archives), Kerry Stokes, Grant Stone (Special Collections, Murdoch University, Perth), J. H. Straczek (Naval History Directorate, Australian Department of Defence), Derek Strauss, Adrienne & Burt Streppel, Richard Summerrell (National Archives of Australia), Anne Summers (The Australian Society of Authors), Penny Sutherland, Ken Sutherland, Tang

Yungmei, Ian Templeman, Colin Thomas (Department of Veterans' Affairs), Peter Thomas, John Thompson (formerly The National Library of Australia), Riet van de Pas, Carolyn van Langenberg, Edgar Vos, Wim Vreedevoogd, Margot Warden, Sheila Watson, David Whiteford (J. S. Battye Library of West Australian History), Noel Whyte, Tim Winton, Catherine Worsley (Random House) and Carolyn Wynn (Mundaring Public Library).

I am deeply indebted to Graham Willett for his initial enthusiasm and ongoing support for this project, from research through to publication; to Tim Curnow, whose long experience as a literary agent and consultant was invaluable as I navigated the publication process; to Robert Dessaix, who alerted me to Glaskin's existence, read my manuscript, provided valuable feedback and agreed to write a foreword; and to Nathan Hollier at Monash University Publishing who decided to publish this biography when others had passed it up.

Above all, I owe much to Gerald Glaskin's partner of 32 years, Leo van de Pas, who convinced me that there was a story needing to be told and then had to put up with my endless questions, to which he gladly responded. Without his initial impetus, numerous referrals and willingness to allow me to pry into his relationship with Glaskin, this book would never have been written.

— *John Burbidge*

Credits and Permissions

I would like to acknowledge the following individuals and institutions for permission to use their resources:

- Sally Bolt, wife of and with power-of-attorney for David Bolt, Glaskin's long-time literary agent, for permission to quote from correspondence between Bolt and Glaskin.
- Fremantle Press (formerly Fremantle Arts Centre Press) for permission to quote from the autobiography of John K. Ewers, *Long Enough for a Joke* (1983).
- The Estate of Han Suyin, Ed Victor Literary Agency, London, UK, and the Howard Gottlieb Archival Research Center (HGARC) at Boston University, USA, for permission to quote from letters of Dr Han Suyin to Gerald Glaskin, housed in the HGARC collection, No. 1415.
- The Estate of Gerald Glaskin, Public Trustee, Department of the Attorney General, Government of Western Australia, for permission to quote from Glaskin's archives, unpublished manuscripts and other material.
- The Graham Greene Birthplace Trust for assistance in tracing a quote from Greene used at the beginning of Chapter 12 from Greene's *A Sort of Life* (1971).
- Ivan King, archivist and historian, Museum of Performing Arts, His Majesty's Theatre, Perth, for making available his interviews with Johan Knollema and Ray Mills; and to Johan and Ray for their permission to quote from this material.
- The Provost and Scholars of King's College, Cambridge and The Society of Authors as the E.M. Forster Estate for permission to quote from the Terminal Note of Forster's novel *Maurice* (1973).

- Trisha Kotai-Ewers for permission to quote from the autobiography of her father, John K. Ewers, *Long Enough for a Joke* (1983) and correspondence between Ewers and Glaskin.

- Leo van de Pas, Glaskin's life partner, for access to all material related to Glaskin in his possession, including photographs, correspondence and the Glaskin family genealogical collections he has created.

- Tim Winton and his publisher, Penguin Group (Australia), for permission to reprint the opening quotation in Chapter 1, My Beautiful Beach, from Winton's book, *Land's Edge* (2000).

I would also like to thank the following for the use of their photographs: Jo Darbyshire, Geoffrey Drake-Brockman, Rae Kean, Trisha Kotai-Ewers, Penny Sutherland, Leo van de Pas and Edgar Vos.

Chapter 1

My Beautiful Beach

*There is nowhere else I'd rather be, nothing else I would prefer
to be doing. I am at the beach looking west with the continent
behind me as the sun tracks down to the sea. I have my bearings.*

Tim Winton
Land's Edge

Flying into Perth over the Indian Ocean one of the first landmarks one notices is the line of Norfolk Island pines, tall and erect as if on sentry duty above Cottesloe Beach. For weary passengers confined for endless hours inside an aircraft, these stately trees are a welcome sign of an imminent end to their journey. But for those who live in this isolated urban outpost, these proud pines carry much more weight. With their widely spaced, parallel branches they symbolise things familiar in a vast and sometimes frightening world, containing within them all the joy and pain associated with the word 'home'. For Gerald Glaskin, Cottesloe's pine trees had a special significance. When he would return to Perth from his numerous trips abroad, the sight of them would evoke deep memories, some pleasant and some he would rather forget. They marked the place where he grew up as a young boy, where he returned to constantly as a writer seeking inspiration, where he had a devastating surfing accident, and where his life came full circle when his long-time companion scattered his ashes off the Cottosloe groyne. Other beaches would figure in Glaskin's life but Cottesloe was his first and very own beach, his 'beautiful beach'.

A short distance from his early childhood home in Palmerston Street, Mosman Park, Cottesloe Beach was a place of refuge and excitement for the young boy who grew up the eldest of seven children, the closest of whom was four years younger and the most distant 21 years younger. The long ribbon of bleached white sand, buttressed on one side by walls of eroding limestone and skirted on the other by a translucent sea, provided an idyllic playground for the young Glaskin, and especially for his ripe imagination. Much of the beach's fascination for him is captured in the character of 14-year-old Gavin in *A Minor Portrait*, Glaskin's second novel. In spite of his disclaimer that 'the book is *not*, in any way whatsoever, autobiographical' – a caveat he might wish to have claimed for later developments in the book but hardly for this aspect – it echoes the strong attachment to this place that Glaskin repeats in correspondence with friends and others throughout his life. In the first chapter of the book he writes:

> Whenever he stepped on to *his* beach, the old sense of proud possession surged within him. He kicked joyfully at the sand that was marked only by wind-waves. Looking backwards as he walked, there were only his own footprints on the virgin sand; it reminded him of the pleasant feeling he always experienced when writing his name in a new book. Dropping his case at the foot of the limestone cliffs, he walked to the water's edge. Yes, the basin was there again, deeper now that the white sand had been scooped out by the winter seas. But towards the end of summer it would fill up again; the water would be shallow, almost too shallow for him to dive from the ledge ... Those were always wonderful days, and the beach the most precious thing in his life; he was quite certain there was not another like it in all the miles of Western Australia's coastline.[1]

Given that his mother, Delia, was an avid swimmer, it is not surprising that the young Gerald might have developed similar proclivities. People would say of Delia, 'You swim like a fish.' 'No,' she would correct them. 'I swim like a seal, equally at home on water or land.' Glaskin followed suit, becoming a keen body surfer and an accomplished water skier, but he also cherished a love for the land that is apparent in several of his books, notably his travelogue, *The Land That Sleeps*, his novel *Flight to Landfall* and his children's novel, *A Waltz through the Hills*.

---

1   Gerald Marcus Glaskin (hereafter GMG) (1957, 7).

Most of the time he lived in Australia, Glaskin resided close to the ocean in Cottesloe and Mosman Park. At 44, in the midst of seven years of alternating between living in Australia and the Netherlands, he purchased a small strata-title unit in Warnham Road, which he affectionately referred to as 'my little box by the sea'. This compact apartment was one of his favourite places to write and to take in the view he treasured dearly. 'Here we live up with the gods with views of the Indian Ocean to Rottnest – and it costs nothing compared to Europe', he said.[2] Rottnest had a mystique for Glaskin, as it does for many Western Australians. References to 'the thin purple line of Rottnest Island' appear in several of Glaskin's novels. Only 20 kilometres from the port of Fremantle, it is visible from the mainland on clear days, standing alone as the last speck of land between Australia and Madagascar. First visited by the Dutch in 1696 and used as a prison for Aboriginals in the Swan River Colony, it has had a chequered history. Glaskin's great-great-grandfather, William Dockwary Jackson, was superintendent of Rottnest from 1867 to 1883. Known fondly as 'Changa' – 'a white man with a white heart' – he gained a reputation for his humane treatment of Aboriginal prisoners.[3]

During Jackson's time on Rottnest, the island was favoured by a visit from the noted British author Anthony Trollope. Trollope was received as a celebrity, with welcoming arches made of wattle trees, elaborate feasting and an Aboriginal corroboree. As Glaskin noted sadly, 'In those days, a writer meant something in Western Australia; not so today. If anything, no one is more disliked, nor treated with distrust and disdain, than a writer, ironically enough especially by his nearest next-of-kin, so to speak, the journalist.'[4] Australia's low regard for its writers is a theme to which Glaskin frequently returned. It became an obsession with him and led to his falling out with many individuals and organisations. Although his passion for the plight of the writer could be attributed to his own vanity and need for approval, that would hardly do him justice. Glaskin was a crusader for a number of causes and this was one with which he had much firsthand experience. He resented the assumption that to be a writer one must first succeed in another occupation in order to be able to afford the 'luxury' of writing, as he himself had to do. For him, stockbroking provided this necessary cushion, although after he had given up his lucrative job in Singapore he continued to apply for a plethora of other positions, from a Southeast Asian liaison officer with the

---

2   No author listed. *The Subiaco Post* (2001).
3   Smith (1953, 95).
4   GMG (1975, 141).

Western Australian Department of Industrial Development to a lecturer in English and creative writing.

Glaskin's never-ending battle to garner respect for writers and to enhance his own reputation went hand in hand with his love-hate relationship with Australia and with Western Australia and its capital, Perth, in particular. Triggered by the reception accorded Trollope in the mid-nineteenth century, he wrote, 'No creative artist can survive in indifference, let alone hostility, and regretfully enough I cannot see any change in this heinous attitude here where the cult of the moron not only prevails but is idolized. The more callous and uncaring, the more "masculine" is the Australian, poor brute.'[5] His lifelong correspondence with the Belgian/Chinese author Han Suyin is riddled with similar references. In 1960 he wrote to her, 'Life here is all decadence from bottom to top, merely to have the biggest TV set, refrigerator, transistor radio – no, smallest transistor radio. Commerce flourishes, culture fades. Writers do exist, readers do not. TV, golf and football.'[6] And again, 20 years later, 'I live on the moon … and on the wrong side of the moon at that.'[7] In *The Eaves of Night*, a memoir of his maternal grandmother, Alice Selina (Nan) Gugeri, he wrote like a tormented soul, 'Oh, the isolation of this exiled outpost of the world!'[8]

However distressed he was about the place of his birth, there were moments when Glaskin did acknowledge his attachment to it. The one thing that would make the pain of Perth's provincialism and isolation bearable was his beach and his favourite pastime, bodysurfing. Choosing a wave just before it curls to break and having it catapult you on an exhilarating ride to shore was a prize, even erotic, moment for Glaskin. 'It may be more spectacular to watch today's youth catching waves on their surfboards,' he said, 'but to me there is an intimacy with the water, almost like the caress of a lover, that can only be experienced with bodysurfing. It could be likened to flying like a bird rather than having to resort to a plane, be it only a glider.'[9]

Ironically, it was while bodysurfing that Glaskin suffered one of several near-death experiences. It was a sunny afternoon in late October 1967 and he and a woman friend had gone to an almost-deserted Cottesloe Beach to sample the surf. A strong northwesterly breeze was stirring up waves over two metres high. Glaskin had just taken one he estimated was nearly

5   Ibid.
6   GMG to Han Suyin (hereafter HS), 20 September 1960.
7   GMG to HS, 2 October 1980.
8   GMG (1975, 109).
9   GMG (1978b, 3).

three metres and was on his way in when his friend decided she would venture into the water. By the time he noticed her, barely half a metre of water was in front of the wave, making it impossible for him to dive under. At the last moment he swerved, managing to avoid a head-on collision, but in the process his left shoulder caught her right hip and he was thrown sideways under the water. Hitting the seabed was like diving onto a block of cement. Had he been only a metre or two to the right he would have hit solid rock. The turbulent water tossed and turned him before dumping him on the beach. Pain raged in his nose and neck. Blood poured from his nose. Although assured by a doctor that his nose was not broken, Glaskin had aggravated injuries he sustained to his neck in the Second World War while serving with the Royal Australian Air Force in Canada. Persistent headaches, increased pain and a tingling sensation in both arms resulted. These lasted for weeks, then months and eventually years. He was forced to wear a surgical collar for much of the remaining 33 years of his life.

Once it became clear that the repercussions of this injury would be with him for the rest of his life, depression set in. His ability to write withered and never really recovered, even though he eventually produced more manuscripts, most of which never saw publication and did not exude the quality and promise indicated by his early books. He felt, literally, washed up. In his unpublished memoir, *Never Again*, he wrote, 'I was beached, stranded and exiled at the wrong end of the earth.'[10]

This was not the first time the beach had proven Glaskin's undoing. On a warm December day in 1960, he had just dropped off his Russian translator Oksana Krugerskaya and her fellow Russian writer Alexei Surkov at their Perth hotel. To refresh himself and to escape 'the relentless press', he headed for a lonely stretch of beach known as the Sun Bowl a couple of kilometres south of the popular Scarborough Beach. A gusty wind made for a rough sea, causing him to be frequently dumped and his yellow racing bathers to become filled with sand. Since the beach was apparently deserted he took off his trunks to reveal a *fundushi* underneath. But according to a couple of police officers who were in the area at the time, Glaskin revealed more than just a Japanese G-string. They claimed he was walking naked along the beach in the presence of at least three other men and charged him with having 'wilfully and obscenely exposed his person'.[11]

Whatever the veracity of the charge, Glaskin was not about to let it go unchallenged. At his hearing in the Perth Police Court, mustering all the

---

10 Ibid., 5.
11 No author listed. *The Daily News* (1961a).

theatrical skills he could, he requested the suppression of the word 'person' from the records and more particularly from press reports, for fear that 'I would soon find a queue miles long from my house of people wanting to view this so generously sized "person", only to disappoint them'. In another reference to the size of his genitals, police witnesses reported being able to identify him as a naked male at a distance of 400 metres. Glaskin's instantaneous response was a smiling 'I'm flattered'.[12] Continuing his remarks on the male anatomy, and a part of it he alludes to a number of times in his writing, 'Buttocks might well be indecent to some but hardly obscene; moreover if two policemen should find them so, they shouldn't be in the police force'.[13] Ripples of laughter spread out across the courtroom. Reporters on the local crime beat hadn't had so much fun in a long time.

Fearful that his decorous courtroom was becoming a decadent cabaret, Magistrate Parker called for order. He made it clear he was not impressed with Glaskin's performance. In closing, he asked if the defendant had any other 'literary comments' to make, to which Glaskin couldn't resist in replying, 'I am now indeed guilty of contempt of court'.[14] Under the circumstances, he was lucky not be charged with that. Instead, the magistrate curtly dismissed Glaskin's *fundushi* claim and maintained that Glaskin had 'wilfully paraded himself, and that his behaviour in doing so was in itself an offence against modesty and decency'. Parker found him guilty, fined him four shillings and placed him on a £10 good behaviour bond for 12 months. Much to Glaskin's chagrin, the courtroom drama didn't escape the attention of the local press. It was reported in both the morning and evening papers.[15]

One columnist, Dan O'Sullivan, described Glaskin's case as 'another blow for Mother Grundyism in WA'. Pointing out that Glaskin could have been gaoled for 12 months, O'Sullivan stated that since Glaskin was prosecuted under Section 66 of the Police Act, his conviction put him in the category of being 'a rogue and vagabond'. He noted that there was no evidence that Glaskin was seen by anyone other than the two policemen who arrested him and no evidence that anyone was offended by his conduct. O'Sullivan stressed that what Glaskin did was 'lumped in with all sorts of sexual obscenity' and that there were other provisions in the law against public nudity with much milder connotations that the magistrate had ignored. Instead, the magistrate

---

12 Alan Seymour to John Burbidge (hereafter JB), personal communication, 24 May 2001.
13 GMG (1995a, 84).
14 Ibid., 85.
15 See *The Daily News*, 4 January 1961, 9 January 1961; *The West Australian*, 5 January 1961, 10 January 1961, 14 January 1961.

ruled that there did not need to be 'some overlay of perversion to substantiate the charge'.[16] O'Sullivan delivered his final blow in Glaskin's defence by posing the question: 'How small would be the percentage of men in this state who could say in truth that they had not enjoyed a nude swim or had never been naked or near-naked on a beach?'[17]

Writing years later in *A Many-Splendoured Woman: A Memoir of Han Suyin*, Glaskin was a little more philosophical about the whole affair. 'Unwittingly, and even internationally, I achieved far more publicity, if not of the right kind, from this one little incident than from all my books.'[18] *The Straits Times* in Singapore, Glaskin's home for 10 years, ran the story, causing a former Singapore colleague to send an anonymous cable with references to characters in Glaskin's Singapore-based novel, *A Lion in the Sun*: RE YOUR PERFORMANCE SCARBOROUGH BEACH CONSIDER YOURSELF SACKED STOP GRANT MACCAULEY LAUGHING STOP NO DUCKS IN OUR FIRM ... JOHN DRAKE.[19] Glaskin acknowledged that the episode caused him to lose some friends and acquaintances, though his family mainly laughed it off. But he also had his loyal supporters. Han Suyin, then Dr Elizabeth Comber, wrote, 'Saw the silly nonsense in the paper – it's absolutely ridiculous, dear Gerry. You know I'm all on your side. I think people have *putrid* minds, anyway as you know they are horrid little lice, nothing else ... Cheer up. I'm cheering for you ...'[20] Han's then husband and acquaintance of Glaskin, Leonard Comber, was equally supportive although more restrained in his comments:

> I was most sorry to see the unnecessary publicity that was given in *The Straits Times* last week to the 'Perth Affair'. My first reaction was 'Good! This will surely have the effect of making your books sell well', and then, secondly, I felt rather unhappy that some people like to make capital out of other people's misfortune. The newspaper report of the whole proceedings did not read smoothly and gave me the impression of having omissions.[21]

Among others who backed Glaskin in his humiliating showdown with the law was fellow Perth writer Tom Hungerford. Never an admirer of Glaskin's

16 No author listed. *The West Australian* (1961c, 14).
17 O'Sullivan (1961).
18 GMG (1995a, 85).
19 Ibid.
20 Ibid.
21 Ibid., 86.

writing – 'It was slipshod and often a lot of sly dirt'[22] – Hungerford represents those who found the police surveillance activities on this isolated stretch of beach and the magistrate's somewhat antiquated notions of prudery equally abhorrent. Some of Glaskin's friends believe he was being hounded by the police. This is not at all out of the question. Given his outspoken and sometimes aggressive nature and the fact that he was often in newspapers or on radio and television, Glaskin would easily have attracted attention in a city the size of Perth. In addition, his regular appearances at the beach and the isolated nature of the place would have lent themselves to intimidatory tactics. Indeed, Glaskin's version of his encounter with the police suggests this. He claims that Constable Doherty, calling himself Detective O'Dowd, exhibited 'almost fanatical belligerence' in demanding his name and telling him to 'get his things or he would knock his teeth in'.[23] According to Glaskin's domestic partner, Leo van de Pas, one of the two policemen tried to extort money from Glaskin in lieu of laying charges. Glaskin refused, so they took him to the police station where he tried a little interrogation of his own. 'Did you see me take off anything after I had dressed myself on the beach', he asked the two policemen. 'No', they replied, at which point Glaskin dropped his trousers and showed his G-string. Now it seemed it was the police who had been caught with their pants down.

But if the beach had been the cause of pain, suffering and humiliation in Glaskin's life, it had also played quite the opposite role. It provided him the space to think, brood and to stretch his imagination to its limits. Although he often admitted to having a lazy quality with which he credited most Australians, his regular beach walks were, in part at least, a chance to let the muse take charge. In an interview with a newspaper reporter, Glaskin described the way he used the beach as an integral part of his writing routine.

> I work for about three hours every morning and by noon I expect to have 2000 words written. After lunch I always go down to the beach unless I have something else I must do. The beach stretches for miles and it's an ideal place to think; there's no telephone to ring or people to get at me there. From the beach, I come home, edit what I wrote that morning and send it off to be typed. At night I sleep on what I've thought out while walking on the beach and next morning it's bursting to get out and on to paper.[24]

---

22 Tom Hungerford to JB, personal communication, 21 September 2001.
23 No author listed. *The West Australian* (1961b, 16).
24 Hetherington (1961a).

Contemporary Western Australian writer and fellow beach devotee Tim Winton expressed a similar sentiment with a different twist. 'On the west coast in summer the morning is for the beach and the afternoon is a time to find shelter. The western summer is ruled by wind. Here the wind is a despot ... The afternoons are the time to be inside on a bed with a book.'[25] Or, if you prefer, writing one. Reflecting on the role of the beach in Australian society, Winton quoted fellow Australian writer, Robert Drewe, who argued that 'almost every Australian rite of passage occurs on or near the beach. The beach is where we test and prove our physical prowess, where we discover sex, it is often the site of our adulterous assignations and where we go to face our grown-up failures. In the end, it is where we retire in the sun to await the unknown.'[26] Glaskin's varied beach experiences would seem to bear out Drewe's argument.

From the writing of his first novel, *A World of Our Own*, the beach provided the wellsprings for Glaskin's creativity. In January 1949, he took up the invitation of his grandmother, Nan Gugeri, and spent six months at her beach cottage at Safety Bay, 50 kilometres south of Perth. Grandmother and grandson, they shared a strong mutual affection, reflected in his later published transcripts of recorded conversations between them, *The Eaves of Night* (in *Two Women*). Her companionship was a welcome relief from his sustained periods of writing, interspersed as they were with breaks for swimming, sunbathing, sailing and crabbing, not to mention sexual exploration. According to his diary, the breaks often won out over the writing, although there were times when he would remain chaste to the task and produce an impressive amount of work – 'Settled down to work straight away and wrote till exhausted at 10 p.m., going consistently from about 2 p.m., completing Chapter Four.'[27]

Apart from those two staples of a Perth summer – 'the temperature at 97 degrees and the flies as prolific as sand grains on a beach'[28] – Glaskin had to contend with other irritations as well. Most difficult of all was the continual stream of family and friends who chose to take advantage of Nan's hospitality. In the midst of these disruptions he managed to churn out a book that told of the challenges faced by ex-servicemen and women returning from the war to civilian life in Australia. Its central character in a rotating cast of many, Alan Ross, wrestles with his relationship with the attractive young Dorothy Reeves, only to finally call off their engagement, ostensibly because of his impotency caused by a war injury. When a friend asks him if that is the

---

25 Winton (1993, 15–16).
26 Ibid., 21.
27 GMG (1949a, 28 January).
28 Ibid., 8 January.

reason he is going away, Ross replies, 'Partly. There are other reasons as well.' What these other reasons are we are left to surmise. Ross quits Australia and sails overseas, as Glaskin was to do within six months of writing this.

Glaskin's difference from other men was brought home to him by his growing awareness that he was sexually attracted to them, an awareness no doubt exacerbated by his wartime experiences in the navy and air force. The war provided abundant opportunities for men to explore their same-sex inclinations, not only because they lived in close proximity with one another in almost totally male environments, but also because they were removed from the restricting mores of their provincial upbringings. Returning to 1950s Perth must have been a difficult adjustment for Glaskin to make. And Safety Bay was not exactly urban Perth, if it could be called urban at all in those days. Given his stunning good looks, this 25-year-old Australian male with Swiss-Italian ancestry would have caught the eye of women and men alike. Glaskin's diary at this time contains several references to his sexual adventuring, although none is explicit about the gender of his partners. And when he does mention friends by name, he carefully avoids any overt reference to a sexual dalliance, although the inferences are lurking between the lines.

The question of matrimony kept stalking the eligible young Glaskin. Pressure to marry would have been immense, he being the eldest of seven children. But his nagging doubts would not go away. Like Ross, he never could quite bring himself to take the leap, although twice he seriously contemplated marriage. One of those occasions was while he was in Canada during the war. Stationed near Winnipeg, he was befriended by the Workman family whose daughter Norma became a close friend. She and Glaskin were engaged to be married, but as she wasn't inclined to leave Canada and he wasn't about to relocate there the engagement was called off. He was barely 21 years old, a long way from home, and still trying to sort out the confusing and competing urges he had had since his earliest sexual awakenings. As he confided to van de Pas, he fell in love with girls but in lust with boys.[29]

While grappling with his ambiguous sexuality, Glaskin threw himself into writing his first novel. It was a challenge that caused him to seriously question his writing ability. He soon discovered a gnawing gap between the quality of what he wrote and what he imagined he could write. His internal critic was fiercely at work, reflected in numerous diary entries, including 'The writing is both involved and immature – far from what I hoped it to be' and 'It is even more stilted in style and distressingly adjectival' or even

---

29 Leo van de Pas (hereafter LvdP) to JB, personal communication, 18 October 2000.

'when I read it through it so disgusted me, I burnt it.'[30] One day, he, like many a young writer, came to the shattering realisation that, 'Perhaps (and more likely) it is just lack of talent with which I thought I was bursting. Enthusiasm is evidently no proof of talent.'[31]

Despite these grave misgivings he produced a book within the six months he had allotted himself for the task. Indeed, he wrote a mammoth 420,000 words, later reduced to around 250,000 and finally to around 125,000. Its length was a major disincentive for publishers to accept the manuscript. After Angus and Robertson rejected it in Australia, Glaskin tried Constable then Heinemann in London with no success. Only when he contacted Humphrey Hare at James Barrie Publishers did Glaskin finally succeed in finding a publisher to take it on, but not without considerable effort. Introduced to Glaskin through Singapore connections, Hare was a literary advisor to James Barrie, the great-nephew and godson of the playwright J. M. Barrie, creator of Peter Pan. He initially rejected the manuscript outright, not only because of its length but also for structural reasons. Not surprisingly, Barrie took Hare's advice, but before making a final decision he sought another opinion – that of noted British writer C. P. Snow. Snow carefully evaluated the manuscript, pro and con, and despite harbouring misgivings about its imperfections, recommended that Barrie publish it but cut certain sections. In his report to Barrie, Snow wrote:

> It is one of the most interesting manuscripts that has come into my hands for a long time. The author ... shows most of the vices that a novelist can show; but he also shows many of the virtues, including the cardinal ones ... [they] come from a complete imaginative abandon to his people and scenes ... he is one of those writers who, without any effort at all, breathes, as the French neo-realists say, in the odour of man. He is very close to them, knows a good deal about them, both how they make love and also earn a living ... The city of Perth itself becomes remarkably sharp ... Like Moliac's Bordeaux, it happens to be a peculiarly evocative literary background ... I take Mr Glaskin seriously. It all depends on his temperament. If he has an ambition directed enough so that he is willing to learn, I fancy he might become an important novelist, and certainly the best spokesman of contemporary Australian society.[32]

---

30 GMG (1949a, 12 February, 13 January and 17 January).
31 Ibid., 3 February 1949.
32 C. P. Snow to James Barrie, 8 July 1954. Typed copy, Glaskin archives, Special Collections, Murdoch University.

A World of Our Own was published on 20 June 1955. When it went to press, Barries had more than 3000 subscriptions for it, which Hare described as 'very remarkable' for a first novel sold at fifteen shillings. A second printing was ordered and by the end of September nearly 6000 copies had been sold, with fresh orders coming in every week. None of Hare's publisher friends could believe the figures.[33] James Barrie was glad he had asked for Snow's counsel and not let his reservations dictate his decision. Glaskin was ecstatic. Six years after those beach-bound days at Safety Bay grinding out chapter after chapter, he had been rewarded for his efforts.

Well, sort of. Not all reviewers were enamoured by Glaskin's literary skills. *The Times Literary Supplement* criticised him for writing 'carelessly and without restraint'. It noted that 'flashback impressionism needs discipline, and the author, overcome by the flow of a lurid imagination, surrenders too uncritically to it.' Despite these and other shortcomings it begrudgingly conceded that the book was 'none the less readable'.[34] Australian literary reviews did not offer much solace either. Writing in *Southerly,* the anonymous H.H. and J.L. declare that Glaskin 'has no natural gift, nor has he set himself to learn those arts of selection and compression which create the illusion of a three-dimenionsal world. His characters do not live or grow ...' They concluded that 'his talents do not lie in the direction of the novel' and suggested he try writing documentaries or radio serials instead.[35] Marjorie Barnard, in *Meanjin*, discerned what she deemed to be flaws of a first novelist – overwriting, too many characters, overplaying realism and a writing style that had a text book quality about it. However, she was a little more gracious in acknowledging that these were faults that time could cure.[36]

But if the literary establishment gave him the cold shoulder, the popular press, both in the UK and Australia, embraced him much more warmly. *The Glasgow Herald* called *A World of Our Own* 'exceptional with its quality of imaginative realism' and the *Liverpool Daily Post* said that it 'makes us wish for more from this promising writer'.[37] Sydney's *Sun Herald* called the book 'authentically and typically Australian'. It singled out his characters as being 'recognisable human beings' and praised Glaskin's ability for 'looking behind the mask of normality and ferreting out what really goes on.' Whereas others

---

33 Three editions (12,000 copies) of the English hardcover were printed. The book was translated into Dutch, French, German and Norwegian. The Dutch publisher alone printed 120,000 copies.

34 No author listed. *Times Literary Supplement* (1955, 345).

35 H.H. & J.L. (1956, 231).

36 Barnard (1957, 205–206).

37 Fiction editor. *The Countryman* (1956, 8).

rejected his technique of telling his story through the individual lives of six men, this reviewer found that it created the effect of seeing 'characters in the round, not just from a certain standpoint.'[38]

A similar sentiment was echoed by John K. Ewers, who reviewed the novel for Glaskin's home audience in *The West Australian*. 'For all its apparently loose construction, here is a novel with a very closely integrated plot. Each character has a direct bearing on the others and the elements of love, sex and tragedy are blended with all the sophistication of a mature writer.' Summing up his review, Ewers referred to *A World of Our Own* as 'a first novel of more than ordinary quality'. He emphasised that with his depth of understanding of human motives and knowledge of human behaviour Glaskin had produced a novel of character, 'a rather rare phenomenon in Australian writing'.[39] In a subsequent article that appeared in the same paper a fortnight later, Ewers described the process Glaskin went through to produce his first novel, calling it 'a story of enterprise, industry and persistence'.[40] Receiving such an affirmative nod from one whom Glaskin regarded as a mentor and adviser must have been most reassuring. It would have confirmed the validation he received four years before when he entered the manuscript in the Commonwealth Jubilee Literary Competition, in which it received the judges' commendation out of nearly 300 entries.

At 27, Gerald Glaskin had arrived. Nineteen more books would follow before his death in March 2000 – novels and short stories, travelogues and memoirs, plays and filmscripts, even a trilogy on parapsychology. They ranged widely in subject matter, style and quality. Mostly through his fiction, he dared to tackle subjects that raised uncomfortable questions about issues many then regarded as off limits, including homosexuality, youth suicide, incest, Australia's treatment of its indigenous people and its phobias about Asia. Several of his novels were acclaimed by critics and readers alike, especially in Europe, and a number were translated into other languages, including Danish, Dutch, French, German, Norwegian, Russian, Spanish and Swedish. Eighteen of his 20 books were published outside Australia and only one in his native Western Australia. Yet in spite of this impressive track record, few people have heard of Gerald Glaskin.

---

38 A.A. *The Sun Herald* (1955, 79).
39 Ewers (1955a, 28).
40 Ewers (1955b, 32).

Chapter 2

A Touch of Class

"Ah, Jo-Jo! We are kindred spirits, aren't we?"

Alice Selina Gugeri
The Eaves of Night

As a young boy, Gerald Glaskin grew up surrounded by relatives from both sides of his family – the Gugeris of his mother, Delia Mary, and the Glaskins of his father, Gilbert Henry. The first of seven children, he was blessed to know all four grandparents, as well as the five unmarried sisters of his maternal grandmother and the 'gaggle' of sisters, brothers, half-sisters and half-brothers of his maternal grandfather. There was no shortage of older relatives eager to dote on this frontrunner of the next generation and Glaskin was quick to learn how to attract their attention and secure their affections. From his earliest years this pretty little boy with blond wavy hair, dark penetrating eyes and a beguiling smile charmed his audience and impressed them with his sharp intellect and zest for life – skills he continued to use and perfect throughout his life. In later years he was much sought after in Perth to open art galleries and give talks to groups as diverse as an order of nuns and patients of the paraplegic annex of Royal Perth Hospital. Cousin and playwright David Buchanan remembered Glaskin's ability to captivate an audience. Recounting a dinner Glaskin was hosting at a Cottesloe restaurant for his nephew and artist Derek Glaskin, Buchanan remarked, 'He ordered fresh basil with clumps coming out of the vase – they never put enough in, he maintained – and entertained the whole table, as only he could. You felt extremely privileged being there because no one else could have handled the situation as well as he did. And it was so seemingly easy for him to do this. You just wonder what he would have done had he been an actor. Life was a stage for him.'[1]

Feeding the springs of his creativity were forebears whose roots go back to the early days of the Swan River Colony and much farther into obscure corners of England and the mountains on the Swiss-Italian border, close to the city of Como in the Swiss canton of Ticino. Glaskin was proud of the fact that he was a fourth-generation Australian on his father's side and a fifth-generation Australian on his mother's. Of the two families, the Gugeris appear to have been the more enterprising and more elitist. Peter Antonio Gugeri, Glaskin's great-great-great grandfather, had seven sons and four daughters. Six of the sons migrated to England, where three of them made their fortunes. The youngest, Andrea Gugeri, had a son, Peter Anthony, who decided to break ranks and go farther afield in search of his fortune. He left England in September 1870 and arrived in Melbourne three months later, from where he took a steamer to King George's Sound (now Albany) in Western Australia, and from there made his way to Perth.

By the time he died 60 years later, Peter Anthony Gugeri had left his mark on the fledgling colony. He was a founding member and later commodore of the Royal Perth Yacht Club, the second club of its kind in Australia; he was a vigneron with 120 acres under vines and a wine merchant whose product was so highly praised by visiting French sailors in 1875 that they ordered 1750 gallons of it; he designed the gothic-style Roman Catholic church in the town of Northam; he was president of the Horticultural Society, a Fellow of the Royal Colonial Institute, president of the Perth Catholic Young Men's Society and a member of the Perth Board of Education; he was a Perth City Councillor, a Justice of the Peace for 38 years, the Clerk of Courts at Guildford and Midland Junction, and became the oldest magistrate in Western Australia. The hills town of Mundaring once bore the name Gugeri's Siding; a Gugeri Road exists in the foothills locality of Herne Hill and a Gugeri Street in the Perth suburb of Claremont. Within a remarkably short time Peter Anthony Gugeri became part of the Western Australian establishment of his day. According to one source, it was Governor Weld who first invited Gugeri to the state for a holiday.[2] Not long after his arrival, at Government House ballroom he met and fell in love with the 16-year-old Catherine Jane Jackson, whom he married three years later on Rottnest

---

1   David Buchanan to JB, interview by author, 12 November 2002.
2   LvdP (1994, 37).

Island, where her father was Superintendent. When she died in 1899, Gugeri remarried a first cousin of his first wife, who bore him eight more children in addition to the eight he already had.

But this talented engineer, enterprising businessman and respected civic leader eventually fell prey to misfortune, for which he was partly responsible. In the early 1890s, the collapse of the Kimberley goldfields, in which he had invested heavily, forced Gugeri to part with his hills property. Then, while he was away in England on business, a combination of exceptional frosts and inaction on the part of his manager caused his entire vineyard to be destroyed. His granddaughter, Yvonne Kelly, described him as 'a most improvident man ... born with a silver spoon in his mouth ... He would borrow money and buy land and forget about it. And then they weren't able to make ends meet.'[3] At the same time, he was an easy take for people who wanted to borrow money, which only compounded his problems. Of the many tales he heard about his great-grandfather, Glaskin particularly enjoyed the one about his decision to sell a large tract of prime Perth riverside real estate for 'twenty guineas and tun of wine' to pay for the coming-out party of his eldest daughter, Maria Constance Josephine, Glaskin's great-aunt Minnie.[4] Glaskin only met his great-grandfather once but the occasion chiselled itself into his five-year-old memory so he could recall it in great detail more than 50 years later. It was a warm spring Sunday morning in 1929 and he was walking home from mass at St. Mary's Star-of-the-Sea church in Cottesloe with his mother and Aunt Minnie. When they reached number 19 Beach Street they ascended to the second storey and came out on the verandah facing north, where the shimmering waters of the Indian Ocean could be glimpsed between houses down a steeply descending street.

> It was here I was left with my great-grandfather. He was seated in a cane armchair with a rug over his legs. It seemed very strange to me that, being at home, he was wearing a hat – a dark trilby, I seem to remember, which somehow added to the aged dignity lent by his white moustache ... I still remember his vividly blue if watery and red-lidded eyes. I suppose I must have spoken to him, but I can't remember his having uttered a single word back to me. He did turn to look at me, but then almost immediately turned away again to gaze out over the verandah rail ... between the roofs of houses to the reaches of ocean north of Rottnest Island – the way ships must pass which might have

---

3 LvdP (1994, 44 and 46).
4 Ibid., 43 and Van Niekerk (1993).

carried him back for one last visit to his ancestral Switzerland. He didn't make such a visit; he died shortly afterwards, at eighty-five. But the small boy did … [5]

If Glaskin inherited any of Peter Anthony's personality traits, it wasn't the man's financial incompetence. Indeed, growing up in the Depression, going to work at 15 to help support his family, working as a stockbroker in Singapore and finally taking the leap to become a full-time writer all contributed to Glaskin's ability to handle money with considerable dexterity and foresight. It was more in the arena of societal connections that he resembled his impressive forebear. Given his relative obscurity as an author, Glaskin cultivated an amazing cross-section of friends and acquaintances during his lifetime, some of considerable stature in their different fields. In addition to numerous authors, both local and international, his contacts included Sir Charles Court, the long-time premier of Western Australia; Sir Paul Hasluck, the former Australian Governor-General; Nigel Thompson, the Archibald Prize-winning artist; Paul Rigby, the noted Australian and international cartoonist; and Kerry Stokes, the Australian business and media magnate, who possesses some of Glaskin's original manuscripts. Glaskin's ability to move effortlessly between the worlds of the arts, commerce and politics and to hold his own in each was something few could claim.

Twenty-five years before Peter Anthony Gugeri was born in London, Frederic Glaskin was born there also, in 1820. He was educated at the renowned Blue Coat School and served an apprenticeship as a goldsmith. His marriage to Louisa Litchfield soon produced three sons, the first still-born. More children followed later. In 1849, while his wife was recovering from childbirth and caring for two little boys, Frederic Glaskin boarded the schooner *Henrietta* bound for Western Australia. En route the ship's captain, knowing he was dying, entrusted the command of the ship to Glaskin and the first mate. They made it safely to Mauritius, where they secured the services of a new skipper to take them on to Fremantle. From this incident Glaskin gained a reputation for responsibility that stayed with him throughout his life. Upon arrival in the colony, Glaskin tramped 100 kilometres east to the town of York, where he worked for several years in a clerical capacity before returning to Perth and becoming a partner in a firm of goldsmiths and jewellers.

---

5   LvdP (1994, 48).

Meanwhile, following the death of her youngest son, Louisa decided to emigrate to Western Australia to join her husband. In April 1852 she and her remaining son joined 29 other passengers and 20 crew members on the 464-ton barque, *Eglinton*, on what became its final and ill-fated voyage. Among its cargo the ship was carrying £15,000 in gold sovereigns for the young colony's coffers. After the long eastward journey from the Cape of Good Hope, Captain Bennett sensed they were approaching landfall and, knowing the treacherous nature of the Western Australian coast, he posted extra lookouts. But in spite of this precaution, on the evening of 3 September, as everyone was celebrating the last night of their six-month voyage, the ship struck an offshore reef and damaged its rudder. Strong westerly winds drove the *Eglinton* over the outer reef onto another a couple of kilometres from shore, where it stuck fast. Bennett ordered the ship's guns to be fired to raise the alarm, but to no avail. Next morning he gave the order to abandon ship. An elderly woman died when a longboat overturned and the boatswain drowned while attempting to save the ship's chronometer he had flung overboard in a fit of drunken rage. An advance party began the 50-kilometre trek south to Fremantle to raise help, which was quickly forthcoming once details of the precious cargo were revealed. Louisa and her five-year-old son, along with 47 others, survived the ordeal, to join her husband and eventually bear him another nine children.

A curious connection exists between Frederic Glaskin and the first ancestor of Gerald Glaskin's mother's family to arrive in Australia, Thomas Jecks II. The 15-year-old Jecks reached the Swan River Colony in December 1829, only six months after it had been proclaimed. Eight years later, he married Elizabeth Jones and they became parents to thirteen children. Jecks is best remembered as the founder/owner of the Rose and Crown Inn (later Hotel) in Guildford,[6] which he established in 1841 and which still exists today as a national heritage site. Once the last stopping place for travellers heading into the unexplored hinterland, it became a popular accommodation spot for country visitors attending the annual Perth Royal Show. It boasted its own brewery, stables and a chapel, and was linked to the nearby Swan River by a tunnel used to receive goods for the hotel that were transported by barge up river from Fremantle. Three years before he died in 1856, Thomas Jecks appointed three trusted relatives and friends as executors of his will. One of those was Frederic Glaskin. Thus, 70 years before his parents' marriage in

---

6   Guildford is 13 kilometres northeast of Perth. Now part of the metropolitan area, it
     was originally the centre of the colony before Perth assumed that role.

1923, Glaskin's maternal and paternal ancestors were linked in this unusual way.

Although he was respected in Perth society as a goldsmith, auctioneer, newspaper reporter, town clerk and a trustee of Trinity Congregational Church, it was as a soap manufacturer that Frederic Glaskin made his mark. When it became clear that there was a drastic shortage of soap in the colony, Glaskin and his jeweller partner decided to manufacture it. Although their initial plant was primitive by the standards of the day, they procured more up-to-date equipment from England and carried on a successful business for many years. In 1866, a box of their soap won a bronze medal at the Melbourne Exhibition and another won a gold medal at the Paris Exposition of 1889. Frederic Glaskin's son, Henry Marcus Glaskin, continued in the soap trade and, indirectly, so did his grandson Gerald Marcus Glaskin. The young Glaskin's second job was with Soap Distributors in North Fremantle and later with their associate company, J. Kitchen and Sons, in Sydney.

However, Glaskin's memories of his paternal grandfather have nothing to do with soap, but rather shoes. Although he worked long hours as a telegraphist after giving up manufacturing soap, Henry Glaskin also put in endless hours in his backyard shed repairing shoes. It was a family joke that he had built the shed – that holy of holies of the Australian male – as far away as possible from the house to evade his wife's pestering voice. There he mended shoes, not just for his own family but for numerous friends and relatives as well. The young Gerald would ride his bicycle the short distance from his house to Grampa's, always to find him working intently, either at his bootlast or polishing shoes until they glittered, while blissfully ignoring Granma's repeated hollerings, 'Dad! Dad!' Henry Glaskin eventually became deaf so didn't need to feign deafness any more. As his grandfather grew older, Glaskin had one of his first exposures to the painful side of aging, something he would come to appreciate much more intensely in the suffering of his own final years.

> When he was over eighty, he gradually became blind. Even with a large magnifying glass, he could no longer see to read the newspaper – from page to page of it, advertisements and all – as he had done all through the years. Instead of poring over it at the dining-room table cleared after dinner ... he took to taking it out to the sunlight in the garden. But soon even this didn't help. So my aunt had to read it aloud to him ... until at almost ninety ... he died the comfortable death he had always hoped for. When I was told the news, I hoped to God he would be provided

with some celestial workshop and the shoes of the angels and saints to repair. Otherwise, for that tiny old grandpa of mine, it wouldn't have been heaven.[7]

Although his male paternal and maternal ancestors provided Glaskin with many a fond memory and in some cases a sense of pride, it was the women who left the greatest imprint on him. And three women in particular: his mother, Delia; her mother, Alice Selina Gugeri or 'Nan'; and Nan's sister, Glaskin's great Aunt Fan (Fanny Flora Jecks), who was also his godmother. In the introduction to his memoir of Nan, *The Eaves of Night*, Glaskin wrote, 'I have been taught by three women – my mother, my grandmother, my godmother – to love [life] to one's utmost ability.'[8] Each woman did this in her own special way and all were present in Glaskin's life from his earliest years. Nan, who eventually outlived both her daughter Delia and her sister Fan, vied for first place in his affections, along with his mother. Recalling the day he and his parents arrived at Nan's stately home, Stoneleigh, in the Perth suburb of Mosman Park from the wheatbelt town of Carnamah, Glaskin fondly mused, 'It proved a happy day; from then on, I had another woman to love as much as I did my mother; at times perhaps even more.'[9]

Nan was born at Almond Grove, a large, rambling house in Guildford with grounds sloping down to a boatshed and jetty on the banks of the meandering Swan River. The front garden was 'a splendour of flower-beds and shrubs while the back had almost every kind of fruit tree and vine and vegetable plots one could think of.'[10] The house boasted telephone Number One in Guildford, something treasured by Nan almost as much as the fact that theirs was 'a *private* home'. This sense of being the best, not in a scathing or snobbish way but more a kind of genteel classiness, is a trait Glaskin may well have inherited from his maternal grandmother. It is easy to imagine his love of fine artwork, smart clothes, exquisite food, proper speech and 'correctly' written prose being inspired by her delight in such things. In some ways Glaskin's classiness was almost old-fashioned, as some have noted.[11] However, in spite of her undisputed femininity, Alice Selina Gugeri was no dainty lady. Born seven months after her parents' wedding, she was the eldest of six daughters. At 14 she suddenly had responsibility thrust upon her when

7   LvdP (1994, 53).
8   GMG (1975, 73).
9   Ibid., 109.
10 Ibid., 85.
11 LvdP to JB, personal communication, 10 April 2001.

her mother died in a dentist's chair from an overdose of chloroform. Nan immediately took over raising her five younger sisters, one of whom was deaf-mute. When she later married Anthony Dennis Gugeri, she bore him six children, one of whom died as a baby from meningitis. She developed a reputation as a good horsewoman and could swing an axe as accurately as any man to cut through tough stands of banksia and jarrah, a task she performed into her eighties. Even in her latter years in a nursing home she would walk a couple of kilometres a day.

Glaskin's experience of his maternal grandmother began when he was four years old and lasted until her death at 91 in 1971. His affection for Nan percolates through much of his writing about her, and particularly in *The Eaves of Night*, which he compiled from interviews with her in her latter years. In one especially poignant disclosure, Glaskin reveals the intimacy the two shared, symbolised by the pet name she had for him, Jo-Jo.

> And I remembered, too, how I had always loved to put my hand … in the crook of her elbow when she wore short-sleeved dresses in summer, for her skin there was both incredibly soft and cool, yet warm at the same time; and she used to laugh when I told her so, and cup my head in her hand when I bowed to bestow a kiss in that sweetly secret cleft of flesh. And she would say, 'Ah, Jo-Jo! We are kindred spirits, aren't we!'[12]

Great Aunt Fan, Nan's younger sister, affected the young Glaskin in a quite different but equally significant way. She opened windows for him into the worlds of art and music, the effects of which stayed with him throughout his life. From his youngest days Glaskin was attracted to pianos. In their house in Carnamah he would watch in wonder as his mother played the pianola and wanted desperately to be able to make the keys move in the same mysterious way she was able to. It didn't take long for him to begin to do so. By the age of five, he maintained, he could play five-finger exercises on the piano and pick out a melody or two.[13] But it was a few years later during his school holidays when he was staying at The Rose and Crown, which his great-aunts Fan and Grace now managed, that he had the chance to let his imagination run free. Seated at their Cable-Nelson pianola he would pedal with all his might to produce Beethoven's *Moonlight Sonata*, then switch moods to 'April Showers' or 'Ain't That a Grand and Glorious

---

12 GMG (1975, 108).
13 GMG (1974a, 20).

Feeling'. Aunt Fan would comment about the pieces and, when she had the chance, display her own talent at the keyboard.

This early fascination with music, and the piano in particular, ran deep in Glaskin's psyche. He often professed that it was his great love, relegating writing to second place. He frequently went with friends to concert halls to listen to classical music, whether his beloved Concertgebouw in Amsterdam or the Concert Hall in Perth. His collection of classical music was prodigious and envied by many. He often said that were it not for the fact that he had both arms broken, he would have aspired to be a concert pianist, although he admitted doubts regarding his capacity to reach such heights. 'I wanted to be able to do all the scriatas and sonatas at the age of 16. At 17 I went into the navy and at 18 the navy busted both arms and that was that. And I never could have done it again. I don't think I would have been a very good concert pianist.'[14] He found his hands unable to manipulate the keyboard in ways demanded by classical music. However, he did develop an ability to play the piano, usually by ear. This came in handy on many occasions, not least during the war when his boogy-woogying skills on the keyboard were popular with his air force mates on many a cold Canadian evening. The closest Glaskin came to musical fame was writing a musical score for his popular children's novel, *A Waltz through the Hills*, but in spite of his best efforts and a bursary from the Western Australian Arts Council, the musical never made it onto the stage or screen. At 62, one morning in a moment of muse and mirth, he composed a small poem that juxtaposed his love of music and writing with this third great passion, nature. He called it 'Change of Heart'.

Pianoforte music once
Was all that seemed to matter;
Alas, I found myself condemned
To typing's endless chatter.

So rather than the growth of words
To squander precious hours,
I've come to put my books away
And watch de growth of flowers.[15]

---

14 Kotai-Ewers (1996). His left arm had been broken when he fell off a ladder as a small boy and due to poor surgery it had to be set several times, leaving one arm slightly shorter than the other. See note 43, Chapter Three, 'Gerald in Wonderland'.

15 GMG, 4 January 1985. Photo album, LvdP private collection. LvdP says this poem describes GMG's three great loves – music, writing and nature, in that order. LvdP to JB, personal communication, 2 April 2003.

One other sister of Nan and Fanny also figured prominently in Glaskin's life, and even after his death. Grace Winifred Jecks was the youngest of the six girls. Small and slim with white wavy hair in her latter years, Grace helped Fan run The Rose and Crown. Apparently it was an environment in which Grace thrived, if her reputation for her love of 'beer, cigarettes and men' can be believed. She worked throughout the huge building and its grounds like a man, and when the hotel was sold she continued tending the garden around the small cottage she and Fan had built in nearby Belmont. Upon Fan's death, Grace, who had never cooked, was left to fend for herself with only help from a meagre pension and a small inheritance from her sister May. Returning from one of his sojourns in Europe, Glaskin heard that Grace was in hospital, dying from pneumonia and malnutrition. He rushed to see her and discovered 'this tiny little bundle of an old woman'. When she finally made out who he was, she turned weeping and reaching towards him, seeking to be gathered like a child into his arms. 'Oh, Gerald, Gerald!' she cried over and over again. 'Look what I have come down to!' Glaskin assured her she would get better once she recovered from malnutrition but strongly encouraged her to sell her cottage and move into an aged person's home where she could be properly cared for.[16] That was the last Glaskin was to see of his great-aunt Grace. Before his next departure overseas, he tried to contact her and was told she had taken his advice and entered a nursing home but had issued firm instructions she did not want to see any family, including him. This pained Glaskin greatly. He sought assistance from the police to locate her but without success. He finally had to resign himself to the fact that if it was her wish to be left alone he should respect it, but it weighed him down with a heavy sense of sadness and guilt.

Grace's decision to distance herself from the family may have been made for a very particular and potentially explosive reason that was to remain secret for another 30 years. Although she never married, she did have children – two or perhaps three, according to Glaskin. Even when her sister Fan died and she was alone and 70 she still had her 'gentlemen callers'. Apparently, one of those was Gilbert Henry Glaskin, her nephew and the father of Gerald Glaskin and his six siblings. This startling revelation didn't come to light until August 2002, when the Melbourne-based daughter of one of Grace's illegitimate children contacted the Glaskins in Western Australia and announced that the father of her deceased father was Gilbert Henry

---

16 GMG (1975, 164–165).

Glaskin. Her father had been adopted at a very young age and, just before he died in 1992, he told his daughter how unhappy he was not having been able to find his natural parents or possible siblings. When Western Australian laws regarding access to adoption information changed, the daughter was able to see her father's birth certificate, on which the names of his mother and father were given as Grace Winifred Jecks and Gilbert Henry Glaskin. Although it would have been unusual for a young man to have sexual relations with his wife's aunt, it would not have been out of the question. At the time of the child's conception, Grace was 34 and Gilbert about 10 years younger. The child was born in September 1926, nearly three years after Gerald and about seven months before his brother Dixie was born. Gilbert and Delia were still living at Carnamah at the time, so the liaison must have occurred during one of Gilbert's rare visits to Perth, presumably over the Christmas holidays.

What prompted Gilbert to do this is open to speculation. There is nothing to suggest that he engaged in extramarital affairs as a matter of course. However, this was not the only pickle Gilbert found himself embroiled in around this time and it is possible that the two incidents are connected. In his job as secretary of the Carnamah/Coorow Road Board, questions began to be asked about financial discrepancies that led to a charge of embezzlement of £443 being laid at Gilbert's feet. He was dismissed without notice and a warrant issued for his arrest. In a desperate effort to stave off prosecution, Gilbert's mother offered to make restitution in full on the condition that the warrant be withdrawn. Gilbert's brother-in-law, Bevil Morris, made a trip to Carnamah on behalf of Mrs Glaskin Snr to plead her case. A special meeting of the Road Board heard out Morris – who had the £443 in his pocket – but after considerable discussion and on the advice of a local solicitor, voted against her proposal. They decided not to withdraw the warrant, but in the event of restitution being made would support any plea of leniency made on behalf of the defendant and would not press charges.[17] What would have led the young Gilbert to jeopardise his job by indulging in such illegal activities is puzzling, unless it was the sheer financial pressure of having to support a wife and two sons in Carnamah as well as a third child in Perth.[18] Every penny counted heavily, if his final claim to the Road Board for payment of £30/0/4 as salary due is anything to go by. In light of the

---

17 No author listed. *The Midlands Advertiser* (1927).
18 If this was a contributing reason for Gilbert's embezzlement, it was probably short-lived since the baby was quickly adopted by a family in Victoria.

above episode, the Board had little compunction in refusing his request and advising Gilbert of its resolution to dismiss him without notice.

Unlike some of his siblings, Gerald Glaskin, had he been alive in 2002, would not have been shocked to receive this news of his father's philandering because it seems he had known about it for some years. He once told his partner, Leo van de Pas, that his father had an illegitimate son by Grace but van de Pas took the disclosure with a grain of salt. Glaskin mentioned his father's liaison with Grace to his three sisters, but not, interestingly, to his brothers. Out of deference to their mother – who seemed oblivious to the whole affair – or out of sheer disbelief, the sisters never pursued the matter. But Glaskin's youngest sister, Hilary, who lived at home with her father until her marriage, sometimes overheard angry conversations between her father and her eldest brother. On one occasion, Glaskin accused his father outright of cheating on his mother and asserted that Gilbert would never have married Delia if she hadn't been expecting. 'Maybe that's where a lot of the spark between Gerry and Dad came from', said Hilary.[19]

While his maternal grandmother and great-aunts played important roles in Glaskin's life, it was his mother, Delia, who took the prize. The relationship between mother and son was unusually close, as evidenced in their correspondence in which he would affectionately address her as 'Old Duck' and she addressed him as 'My dear first-born' or sometimes, with more tongue in her cheek, 'My dear wretched first born'. The tone and content of their letters suggests an exchange between peers or intimate friends rather than a more traditional mother-son relationship. It was honest, humorous and caring. Delia seemed to go to some lengths not to favour any of her seven children and was well liked and respected by all of them, and many of their spouses as well. Audrey Glaskin, wife of Gerald's next younger brother, Dixie, recalled an incident that reminded her of Delia's pleasant nature. 'One day, she made a surprise visit and commented how nice the windows looked. I'm definitely not one for housework; I must have just been in the mood for cleaning! But she would never come up and say they were dirty or anything like that. She had a lovely way with her.'[20] Delia was the glue that held the family together. She organised family outings and picnics and often went on holidays with relatives, especially all-girl affairs with sisters and nieces. After her death, relationships among some family members began to fray, and rifts that had been hidden became more visible and deepened.

---

19 Hilary Heath to JB, interview by author, 29 November 2002.
20 Audrey Glaskin to JB, interview by author, 3 December 2002.

In spite of her efforts to care for all family members, Delia carved out a special place in her heart for Gerald, and he for her. In Glaskin's mind, the carving began at his conception. Delia confided in him that he was his parents' love child and her 21st birthday present to his father, being born on 16 December, just six months after their marriage and nine months after Gilbert's 21st birthday. She was quick to point out that his six other siblings were also conceived in love but 'with such expectancies expected from Roman Catholic mothers, even with a Protestant father.'[21] Glaskin resembled his mother in many ways. Reflecting on his mother's own childhood habit of wandering off alone he recalled, 'She had wanted to escape down the street from some house or another all her life. And I have inherited that urge from her ... She was like that ... till the day she died. And so am I.'[22] There were other similarities, too. Both were fond of the water and were strong swimmers; both enjoyed going to movies and plays; and both loved a good time. In a letter she wrote to him from Japan after Gilbert had been stationed there with the British Commonwealth Occupational Force she reported, 'I enjoyed a slap-up time at the Mess last night. I was the only lady at our table of 20 soldiers, sat next to my mate who, after many drinks bashes my ear and tells me he wishes I wasn't married ... and he loves my smile!'[23] Like her eldest son, she knew how to be thrifty and make do with little when she needed to, but she also enjoyed spending money on herself from time to time. In another letter from Japan she proudly announced that she had indulged in buying a second string of pearls, a tailored coat and the latest style folding umbrella – 'a 3000 [yen] touch but wait until Perth sees it!!' However, in a final and more sobering note, she wrote 'It's happy spending up here. Never happens at home.'[24]

Managing finances at home must have been a challenge with a family of seven children, particularly during the Depression and the Second World War. From the time he left school at 15, and especially once he moved to Singapore and began work as a stockbroker, Glaskin provided financial support and gifts for his family, although the extent of this support is contested by some of his siblings. Glaskin paints a picture of a family that struggled to make ends meet in their early years; yet they were not destitute. 'We always had chooks and veges in the backyard', recalled brother Llew.[25]

---

21 GMG (1998, 1).
22 GMG (1975, 126).
23 Delia Glaskin to GMG, 8 February 1949.
24 Delia Glaskin to GMG, 28 January 1949.
25 Llew Glaskin to JB, interview by author, 22 November 2002.

Glaskin often recounted the story of how shocked he was as a young boy to come across his father working on a road gang as he walked home from school one day with his mates. The boys were making fun of the men until suddenly Glaskin realised his own father was among them and he was filled with a deep sense of shame. He fictionalises this event in *A Minor Portrait*, where the protagonist, Gavin, has the same experience. It is possible that this incident precipitated his decision to leave school after completing his Junior Certificate in order to get a job to help support his family. Unlike Gavin's mother who did dressmaking from home and eventually became the financial backbone of the family, Delia didn't do this for a living once she was married, although she often made and mended clothes for her family, as many mothers of her time did.

However, Glaskin was generous in helping his family, and his mother in particular, a gesture his father did not always appreciate, given his assumed role as family provider. Once Delia had her heart set on an elaborate new bedroom suite but Gilbert couldn't afford to buy it. Glaskin promptly went out and purchased it, an action that resulted in a huge tiff. This financial inequity between father and son created a difficult situation and one that was exacerbated by the fact that Gilbert was laid off work for periods of time with bronchial asthma he contracted while working in army food storage freezers in Japan. But other problems of his own making added to his trials, not least his love of whisky and betting. When Delia first realised he had bought another bottle of whisky she would throw the same amount of money down the toilet to try to shame Gilbert into changing his ways, but when this didn't work she would buy herself a hat and say, 'At least one of us has something to show for the money!'[26] After returning to Perth from Japan, Gilbert secured a war service home, Fairholme, in Brockway Avenue, Graylands, but by the late 1950s he had trouble making payments on the house. By this time Gerald was earning substantial money as a stockbroker in Singapore, so he offered to pay off the mortgage on the condition that the title was transferred to his name and that his parents could live in the house rent-free for the rest of their lives.[27]

Unfortunately, Delia was only to live there another couple of years before her tragic death in March 1960 from uraemic poisoning of the kidneys. She had known for some years that she had a kidney problem. In a letter to Glaskin in 1949, she acknowledged 'fat around the kidney' but laughed

26 LvdP to JB, personal communication, 8 April 2001.
27 Gilbert Glaskin to GMG, 2 November 1966.

it off as something she had 'seen many times in the butcher's shop' and although she was on a diet, she expressed scepticism about whether it would make any difference.[28] Just the previous December it appeared that she was in good health because, writing to a friend, Glaskin remarked, 'both mother and dad are much better than I have known them to be for years. In fact, they have both made what one might call "miraculous" recoveries.'[29] But by early February things had taken a turn for the worse. Glaskin had been invited to Canberra for the farewell of the Governor-General, Sir William Slim. He was planning to stay six weeks but returned home early on the news that his father had suffered a severe heart attack and was hospitalised and his mother had had a relapse of her kidney condition. Her last remaining kidney had stopped functioning and she was haemorrhaging to death. Her doctors said they could give her a blood transfusion that might prolong her life for a month or so but her death was inevitable. Given his father's condition, the doctors deferred to Glaskin to make the decision. He ordered the transfusions and after a week brought her home again. He took her driving and swimming and the whole family did all they could to make her last days as happy as possible. But the month turned out to be only a fortnight. The final stages of uraemic poisoning set in and she had to go back to hospital. It was an agonising time for everyone but especially for Glaskin and his mother. Writing to a friend a short time later he divulged the full extent of the pain.

> Had they told me the kind of death she would suffer, I would never have had the transfusions done. I was with her for the last five days and nights, taking stuff to keep me awake, as she didn't want me to leave her. I have never seen anything so hideous as her last convulsions of uraemia but even the special nurses couldn't manage at times and I had to help turn her over, give injections, and feed her with sips of water every few minutes. Ironically, when she had finally lost consciousness, I left her for about a half an hour to go home to change my clothes and while I was away, she died.[30]

And to Han Suyin he wrote,

> I prayed for her to be released by death. She couldn't speak or even make any recognisable signs because of the terrible spasms and her eyes were

---

28   Delia Glaskin to GMG, 21 February 1949.
29   GMG to Hanspeter Schlieper, 16 December 1959.
30   GMG to Lyn Robinson, 28 April 1960.

open nearly all the time, always watching me. Sometimes they would suddenly fly open and then snap shut again. Seeing that I could think of only one thing. Man has perpetrated some fiendish deaths and tortures on his fellow man but none so devilish as those devised by God.[31]

A Maltese priest said the last rites and pronounced final absolution for Delia. At her request, her body was taken to the little Star-of-the-Sea Roman Catholic church not far from Cottesloe beach that both she and Glaskin loved so much. Here, the same priest said a requiem mass for her. The loss of his mother was almost unbearable but at the urging of friends Glaskin managed to resume writing *A Waltz through the Hills*. When that was complete, he joined his Chinese Malay friend Paul Lee and took off on a safari north to gather material for *The Land That Sleeps* and *Flight to Landfall*. With a car accident in February and his mother's death in March, 1960 had already proven to be a disastrous year for Glaskin but little did he know that before the year was out more strife would be in store for him. It truly was his *annus horribilis*.

If Glaskin idolised his mother, his adoration was reciprocated. Delia exhibited the pride a mother feels when her children accomplish something of significance. Writing to a friend in 1959 Glaskin stated, 'Mother can take all this publicity nonsense in her stride, much better than I can, for I've had quite a basinful of it since arriving back as "the first West Australian author to have had anything accepted for films" (that's how small the place is). Mother laps it all up.'[32] There seemed little wrong that her first-born could do. Even his sexual orientation she seemed to embrace in ways that Gilbert and Glaskin's brothers did not. However, the circumstances of its revelation were a shock for everyone, not least Delia who, according to Glaskin's brother Llew, was initially very upset at the news. It was news that would not have been easy for any mother to accept, especially in 1950s Perth, where the notion of having a gay family member was virtually unheard of. At the time, Glaskin occupied the front bedroom at Fairholme. One morning, Gilbert entered the room expecting to find Gerald there alone and instead found him in bed with one of his male friends. Gilbert exploded; Gerald retaliated and shortly afterwards moved out to a flat of his own on Stirling Highway. This was the same flat to which Gilbert was called to rescue his son from the attacks of one of Glaskin's lovers not long afterwards. Glaskin was so severely beaten that his father brought him home to recuperate.

---

31 GMG to HS, 21 March 1960.
32 GMG to Robinson, 5 September 1959.

Glaskin fictionalises the incident in *No End to the Way*, no doubt embellishing it to entrance the reader.[33] In the novel, a wild and drunken Cor pursues Ray down the street and brutalises him to the point where he has to be hospitalised. What is interesting are the comments of both Ray's parents when they visit him in hospital, comments that may well have reflected the attitudes of Delia and Gilbert to their son's predicament. His mother regards it as 'unfortunate in being kind to a foreigner ... only to be repaid with a bash over the head ... and dismisses all foreigners as a kind of subhuman species.' Ray's father on the other hand has a more sympathetic response. With a 'your-old-man-does-know-something-about-these things look on his face ... and with a sly pat on the knee', he says, 'Don't worry about it, son. You'll soon be rid of him when you leave for London. There's no fury like that of a woman *spurned* ...'[34] Glaskin told van de Pas that the last sentence was the exact one his father used to comfort him after his own attack. In what was probably a rare gesture of empathy on his father's part, it suggests that Gilbert may have experienced something similar himself.

Although this response by Ray's mother to her son's homosexuality seems lukewarm, it appears that Delia's response to Glaskin's sexual orientation was more sympathetic. When Glaskin's young sister Myree came home from school one day she found her brother in the backyard, sitting on a bench near the rotary clothesline and crying his heart out. He was deeply distressed and his mother was comforting him. Myree didn't know what had happened but from what she could infer it seemed to have to do with her brother's rejection by a male friend. Myree's younger sister, Hilary, also experienced their mother's unusually close bond with their elder brother. A few years before Glaskin died he sent Hilary a bundle of letters that he and Delia had written to each other, letters that left no doubt that she had come to terms with having a gay son, perhaps even delighted in it. While Hilary could not remember the precise contents of the correspondence, she never forgot their confidential and familiar tone. 'They were the most strange letters', said Hilary. 'I couldn't imagine my mother writing the things she did. I was so horrified that I threw them out.'[35]

One other episode of destruction of correspondence happened in Glaskin's life, more devastating than this, at least as far as Glaskin was concerned. Throughout his time abroad, Glaskin wrote thousands of letters to hundreds of people as a substitute for keeping a diary. One of his long-time

---

33 Jackson (1965, 221–230).
34 Ibid., 234.
35 Heath to JB, interview by author, 29 November 2002.

correspondents was his father's sister, Aunt Alma. A spinster schoolteacher, Alma Glaskin had been a great help to her nephew when he began writing. Being a faithful and fastidious adherent to 'the Queen's English', she edited much of Glaskin's work with zeal and precision. She was also well read and knowledgeable on a range of subjects, qualities that inspired Glaskin and which he seemed to absorb from her. According to him, he intended his aunt to keep the letters so he would have a record of his life and work that he and others could draw upon. Either he did not make his intention explicit or Alma became overwhelmed by the sheer quantity of letters, but his aunt finally disposed of them. Glaskin only discovered this when he wrote to her to ask about the possibility of having their correspondence placed in Western Australia's Battye Library. Alas, she had thrown them out less than a month before. Said Alma, 'I've got to the stage where I'm often discarding things with the idea that there will be so much less for somebody else to do when I shuffle off this planet for regions afar.'[36] Glaskin's response to her was restrained but seeping with despair and sadness. He castigated himself for not having made carbon copies of his letters – a practice he later followed religiously. To others, however, he revealed how angry he was over the whole affair, which he attributed to an entirely different cause.

At least two of Glaskin's novels were translated into Russian and sold in the then Soviet Union, although he never received payment for them.[37] However, he did have the gratification of seeing the books in stores when he visited Russia in 1966. While there, his Russian translator, Oksana Krugerskaya, asked about his family origins. He told her he thought the Glaskins could be traced back to England, the north of France, the Jordaan district in Amsterdam – a well-known Jewish quarter of the city – and before that Russia. Krugerskaya suspected this might be the case since the name Glaskin was quite common in and around Moscow. It was Jewish, she explained, and meant 'little eye', a name possibly attributed to them for the dubious distinction of being police spies.[38] Glaskin was fascinated by this. He dashed off a letter to Aunt Alma and even addressed her name on the envelope in Cyrillic script. Later, when he returned to Australia and discovered she had destroyed all his correspondence, he wondered if his enthusiasm over this discovery had triggered a reaction in her. She told him that she considered there was too much in the letters that might

---

36 Alma Glaskin to GMG, 30 August 1966.
37 *A Lion in the Sun* and *A Waltz through the Hills*.
38 In Russian 'Glazkov' means 'little eye' so Krugerskaya's comment appears to be inaccurate.

prove embarrassing or damaging to other family members. What she didn't tell him was that before doing away with the letters she had sought legal advice that confirmed that as the owner of the correspondence she could do whatever she liked with it. This suggests a more premeditated action on her part than she had intimated to Glaskin. When he learnt this, Glaskin was livid. He severed all contact with his beloved aunt, a response he repeated with a number of people throughout his life, especially in his latter years. Alma Glaskin took it very hard.

Glaskin's own relationship to his ancestry was as fickle at times as his Aunt Alma's was to hers. After the debacle with his aunt, he resolved never again to involve himself in anything to do with family where, he maintained, 'some standards or demands can be set far too high'.[39] Yet later on he delighted in the fact that his partner and genealogist, Leo van de Pas, offered to trace Glaskin's roots on both sides of his family and write personal biographies. Together they spent considerable time and energy on the project, which resulted in a self-published book, followed by a second some years later.[40] He was proud of his heritage as a Glaskin-Carter and a Gugeri-Jecks, but he preferred the latter over the former. Bemoaning the difficulty of Australians trying to pronounce Glaskin correctly and fed up with his father's ill temper, he considered changing his surname to his mother's family name of Gugeri, because he felt 'so much more akin to them than to anyone in my father's [family]'.[41] Then it occurred to him that Gerald Gugeri would have been just as much, if not more, a tongue twister than his current name. He also detested Gerald as 'foppish-sounding' and so opted for G. M. Glaskin, at least for his writing life.[42] As a young child Glaskin had the fair-haired looks of the Gugeris, but from his fifties onwards he looked much more like a Glaskin with what his brother Llew called 'those brown cow-like eyes'. As a young man his dark skin and noble appearance earned him the name of 'the Indian prince', a title he would have relished and perhaps flaunted for all its mystique and charm. This variable aspect of Glaskin's appearance underscored his mercurial and sometimes contradictory nature in both public and private life. It led him to be revered and hated, sought after and ignored.

---

39 GMG (1985a, 6).
40 LvdP (1994 and 2010).
41 GMG (1975, 157).
42 Ibid., 158.

Chapter 3

Gerald in Wonderland

Not only did these letters open up a whole new world to me ...
but also started me on the road to becoming an author.

Gerald Glaskin
One Way to Wonderland

Soon after his birth in December 1923, Glaskin's parents moved from their cramped West Perth flat to Carnamah, a small mid-west town 300 kilometres north of Perth, where his father had been appointed secretary of the Carnamah/Coorow Road Board.[1] 'Town' may be too grandiose a term to describe Carnamah at that time. A large amount of the present town was bush or bare ground. In the words of one local resident, 'There were no streets. Somehow by chance houses and buildings ended up in good enough places to make streets!'[2] Glaskin's first memories were formed in the few years he spent in this dusty rural community, where the overpowering smells of wheat-laden silos and shorn sheep competed for a place in his consciousness with the familiar hoot of freight trains passing through in the middle of the night. His family's compact, black weatherboard house stood at the end of an unsealed road that stretched endlessly to a vast, flat horizon and a mostly cloudless sky. From his favourite vantage point on the front verandah, the

---

1 The Road Board had only been formed in 1923 and included the towns of Three Springs, Carnamah, Winchester and Coorow, as well as the land between these towns and the coast. It was an enormous area, about three times the size of the present Carnamah Shire.
2 Andrew Bowman to JB, 12 December 2003.

young Glaskin could peer out onto the world that beckoned him to come and discover its mysteries. Beyond the fence of wooden palings and cyclone wire he could see a rambling stone building that he was later to learn was a hotel. At one end of the verandah was a cane lounge on which his mother rested; at the other was a cage with his very own companion, a pink-and-grey galah named Cocky-Dick.

Carnamah was where Glaskin first discovered the world could be a frightening and dangerous place. One particular event revealed this to him. There was no kindergarten or preschool in the town in those days and few children his age to play with. He once claimed that he didn't see any white children until he came back to Perth in 1927, and it may well have seemed like this, except for one incident he described that involved their nearest neighbours, the Sheridans. Mrs Sheridan had visited Delia to discuss the possibility of her two sons, just a little older than Glaskin, coming to play with him. All was agreed but the boys never appeared, so Glaskin decided to seek them out. Their house was about a kilometre from the Glaskin's, down a narrow dirt path and shrouded by a grove of gum trees. Between the two houses was a large wheat field. When the young visitor appeared on their doorstep Mrs Sheridan informed him it was lunchtime so the boys were not available to play and he should return home. Disappointed and dejected, Glaskin turned around and started to retrace his steps. Suddenly, to his right, he glimpsed what appeared to be a huge monster bearing down on him with alarming speed, churning up an angry cloud of dust in its wake. He ran screaming to the wire-netting fence at the back of their house, which was much higher than at the front.

His father came running from the house to see what was wrong. Had the boy seen his first dugite snake or racehorse goanna? The young Glaskin was petrified and tried feverishly to scale the fence that separated him from this evil creature rapidly gaining ground on him. In the nick of time, Gilbert came to the rescue. Calmly but firmly, he inserted his upturned hands with clenched fingers through the wire so his young son could use them as a ladder to climb up and over the fence. When he reached the top, his father hoisted him over to the safety of his own backyard. As the child's screaming was replaced by sobbing, Gilbert wiped the boy's eyes and said, 'There, there, son. It's only a tractor! It won't do you any harm.' This explanation didn't mean anything to the young boy at the time but in a quieter moment, Gilbert explained to his son what a tractor was. Glaskin assimilated this information with the wonder and scepticism of a small child and used it to advantage in his next encounter with a machine. 'In no time at all, I had overcome my fear of tractors and all species of automobiles by trying to drive them myself – with disastrous results to my parents' car when I was four-and-a-half.'[3]

Other lessons followed. The lid of his favourite player-piano came crashing down on his tiny fingers; in his eagerness to pry loose a sizable book from the shelf above him, it fell down on his head; and while standing on the kitchen table to pull down a biscuit tin, he brought with it an iron that had been heated on the wood stove. Still hot from use, the iron knocked him to the floor and hit his right thigh, where it seared the tender skin and left a permanent scar.[4] This incident was a precursor of other painful injuries that Glaskin's body would be subjected to throughout his life. Strangely, the scar would come in useful years later. Working to repair damage to his right arm sustained during a naval accident, doctors were able to graft the hairless skin of the scar tissue to the place just above the elbow where his arm had almost been torn off. But for now the young Glaskin was learning by trial and error. He soon discovered that such calamities happened without warning, and there was little he could do to prevent them. What he could do was choose how to respond to them. Rather than let his fear of the unknown and unexpected paralyse him, he decided to confront it head on. It was a choice that would characterise his response to many situations in life, in some cases to his detriment.

Carnamah was also where Glaskin first came to know that the world was made up of people very different from himself and his parents. Like many Australian country towns of its day, Carnamah's population included a number of Aboriginal people, mostly of mixed blood, who lived on the fringe of the town at 'the reserve'. But the young Glaskin didn't have to go looking for Aboriginal people; they came to him. One afternoon as he was playing in the backyard, he happened to look up and saw the strangest thing. Just on the other side of the six-foot wire fence were two figures, as tall as his mother and father but more straight up and down and with hardly anything covering their bodies. Their skin was a deep chocolate brown, something he had never seen before. Their tangled hair was even blacker than their skin and their eyes were sunk beneath prominent eyebrows, their black irises making a startling contrast with the white background. Glaskin didn't know what to make of them but unlike the monster tractor they didn't seem to be threatening. Nevertheless, it was a scary experience for the four-

---

3   GMG (1974a, 20).
4   Ibid. In this essay, Glaskin refers to the iron as electric, whereas in his autobiographical notes (1998), he says it was 'an iron made of iron heated on the wood stove'.

year-old. He dropped his toys and stared at his visitors. Two small boys, completely naked, stood alongside the grown-ups. His eyes scanned their skinny bodies with intense curiosity. Their hair was shorter than the adults' and lighter at the ends, although just as matted and dirty. Unlike his, their pee-pees were covered with skin at the end and thick strands of snot hung from their noses.

As the two boys stood there, they poked their upturned hands through holes of the wire netting and gestured with their cupped hands to their mouths. Glaskin soon got the message. He ran inside the house and found pieces of stale bread, which he offered to them. No sooner was each bread-laden hand outside the wire-netting than a larger black hand grabbed it and plucked the bread, leaving the boys to plead for more. Back to the kitchen he ran but there was no more bread. What should he do? He decided to break the rule and wake up his mother who was resting on the front verandah. 'What is it?' she asked sleepily. 'I ... I need more bread for the blackies', he stammered. She didn't understand what her son was saying so she heaved herself off the cane lounge and strode down the passage to the back door. She looked outside, banged the door shut, locked it, and then ran back to the front and did the same with that door. Grabbing her son's hand, she hurried him along to the storage room they always kept closed. Holding him close to her, Delia sat and waited until Gilbert came home from work. When he did, he went straight to the backyard to look for the intruders, but no one was there.

Glaskin had just had his first lesson in 1920s Australian race relations. It had left him with a sour taste in his mouth and many puzzling questions. Why didn't they wear clothes like he did? Why were they so hungry? Why didn't they talk to him and not just gesture? His mother's reaction to his efforts to help the 'blackies' was even harder to fathom than their sudden appearance and disappearance. After their initial visit, Glaskin would watch out for them but they never appeared again. He felt sad and confused. But this experience left its imprint on Glaskin. Throughout his life he demonstrated a concern and compassion for Aboriginal people beyond that shown by most white Australians of his day. They appeared in some of his short stories and several of his novels, usually as heroes or heroines who came to the rescue of their white counterparts.[5]

Carnamah may have been a sleepy little town in the mid-1920s, but for Glaskin it provided plenty of days filled with wonder and awe, questions

---

5   See Chapter 8, 'Writer in Search of a Cause'.

and puzzles, as well as fear and terror. It was as though life was bent on teaching him one lesson after another. One of these occurred on his third birthday, a day that began in grand style. He awoke to find a pillowcase filled with toys – a train with carriages, a car, a truck, a ball, and blocks with numbers and letters on them. But the prize that stole his heart was a tricycle, which he raced with all his might up and down the path leading from the house to the front gate. Last in this deluge of presents was something he didn't pay much attention to at first, another bird as a companion for Cocky-Dick. It was much smaller but prettier than Cocky-Dick, with green and blue and a yellow neck-stripe. He had become the owner of a beautiful ringneck parrot.

Before Christmas had even arrived, the parrot was to become Glaskin's first and possibly greatest horror. Despite its being so much smaller, it attacked poor Cocky-Dick mercilessly. The galah's shrill and desperate shrieks could be heard all over the house. The first time it happened, Glaskin ran to the cage on the verandah to see what was the matter. What a sight confronted him! Both Cocky-Dick's feet were bleeding on the top of his claws. The parrot chased the galah around and around the tiny cage until the floor was bloodied all over. Not one to equivocate in such situations, Glaskin decided to teach the aggressor a lesson and save his poor Cocky-Dick from further pain and suffering. Taking a piece of dowelling, he poked it between the rungs of the cage to try to separate the two birds. When the parrot persisted he gave it a poke. When that didn't do the trick, Glaskin kept poking until the bird fell to the bottom of the cage and lay motionless.

As soon as Gilbert and Delia realised that the screams they were hearing were no longer Cocky-Dick's but their young son's, they rushed to the verandah and were aghast at what they saw. Keeping his emotions under control, Gilbert explained to Glaskin that he had just killed the bird and the seriousness of his actions. His father stressed that he should never do such a thing again. If something was troubling him, he should come to seek their help before leaping in and taking actions he might regret and whose consequences he could not foresee. This point Glaskin would have found hard to grasp, not only then but throughout his life, as he demonstrated time and again when he found himself in similar predicaments. Often enraged over what appeared a gross violation or injustice to himself or others, he would jump in and go on the offensive, with little concern for the possible effects of his actions. His words and deeds at such moments often ended relationships, some of long standing. He later wrote of this episode, 'The horror of it was to haunt me for the rest of my life.'[6] Just how emblematic it was of much of the rest of his life seemed to escape him.

Glaskin's time at Carnamah was short-lived. When his father's job with the Road Board was abruptly terminated, he took his young family back to Perth in search of much-needed work.[7] It was one of many moves Glaskin would make in his life, from house to house and country to country, but it was a highly memorable one. Gilbert and Delia loaded up their 1927 navy blue Chevrolet, with young Gerald pinioned amid cases, clothes and the squawking Cocky-Dick in its cage in the back seat. After the long and tiring journey to Perth, they were delighted to be welcomed into the open arms of Delia's mother, Nan, in her stately home, Stoneleigh, at 61 Palmerston Street, Mosman Park. The grand house was a refuge from the hardship of the outside world and a far cry from the tiny weatherboard structure they had known in Carnamah. Glaskin's description of Stoneleigh as 'a paradise for children' situated midway between ocean and river sounds idyllic …

> with its grounds of almost half an acre, its huge fir-tree hedge in which children could hide and almost become lost, its tall palm-trees and enormous Moreton Bay Fig tree, its almost as enormous Adam Fig tree, masses of grapevines, labyrinths of fowl-runs, flower gardens, vegetable gardens, orange and lemon trees, plantain banana trees and passion-fruit vines, lucerne trees with their white pea-like blossoms and tender green pea-like pods …

And of the house itself, Glaskin basked in its

> four beautiful big rooms, all with ceilings much more than twice a man's height, one a sitting room and the other three bedrooms, each with beautifully worked fireplaces … windows that opened up vertically on to that long, long and so wide front verandah which, enclosed with canvas blinds, provided masses of sleeping room for at least us three elder children and the occasional destitute uncle or visiting friend.[8]

Stoneleigh was not only a fine house but, as Glaskin referred to it, a true home. Its location was as significant as its style and ambiance. Palmerston Street was then in the locality of Cottesloe Beach (later Buckland Hill and later still Mosman Park), a young and growing middle-class suburb of Perth but not quite the scintillating diamond it is today with river-view homes that

---

6   GMG (1998, 4).
7   See Chapter 2, 'A Touch of Class'.
8   GMG (1975, 129–130).

comprise some of the wealthiest real estate in Australia. Nevertheless, that the Glaskins lived there after arriving 'penniless' from the bush must have inflated their self-image considerably. At the same time, it must have felt quite incongruous, both to them and to those aware of their circumstances. They stayed there nearly two years before moving to a rented house at 72 Mason Street, the main Perth-Fremantle road that was later renamed Stirling Highway. But as the Depression set in, even the pound-a-week rent they paid their landlord at Mason Street proved too demanding and they moved back to Stoneleigh for a second time.

Finally, in 1938 when Glaskin was 15, the family moved into its own home at 35 Johnston Street, Peppermint Grove. Although this was only around the corner from Stoneleigh and a very plain, simple dwelling compared to most other houses in the area, it had the magic address of Peppermint Grove. Likened to Melbourne's Toorak and Sydney's Vaucluse, Peppermint Grove was the crème de la crème of Perth addresses. Its 104-hectare shire is the smallest local government area in Australia, but also one of the most sought after with one of the highest per-capita incomes in the state. Begun in the gold-boom 1890s, its population is less than 1600 today. It has been the home of Perth mayors, state premiers and numerous high profile professional and business people. It boasts several private schools within its borders, as well as a number of historic homes. Clearly, 35 Johnston Street was not among them. At the time they moved there, Gilbert worked as a projectionist at Lew Hatfield's cinemas in the area. It was a full-time job that caused him to be away from home on evenings and weekends. Young Gerald obtained his first job assisting his father, changing film reels and cleaning up the picture theatres after the show, but neither father nor son earned a great deal. However, given the times, gainful employment of any kind was a blessing and not to be sneezed at.

To say that you lived in Peppermint Grove elevated you in the eyes of many, regardless of the rung of the socio-economic ladder on which you perched. But it also had other practical advantages. Located midway between Perth and Fremantle with a major highway and rail service connecting the two cities meant that the locality had easy access to the facilities of both, not least some of the best schools of the day in Western Australia. Glaskin had a fair sampling of these institutions. He attended six schools in nine years, beginning at age five at the Iona Presentation Convent down the end of Palmerston Street, the same school his mother had attended two decades earlier. It was here the young Glaskin had his first encounter with authority outside the home and he didn't take to it too kindly. He had just created a house of cards when, for reasons he fails to mention, Sister Patricia blew them down. Without hesitation he smacked her across her red cheeks. The principal, Mother Mathews, promptly caned the obstreperous child, who ran home to report the heinous crime inflicted upon him. Not long afterwards he was transferred to Christian Brothers College in Fremantle, where again he found the authoritarian style of the Catholic education system impossible to deal with. He was there only a week when one of the brothers whacked him across the legs with a stick. Instantly, Glaskin grabbed the stick, slapped the teacher across the face with it and walked out. From then on he attended state schools, at which he fared much better, but by this time his knee-jerk response to aggression was firmly implanted in his psyche. It was something he would fall back on time and again and served notice that he was no doormat to be walked over or milquetoast to be taken lightly. But it also may well have contributed to his lack of success in dealing with opposition of any kind throughout his life. Publishers, agents, neighbours, police officers, magistrates, librarians and others could attest to this.

By the time he was transferred to Cottesloe State School for his third and fourth standards Glaskin had begun to show signs that his academic prowess was as impressive as his temper. He found himself in an intensely competitive scholastic environment and was in his element. Casting her mind back to those early years, fellow classmate Ila Dellar had recalled, 'Weekly testing and assessments, together with the rearrangement of the student's place on the progress ladder meant that great (but friendly) rivalry was the norm, and most of us thrived on it. I have no trouble in identifying Gerry with that highly flexible list.'[9] In the latter part of 1933 Glaskin was moved to nearby Buckland Hill State School, where he emerged at the end of sixth standard as top boy. His natural intelligence began to be complemented by an array of interpersonal skills that contrasted boldly with his earlier retaliatory efforts in dealing with overbearing and impulsive teachers. In his final report, headmaster Harold Jeans commented, 'Gerald has shown himself to be a very willing and apt pupil. He took a keen interest in his work, which was always neatly and carefully done. In conduct, he was exemplary. I found him to be very well mannered and thoroughly trustworthy.'[10] Similar words of praise were lathered on Glaskin at his next school, Fremantle Boys, where he not only graduated as top boy once again, but also earned the unique distinction of being the only pupil in the entire Fremantle district to win a

---

9 Ila Dellar to JB, 28 April 2001.
10 GMG's report from Buckland Hill State School, 28 October 1936.

scholarship to the highly prized Perth Modern School (PMS). Writing a reference for him, his class teacher Jerry Dolan described Glaskin as 'a fine type of boy in every way, appearance, character, behaviour and ability'.[11]

Winning a scholarship to Perth Modern School was no mean achievement. In 1940 fewer than 50,000 children were enrolled in government schools in Western Australia and of these just over 400 or less than 1 per cent went on to secondary schools beyond the third year.[12] Only students of high academic ability attended PMS, many of those on a scholarship to cover fees, books and in some cases travel to and from home. PMS was a model school. With a battlement clock tower from which flew the school's blue flag with its gold sphinx emblem, and a great hall with a high-panelled ceiling, hammer-beam roof trusses and inset dormer windows, the building was formidable, if not intimidating. Opened in 1911, the school emphasised science, mathematics, modern languages and other subjects considered vital to the development of Western Australia. It was intended to provide educational benefits to gifted children whose parents could not afford the high fees charged by private schools. At first a fee of £6 per year was charged, but for children whose parents could not afford this, government scholarships were instituted. Fifty were allotted each year and in 1937–38 Glaskin was one of the privileged recipients. Although it was the first co-educational government high school in the state, PMS maintained a strict separation of the sexes in the assembly and play areas of the school grounds, as well as during classes in the first and second years. Mixing outside the classroom was not encouraged.

A tradition the school established early in its existence was its success in gaining exhibitions – scholarships awarded to students who gained the highest marks in the state in each subject in the final Leaving Examination. It often won more than half of the 10 awarded in open competition with fee-paying colleges. But with an annual intake of a hundred hand-picked students each year, it was perhaps inevitable that PMS would turn out men and women who, in the years to come, would make their marks in various walks of life, not only in the local community but throughout Australia and the world. Among these are former Australian Prime Minister Robert Hawke, former Governor-General Sir Paul Hasluck, feminist activist Irene Greenwood, entertainer Rolf Harris and, somewhat ironically, the Hon. Roy Vivian Nevile QC, Judge of the Supreme Court of Western Australia

---

11 Reference by Jerry Dolan and co-signed by C. C. Stewart, Head Teacher, 18 March 1937. Glaskin archives, Special Collections, Murdoch University.
12 John Curtin Prime Ministerial Library (2002).

and President of the Industrial and Arbitration Court. Nevile was one of two Western Australian justices whose names Glaskin is said to have used to create his pseudonym – with a slight change of spelling – Neville Jackson, for his banned novel, *No End to the Way*.[13]

One graduate of PMS who had a major influence on Glaskin's life and work was John Keith Ewers who lived just around the corner from the Glaskins in Peppermint Grove. Ewers entered Glaskin's life soon after Glaskin had returned from the war. Glaskin's mother first made contact with Ewers, in his capacity as air raid warden for their neighbourhood. Doing his rounds one night during the blackout, Ewers noticed a light coming from 35 Johnston Street. He notified Delia of the problem and helped her deal with it. He also discovered that with her husband and two eldest sons away at war, she had her hands full with five children and a large house to take care of. Ewers often dropped in at the Glaskins' after that to chat over a cup of tea and see if everything was all right. In the course of conversation, he realised that her eldest son was the same Gerald Glaskin whose byline he had become familiar with on short stories published in the local papers. Ewers was impressed with Glaskin's promise as a writer and indicated he would like to meet the young man, so Delia passed on his request to her son. Glaskin's immediate response was a mixture of astonishment and delight. 'Oh my god,' he said, 'I've read his books.'[14]

When the two eventually met some years after Glaskin had left PMS, Ewers asked him point blank, 'When are you going to write a book?' The 21-year-old Glaskin was a taken aback. 'Some day', he replied. 'Take my tip', said Ewers. 'Don't leave it too long. Write while you're young. Don't wait till you get middle-aged. You can only write young books when you're young. When you're middle-aged, so are your books.'[15] Glaskin took Ewers' words to heart, although it was another three years before he finally gave up the security of a regular job and dared to attempt to write his first novel, *A World of Our Own*. Little did Glaskin realise then that it would take another six years to see the book in print. When it did finally see the light of day, *The West Australian* asked John K. Ewers to review it.[16] His sympathetic appraisal of the book appeared along with a review of *Keep Him My Country*, the first novel by another promising young Western

---

13 See Chapter 9, 'Love', for further details.
14 It would not be surprising that Glaskin had read Ewers' books because Ewers was well known for several of his novels, as well as for the text books he authored.
15 GMG (1978a).
16 See Chapter 1, 'My Beautiful Beach'.

Australian writer, Mary Durack, with whom Glaskin would develop a lasting and close friendship.

Like Glaskin, Ewers came from a lower-middle class family that often struggled to make ends meet. Also like Glaskin, he succeeded in gaining a scholarship to attend Perth Modern School (PMS) but he was in the 'second fifty' who had to pay for their own books. In contrast to Glaskin, however, Ewers completed the full five years at the school, where it was impressed upon students 'the privilege it was for us to be there' and the necessity of 'behaving with a dignity befitting its reputation'.[17] Ewers remembered with pride having his own desk with a top of polished jarrah unmarked by the slightest scratch or blemish. He also recollected how, like many Australian schools of its day, PMS's curriculum lent heavily towards England and almost despised things Australian, especially in the realm of literature. 'If Russia or Germany or Italy or France had literatures worth studying, we heard nothing of it. America, too, was presumably illiterate, and as for Australia, well that was unmentionable in a literary sense. In this attitude, Perth Modern School was not alone. It was part of the general teaching practice of the day.'[18] By the time Glaskin entered its hallowed halls, PMS had already had a quarter of a century to establish its traditions that were highly reminiscent of an English public school. With masters and mistresses wearing black academic gowns, it would have been easy for students to imagine they had been transported from Australia back to England.

One of the chief architects of Perth Modern School was its second headmaster, Joseph Parsons. Parson's tenure (1912–1939) was marked by four tenets: academic excellence, self-development, self-discipline and pride in corporate tradition. He eschewed corporal punishment, believed that scholarship should be its own reward and that the student should be preparing him or herself for lifelong education. For all his virtues, Parsons had a tongue which, according to Ewers, 'could make anyone who suffered his displeasure cringe with shame'.[19] More serious breaches led to expulsion and during Ewers' time there some boys simply disappeared and didn't come back.'[20] Glaskin avoided such a fate. He didn't stand out particularly from the other 600 students at PMS, although he completed the usual three-year

---

17 John K. Ewers (1983, 44).
18 Ibid., 64.
19 Ibid., 63. Ewers also mentions that Parsons is thinly disguised as Joshua Bishop in the novel *The Iconoclast* by Leo Conon (1957).
20 Ibid., 44.

lower school course in two years.[21] Writing in Glaskin's final report, Parsons summed up the boy in a most nondescript way – 'a lad of a quite unassuming nature coming from a good home, he has good manners and a nice presence that with his other qualities, should commend him to an employer.'[22]

Academically, Glaskin performed moderately well, passing his Junior Certificate in eight subjects and failing in two, German and history. That he attempted 10 subjects when he needed only seven to pass was typical of Glaskin. As one teacher noted, 'he tries to go beyond his limits', a comment referring specifically to the fact that he was prone to fainting spells in gym class – probably due to his severe asthmatic condition – although it might well describe Glaskin's relationship to life in general. Asthma caused him more problems than just physical. He attributed the tormenting he received from other students to his wheezing. Although it may well have been a contributing factor, it appears there were other reasons also for the kind of chiacking he was subjected to. One curious note appears in Glaskin's PMS file – 'done well for a boy in his position'. Although this would seem to refer to his family's meagre income level, one person took it to be a reference to the fact that Glaskin was known to have 'homosexual leanings'.[23] While it seems unlikely that teachers would have made such a remark, albeit euphemistically, it would not be at all surprising that some of his peers might have. And it seems they did. According to one fellow pupil at the time Glaskin was commonly called 'Gertie Glaskin'.[24] Another student recalled several incidents in which Glaskin was on the receiving end of schoolyard bullying, including one in which a group of boys pushed him over a fence. 'I saw it from a distance. It was a wonder they didn't break his back', said James Glance. 'I don't know why he came in for that sort of treatment. I was just as girlish as he was at school and I never had any problems. Of course, he was very good looking.' But Glance's overriding memory of Glaskin at PMS was that he wasn't happy at school. 'I don't know what it was but he didn't seem to get on with people. He was always starting at the wrong end. Long after we had left school he was still very bitter about it. The school he

---

21 There is ambiguity about this, although Parsons confirms it in GMG's report and GMG reiterates it elsewhere. However, according to PMS archivist, Carole Stabb, he probably did his first year of high school at Fremantle Boys School, then took an exam that PMS set for all their incoming students, which would have allowed him to go straight into second year instead of having to repeat first year.

22 Final school report of GMG, 28 November 1938.

23 Carole Stabb to JB, personal communication, 2 December 2002.

24 David Buchanan to JB, interview by author, 12 November 2002. Buchanan reported that his father, a student at PMS in the same year as GMG, told him this.

described was not the school I went to at all', he said.[25] Never one to suffer fools lightly and ever sensitive to perceived threats, Glaskin displayed his combative nature that would cause him much grief in later years.

But there was one arena of school life in which Glaskin was beyond intimidation – his English class. When assigning an essay, his English teacher, Frank Constantine, would say, 'Everybody will do no less than five pages but you, Glaskin, will do no more than twenty.'[26] It seems that his propensity to overwrite was well entrenched, even in those early years. Quite unwittingly, Constantine opened a door in Glaskin's life that would have repercussions for the rest of his days. One autumn morning in May 1938, Constantine stood before his class and produced a letter he had just received addressed to 'The Head Master, a High School, Perth, Western Australia'. It was sent from another English teacher on the other side of the world and contained a note from his Dutch son, Sjoerd Steunebrink, who was seeking an Australian penfriend. When Constantine asked who would be interested in taking up the offer, he was met by a sea of hands and shrieks of 'Sir! Oh sir!' Glaskin was the lucky chosen one. He immediately penned his first note to the Netherlands. Fifteen years later almost to the day, he would finally meet Steunebrink in Amsterdam. They wrote back and forth with increasing regularity until the onset of war and censorship put a halt to their correspondence. After the war, Steunebrink's father, then in his eighties, found Glaskin's letters to his son stored in a hiding place for safekeeping. Ironically, while these letters survived, most of Steunebrink's letters were destroyed in a fire in Perth. From what he was able to salvage, Glaskin compiled a book, *One Way to Wonderland*, which after many attempts was finally published in 1984. Sales were not impressive but the glimpses it offers of Glaskin's boyhood and the time and place in which he grew up make it a valuable document.

Glaskin's association with Steunebrink was important for several reasons. First, it marked the beginning of a lifelong love affair between Glaskin and the Dutch.[27] Second, it reinforced his love of writing that had already revealed itself in his efforts to write stories, articles and poems for school magazines and other publications. Steunebrink's father, impressed with Glaskin's writing style, grammatical correctness and attention to detail, predicted that Glaskin would become a writer.[28] Third, it whetted his appetite

25 James Glance to JB, interview by author, 20 November 2002.
26 Willett (1999, 2).
27 See Chapter 7, 'Going Dutch'.
28 GMG (1984, 91).

for exploring the world beyond Australia. He would daily scan the shipping schedules in the morning paper and when something caught his imagination, promptly make his way to Fremantle harbour where he would board ships and imagine himself being on them one day. This proved to be the case many times over. Perhaps most of all, his association with Steunebrink confirmed for Glaskin something he already knew but was still dawning in his consciousness at age 14 – his undeniable attraction to members of his own sex. Although their relationship initially was just a boyish infatuation with boyish things, it led to a more self-conscious realisation that Glaskin – and, strangely, Steunebrink too – was homosexual.

The content of Glaskin's letters to Steunebrink reflects the interests and concerns of a young boy growing into a young man in a place he was proud to call home but one far removed from the world's trouble spots in a time of incipient war. They are laden with detailed descriptions of Perth and places Glaskin visited in Western Australia, peppered with facts and figures and maps meticulously sketched in Glaskin's own neat hand. Steunebrink reciprocated with colourful brochures and postcards of his hometown of Leeuwarden in his native Friesland, along with packages of coins, stamps, seeds and other paraphernalia. There was an element of friendly one-upmanship about their exchanges, some of which would have cost no small sum to send via airmail. Both families became part of this international dialogue, each eagerly awaiting the arrival of the next instalment from the other side of the world. Steunebrink's father would annotate Glaskin's letters where words and phrases were beyond his son's grasp of English. The tone of Glaskin's letters is intriguing. It tends to be formal and pedagogical – 'You had better get your atlas out now' and 'I think I have told you enough about physiography for today'[29] – and at times business-like. While this style no doubt reflects a stiffness encouraged by teachers of the day, and perhaps was Glaskin's attempt to make his writing intelligible to second-language English users, it is also the kind of mannerism that later caused one of his close associates to refer to him as 'a rather haughty man of patrician personality'.[30]

All this bonhomie, however formalised, was taking place against the backdrop of ever-menacing developments in Europe, as Hitler continued to assert his power beyond Germany. In May 1940, the flow of mail came to an abrupt halt when two of Glaskin's letters were returned to him heavily

---

29 Ibid., 17 and 51.
30 Alex Cohen to JB, personal communication, 3 June 2001.

censored with Indian ink and razor blade cutouts. When Glaskin heard of Germany's invasion of Holland, he feared the worst for his Dutch pal and his parents. He became obsessed with Steunebrink's safety, to the point of fantasising about joining the RAAF so he could parachute into Leeuwarden and rescue his friend. But not being able to join the air force at 17, he opted for the navy instead. The absence of news grew unbearable. 'It was the *not* knowing what had happened to him that was so difficult, so terrible to bear', he wrote.[31] Meanwhile, the reality of war impressed itself on Glaskin by the increasing number of convoys of troop ships coming and going from Fremantle, the frequent blackouts and the rationing of food and petrol. When his mother joined the Red Cross and his father the army, the reality of the times inserted itself into the Glaskin household. 'They were terrible years, truly terrible', he recollected.[32]

As well as expressions of concern for the safety of Steunebrink and his parents, Glaskin's letters reveal a level of feeling for the young Dutchman that suggests a growing affection, and one that was reciprocated. Glaskin had several other penfriends in different countries but they did not rate in comparison to his Dutch friend. Referring to a friend in Toronto, he wrote to Steunebrink, 'I told him from the very beginning that you were to have the first & best of everything and that he should have what remains. No-one, Sjoerd, could ever rise half as far as you have in my esteem.'[33] And of a young English girl Glaskin asserted, 'I would rather have you than 1000 of her.'[34] Steunebrink displayed his feelings for his Aussie mate by naming his yacht 'The Gerald', a gesture that touched Glaskin deeply. When the agonising war-induced silence between them was broken on VE-Day, both sent jubilant cables to each other almost at the same hour. Glaskin was elated that Steunebrink had escaped the Nazi onslaught by hiding out on a neighbour's farm. Although he had an intense yearning to meet this lanky, fair-haired Dutchman, he would have to wait another eight years to do so. When the day finally came, Glaskin was not at all disappointed. 'After all those long years, our right hands were at last clasped together in handshake, our other hands pumping each other on the shoulders. It had all been worth while. It had all been very much worth the while ...'[35]

31 GMG (1984, 150).
32 Ibid.
33 Ibid., 140.
34 Ibid., 56.
35 Ibid., 156.

Prior to their meeting in Amsterdam in 1953, a major turning point in their relationship happened with the arrival of a letter from Steunebrink in August 1948. It was the kind of letter that could only have been sent between trusted friends. At 25, Steunebrink couldn't stand the agony any longer. He had to share with someone the fact that he was attracted to his own sex and had found immense pleasure in his sexual encounters with other young men. Racked with guilt and unsure how to reconcile this part of himself with the dutiful only son of two conservative parents, Steunebrink poured out his heart to Glaskin. Glaskin responded with a 13-page epistle which, true to form, was both highly supportive and overflowing with advice from one-who-has-been-through-it-all, even though he was a year younger than his Dutch friend. He prefaced his remarks by acknowledging that he himself had just passed through a period of 'chaos and confusion' and that he was only on 'the first rungs of a ladder on which to climb out of the "slough of despondency"'. Although he still had many questions, Glaskin boasted that he had 'ascertained the meaning of life in a very broad sense' and had learned to achieve 'inner peace' by reconciling the warring parts of his own psyche – the public self with the private, the good with the bad, the too-bright with the too-morbid.[36] Predictably, homosexual thoughts and actions belonged in the latter category, thanks in large part to prevailing societal attitudes and conventions. With a passion of a young student arguing his heartfelt thesis, Glaskin removed same-sex feelings and behaviour from the realm of 'defect' and 'sin' and portrayed them as natural, god-given and ineradicable. Same-sex behaviour itself was not immoral or distasteful; only if it did harm to others and oneself. He presented a well thought through and convincing case, one in which he obviously had much invested. Whether it was influenced by the publication of the Kinsey Report that same year is impossible to say, but Glaskin's comments indicate that he had done significant reading on the subject in coming to his own conclusions.

Glaskin's discourse was as much a response to Steunebrink's pleas for re-assurance about his sexual confusion as it was about Glaskin's attempt to document his own journey of self-discovery. He was only 24 and having recently experienced life in the services, where opportunities to have sexual encounters abounded in ways previously unavailable to him, he was on the cusp of creating a new identity for himself. To Steunebrink's confession that he was 'wild with sex', Glaskin shot back an immediate 'So am I. Who isn't?' While Glaskin admonished Steunebrink to 'face up to the realisation

---

36 GMG to Sjoerd Steunebrink, 17 August 1948.

that your natural tendencies are towards the homosexual', he chose not to wear the same label. Instead, he referred to himself as bisexual. At the same time, Glaskin responded positively to Steunebrink's sexual overtures to him, sometimes subtly insinuated by terms of endearment in his letters and sometimes more overtly. When Steunebrink described his masturbatory fantasy of a 'flying man', induced by a photograph of Glaskin on a motorbike, Glaskin was not the least shocked or disgusted. On the contrary, he seemed eager to reciprocate Steunebrink's affection for him, on one condition: 'If you were to come to Australia, or I go to Holland, and you showed to me that you wanted to show your affection to me physically as well as mentally, I must admit to you now that I would acquiesce. If, however, it meant that I should lose your mental affection and friendship, it would be the last thing I wanted.'[37]

Glaskin had been trying to fathom and come to terms with his perplexing sexuality since childhood. His earliest recollection of a sexual experience occurred when he was about four years old at the hands of a 14-year-old boy. Details of the episode are not known but presumably it happened at Carnamah or soon after the family moved back to Perth.[38] But the event that did mark a sexual epiphany for Glaskin happened at Easter 1939 when he attended a Boy Scout camp near the town of Mandurah, 70 kilometres south of Perth. Boy Scout camps are notoriously fertile grounds for sexual enlightenment of the young and inexperienced and this was no exception. Glaskin devotes nine pages of *One Way to Wonderland* to describing the camp in exquisite detail, replete with maps, references to the role he played as leader of the Kingfisher Patrol and the fun had by all in staging a campfire concert for local residents. But there is not an inkling of a reference to what was undeniably the shattering revelation of the entire camp. That had to wait sixty years when, asked in an interview about his early sexual experiences, Glaskin was more forthcoming. 'There were two or three of them who I think were gay, who had had anal sex, including twin brothers who had sex with each other. The slightly younger one was very tall. They weren't look-alikes at all ... that was the first time and I was so surprised that anal sex was even possible. It was incredible.'[39]

If Boy Scout camp was Glaskin's awakening to the possibility and pleasures of homosexual activity, it was his decision to join the navy in 1941 that was his raw initiation into its ranks. From 20 November 1941, when he began

---

37 Ibid., 8.
38 See Chapter 9, 'Love', for a fictionalised account of this experience.
39 Willett (1999, 9).

service at HMAS *Cerberus* in Victoria, he entered a world populated by men – many about his same age, from all walks of life and all parts of the country. For the first time they were free from the shackles of parental authority, restrictive mores or reputations they may have accrued back home and were able to recreate who they wanted to be. It was a rare chance to experiment, to let their urges take them where they would and not be confined by morality and convention. Given that they were surrounded day and night by other men, a certain percentage of whom had no short measure of good looks and charm, the opportunity to enter into liaisons was like a dare waiting to be taken up. For those who, like Glaskin, had already had a taste of homosex and found it to their liking, this was a made-to-order situation.

After five months at HMAS *Cerberus*, Glaskin received his first posting to the HMAS *Manoora*, a converted armed merchant cruiser used mainly to escort other naval ships in the Pacific and Indian Oceans. Glaskin was only on the *Manoora* two months before he was transferred to another converted armed merchant cruiser, HMS (later HMAS) *Kanimbla*. During his time on the *Manoora*, it escorted ships from Australia to Noumea twice before returning to Sydney for maintenance, where it remained for all of June 1942. The exact reason for Glaskin's transfer to the *Kanimbla* is not recorded but it seems likely that he was part of a batch of Western Australian ratings who were exchanged between the *Manoora* and the *Kanimbla*, which was expected to depart soon for their home port. There is no mention of misconduct or illness on Glaskin's part. However, comments Glaskin made to others and an inference passed on to his younger brother Llew suggest that Glaskin may have been sexually active with other men while at sea. Long after the war, Llew was drinking with a couple of mates one day at a Perth yacht club when the name Glaskin came up. One of the men recollected that he was in the navy with a Gerald Glaskin. They were on the *Manoora* together before Glaskin was transshipped to the *Kanimbla*. 'The funny way he said, "I knew him on the *Manoora* and well ..." was if he was a bit of a sailor's boy', reported Llew.[40]

Whatever pleasures Glaskin may have been indulging in on board ship were severely curtailed, if not completely halted, when he became the victim of a traumatic accident. He gives a fictionalised account of the accident and its aftermath in *A Lion in the Sun*.[41]

---

40 Llewellyn Glaskin to JB, interview by author, 20 November 2002.
41 GMG (1960a, 16–17).

And just at that time, after our first taste of action, with its brief but horrifying glimmer of the meaning of war, and its hideous stench of young death, I had the misfortune to be injured – not in the action itself, but a few days after it was over. I was serving on an armed merchant-cruiser that had not been intended to see such action. I was a mere Able Seaman, serving my seatime for Officers' Training Course at Flinders in a few weeks' time, when, ironically, I was a victim of one of those stupid accidents that should never happen. Our signal halyards had been blown away. The replacements, when they were brought up from below, were found to have rusted on to their drums and had to be unwound from one drum to another. New ratings, like myself, almost fresh from the naval training depot, were operating the winches. The one taking up the rusted wire was straining under pressure to wrench the wire from the old drum. But the wire was rusted only an inch or so down and, when the clean wire was reached, the winches suddenly ran free with a hideous screech and the hiss of flying wire.

I had been standing lookout on the nearby gun and, hearing the sudden shouts and this unknown hissing in my ears, I span around. Great whirling coils reared up and lurched along the deck. At first I could not understand what these writhing circles could be, but involuntarily I raised my arms to protect my face just as the first circles struck me. The binoculars were dashed from my hand. A sudden heat seared across one cheek. Before I could move out of the way, some of the coils had wound themselves around my arms. Just then, the winch taking up the slack wire got out of hand and raced at an insane speed, suddenly tautening the coils. One of the coils caught around my right arm, just above the elbow. It drew tight. The pain was like a hot knife slicing through my flesh. A sudden jerk of the wire threw me off my feet, knocking off my steel helmet.

Fortunately, it also knocked me unconscious. Afterwards, they told me I was dragged, like a limp rag, screaming, along the deck and over the winch. The sailor operating the winch hadn't known how to stop it. The impact smashed my left arm. The right one, almost severed by the wire, was freed miraculously by the wire snapping in the fraction of an inch between my arm and the winch. Otherwise, I should have lost it. As it was, it would have been amputated immediately in the sick bay had it not been for two things: I was still unconscious and unable to give my consent to the M.O. [Medical Officer] to perform the operation; secondly, as I was under twenty-one, the consent of my parents had to be obtained, and communication between ship and shore was prohibited. So I kept my arm and I have it still.

I was kept doped with morphia until we were scheduled to reach Sydney. But we did not go to Sydney. Owing to the scare of Japanese submarines we were ordered on to Melbourne. Before Melbourne was reached, the urgency of transporting troops from Fremantle to the eastern states changed our orders again. We bypassed Adelaide, crossed the Great Australian Bight, and, to my half-crazed delight, I found myself being put ashore at Fremantle, my home port.

At the Hollywood Military Hospital, they told me that, although there was nothing serious now about my injuries, it would take several months before I would again have even restricted use of my arms.

Given Glaskin's propensity to be strikingly autobiographical in much of his writing, this is probably a fairly accurate description of what happened, although separating fact from fiction has required considerable effort. Medical records at Hollywood Private Hospital – then the 110th Australian General Hospital – confirm that Glaskin was admitted on 9 July 1942, although they are inconsistent when referring to which arm suffered the most severe damage.[42] It appears that it was his right arm, which is corroborated by medical reports from later life. He had already damaged his left arm as a child and it had never been correctly reset.[43] However, the precise nature of the accident, its severity, and the time and place when it occurred are

---

42 The 110th Australian General Hospital report reads: 'This rating was injured on 24.6.42 in the following manner. A wire being led between two winches became looped around his upper arm under strain. He sustained a circular bruising of the arm and damage to the superficial nerves. On examination, [there was found] some swelling of the lower one-third of [his] upper arm, no skin sensation from sore line down. X-ray no bony [sic] damage. Since this date the sensation has gradually returned to the forearm and hand, and movements are good except extension of elbow. There still appears to be some oedema in the area of the insertion of the triceps which interferes with the movement. He is forwarded for admission and treatment please.' Department of Veterans' Affairs, Perth, 18 January 2004.

43 His left arm he fractured as a young boy. He fell from a ladder while trying to help his Uncle Alan pick loquats and was rushed by car to Perth Children's Hospital. Shortly after, he tripped and fell and broke it again. It was set a second time but done crookedly so it had to be broken and reset. The result was his left arm was about two inches shorter than the right one. GMG (1975, 100–101).

open to question.[44] The hospital records state that Glaskin was injured on 24 June 1942. If this is true, the incident occurred a day or two after Glaskin had been transferred from the *Manoora* to the *Kanimbla*, which was still in Sydney where it had been since 25 May undergoing maintenance. It left Sydney on 27 June and reached Fremantle on 4 July. However, Glaskin was not drafted ashore to HMAS *Leeuwin*, the naval depot for Fremantle, until 9 July. Clearly, his injuries were not severe enough for him to be hospitalised in Sydney, nor was hospitalisation deemed urgent enough that it couldn't wait another 15 days until he reached Perth and then another five days after berthing. Naval records, including war diaries for both the *Manoora* and the *Kanimbla*, contain no reference to any accident of the kind described above having occurred on either ship during the time Glaskin was on them. A signalman who served on the *Kanimbla* contradicted some of the details in the fictionalised account of the incident.[45] Finally, there are no recorded deaths on either ship during this period. This would make the story that Glaskin sometimes told that two sailors standing near him were decapitated in the accident appear to be fictitious, probably added to accentuate how close he came – once again – to death. However, 96-year-old Frank Davey was able to confirm parts of Glaskin's story. While the *Kanimbla* was in Sydney he was on watch one day when a young rating's arm was injured in an accident involving loose wire. Davey also confirmed there was no decapitation.[46]

But the story in *A Lion in the Sun* is interesting for another reason. It is set in Perth and Singapore in the midst of the Second World War and the years following. It begins with the narrator, Geoffrey Graham – whose initials happen to be identical to Glaskin's[47] – recuperating in Perth's Hollywood Military Hospital from wounds he suffered while serving on an armed

44 Loris Carberry (GMG's oldest sister) to JB, personal communication, 12 December 2003. She thought it was his right arm that was broken, caused by an anchor chain twisting around it.

45 Alan Roberts to JB, 1 December 2003. 'Being a Signalman myself, I can vouch that *Kanimbla* did not have wire halyards, but rope. The signal lockers on "K" were on the Compass Platform, and the closest gun to where he was standing was a deck below outside the wheelhouse. There were no winches in either area for wires to be hissing around.'

46 Frank Davey to Alan Roberts, 2 February 2004.

47 GMG initially used his own name as the narrator of this highly autobiographical novel but his editors strongly objected, for two reasons – it could increase the risk of libel, especially in a close community like Singapore, and at this stage of his career they thought it unwise for him to identify himself in the minds of his readers with any particular circumstances. After some debate, GMG finally gave in but only partly – he changed the names but kept the same initials.

merchant cruiser. Graham strikes up a friendship with fellow patient, Bradley Chase, a journalist-cum-poet who is recovering from injuries he received in the air force. Thrown together by fate, the two men develop an intimate relationship that stretches Aussie mateship to new bounds. Describing their efforts to help each other bathe, Graham reflects that, 'There can be nothing more personal than having someone else dry your buttocks and genitals, or even between your toes.' As Graham places his arms around Chase's neck to lower him into the bath water, Chase responds, 'Now kiss me mate and make my life complete!'[48] If this episode is anything close to what Glaskin actually experienced at Hollywood Hospital it would seem that his shipboard escapades continued unabated on land. After two months, Glaskin was released from hospital and in February 1943 was discharged from the navy 'Physically Unfit for Naval Services' (PUNS), although he later claimed he was certified unfit for all service, possibly to avoid being drafted into the army for national service. His naval records do not give the exact reason why he was declared PUNS but they do mention his problem with asthma, which recurred while he was in the navy after it had lain dormant for several years. Glaskin claimed that he was discharged for both his asthmatic condition and for injuries he sustained.[49] He was granted a pension of 10 shillings a fortnight and went back to civilian life at the ripe old age of 19.

But not for long. Having tasted life in the services and all that came with it, he was eager for more. Glaskin moved to Sydney where he boarded initially with his great-aunt May and her Scottish husband, Archibald MacPhail. Using the excellent reference he obtained on leaving Soap Distributors in North Fremantle, he quickly found a job with the company's Sydney counterpart as a sales statistician and advertising copywriter. After hours, he no doubt found time to explore Sydney's alluring nightlife of King's Cross and its gay nooks in particular.[50] Given that the city was awash with visiting American servicemen in these years, opportunities for Glaskin to continue his sexual exploration would have been rife. However, with the prospect of national service looming and possible recruitment into the army, he decided to try his luck with the air force instead. Since he had been discharged from the navy PUNS, he knew that his chances of being accepted into the air force were slim, so he took the precautionary measure of changing his name

48 GMG (1960a, 25–26).
49 GMG (1975, 133).
50 For a fictional account of gay life in Kings Cross during this period, see Jon Rose's book, *At the Cross*.

from Gerald Marcus Glaskin to his full Gerald Marcus Leonard Glaskin.[51] A meticulous RAAF officer might have quickly latched on to this ploy had he bothered to ask the right questions or had he the means at his disposal to check, but that never happened. Besides, the air force's desire to attract, and not deter, young men from signing up no doubt worked in Glaskin's favour. However, his clever manoeuvre was uncovered nearly a year later. The episode is described by the Melbourne-based author and journalist, John Hetherington.

> He trained in Canada as a navigator. All the time he was worried that his RAN past would catch up with him, but nothing happened until the day he graduated at Winnipeg. Then he was summoned to the presence of Air Vice-Marshal S. J. Goble, RAAF liaison officer in Canada. Goble handed Glaskin a sheaf of papers and asked, 'Any connection?' They were Glaskin's RAN discharge papers. Knowing he could not lie his way out of this one, he said, 'Yes, sir.' Goble looked severe, but his eyes twinkled. 'You've been a very very naughty boy,' he admonished. 'Don't do it again!' That was the only reproof Glaskin ever suffered for his irregular entry into the RAAF.[52]

Yet the real test for Glaskin joining the RAAF was yet to come. He still had to undergo a physical examination. His account of how he did this borders on the incredible and one wonders if the old adage of 'never let the truth get in the way of a good story' prevailed. While Glaskin was waiting for his turn at the horizontal bar, an officer approached him and asked if he was a Glaskin from Western Australia. When he replied yes, the officer introduced himself as Sergeant Ronald Glaskin, also from WA and a cousin of Glaskin's father. While chatting together, Glaskin kept an eye on his place in the queue and when they had passed the horizontal bar he excused himself and continued with the tests.[53] He was accepted into the RAAF and sent to Winnipeg in Canada for training as a navigator as part of the British Commonwealth Air Training Plan.[54]

---

51 GMG claimed he did this. However, the name on his RAAF enlistment papers is simply Gerald Marcus Glaskin.
52 John Hetherington (1961b, 18 and 1963, 229).
53 LvdP (n. d., 62).
54 The British Commonwealth Air Training Plan (BCATP) was a joint undertaking of Australia, Britain, Canada and New Zealand – with other participants from Belgium, France and Poland – that took place in 107 schools across Canada. The program, which ran between May 1940 and March 1945, took in more than 167,000 students and had

Once in the air force, Glaskin wasted no time demonstrating his innate leadership abilities. While stationed at Bradfield Park Embarkation Depot near Lindfield, NSW, he organised basketball games for his fellow trainees. In the early hours of 1 July 1944, he and hundreds of other servicemen boarded the USS Cape Perpetua and set sail for San Francisco. During the three-week crossing, Glaskin was appointed Liaison Officer for the Australian contingent on board and elected their official buyer at the American PX (post exchange) canteen, for which he gained a reputation for accurate purchasing and fair distribution. Upon arrival, the Australians were given a thorough medical examination, then hosted royally by their American counterparts before being put on a troop train north to Canada, a journey that amazed the Aussies with its excellent service and fine meals, a far cry from what they were used to at home. It also introduced them to the alien custom of tipping. This led to Glaskin exhibiting another aspect of his personality that has not always attracted the same attention as his more belligerent and bullying nature. Fellow Western Australian serviceman Noel Whyte, whose family had lived next door to the Glaskins, remembered this event vividly.

> Our head waiter was a middle-aged black American named Godfrey, who was the father of nine children and who had to sleep on the dining car tables overnight. He was a lovely bloke and gave us all an endless supply of Californian chilled Sunkist oranges. As we approached Calgary, Gerry collected a US dollar from each of the sixty of us in the carriage and presented the $60 to Godfrey. He burst into tears, saying that this was the most money he'd ever had in his life and would remember us Australians for years to come. This was Gerry's intuition and compassionate heart shining through.[55]

Once they arrived in Winnipeg the Australians were put to work for seven weeks without a break, to make up for a week they lost by being sent to the wrong training base en route. At the end of five months crammed with classroom lessons and practice flying, Glaskin graduated a commissioned Pilot Officer, Navigation. To celebrate his achievement, he led a group of Australians on a two-week trip to Toronto and New York. After soaking up the sights and sounds of The Big Apple, Glaskin and another Australian, Bill de Meyrick, spent a relaxing week with the

---

a significant impact on allied air operations in Europe, Asia and Africa. Sources of information: Martin (2002, 65–69) and Juno Beach Centre (2003).

55 Noel Whyte to JB, 27 August 2001.

Blattner family in Mountain Lakes, New Jersey. This became the setting for his short story, 'The Ice Yacht', although the events that unfold in this tragic tale of a family in disarray are no doubt figments of Glaskin's fertile imagination or clipped from other experiences in his life. De Meyrick and Glaskin also shared another family visit together, one that potentially could have had much more significant long-term consequences. The Workmans were one of a number of Winnipeg families who offered to host Australian air force trainees stationed in their city. De Meyrick and Glaskin spent most of their weekend leaves together at the Workmans' home. They were delightful hosts, with the added attraction of having a very pleasant young daughter, Norma, of whom Glaskin grew extremely fond. Their friendship developed into an engagement. However, this is where it ended. Glaskin gives different reasons for its termination – she didn't want to leave Canada and he didn't relish their cold winters, and 'sexually we were suited but intellectually we were on separated planes'.[56]

This was not the first time Glaskin had shown serious interest in a relationship with a woman. As a 17-year old in the navy, he fell in love with Jean Snell, the proverbial 'girl back home' who lived near the Glaskins in Palmerston Street. They corresponded frequently until the day Glaskin met a friend who was on a supply ship in the Pacific. In the midst of their conversation his friend casually mentioned, 'Oh, I've just had a letter from Jean.' Glaskin had the presence of mind not to tell him that he had also. His friend showed him the letter. It was identical to one Glaskin had received. This moment of truth quickly ended Glaskin's romantic fling. Later on, in Singapore, Glaskin met Valerie Hill and became enamoured with her. But again this relationship fizzled. Glaskin attributes its demise to the fact that she didn't want to give up her position and that he had other offers, but doesn't elaborate on the nature of them. Unlike with Jean, Glaskin and Hill remained in touch, even after she married and settled in Sydney. Between these two encounters, while he spent six months at Safety Bay writing his first novel, Glaskin enjoyed the company of another young woman, Eileen Baxter.[57] His diary suggests that she sometimes spent the night with him, as well as cooked meals and that they enjoyed times together at the beach. Apparently, Eileen came a lot closer than Norma Workman to meeting Glaskin's high standards for intellectual parity and outlook on life. 'Twenty-one, green-eyed and easy to look at. If I could consider matrimony

56 GMG to Sjoerd Steunebrink, 17 August 1948.
57 Not to be confused with his mother's sister, Eileen, was who just 14 years older than GMG and with whom he had a close relationship for much of his life.

now, then she just about fills the bill. Well educated with a little culture, she is genuine, broad-minded and so sensible. A rare specimen, in fact.'[58]

But while he was tossing up the pros and cons of life with Eileen, he was also having a lot of fun with a guy called Harry. A well-known Perth footballer, Harry visited Glaskin frequently during his half year at Safety Bay. Harry's tender blanched skin contrasted to Glaskin's ever-darkening tan, but what Harry lacked in pigmentation he made up for in strong doses of ockerism. On one occasion, after Glaskin had waited anxiously all day for him to arrive, Harry finally showed up after five o'clock stone drunk and insisted on taking Glaskin to a pub in nearby Rockingham to get him 'rotten', because he thought his writer friend had been working too hard. The next day Glaskin wrote in his diary, 'A restless night with the acute awareness of Harry sharing the double bed'.[59] But Harry was not just another bed mate for Glaskin. He also read and critiqued his writing. And, it appears, he was the subject of at least one piece of Glaskin's writing, albeit two short stanzas. Fifteen years later, while Glaskin was taking a working holiday on the island of Mallorca, he wrote the following poem, called 'Harry, look …'

> Look at the way the sun shines, Harry,
> Over the hills and into the trees,
> Falling on ground that holds it, Harry,
> Much in the way that you hold me.
>
> Look at the way the sun sets, Harry,
> Burning its beauty away in death;
> Help me to leave you that way, Harry,
> Loving you with my dying breath.[60]

Such a tender expression of affection cannot be dismissed as a passing fad. Clearly, Glaskin had sexual interests in both men and women. He admitted as much. 'I used to fall in love with girls from the age of 14 but I loved to muck around with guys', he said in a 1999 interview.[61] In the next breath, he added almost offhandedly, 'But girls were a bit unfortunate in

---

58 GMG (1949a, 14 January).
59 Ibid., 23 January 1949.
60 Written at Palma de Mallorca, 9 August 1964. A version of this poem later appeared in the journal *Artlook* with a generic 'lover' substituted for Harry. GMG (1977, 28).
61 Willett (1999, 3). Another version of this reported by LvdP was 'I used to fall in love with women but in lust with men'.

my career.' However, Glaskin didn't always refer to himself as bisexual. His favourite aphorism was, 'I'm trisexual – I try everything at least twice in case I don't like it the first time'.[62] Not surprisingly, Glaskin became intensely interested in the subject of sexuality, as well as the practice of it, which he discovered could be unpredictable. He admitted being shocked when a close air force friend of his who was married disclosed that he 'preferred a gent every now and again'.[63] He also claimed to know a number of women whose husbands had no idea that their wives had liaisons with other women. He began reading as much as he could on the subject and became convinced that human sexuality was a spectrum with various combinations and permutations within it. This realisation led him to want to write a trilogy of novellas on sexualities to be called *O Love, O Life, O Loneliness*. But this wasn't to be, at least not in this format.[64]

While the war provided abundant opportunities for Glaskin to explore his sexuality and demonstrate his leadership abilities, it also was the backdrop to several of his most severe injuries that would plague him for the rest of his life. In addition to the broken arms he received in the accident on the HMAS *Kanimbla*, he was also involved in two incidents in the air force in Canada, one of which would have repercussions later on. The first occurred one evening when, in order not to let down his co-navigator from taking a few 'star and moon' shots required during flying exercises, he flew with a poisoned foot. On the way to give the pilot a change of course, Glaskin tripped over a bulwark and knocked himself unconscious. The pilot was forced to make an emergency landing so Glaskin could be taken to hospital, where he remained for several days before being discharged. The other incident was of greater consequence. The Avro Anson aircraft he was in hit an air pocket and suddenly lost altitude, causing Glaskin to shoot up and hit his head on the ceiling of the plane. This left him with neck injuries that were exacerbated when he had his near-fatal surfing accident at Cottesloe Beach in 1967.[65] Over the rest of his life he was also involved in two car accidents, in one of which the car rolled over several times. Glaskin's claim

---

62 Ibid. The same quote also appears in Cover (1994b, 19).
63 Ibid., 2.
64 See Chapter 9, 'Love', for details.
65 It seems that in spite of his injuries, GMG fared better than some during his time with the BCATP. In the course of the program, 856 trainees died, and if training staff and non-operational units are included, that figure increases to at least 1713 fatalities and possibly more. The RAAF sent 9606 trainees, of whom 65 were killed during the program. Martin (2002, 65–69).

that he lived a charmed life of the feline variety seems to have some validity to it.[66] Scars on his right thigh, elbow, forehead and left leg bore testimony to it.

Ironically, Glaskin never put his navigation training into effect because upon its completion the war in Europe ended, so his anticipated transfer to the Pathfinders Squadron never happened. He did only one sortie with the Americans over the Aleutian Islands before being reassigned back to Australia in March 1945 to help fight the lingering Japanese campaign. Crossing the Pacific on the Victory Class liberty ship USS *Frederick C. Ainsworth*, Glaskin again displayed his qualities that caused Noel Whyte, Bill de Meyrick and other fellow servicemen to refer to Glaskin as 'a born leader' and 'a good mixer'. He recorded the names and addresses of all 700 Australians on board and wrote a small booklet as a memento of their journey, which he mailed to them once he was back on Australian soil. The voyage home was a circuitous one via the New Hebrides, Guadalcanal and Noumea, but free from mishap. After disembarking in Brisbane, Glaskin joined the other Western Australians on their five-day train journey to Perth, where he was granted two weeks leave. When the rattling wooden carriages of *The Westland* pulled into Perth Railway Station, one chapter in his young life was close to ending. But not quite. In May, he was posted to Port Pirie in South Australia to adapt the navigational training he had received in Canada to southern hemisphere conditions. He would have to wait four more months for the war to end with the bombing of Hiroshima and Nagasaki in August. Glaskin was discharged in November and finally demobilised on 6 February 1946. At that time, his earnings and other credits from his RAAF service amounted to £654, a useful sum in those days. He now had to decide what to do with the rest of his life, a question postponed by the onset of war.

His family came to the rescue. His mother's brother, Noel Gugeri, offered Glaskin a job as departmental manager at his sports store in Fremantle. Although Glaskin described it as 'selling sporting goods and toys and restringing tennis racquets',[67] he was glad to take it on while trying to figure out what kind of future he really wanted for himself. After 10 months, he moved to the Ford Motor Company in North Fremantle, where he worked for two years as a sales statistician, a job that may have suited the rational, ordering side of Glaskin's brain but definitely not his creative side.

---

66 GMG to HS, 25 November 1983.
67 GMG (1994–1999, 6).

Providence stepped in in the person of Foster Wearne, a car dealer with a flourishing business in Singapore whom Glaskin had met while working at Ford. Impressed by what he had seen and heard of Glaskin, Wearne offered him the job of manager of his spare parts department. Glaskin jumped at the opportunity, but not before he negotiated with Wearne a six-month hiatus during which time he took his air force pay, moved down to Nan's cottage at Safety Bay and hammered out the first draft of his first novel. He had now secured a steady income and found ways to create the time and space to do what he most wanted to do – write.

Even though he had achieved this important milestone there was one question that kept needling him. When he left school at 15, with a scholarship that most likely would have continued through the remaining two years of high school, his formal education came to a halt. He nursed a yearning to go back and do further study, at least to a bachelor's degree at the one institution in Western Australia that offered it at the time, the University of Western Australia. As a returning serviceman twice over – RAN and RAAF – he was entitled to a scholarship that would have supported him in this endeavour. However, this was not to be, due to an ironical twist of fate. Professor Walter Murdoch, then head of the university's English Department, interviewed Glaskin for the scholarship. He asked the young man what he wanted to do with a degree in arts. Without hesitation Glaskin replied that he wanted to be a writer. 'But aren't you the same Glaskin who is already writing?' inquired Murdoch, having seen some of Glaskin's short stories in local and national magazines and newspapers. 'Then go away from here and write or you'll end up a dilettante old essayist like me!' A dejected Glaskin found this advice hard to take. 'No doubt he meant well and was convinced he was doing the right thing at the time' he said. 'But he couldn't have been more wrong. Now I suffer from a defect that can't be rectified.'[68]

One wonders what might have happened had Glaskin undertaken university studies. Quite possibly, he would have refined his craft as a writer as he came into contact with fellow writers and broadened his range of reading material. He may have learned the art of reasoned debate and logical argument rather than impulsive and emotional reaction, which doubtless would have served him well in his abrasive encounters with individuals and organisations in later life. But this was not to be. He left academia and Australia behind him and went off to conquer wider horizons and new challenges. He was 25, had travelled halfway around the world and back, worked

68 GMG (1978b, 39).

in five different jobs and had the draft of his first novel in hand. He was now also the eldest of seven children. Although he had had a rich childhood, it had been curtailed by the onset of the Depression and war. He had grown up quickly and discovered he possessed qualities of leadership that may have surprised even him. It is little wonder that he slipped so effortlessly into the role of 'the managing elder brother'.

Chapter 4

The Managing Elder Brother

*Most writers wear a mask, a leaping clown we put up to
entertain the crowd while we observe, take notes, and
the managing elder brother may have been Gerry's disguise.*

Ethel Webb Bundell

Being the eldest of seven children, the youngest 21 years his junior, it was natural that Glaskin would find himself called upon to play an adult role with his siblings. His youngest three siblings – Roland, Myree and Hilary – barely knew their elder brother because much of the time they were growing up he was away at the war or working in Singapore. Glaskin was godfather to Myree and often acted out that role with all the seriousness of a substitute parent. He was generous with money and gifts to the rest of the family, especially when he lived abroad and earned significant income from stockbroking, and at times from his writing. He was equally generous in dispensing advice to his brothers and sisters, a propensity of his not especially appreciated by the rest of the family. With a sharp wit and a cutting tongue, he could quickly put them in their place, just as his father had using 'the Glaskin stare'. On occasions he didn't hesitate to use his physical strength to take on his brothers by swinging a punch or wrestling them to the ground. Not surprisingly, Glaskin's siblings didn't hold their elder brother in the high esteem one might have associated with having a well-published author in the family. Where this happened, it was usually with the next generation of nieces and nephews, some of whom respected, even adored, their 'Unc', or as they sometimes jokingly called him, 'Auntie Gerry'. But for his six brothers and sisters, and others outside the family who encountered him, Glaskin was, unapologetically, 'the managing elder brother'.[1]

The first of his siblings on whom he was able to cut his teeth as elder brother was Dixie, who was born a couple of months before the family returned to Perth from Carnamah in June 1927. After being the sole object of his parents' and relatives' affection and attention for four years, Glaskin suddenly found himself having to share the limelight. At best their relationship was one of mutual co-existence and at worst it was one of loathing and intolerance. Of Glaskin's three brothers, Dixie had the hardest time accepting Glaskin's homosexuality. According to Dixie's wife, Audrey, he never did. She remembered an incident one evening shortly after Leo van de Pas had arrived in Perth from the Netherlands to take up his position as Glaskin's 'assistant'. Apparently, this euphemism didn't win favour with Dixie. 'They [Glaskin and Dixie] were both sitting out the back having a few glasses of wine when they got into a real ding-dong argument. They were going at it hammer and tongs. It all had to do with Gerald being gay', she said.[2]

Right from his birth Dixie posed a challenge to Glaskin. Although they were both born in the same maternity home, Glaskin was quick to point out that, whereas he only had a nurse present at his birth, Dixie was attended by a doctor, Dr Dixie Clement, after whom Delia named her second son. In *The Eaves of Night*, Glaskin not only mentions this but also debates with his beloved maternal grandmother which of the two boys was the heaviest at birth, a seemingly inconsequential detail but one that Glaskin considered worthy of inclusion in this family memoir. Regardless of their respective birth weights, as adults the two brothers developed quite different and distinctive appearances. Glaskin's commanding near-six-foot frame, chestnut brown eyes and wavy hair contrasted starkly with Dixie's short, wiry build, close-cropped hair and blue eyes. With a hint of one-upmanship, Glaskin couldn't resist commenting on this in the one book, albeit unpublished, he dedicated to his younger brother – and 'for my brother Dix who prefers his fiction the same way he is: short.'[3]

Like his elder brother, Dixie attended Fremantle Boys School but instead of shining academically as Glaskin did, he earned the honour of being

---

1   Ethel Webb Bundell to JB, personal communication, 18 April 2001.
2   Audrey Glaskin to JB, interview by author, 3 December 2002.
3   *Any Girl Will Do: Stories Not in a Literary Style*. Unpublished. The full statement is: Dedicated to Hugh Bainger, who not only published my first short story but asked for more (and got them) and for my brother Dix who prefers his fiction the same way he is: short. GMG (1972b).

champion swimmer, an achievement of no small measure in sports-crazed Australia. He went on to claim the same title at the Cottesloe Surf Club where he met his wife-to-be, Audrey, also a good swimmer. As a young man, Dixie often helped out his maternal grandmother, Nan, who lived on a four-hectare property in the foothills at Herne Hill about 45 kilometres east of Perth. This block had originally been part of a much larger tract of land owned by Glaskin's great-grandfather Peter Anthony Gugeri but had been whittled down by the old man 'to provide him with the style of living from which he never became accustomed to having to abandon'.[4] When Nan's husband died, Dixie went to live with his grandmother to keep her company and ended up staying nearly 18 months. In appreciation of the assistance he had rendered over the years and in an effort to give a young couple a start in life, Nan gave part of the property to Dixie and Audrey when they married in 1950. In the style of true Aussie battlers, the pair built their own house from scratch, even making the concrete bricks themselves. Dixie carried bags of cement one by one from nearby Kalamunda on his motorcycle by placing them across the fuel tank and resting them on his knees.

Glaskin fictionalises these events in his short story *A Small Selection*, the title story in his first volume of short stories published in 1962. The narrator, George, is a writer who has just returned from overseas and is basking in the glory of having his first novel published in London. While he has been plugging away at his second novel in his Singapore flat, he has been admiring from afar the tireless efforts of his young friends Derek and Anne, to create their own home in the bush. He builds with words while they build with bricks. After years of backbreaking labour they finally have a small house and property they are proud to call home. But circumstances dictate otherwise. The long drive to the city and back every day for Derek, the absence of amenities and services, not to mention the separation from their favourite beach, take their toll. After seven years of sweat and toil, Derek and Anne sell their beloved place in the bush to a retired Malayan couple and move back to a pokey little house in a boringly repetitive, working-class suburb. When George returns to Perth and drives his friends to see their 'small selection', they are confronted with a heart-stopping sight. The house has been demolished and a sign has appeared announcing that a brick factory is to be erected on the site. Their dream home has been sold out from under them, no doubt for a tidy sum. All the sweat from their toil is now replaced by tears of angst and bitterness. Anne makes a valiant gesture in proclaiming

---

4   GMG (1975, 146).

they will build again, this time close to the ocean, but the pain remains. It is a touching story in the great tradition of the Australian underdog, fighting hopeless odds to carve out a place for himself in the world, only to have it unceremoniously ripped away from him. And in this case it was partly true.[5] In the story Glaskin makes an indirect tribute to his brother when he says of Derek, 'I could not help marvelling, with profound respect, at his courage and resolution.'[6]

Throughout the story most of the correspondence referred to is between the narrator and Anne. Twice the narrator is on the brink of writing to Derek but just can't do it. This mirrored the relationship between Glaskin and Audrey, whose chatty, no-holds-barred approach to life Glaskin responded well to. But he didn't share the same rapport with his younger brother. They were made of different stuff and walked down different paths most of their lives. On one occasion, when Glaskin was preparing to ship his car to Singapore, he was struggling to detach the aerial from the mudguard. It was growing dark and he had trouble seeing what he was doing, lying on his back under the vehicle. Dixie happened to come along at that moment. 'What are you trying to do?' he asked, suggesting his brother was making tough going out of something quite simple. Knowing his brother's natural aptitude with things mechanical, Glaskin handed him the spanner. Dixie had the aerial off in a flash. 'Gerald had a bit more in the head,' said Audrey, 'whereas Dix was good with his hands'.[7]

He was good with hands in other ways too. Like Glaskin, Dixie served in the navy, where no doubt he kept his strong swimmer's body in good shape. Not long after his discharge, he was home one evening with Glaskin and their next brother, Llew.[8] Glaskin was in the bathroom getting ready to go out and Llew, who had just arrived home filthy dirty from his job as a motorcycle mechanic, was leaning against the ice chest in the kitchen. Delia said something to Llew but since he was engrossed in reading the paper he didn't reply. Instantly, Glaskin snapped, 'Why don't you answer your mother?' Not taking kindly to his older brother bossing him around,

---

5   According to Audrey Glaskin, it is 'more fictional than fact'. She and Dixie never met the buyers of their Herne Hill property, she didn't think the house was demolished, nor did she believe that a brick kiln was erected on the site. Furthermore, she didn't assist Dixie making bricks. However, they did sell the property and rebuilt close to the ocean at North Beach with the aid of a war service loan. They put the proceeds from the sale of their hills property towards the purchase of a Holden panel van. Audrey Glaskin to JB, 27 September 2003.

6   'A Small Selection' in GMG (1962b, 246).

7   Audrey Glaskin to JB, interview, 3 December 2002.

8   His full name is Llewellyn.

Llew retorted, 'Who's talking to you, God Almighty?' The next thing he knew a fist came straight through the paper and hit him in the face. Within seconds Glaskin had zipped from the bathroom and delivered his blow. Llew grabbed Glaskin around the neck and started dragging him out the front door. He whacked Glaskin with his fist and was determined to choke him to death. Their mother stood by horrified, uttering pleas of restraint that fell on deaf ears. At that moment, Dixie joined the fray and pulled his two warring brothers apart. 'If you come outside, I'll break both your bloody necks', he screamed. The two relented and calm was restored. Summing up Dixie's skill, gumption and presence of mind, Llew quipped, 'He was a tough little bloke.'[9]

There was a tension between Glaskin and Dixie that didn't manifest itself with his other younger brothers, Llewellyn and Roland, at least not to the same extent or in the same way. With Dixie's arrival on the scene Glaskin had a rival to deal with. If Glaskin was the apple of his mother's eye, Dixie claimed the prize from his father, much to the chagrin of the other siblings who came later. Said Llew, fourth in line, with a smirk, 'Dixie was Dad's boy. Loris [third child and first daughter] was Dad's girl, and I was a pain in the butt!'[10] Both Glaskin and Dixie were extremely fond of their grandmother Nan, who skilfully dispensed her affections between the two, although Dixie was the lucky recipient of the gift of land from her, a gesture that Glaskin might not have received so well. Another relative who was the envy of both boys was their Uncle Alan, their mother's younger brother who lived alone on the family property, Acacia Springs, near Glen Forrest in the Darling Ranges. Before his tragic death at 22, Alan had been adored by his two young nephews. How difficult it must have been for Glaskin to accept the fact that his uncle, whom he called 'a marvel of a hero', preferred Dixie to him. In a confessional moment he wrote, 'Dixie was Alan's pet and I was inordinately jealous of this.'[11]

For most of their adult lives Glaskin and Dixie lived in separate worlds. When Gilbert took his family to Japan at the end of the Second World War with the British Commonwealth Occupational Force, Glaskin and Dixie remained behind in Perth. But instead of sharing a flat they lived at separate residences just down the road from each other. When Dixie died on Christmas Day 1996 at age 69, Glaskin did not attend the funeral. This

---

9   Llew Glaskin to JB, interview by author, 20 November 2002.
10 Ibid.
11 GMG (1975, 110 and 114). For more on the life and death of Alan Gugeri, see Chapter 8, 'Writer in Search of a Cause'.

surprised and shocked some members of the family. But his absence was due to the fact that he spent most of the day lying prone on his bed barely able to move. Nineteen ninety-six had been a tough year for Glaskin. In addition to his usual assortment of ailments and accidents he also had several altercations with his apartment neighbours, one of which led to his being charged with assault, although he was finally acquitted and awarded damages. His neck and head were still in pain from the attack on him 10 months before. As soon as he stood up, the pain increased. It was months before Glaskin would walk again outside his unit. In his diary that day Glaskin wrote, 'Not a word from any of the family. Dix's death bears out what Mother said to me in Singapore circa 1957 – "I love my children, they're my children, but I don't really like them" … Neither do I!'[12] Three years later when Glaskin himself was close to death and heavily drugged with morphine, he was often heard calling out names of family members, among them his mother, his great-aunt Fan and Dixie. Perhaps this was Glaskin's last attempt to bridge the gap that had always existed between him and his younger brother.

One thing that Glaskin and Dixie did have in common was a willingness to care for their father in his latter years, in spite of differences both had with Gilbert. Most of the other siblings washed their hands of their father. In 1976 Gilbert had a yearning to revisit the homes of his childhood, two in the Eastern Goldfields towns of Kalgoorlie and Coolgardie and the other in South Fremantle, where he was born. Sceptical that his father would recognise the dwellings and hoping they still existed, Dixie agreed to his request. When they reached Coolgardie all they found was an empty block of land but Gilbert was sure it was the right place, even though he would have been only about three at the time he lived there. But in Kalgoorlie, where he lived as a five- or six-year old, Gilbert pinpointed the exact house, facing south on to a park and with 'funny scrolls' on the front. Dixie was amazed at this father's memory. Gilbert wasn't well at the time but lived another 10 years before he died in a nursing home, which Dixie had arranged for him to move into. During this period Glaskin also spent time with his father, recording some of his life stories. On one occasion, wheezing for breath from bronchitis, Gilbert asked his eldest son if he could do something to help him 'follow your mother'. Glaskin jokingly replied that, short of dropping him on his head out of a three-storey window, he couldn't think of a thing. His father smiled and patted his son's hand. It was in these moments of reconciliation that Glaskin learned how proud his father was of his achievements as an

---

12 GMG (1996, 30 December).

author. Gilbert astonished his son by recalling episodes from his books that he himself had forgotten. When his father died at 83 of a 'quick and easy death' Glaskin was generous in his comments about him. 'My father had a long life but, compared with my own, not at all a good one. He had the intelligence and application to achieve a good deal more than he did, but never the opportunity.'[13]

If Glaskin found his next male sibling distant and divergent in interests and values, his relationship to his first sister was quite the opposite. Loris Winsome was born seven years after Glaskin, when the family was living at 72 Mason Street (now Stirling Highway) in Cottesloe. Her first recollection of her eldest brother was of him playing the piano with his pet pink-and-grey galah perched on his shoulder. To the impressionable young girl, Glaskin must have cut quite a startling figure, able to perform so competently and entertain at the same time. Being number three in line and a girl at that, she probably didn't present quite the challenge to Glaskin's male supremacy in the sibling hierarchy that Dixie did. As they grew up together, Glaskin and Loris developed quite close ties. She above all his siblings was the one who returned his affections most readily and most consistently. He referred to her by her nickname, Pops, a reference to the fact that she was born on Anzac Day. Each year until her 21st birthday Loris was the recipient of a bright red poppy that was pinned to a sash her mother had made for her.

But the bond between Glaskin and Loris was put to the test when, at 18, Loris decided to marry an Englishman, Christopher Carberry. As the marriage began to show signs of strain, Glaskin decided it was time for him to assert his role as elder brother, much like his Swiss-Italian ancestors may have done in a culture where it is the brother's duty to defend the honour of his sister. Unable to stand aside and let his sister handle her own problems, Glaskin threw himself into the fray. Although never married himself, he had abundant advice for his young sister about how she should handle her marital discord. His bottom line was that Loris should seek a divorce. Being brought up a good Catholic, she couldn't contemplate such a thing. Not surprisingly, Carberry resented his brother-in-law's attempts to interfere in his personal life and, in an effort to get Glaskin to desist, wrote him a letter in which he asked Glaskin to stay away from the Carberry family. Loris and her husband finally parted company, although with the understanding that each would care for the other as needed. In the meantime, she was able to obtain some distance on her situation by spending half of each year in

---

13 LvdP (1994, 64).

England, a practice she has continued to follow for much of her adult life. In Glaskin's latter years, the rift between him and Carberry appeared to heal. In spite of his deteriorating health, Carberry was present at Glaskin's funeral, a gesture that did not go unnoticed, especially by van de Pas, who was quite touched by it.

Just before her brother died, Loris was a regular visitor to his bedside, as she had been throughout Glaskin's life. She sat with him during his last day, talking with him about their mother, before he finally ebbed out of this world early the following morning. They had shared a number of intimate moments over the years, trusting each other with secrets and feelings that neither would have so easily divulged to other brothers and sisters. One such experience involved their great-aunt, Grace Winifred Jecks, known as 'Snowy' for her wispy white hair. Loris and her husband kept in close touch with Grace for many years so it wasn't surprising that Loris, like Glaskin, was privy to the news of Grace's liaison with their father, Gilbert Henry Glaskin.[14]

If Loris was Glaskin's favourite sister, Llewellyn, or Llew as he was known, was Glaskin's favourite brother, fist fights and other physical confrontations notwithstanding. Llew was born when Glaskin was nine so didn't represent a threat to Glaskin's ascendancy in the family. Besides, with Loris's birth two years before Llew, the Glaskins had begun to grow into a sizable family with room for a range of personalities and relationships. Glaskin's affection for Llew is captured in many of his letters where he would address his brother as 'Llew love' or, with an alliterative flair, 'Lululuv'. Why Llew should have been the chosen one is not clear because he didn't reciprocate Glaskin's affection, at least not to the same extent. But one event in their childhood could have had something to do with it.

When Llew was around five or six years old, the family went for a picnic at Bibra Lake, south of Perth. Dixie was about nine and Glaskin around 14. It had been a particularly dry year, which had left a wide strip of boggy mud out from the reed-covered edge of the lake. Beyond that was a hard crust of yellowish sand but in order to reach the sand, you needed to traipse across a line of stepping stones. Dixie had ventured out onto the sand and Llew was keen to follow. He yelled out to Dixie, 'Is it hard out there?' 'Yeah,' replied Dixie, 'but you'll have to jump over the muck to get here.' Llew retreated far enough to get a running start and, with all the power he could muster in his

---

14 Loris Carberry to JB, 12 December 2003. However, Loris reported that it was GMG who told her about the affair and the child that resulted from it.

two little legs, took a gigantic leap. The next thing he knew he was up to his neck in mud and sinking fast. Dixie took off like a rabbit, screaming for help. Glaskin suddenly appeared on the scene. He raced to the stones and lent over the side. He was just able to grab Llew's hair and yank him out of the morass. 'I can remember vividly coming out', said Llew. 'I was hurled through the air, landed on the ground with a bonk, and had this stinking mud falling off me.' He was taken to a nearby dairy farm where his father borrowed a hose and washed him down. The dairyman's wife reminded him how lucky he'd been to escape with his life. 'Oh, it's dangerous you know', she said. 'It's almost like quicksand. We've lost cows in that because they've wandered in there.'[15]

Glaskin's prompt action in rescuing Llew reflects a maturity beyond his years and a propensity to take charge of situations without question. He would say what he thought, act as he felt impelled to, then later weigh up the pros and cons of his behaviour. And he would not hesitate to use others if he thought it would reinforce his case. Even when he was in his seventies, he called on Llew to play such a role. When Glaskin became enmeshed in a series of incidents with other residents of his strata-title units, the police cautioned both parties not to have any physical contact with each other. Glaskin heeded this warning but decided on another tactic to keep his neighbour in line. One day when Llew came to visit him, Glaskin spotted his neighbour moving around downstairs. He opened his back door, lent over the railing and announced scathingly, 'Come up here now, you fucking bastard. My brother's here and he'll flatten you.' Somewhat taken aback by his newly acquired role of Glaskin's goon, Llew said, 'Now, hang on Gerald, if you don't mind!' Glaskin wouldn't say exactly what he had told his neighbour about his brother's fighting skills but the man didn't show his face for days afterwards.[16]

Apart from Llew's physical prowess, Glaskin respected his brother's business acumen and trusted him to handle his financial affairs when he lived outside Australia. Glaskin gave Llew power of attorney and often recommended stock for him to buy and sell on his behalf. They also helped each other with property transactions at different times. When Llew needed money for a deposit on his first home, Glaskin willingly obliged. Later on, when Llew had acquired a block of land near Mandurah, Glaskin became interested in doing the same, so Llew organised that on Glaskin's behalf.

15 Llew Glaskin to JB, interview, 20 November 2002.
16 LvdP remembered this episode differently. He says Glaskin abhorred violence and was worried that Llew would go downstairs and 'sort out' his neighbour.

Two or three years before he died, Glaskin phoned Llew and asked him to be the co-executor of his will, along with the Public Trustees Office.[17] Llew was at first puzzled by this request, given the solid reputation of the Public Trustees Office. 'Because you've been an accountant and know all these things, I'd like you to ensure that what I've put in my will is done as per the will', Glaskin explained. 'Not that I don't trust the Public Trustees but sometimes they get a bit tardy or they shove it to one side.' Llew understood his concern and agreed to do as his brother asked.

Glaskin relied upon Llew more than either of them probably realised. In the last few years of his life, when he began to terminate a number of close relationships, Glaskin had little contact with most of his immediate family, which he deeply regretted. He became indignant. After all he had done for his siblings over the years, when he needed them most they were not there. During his final days in Hollywood Private Hospital, he had a number of visitors, mostly friends and nieces and nephews, apart from van de Pas's near-constant presence. With the exception of Loris, his brothers and sisters were notable by their absence. And Llew's absence pained him more than that of the others. One day, desperate to talk to Llew and unable to dial the phone himself, Glaskin managed to get one of the nurses to dial Llew's number for him. Llew's wife answered and told Glaskin that her husband was not at home but that she would pass on his message to him. Her efforts to mollify her angry and pleading brother-in-law and to justify his brother's absence didn't pass muster. But Llew had his own excuses that went beyond inertia or lack of caring. 'My own granddaughter was extremely ill with a tumour on the brain. She was susceptible to anything. Since Gerald had a notice on his hospital door warning visitors not to touch him, I was worried I might pick up a bug and transfer it to her, so I stayed away'.[18]

The same could almost be said for Glaskin's youngest brother, Roland, although he did make several attempts to see his brother before Glaskin died. His last visit was about a week before Glaskin's death and it gave him

17 In 1988, GMG asked his friend and fellow writer David Hough to be his literary executor. He was concerned about the fate of his manuscripts when he died and felt Hough would be a good person to deal with such matters. However, two years later GMG became entangled in a dispute with the Library and Information Services of Western Australia over his manuscripts and informed Hough that, regretfully, because of the complexity of the situation in which he now found himself he could no longer use him as his literary executor. David Hough to JB, interview by author, 19 November 2002.

18 Llew Glaskin to JB, interview, 20 November 2002.

quite a shock. 'He looked dreadful', said Roland. 'He was in a bit of a coma. I didn't get to speak to him. I just sat by his bedside for some time. He seemed to be dreaming or hallucinating and he looked ghastly. His feet were sticking out over the end of the bed and his toenails hadn't been cut in ages. It was gross.' This last cameo of Glaskin was a far cry from some of the earliest memories Roland had of his eldest brother. One of these was when Roland was about seven or eight and Glaskin had just returned home from the war. Roland used to spend a lot of time down at the Swan River, which in those days flooded nearly every winter. He would wander down there after school and fossick among the debris that floated onto the shore, looking for treasures. One day, he came upon a sizable turtle. Like a young pup wanting to show his master its prize pick-up, Roland thought he would take it home to delight his mother and add it to the goldfish pond in the backyard. But Glaskin thought otherwise. The next thing Roland knew he was being forced marched all the way back to the river with the turtle, under the military-like thumb of his eldest brother. 'He even gave me a shove to make certain I would put it back in the water', said Roland.[19]

Soon after this, Roland joined most of the rest of his family in Japan. During this time, Glaskin was working as a stockbroker in Singapore and often sent gifts to family members. Roland's prize was the stamps that Glaskin had his business colleagues collect from mail they received from all over the world. He would soak them off their envelopes and send them by the boxful to Roland, who soon became an avid stamp collector. While he was in Japan, and encouraged by his mother, Roland wrote frequently to Glaskin, regaling him with stories about earthquakes and typhoons and snow – things his older brother would not have experienced. Glaskin was quick to notice that Roland possessed a gift with words that he prided himself having. As he often did with promising young writers, Glaskin encouraged Roland to expand and refine his stories and send them to *The Western Mail* in Perth, which had published Glaskin's first stories. Soon a second Glaskin was being published in the newspaper. Roland was thrilled and for a while considered trying to follow in his brother's footsteps. Before mailing off his manuscripts to the paper he would send them to Glaskin for his comments. In an editorial style characteristic of Glaskin, they would come back to Roland riddled with corrections and suggestions for improvement. He persisted for a while but when the rejection slips became too numerous and too deflating he decided to leave writing to his older brother.

---

19 Roland Glaskin to JB, interview by author, 20 November 2002.

Most of the time Glaskin and Roland had a fairly amicable relationship, perhaps in part due to their 14-year age difference and perhaps because they didn't spend a lot of time living under the same roof. Glaskin was quick to offer his younger brother financial help when he needed it. Before he married, Roland and his fiancée decided to have a joint 21st birthday party at the reception room in a high-rise city building. Both sets of parents came together to discuss arrangements and agreed to share costs. When it came to the crunch, however, Gilbert didn't have the money, neither did Roland. His mother asked Glaskin to pay half the bill, which he did. Not long after, when Roland and his wife went on their honeymoon, Glaskin lent them his 1959 FC Holden station wagon, an export model with all the latest bells and whistles, which Glaskin had brought back from Singapore. 'It was very kind of him', said Roland. Like his eldest brother, Roland was drawn more to the Gugeri side of the family than to the Glaskins. Following Glaskin's example, he too spent holidays with his great aunts at The Rose and Crown hotel in Guildford, especially when his mother had her hands full coping with two little girls. In contrast to Glaskin, however, he had a hard time relating to his paternal grandfather and grandmother. 'They were the most unfriendly people', said Roland. 'Especially grandpa who would go out of his way to frighten me by popping out his false teeth!'[20]

Growing up, Roland had always put Glaskin on a pedestal, especially as a writer. 'I used to feel proud when people would say, "Glaskin, eh? Are you related to Gerald Glaskin? I've just read one of his books."' But this deep sense of pride and adoration was shattered the day he discovered his eldest brother was gay. 'I was 17 or 18 when the old man came across Gerald in bed with one of his friends. They had such a fierce argument over it. Oh god!'[21] Roland had no way of dealing with this kind of revelation. As a young man himself, he was no doubt exploring his own sexuality at the time. But not having been exposed to the ways of the world as Glaskin had in the armed forces and cosmopolitan Singapore, he had a much more limited frame of reference in which to try to make sense of this devastating news. All he had to fall back on was the prevailing attitude towards gays in 1950s Australia, which dubbed his brother into the semi-human category of being 'just a bloody poofter'. This was such a far cry from the sophisticated, successful, outgoing and caring brother he had known and worshipped that it didn't make any sense to Roland. Perhaps even harder to take than the revelation

---

20 Ibid.
21 Ibid.

itself was the total silence that surrounded it. Homosexuality, and having a homosexual family member in particular, was not a subject for dinner-table conversation, nor any conversation. 'I never discussed it with Gerald. He never discussed it with me. There was no discussion. You just had to accept it. Mum never mentioned it to me either. And with Gilbert, the knife went in deeper.'[22]

As shocking as this disclosure was to Roland, it was as though it was preparing him for another moment that would occur later in life, when his third son, Rodney, came out to his parents as gay. Glaskin greeted the news of having a gay nephew with utter delight, even if complete surprise. When he invited Rodney to Christmas dinner one year his nephew asked if he could bring a friend, to which Glaskin gladly agreed. When Rodney arrived with a male friend Glaskin was speechless. 'I nearly flipped,' he said, 'I just couldn't believe it. Naturally, we've become very close.'[23] A bit too close, at times, according to Roland. 'He was quite fond of my younger son, Rod. He would phone me up and ask what's Rod doing these days and why isn't Rod in his own home. Then he would start to pester me about it, saying that if I couldn't lend Rod or give Rod the money as a deposit on his house, then he would. I finally got sick of it. It wasn't that I wasn't prepared to give Rod the money. The banks didn't want to lend money based on a deposit that someone else had given you. Gerald gave me a hard time and he tested my patience a lot. He was interfering, being forceful. I guess he had Rod's best interests at heart but it was the way he was going about it that I wasn't very impressed with.'[24]

Glaskin's other siblings expressed similar sentiments about the interest he expressed in the well-being of his nephews and nieces, and the former in particular. It is an intriguing aspect of Glaskin's personality that warrants closer scrutiny. It is as though at times 'the managing elder brother' crossed over and became 'the interfering elder uncle'. At its most basic level Glaskin's desire to be of assistance to young people, whether inside or outside his family, appeared to have all the manifestations of genuine, altruistic, selfless concern. Indeed, many have commented on Glaskin's ability to relate to young people and his willingness to go out of his way to help them.

One of those was his long-time friend, Rae Kean, herself the mother of two sons and a daughter. Glaskin met Kean and her former husband and children in 1967 while going to the Netherlands on a Dutch freighter on

22 Ibid.
23 Cover (1994b, 19).
24 Roland Glaskin to JB, interview, 20 November 2002.

which they constituted over half the passengers. This introduction developed into a life-long association between Glaskin and Kean that both greatly cherished. At one time Kean and her husband were hosting a Rotary exchange student at their home. He was a young South African who, like her own eldest son, was musically talented. 'He was a very bright and highly gifted young man but had lived a rather sheltered life. Gerry went to enormous lengths to help him', she said. 'They weren't grandiose gestures but they were very thoughtful things. He would buy the boy music or CDs. He freely gave of his time to discuss things with him, which I think is the real test of generosity.' Kean added, 'Gerry had a way of communicating with young people that was very effective. He always treated them as adults, even from quite young. He would speak to six- or seven-year olds on an equal footing and they responded accordingly.'[25]

Others echoed Kean. Kevin Pearce, a travel entrepreneur and Glaskin's long-time friend, experienced this side of Glaskin on many occasions. 'Gerry loved young people and had a wonderful ability just to be with them, even though he was a generation older', said Pearce. 'When he lived at Cottesloe, he'd go down to the beach and get talking to someone and invite them back for coffee. I'd often pop in at his flat and he'd be chatting away to some young person he'd just met.'[26] Another close friend of Glaskin, David Harrop, noticed the same propensity in Glaskin in the realm of art and music. 'He was very encouraging to artists, particularly young people, students and those having their first exhibitions. I never heard him put down anyone for their efforts. He usually had some anecdote he would use to compare their work to that of a master, such as "yours is the style of so-and-so's painting" or "your music is like Beethoven".'[27]

But what appeared to be a genuine sense of caring for young people and a willingness to go out of his way to offer them advice and support would sometimes develop into a meddlesome intrusion into their lives and the lives of their families. Glaskin's youngest sister, Hilary, experienced her brother this way in his dealings with her two sons as they were growing up. According to her, Glaskin used to encourage her first son, Mark, to spend time with him, but Mark didn't have the time or the desire to take up his uncle's offer and his parents didn't encourage it. When Mark married, Glaskin was not invited to his wedding, which hurt Glaskin a lot. Following this, Glaskin redirected his energies to her younger son, Aaron. When

---

25 Rae Kean to JB, interview by author, 13 September 2001.
26 Kevin Pearce to JB, interview by author, 21 November 2002.
27 David Harrop to JB, interview by author, 2 December 2002.

Aaron was about eight Glaskin arranged a penfriend for him through one of his friends in Singapore, a gesture no doubt prompted by the life-changing experience Glaskin had in his own relationship with his Dutch penfriend, Sjoerd Steunebrink.[28] Aaron also had an interest in English literature and showed early promise as a writer, something Glaskin no doubt was keen to encourage. Said Hilary, 'Maybe he did it in Aaron's best interests but Aaron didn't really get along with Gerry. It was quite sad. Gerry would ring up and say, 'I want to have a chat with Aaron about something.' He never wanted to chat with me, it was always with Aaron!' After a while Aaron tried to avoid his uncle's phone calls and Hilary found herself in an invidious position. 'Because he never had any children of his own, I think Gerry tried to parent through his brothers' and sisters' children. My two were just the last.'[29]

Apart from his dealings with her sons, Hilary had her own troubles with her brother, 21 years her senior. One of these concerned the use of Fairholme, the war service home Gilbert had acquired upon returning from Japan in 1949, but whose mortgage payments and ownership Glaskin had assumed in 1958. After Delia died in March 1960 and Myree and Roland each married and moved out later that year, Gilbert and Hilary were left alone in the house. To help support the two of them, Hilary gave up her desire to be a teacher and sought other work. As soon as he was well enough, Gilbert also obtained a job with an electrical goods retailer. It was initially a part-time position but with his smart clerical skills and elegant handwriting he soon upgraded to a full-time employee. At home Hilary did the housework and Gilbert helped with the cooking on weekends. It was a mutually convenient arrangement that lasted until 1966 when several things happened. Not being in good health and having the support of two pensions, Gilbert announced he was planning to retire. About the same time, Hilary met Noel and wanted to get married in September. Tiring of Dutch winters and concerned about his father's ill health, Glaskin decided to return home later in the year. In August, Gilbert wrote to Glaskin asking if he would mind if Hilary and Noel stayed at Fairholme for a short time after their marriage until their house was available or they knew where Noel was to be posted. Gilbert confessed that he had an ulterior motive in making the request – it would compensate for the loneliness he so feared once they moved out.

A flurry of letters ensued between Perth and Amsterdam among all three parties. The exchanges became more heated, especially between Glaskin and

28 See Chapter 3, 'Gerald in Wonderland'.
29 Hilary Heath to JB, interview by author, 29 November 2002.

his father. Glaskin made his position clear. He didn't mind if Hilary and Noel stayed on, as long as he could have back his old room, which they were then occupying. This was a condition he claims he always stipulated. To Glaskin the solution was simple. They would have the larger room at the front of the house, his father would occupy Hilary's old room or the back verandah and he would have his old room. But the memory of her mother's agonising last days and weeks in the front room were too much for Hilary to contemplate. Glaskin dismissed her concern and suggested that she and Noel find other accommodation before he arrived. Fortunately, Hilary and Noel had already come to the same decision. They rented a flat in which they lived until their home was ready. The elder brother had spoken and they had no desire to exacerbate the situation. But as they soon discovered, Glaskin would not be out of the picture, especially once their two sons were born and he found a new role for himself as the guiding uncle and parental advisor.[30]

Gilbert didn't take his son's pressure tactics so lightly. In his letters, Glaskin reprimanded his father about the way he had treated Delia, charging that he only took over payments on the house because 'you made conditions for her insupportable'. Furthermore, he added, 'Over the years, whenever I have returned [to Perth], you have seemed to delight in making conditions incompatible, and this time you started even before I returned … You would make life unbearable for even a street-cleaner, let alone for someone trying to write.'[31] Gilbert was quick in responding to his son's 'abusive letter', answering some of his charges and leaving others until Glaskin's return. He let Glaskin know that certain relatives had hinted he was returning to Perth with the intention of settling his affairs, selling the house, and going back to live permanently in the Netherlands. 'This flattened me', wrote his father.[32] At least part of this was true. After Glaskin returned to Perth in January 1967, he spent five months looking for a suitable apartment for his father. At last he found what he considered to be the perfect situation in Warnham Road, Cottesloe. But Gilbert loathed living in a flat and refused to take up his son's offer. Ten years later he still hadn't set foot in the place. Glaskin next tried to convince Loris to take Gilbert by having a bed-sit built on to her beach house at Safety Bay. Loris was willing to entertain the idea but

---

30 LvdP disputes that GMG played such an interfering role with his nephews and nieces. He claims that GMG would only have seen Hilary's sons half a dozen times in all the years he was living with GMG, and then only at family gatherings. However, Hilary's comments pertained mostly to phone calls GMG made, to which LvdP would not always have been privy.

31 GMG to Gilbert Glaskin, 4 November 1966.

32 Gilbert Glaskin to GMG, 11 November 1966.

in the meantime Gilbert rented a room on the back verandah of a house in the suburb of Morley. The only snag was the room needed to be finished. Glaskin paid to complete and outfit the room.

In his same letter Glaskin complained that, 'It seems that whenever I try to do something for some members of the family, I can expect not thanks for it but only abuse.' But therein lay a large part of Glaskin's struggle – he always tried to do things *for* others, in his family and beyond. He always thought he knew what was best and would act on it, often impulsively and sometimes in a high-handed manner. It probably never occurred to him to consult the other party first and solicit their thoughts on the subject or to involve them in the decision making. He had the know-how, the skill, the articulateness, the courage and, above all, the resources to discern the problem, devise the solution and implement the action required. In this sense, he was more like the benevolent dictator, whereas he imagined himself to be, and portrayed himself as, the caring provider. He couldn't fathom why others were often so ungrateful for his munificence, both monetary and advisory.

In some cases, however, his dismay was justified. He complained that his father, for one, could never understand, let alone appreciate, the sacrifice he made in diminishing his share in his partnership in the stockbroking firm of Lyall and Evatt in order to help buy Fairholme.[33] Considering that he offered to pay the £1,528 owing on the mortgage, which was no mean sum in 1958, he had some reason to resent his father's attitude. But in other cases his claims of supporting the family through tough times appear somewhat exaggerated. Glaskin's assertion that he helped put his two youngest sisters through school was met with scepticism by both Hilary and Myree.[34] When the girls returned from Japan they went to St. Thomas's Catholic School in Claremont for a while, but Myree, emulating the style of her elder brother, hit a nun who had wrongly accused her little sister of a misdemeanour. She curtly left and refused to go back to the convent. Their mother then took the girls to Claremont High School, where they stayed until the end of their third years. Myree completed her fourth year at John Curtin High School in Fremantle before going on to dental school. While Glaskin may well have helped offset the cost of his sisters' uniforms, books, travel and other incidentals, these would not have been huge sums of money. As far as Myree

---

33 GMG (1978b, 6).

34 LvdP is sceptical of their claims. He maintains that as teenagers, they would not have been made aware of how the family finances operated and would not have been told of any contributions GMG would have made, knowing how much this grated on Gilbert.

was concerned, she never remembered the family having to scrimp to put her and Hilary through school. 'We were always well dressed and well fed', she said. 'My father made a reasonable amount of money and my mother was a very good manager. She was a dressmaker before she married.'[35]

Myree may not have been aware of her brother's financial aid to her, but she had other reasons to remember him. 'We were both the black sheep of the family', she said. 'He liked to travel and so did I. I lived in Sydney for nearly 22 years. He and I both went off and the others stayed.' In her younger days, Myree adored her elder brother. 'I absolutely idolized him', she said. 'He was charming, polite, well spoken, artistic. And a very caring person.' Glaskin would visit Myree on his trips to Sydney and they exchanged birthday cards. Myree enjoyed his company, whether in private or public. They once went to a theatre together and were waiting in the foyer before the show. Myree couldn't recall the exact play but it involved a king. Never one to miss an opportunity for a laugh, Glaskin quipped, 'You're going out to see a king with a queen, you know!' Not surprisingly, Glaskin found it much easier to joke about his sexual orientation with his sisters than his brothers. In a letter to Loris he once wrote, 'My dear sister. What are you doing growing pansies? There are more than enough in the world as it is!'[36]

Glaskin's relationship to Myree was coloured by the fact that not only was he her eldest brother, 19 years her senior, but he was also her godfather. As such, he tended to be even more liberal in giving advice and intervening in her life than he otherwise might have been. One of the first times he demonstrated this was when Myree became pregnant at 17. The rest of the family was still reeling from Delia's death a few months before and not ready for another shock. Myree turned to Glaskin for advice. At first, he was appalled and told her she should have the child adopted. However, he was outvoted. Myree wanted to keep the child, as did both her own father and the grandfather of the child. The result was a shotgun wedding, but not the 'quiet and pleasant little church wedding and reception' Glaskin envisaged.[37] The child's father came from a prominent, well-to-do Perth family and his own father was the state Minister for Health. The wedding hit the Perth newspapers and guests included several cabinet ministers and the wife of the premier. The premier himself, who was in Canberra at the time, sent a congratulatory telegram. Writing to Han Suyin, Glaskin noted sardonically, 'So the next announcement in November may come somewhat as a surprise to many, except that Myree, as she was leaving the reception, gaily waved a pressure cooker and said she knew how to use it. The house will be quiet, no, less noisy, without her, and my telephone bills much cheaper.'[38]

Although Myree had now embarked on her own life she had not left Glaskin's sphere of influence. This marriage ended in divorce, as did her next two. Glaskin was always there to advise – and in one case, accuse. When Myree's third husband committed suicide, Glaskin blamed her for his demise.[39] But his judgement may well have been clouded by another event that had taken place, which caused Glaskin to sever all contact with Myree for the rest of his life, much to her chagrin. After splitting with her last husband, Myree decided to sell her house and needed a temporary place in which to live. Since Glaskin owned the unit next door to van de Pas's in the Mosman Park apartments but didn't really use it, he offered it to his sister for a modest rent of $130 a month. Her daughter and son also had keys to the unit and often came and went. Not long after she had moved in Myree was diagnosed with Hodgkin's disease[40] and was immediately hospitalised. When her daughter visited her in hospital she told her mother that the police had just called on her and her brother, because somebody in the apartments had accused them of drug dealing. The same person had also rung up the electricity company and had the power cut off. Myree was mystified and distressed. She asked her older sister, Loris, to talk to Glaskin about it and see what he could do. Loris did and came back to tell Myree that Glaskin wanted her to hand over the keys to the unit. Perplexed, she asked why. 'Because of the drugs charge', said Loris. 'He doesn't want the police going through the unit.' Myree was furious. When she confronted Glaskin, she could no longer restrain herself. 'I was so angry I screamed at him. I couldn't understand what he was doing. He just stood back. He didn't care. I could have been anybody. He didn't care that I was so ill. He told everybody that I was a lunatic and should be in a psychiatric centre and that I probably had AIDS. That's what I got from my absolute fabulous brother who had done just about everything in my life for me.'

According to Myree, Loris gave Glaskin the wrong story. But Loris categorically denied this – it was one of Glaskin's neighbours with whom he had many unsavoury encounters and whom he later claimed was mentally ill

38 GMG to HS, 27 June 1960.
39 Denny's ex-husband asked her for money, which she refused. GMG claimed that this led to his suicide, which he then blamed on Myree.
40 A malignant disease of lymphatic tissues usually characterised by enlargement of the lymph nodes.

who planted the drugs story, she maintained. Myree was adamant; it was not drugs but take-away food that the nosy neighbour had spotted being brought into her unit. Her son and daughter lived together and worked in a teen-scene pub so kept odd hours. They often ordered in five-dollar meals from Dial-A-Dinner, which would deliver the food by car in a covered basket. Glaskin didn't buy this. Or perhaps he just resented the histrionic way his sister tried to convince him of her children's innocence, a mannerism that he too so often used on others. He cut all ties with Myree. She later regretted the way she tore him to shreds and pleaded with him to try to listen to reason but Glaskin wouldn't budge. Although she was seriously ill, he didn't visit the hospital or even send a card. He told her to move out of the unit right away. Even her separated husband tried to convince Glaskin to back down but he made no impression.

Glaskin's decision to cut his sister out of his life pained Myree. 'It was like I didn't exist any more. If we had passed in the street he would have totally ignored me', she said.[41] Finally, she got her own back on her brother for his mistreatment of her, in an indirect way. Just as Glaskin had not attended Dixie's funeral, so Myree did not attend Glaskin's. But it was not a straightforward decision. Before the funeral, one of her nieces rang Myree to ask if she was planning to attend. Myree said she wasn't, but since the rest of the family seemed to think she should be there she would consider it. Then, in a polite but firm tone, her niece told her that she had been asked to tell her not to come. Feeling he was carrying out Glaskin's wish, van de Pas had asked that Myree stay away from the funeral. Since Glaskin had insisted on no further contact with Myree when he was alive, van de Pas thought it only right that she not try to honour him in death. Other siblings were divided on the issue. Torn between conflicting advice and personal feelings on the matter, she decided to stay away. On the morning of his funeral, Myree went down to the beach at Rockingham, sat and read the paper, and went to the hairdressers. 'The only thing I regretted is that he would never listen to me so that I could explain things', she said sadly.[42]

Glaskin's relationships with his family, and his siblings in particular, were often strained. His keen wit and sharp intellect, his unabashed homosexuality, his often haughty public persona and his I-know-what's-best-for-you attitude no doubt all contributed to this. For much of his life, they lived in different worlds, literally and metaphorically. But in spite of

---

41 Denny to JB, interview, 29 November 2002.
42 Ibid.

appearing confident, articulate and assured, Glaskin often masked his own need for support from other family members and, perhaps without intending to, pushed them away or kept them at arms-length. After his surfing accident in 1967, in which he was virtually immobilised for months and found it excruciatingly painful to sit at his typewriter, he sat alone in his recently acquired Cottesloe apartment, bemoaning his fate and the lack of attention paid to him by his closest family members. In *Never Again*, he wrote:

> Six months had passed since the accident, and since then only a very few of my closest friends had come to see me. Even my own family – I don't count my father, but all those brothers and sisters most of whom I had helped purchase homes, or blocks of land on which to build them, or something or other – seemed to have deserted me. If they did come at all, it was invariably rather briefly and with a wary look of enquiry as though apprehensive of just how handicapped I might have become. It was never said but I fear that, whether or not I malign them, I could not help suspecting that they were concerned that I might become a burden to them, both physically and financially, which was pretty much what I had become to myself.[43]

Not all family members, especially the less immediate ones, found Glaskin a burden. Some even relished his quirky eccentricities and outgoing style, his audaciousness and theatrical flair. One of those was Glaskin's cousin, David Buchanan. He recalled one occasion in which van de Pas and Glaskin had been invited to dinner at a relative's home. 'Gerry was talking about placenta pink and penis blue. He outraged the whole evening and then promptly left, having entertained everyone from go to woe', he said. Buchanan not only delighted in Glaskin's personality but noticed that a number of other members of the Glaskin family – his mother Mary Glaskin and his uncle John Glaskin among them – 'suffered from the same condition', which he called 'Glaskinitis'. Buchanan ranked family members who had the condition from one to 10 and did not hesitate to put Glaskin at the top of the list. According to Buchanan, the main characteristics of Glaskinitis are:

- amazingly exuberant and extrovert (and occasionally introvert)
- enormously entertaining and charming
- almost narcissistic but not quite (it's more complex than that)

---

43 GMG (1978b, 15).

- given to fits of pique in which one and all can be completely dismissed
- hugely hysterical (where the cutting, bad scenes come in)
- loves a stoush and will take offence at almost anything from time to time
- willing to engage in meaningless battles over almost nothing forever.

Glaskin fits comfortably into this psychological template. Broadly speaking, its characteristics fall into three groups. The first two characteristics depict his conviviality and highly developed social skills, while the latter four point to his more bellicose nature and almost stoic refusal to give up the ghost. The third one captures Glaskin's capacity for reflective introspection, at times to the point of self-absorption. Glaskin's life is filled with examples of all three. Some who encountered him predominantly in one of these facets of his personality found it difficult to reconcile it with the other two. Buchanan, perhaps, was one of the few able to put together the pieces of the jigsaw puzzle that was Gerald Glaskin and celebrate the man in his wholeness, warts and all.

Growing up, Buchanan never knew Glaskin because their two families had no contact with each other. But he certainly knew of his famed cousin and his Dutch genealogist partner, almost as mythical figures. When he was 19, Buchanan went through a difficult period and contemplated getting in touch with Glaskin for advice and support. He had read Glaskin's *No End to the Way* and was impressed with its fluid, descriptive writing. Buchanan thought Glaskin might have been able to help him through his current crisis but he never could quite bring himself to pick up the phone or write a note. Instead, he went to Europe for four years and by the time he returned to Perth he had become a musician. Ironically, it was Glaskin who contacted him, after he had heard Buchanan's music on the radio. Van de Pas, who was working on the Glaskin family genealogy, contacted Buchanan and told him that Glaskin would love to meet him. Buchanan was intimidated by this larger-than-life man he was about to meet but he finally plucked up courage and knocked on Glaskin's door. Within minutes of meeting Glaskin all Buchanan's misgivings dissipated. His first reaction was, 'God, this guy is so much like my mother – vivacious, charming, witty … a wit that could cut air. And warm, above all, warm. Exuberant. It was a wonderful combination.' As he came to know him, Buchanan was struck by Glaskin's garrulous and comic nature. 'He talked effortlessly. He would often derail from his main topic because his mind was so full of thoughts. But you wouldn't be lost or left behind because he was so eloquent. And all the time he would use humour to bridge the gap. I spent nights with him and Leo over dinner when I laughed almost nonstop for hours. He could be so incredibly funny that I felt privileged to be with him.[44]

Some of Glaskin's more dramatic performances are firmly etched in Buchanan's memory. When they both lived in Mosman Park, he and Glaskin shared the same butcher shop owned by a young couple who kept up with the life and work of their customers. One day, right after Buchanan had had his first play performed and received favourably by the critics, he was in the shop talking to the butcher about the reviews in the paper that morning. Just at that moment, Glaskin walked in. In contrast to Buchanan's more self-effacing style, Glaskin had the kind of imposing demeanour that filled the whole shop and made people turn and look. He immediately picked up on the conversation and without seeming to take a breath announced, 'He comes from a very talented family. Mine!' Buchanan also never forgot some of Glaskin's most piquant one-liners. During a period when Glaskin and he were very close, Glaskin would phone Buchanan frequently. Buchanan never knew what Glaskin would have in store for him. One of Glaskin's most unforgettable opening lines was, 'Hallo, Gerry Glaskin here, second cousin once renowned!'[45]

Part of Glaskin's capacity to entertain was his delight in crossing the line of acceptability in public discourse. He possessed the audacity that would allow him to say things others would like to say but dared not. With his astute sense of timing, elegant poise and dramatic effect he could get away with it. Kevin Pearce, who led tour groups to Indonesia and Malaysia, enjoyed having Glaskin along on his trips for a number of reasons. 'He was very popular, especially with the women. He was gregarious, outgoing and amusing. And of course, he was extremely good-looking. But more than that, he had the ability to be a little bit outrageous and they loved it.'[46] Pearce also witnessed Glaskin's ability to outrage back home in Perth, where he was in demand as a guest speaker. On one occasion, Glaskin was invited to a convent to address a group of nuns on the quirks of the English language. Instead of limiting himself to humorous eccentricities or weird anomalies of his mother tongue, he chose to go for the jugular. He told his pious audience that a 'fuck' was an ancient plough and described the implement in great

44 David Buchanan to JB, interview by author, 12 November 2002.
45 Ibid.
46 Pearce to JB, interview, 21 November 2002.

detail. Just to drive home his point, he looked the devout ladies straight in the eyes and let loose with, 'So there. You can say it. Fuck, fuck, fuck!'[47]

Another time Glaskin was asked by his fellow writer and friend, Bert Vickers, to fill in for him as the presenter to a group of paraplegic and quad-riplegic patients at Royal Perth Hospital. Vickers warned him that he could expect some antagonism and even rudeness from his audience, some of whom were still struggling to adjust to the horrible handicap inflicted upon them. Because of this, Vickers stressed the need to establish rapport with his audience right from the start. Glaskin took up the challenge. Watching from behind a window as the patients were wheeled into the room, he decided they could be as rude as they liked but he would get the upper hand by being rude to them first. Taking a deep breath, he strode to the table in the centre of the room, looked around the group from one to the next and took the plunge. 'Oh, please don't bother to stand up just because I've come into the room!' he proclaimed. Stunned silence. His audience just stared uncomprehendingly. He had shown his hand and lost. Or so it seemed. Then first one, then another, and finally all of them laughed and clapped. The gamble had paid off. He had achieved the breakthrough he sought and established a rapport with this group that enabled him to keep coming back month after month. But he was lucky not to end up as a patient himself. During this time Glaskin suffered his own tragic surfing accident and was forced to wear a neck collar most of the time. He decided it was the perfect device to strengthen his bonds with the group. With head high and neck stiff in the collar, he walked in on his audience. Once again he said nothing but eyed his group slowly while they stared back at him. Was this some kind of joke, they wondered? Then, breaking the ice, Glaskin said, 'Well, you might at least have told me that it was contagious!'[48] Laughter filled the room and this time included Glaskin's own as well.

Along with his stinging intellect, clever use of language and consum-mate stage presence went enormous hubris. He didn't hesitate to dismiss the work of other established writers with the flick of his wrist, especially some of his fellow Australian writers. He found Randolph Stow 'rather dull and immature' and Hal Porter 'much too pretentious'.[49] Of the early works of the young Tim Winton, then a mere minnow of the literary figure he was to become, Glaskin said, 'I can read only a sentence at a time and then I have

47 Ibid.
48 GMG (1978b, 13).
49 GMG to Alma Glaskin, 12 November 1966.

to put him down. It's so thick.'[50] But he reserved some of his greatest disdain for Patrick White, while begrudgingly acknowledging that the man had some virtues. When the celebrated Australian writer won the Nobel Prize for Literature in 1973, Glaskin wrote to Han Suyin, 'It's marvellous for Australia but disastrous for the Nobel Prize.'[51] To his friend Peter Hurford he caricatured White as 'an old lady sitting with her knitting'.[52] And with a strange mix of sarcasm and envy Glaskin often proclaimed, 'I wish I could write like Patrick White but, thank God, I don't.'[53] Glaskin once wrote to White, suggesting that he might write a screenplay for *The Twyborn Affair*, White's complex three-part novel with a sexually ambivalent protagonist. White wrote back a short note in his scrawling longhand, turning down Glaskin's offer. 'Having been bitten once over a film I'm not inclined to become involved again in a hurry. In any case, *The Twyborn Affair* will only be made if one has a really extraordinary actor, scriptwriter and an exceptional director. The actor is the chief difficulty and if there is such a person, he will come to light in time … I am biding mine.'[54]

Just as Glaskin found it easy to point out the flaws in others' writing, so he found it hard to accept criticism of much of his own work. This was particularly true in his latter years, when he sent manuscript after manuscript to publishers in Australia, the UK and the USA, only to be rejected. Works like *Carnal Assault*, *Never Again*, *The Way You Went* and *At the End of It All*, which he rated among his best writing, failed to impress. But many of these manuscripts give the impression that he churned them out at prolific speed with seemingly little reworking and polishing. They have an off-the-cuff, stream-of-consciousness feel about them. They suggest Glaskin believed that because he was a successfully published author – in Europe no less – anything he wrote henceforth must be good and that he didn't need to spend a lot of time refining it. But what appears to be sloppy craftsmanship in his latter years was no doubt fed by other things happening in Glaskin's life, not least his failing health and a growing inflexibility and stubbornness in dealing with others, be they writers, publishers, agents or neighbours. Said Buchanan, 'In a sense, he was so dented that his only recourse was to become more narcissistic and gaze more longingly into the pond. At one stage, I used to call his flat "The Pond" because that was where he was and he

---

50 Buchanan to JB, interview, 12 November 2002.
51 GMG to HS, 24 December 1973.
52 Peter Hurford to JB, personal communication, 24 April 2001.
53 LvdP to JB, personal communication, 15 April 2001.
54 Patrick White to GMG, 7 January 1981.

wouldn't leave it, no matter how awful it was.'[55] Even when the pond became a raging sea, it seems. When Glaskin became embroiled in skirmishes with his neighbours, he tried to get Buchanan to take his side. Buchanan was reluctant and suggested that Glaskin and van de Pas remove themselves from what seemed to be an insuperable situation.[56] Glaskin wouldn't hear of it. Buchanan summed up Glaskin's position as, 'I'm Gerry Glaskin. I cannot be taken down. I will win this. I will take on the police if I must.'[57] And he did.

At times like these, Buchanan was thankful that he didn't seem to have inherited the Glaskinitis genes. While he revelled in the more uplifting manifestations of this family-like condition, he was clear it had its limitations as well. 'If I could get you Valma Glaskin, my mother Mary, John and Gerry in the same room, you'd be amazed. You'd be entertained almost to the point of tears with their wit and repartee. And then something would happen, you wouldn't know quite what it was, and there could be hell to pay at any moment.'[58] Glaskin repeated this pattern over and over with individuals and institutions. Several people have commented on it. As Myree noted, 'Everybody had a beaut thing going with Gerry and then something happened, and that was it'.[59] It was as though he drew a line in the sand and the moment you stepped over it there was no going back to your former relationship.

One of the most memorable yet painful instances of this occurred in 1973 between Glaskin and another well-known Western Australian writer and lawyer, Nicholas Hasluck. Hasluck was one of two sons of Alexandra and Paul Hasluck, both acknowledged writers in their own fields but better known as the former vice-regal family of Australia. Nicholas Hasluck had met Glaskin on several occasions in the early 1960s when he would drop by the Hasluck home for a drink or to discuss matters with his mother and Henrietta Drake-Brockman, all of whom were involved in the local chapter of the Fellowship of Australian Writers (FAW). When Hasluck returned from overseas in the late 1960s Glaskin had assumed the presidency of FAW in Western Australia and Hasluck attended some of his writing seminars. He remembered Glaskin as 'urbane, genial and helpful'.[60]

---

55 Buchanan to JB, interview, 12 November 2002.
56 Buchanan wasn't the only one to suggest that GMG and LvdP move. GMG did look at other properties but didn't find anything suitable. Finally, according to LvdP, he simply became too old to relocate.
57 Buchanan to JB, interview, 12 November 2002.
58 Ibid.
59 Denney to JB, interview, 29 November 2002.
60 Nicholas Hasluck to JB, personal communication, 22 May 2001.

Towards the end of 1973, Hasluck and Glaskin found themselves invited to the same party at the newly formed Fremantle Society. Assuming Glaskin would remember him, Hasluck began chatting to him in a friendly, collegiate tone. He asked the 50-year-old Glaskin what he thought of newly emerging Australian writers such as Frank Moorhouse and others. Glaskin made some contemptuous remarks about them, whereupon Hasluck ventured to ask – perhaps a little too legalistically, he later conceded – why Glaskin was so down on the younger generation of literary Australians. Hasluck had pressed the wrong button. Glaskin flew into a rage, accused him of constant nitpicking and stalked off in a huff. Hasluck stood there stunned. He had scarcely collected his breath when Glaskin reappeared to say he had just found out who Hasluck was. He said he was sorry to hear that his brother, Rollo, had died a few months before but he didn't take back anything he had just said because as far as he was concerned Hasluck was a disgrace to his family and a disgrace to Australian literature. Whereupon Glaskin stalked off again. After gathering his composure, Hasluck was more bemused and bewildered than offended by the whole episode. But he gave Glaskin a wide berth thereafter and only saw him from afar on a few occasions.

Van de Pas was also present at the party and witnessed the exchange between Glaskin and Hasluck. He attributed Glaskin's belligerence to two factors – his failure to be deprogrammed to react aggressively to opposition at the end of the war, and the fact that earlier that same evening several people had needled Glaskin about his failure to have his books published in Australia. Glaskin's retort to the latter assertion was, 'Don't they realise, it is much harder for Australians to be published in England because they have to compete with so many English writers.'[61] Upon reflection, Hasluck admitted that Glaskin was probably unfairly underrated in the Australian literary world – a fate shared by a number of other Western Australian writers, he possibly among them. Hasluck admired some of Glaskin's early novels, particularly *A World of Our Own* and *A Minor Portrait* and did not hold this one outburst against him. With the passage of time, and as an older writer whose name means little to an emerging generation of writers, he empathised with Glaskin. 'I can well understand the irritation that Gerry must have experienced on the night in question when a younger writer – namely, myself, on that occasion – began singing the praises of a new generation of writers, paying very little regard to his

61 LvdP to JB, personal communication, 15 May 2001.

own achievements as a writer. Such is the wisdom that comes with the passage of the years.'[62]

This event captures the stormy, reactive side of Glaskin, full of venom and quick to take offence at threats, perceived or otherwise. It embodies some of the less pleasant qualities of Glaskinitis that Buchanan enumerated. There were many times in Glaskin's life when these proclivities showed through, especially in his dealings with individuals and institutions in the literary world, from libraries to publishers, agents to writers' organisations. But this isn't the whole story. There was also a caring side of Glaskin that was part and parcel of his kaleidoscopic nature. Said Buchanan, 'He was so much more complex than your average litigious, loquacious and narcissistic personality. At times, he was capable of a kindness and warmth that I haven't seen.'[63] But perhaps fellow writer Ethel Webb Bundell summed him up best of all. 'I found Gerry very supportive in a bullying sort of way. When I realised he behaved the same with everyone – it wasn't personal – it dawned on me that he was acting like an older brother, which he was, and wanted the best for all of us.'[64]

---

62 Hasluck to LvdP, 15 May 2001.
63 Buchanan to JB, interview, 12 November 2002.
64 Bundell to JB, personal communication, 18 April 2001.

Chapter 5

A Singapore Fling

The oft-repeated cliché that Singapore was a first-class place
for second-class people was, in my opinion, way off the mark.

Bob Dawson
Former Deputy Lord Mayor, Perth

In a 1997 letter to Singapore friend Harold Tay, Glaskin wrote affectionately about 'those halcyon days of water skiing at Ponggol'.[1] He was sending Tay a tin of old cinefilms taken 40 years before that he discovered when sorting through stuff in his apartment. Water skiing at Ponggol was a regular Sunday affair for Glaskin and his Singapore friends, both Chinese and European, who applied themselves to it with almost religious fervour. According to Glaskin's brother Llew, who also came to know Tay, he was a highly skilled water skier whose risky acrobatic feats using circular boards and chairs were something to behold. 'He was built like a human tank', said Llew. 'Big bulging muscles and rippling chest. He was Mr Singapore one year.'[2] Glaskin and his coterie of water skiing enthusiasts clubbed together to buy a speedboat, which one of his Chinese friends named after Glaskin as *Hum Sup* or 'Dirty Old Man'.[3] The Chinese penchant for calling a spade a spade was no doubt well deserved in this

---

1 GMG to Harold Tay, 19 April 1997. Tay and GMG were very close. In one letter to GMG, Tay refers to him as 'the dearest friend I have ever had'.
2 Llew Glaskin to JB, interview by author, 20 November 2002.
3 *Hum Sup* appears to be the name the group also used to refer to itself and their Sunday morning frivolities. In a letter to GMG after GMG's indecency charge on a Perth beach, Tay reminds him that 'not only did we go naked on the beach, but we

case. Just how well is a matter of speculation. Apart from their proficiency as water skiers, some of them also shared striking physiques and alluring good looks. Glaskin's bronzed Aussie tan and penetrating chestnut eyes were as attractive as the smooth-skinned, curvaceous bodies of some of his Chinese friends. Their athletic prowess and appealing appearance could well have been a source of mutual attraction. As Vera Vaughan Bowden, one of Glaskin's British friends who lived in the same apartment block as he, recollected, 'I would know it was Sunday morning because a number of young Chinese guys would show up at his place. They would pack into a car and go off down the East Coast Road to Loyong Ponggol. He was known as "Gerry and his little boys".[4]

But it was not just water skiing that made Glaskin regard the 10 years he spent in Singapore as his halcyon days. He had, quite literally, the time of his life. He went there when he was 25 and had just completed his first novel, and would go on to write four more before returning to Perth at the end of 1958. He embarked on a new career as a stockbroker which, as well as teaching him some tough lessons about the cut and thrust of the corporate world, earned him significant income for the first time in his life. He also formed a friendship with the young Belgian-Chinese writer, Han Suyin (then Dr Elizabeth Comber), that would last for the rest of his life.[5] It was a source of inspiration, if not adoration, that culminated in his writing *A Many-Splendoured Woman: A Memoir of Han Suyin*, his last book to be published. Most of all, he developed an understanding of, and deep appreciation for, the people and cultures of Southeast Asia at a time of immense political upheaval and historical change that left many Australians either fearful or ignorant of what was happening in the neighbouring countries to their immediate north. His Asian-based novels – *A Lion in the Sun, The Beach of Passionate Love* and to a lesser extent *Flight to Landfall* – reflect this sensitivity to Asia and a willingness to see things from an Asian perspective. This, arguably, is one of Glaskin's most important and least acknowledged contributions to Australian literature.

When he stepped off the ship from Fremantle in July 1949 Glaskin entered a world vastly different from anything he had known in Australia. His one link between the two was Foster Wearne, who had offered him a job in Singapore. Wearne was one of two brothers who owned a large and prosperous

---

also skied naked' and suggests GMG come back to Singapore where people are more broad-minded than in Perth.

4   Vera Vaughan Bowden to JB, interview by author, 22 August 2001.

5   See Chapter 6, 'Dear Old Thing'.

company that imported and repaired foreign cars. Legend has it that their father began the business by selling one of the first cars in Singapore to a wealthy Indian who needed a car that could negotiate the steep driveway up to his house. Putting the car in reverse, the strongest gear, the senior Wearne had no trouble in meeting this requirement. He sold the car, made a nice profit and never looked back. In the highly autobiographical novel *A Lion in the Sun*, Glaskin describes a company that mirrors the Wearne's business – a multimillion-dollar organisation with subsidiary companies and branches throughout Singapore and Malaya. He portrays his protagonist's employer as one whose 'every moment would be devoted to some interest or hobby with relentless zeal, self-preoccupied, self-sufficient, detached from the interests of others.' But he also assesses him to be 'firm and just, his decisions impartial and, once made, rarely rescinded; a man of fixed purpose and fore-ordained progress'.[6]

Wearne's invitation to Glaskin to come to Singapore was to help sort out the company's storage of car parts, a task well within Glaskin's capabilities.[7] After a few months he decided he needed to look for something more challenging and took up a position as sales manager with McMullen and Company, importers of office equipment, furniture and stationery. He kept this job for just over a year before the lure of the stockbroking world became too much to resist. McMullen's were sorry to lose Glaskin, whom they found to be energetic, conscientious, capable and highly liked by their customers. In spite of his departure from Wearne Brothers, Glaskin's friendship with Foster Wearne and his wife Wynne continued until Wearne's death in the early 1970s. They represented the kind of wealthy Australian who found Europe a welcome contrast to their own country and tended to use it as a kind of playground, money being no object. Glaskin delighted in telling one story that illustrated this. When he was travelling in Europe and the Wearnes were staying at their home in England, they decided to visit him at Calella de Palafrugel in Spain. They shipped their Rolls Royce to the Continent and started to drive to Calella. Along the way, the car became stuck in a small village, so they flew over a chauffeur from England to try to extricate it. He could not deal with it either, so they ended up getting a crane to lift out the car.[8]

While the motor vehicle industry was one Glaskin knew something about, it was never his cup of tea. It was, however, something that seemed to attract

---

6   GMG (1960a, 129).
7   Wearne Brothers also asked him to write a company history but he declined due to pressure of other work. GMG (1994–1999, 7).
8   LvdP to JB, personal communication, 4 June 2001.

a number of Australians to Singapore. As Vaughan Bowden put it, 'There weren't too many "cultured" Australians in those days. They were mainly car mechanics. Rough, tough guys. Real beer drinkers.'[9] Clearly, this was not Glaskin's set, no matter how friendly he may have been with Foster Wearne. His sharp intellect, urbane manner and oozing charm would have only brought tirades of derision from this crowd. He was much more a Chablis man, who would have preferred reading a Graham Greene novel with Beethoven playing in the background to slugging it out with the lads down at the local bar.

Exactly how and why Glaskin was offered a job in a stockbroking firm is not clear but the most likely explanation has to do with another young Australian, John Donnell, whose father, R. B. B. Donnell, ran the firm of Lyall and Evatt. Donnell Jnr and Glaskin became friends, flatmates and some say lovers or, as a fellow stockbroker delicately put it, 'very, very *friendly*'.[10] They lived together at 18J Dunearn Road in the Bukit Timah neighbourhood, a normally quiet part of town that was ideal for Glaskin to pursue his extra-curricular activity of writing. But it wasn't always so quiet. On one occasion a friend of theirs had just flown in from Karachi and called to make contact. He was told to 'get your arse around here right away'. When he arrived at the flat he found Glaskin and Donnell entertaining a group of young British soldiers on R & R who were waiting to be flown back to England. 'A great party was going on and after a while bedroom doors began to be closed', he said.[11] The BORs or British Other Ranks had a reputation in Singapore for their partying skills, often outshining gay men at their own game. One night, Glaskin had popped into a party in full swing, only intending to stay for a short time. Preoccupied with his own agenda, he hadn't realised that one young BOR had been following him around since he arrived. When Glaskin didn't get the hint, the Britisher came up to him and poked him in the chest and said, 'What's wrong with fucking me! What's wrong with fucking me?' Glaskin let loose with one of his trademark one-liners: 'Is that an adjective or a verb?' The young serviceman was crestfallen at being turned down.[12]

Like Glaskin, Donnell was a refined type, somewhat flamboyant but also quite manly. He was always impeccably dressed, usually in a blazer, but not easily identifiable as gay. This ambivalence no doubt attracted Glaskin to

9   Vaughan Bowden to JB, interview, 22 August 2001.
10 Andrew Clinton to JB, 30 December 2001.
11 Charles Kissane to JB, personal communication, 28 October 2001.
12 Cover (1949a, 15).

Donnell, since it partly reflected his own self-image. As one of his British agents described Glaskin, 'Homosexual, but you would never have guessed it: tanned, handsome and very fit looking. Typical macho Australian.'[13] But for all his outward appearances Donnell wasn't known to be the most pleasant of men. 'An unhappy, grumbling malcontent' was how one colleague described him.[14] His relationship with Glaskin soured and ended in a ferocious row. Donnell eventually returned to Australia where he died an alcoholic.

If Donnell was Glaskin's entree into the world of stockbroking, Glaskin soon established himself in his own right. Lyall and Evatt was one of a handful of stockbroking houses in Singapore in those days, mostly branches of their British parent companies. In this case, the parent was the rubber broker, Lewis and Peat, an old London company headquartered in Mensing Lane, the home of British broking houses. On the firm's letterhead was printed 'Established about 1780', giving it a regality all of its own. Michael Redhill, an Englishman born in China, raised in Malaya and who could speak street Malay with a Chinese accent, joined Lewis and Peat at 18. He was the company's first Singapore employee sent to the London office for six months on an exchange with another employee to find out how each end of the business worked. He soon became referred to as 'our young man from the East'. 'The big money spinner was Singapore', said Redhill.[15]

So successful was Lewis and Peat that by the mid-1950s a group of accountants and lawyers in London made a takeover bid for the company. When they caught whiff of this, staff in the Singapore office became very nervous. Redhill explained. 'As rubber brokers, we would buy and sell between clients. We would either sell ordinary or sell guarantee. The latter meant that the seller wanted to keep their name confidential, so they would sell to us and we would sell it on. Because we were the largest brokers in the world, it was imperative that our solvency be without question. If accountants and lawyers were to take over this little pot of gold, our solvency may well have been questioned and companies wouldn't deal with us.'[16] As a result, the Singapore chairman flew to London to plead their concern but it fell on deaf ears. The head of the takeover consortium, the Russian-Jewish-English Lord Kissin tried to reassure his colleague from the orient he had nothing to worry about. The takeover went ahead. The day it was announced, all the Singapore directors gave three months' notice. Two months later all the

---

13 David Bolt to JB, personal communication, 12 June 2001.
14 Michael Redhill to JB, personal communication, 28 November 2001.
15 Michael Redhill to JB, interview by author, 2 December 2001.
16 Ibid.

management staff gave one month's notice. Two weeks later, the clerical staff gave two weeks' notice. On a Friday at the appointed hour, everyone closed their books and walked out. On the following Tuesday they opened up a new business called Holiday, Cutler and Bath, the names of three directors of the new company. 'It was a roaring success', said Redhill.[17]

This shift in ownership may have had repercussions for Lyall and Evatt too, although under different circumstances. In his memoir of Han Suyin, Glaskin alludes to a change in management at Lyall and Evatt, but it seems a more local affair than the Lewis and Peat episode. He refers to new recruits that Donnell Snr had brought in to assist Glaskin in the absence of himself and his son who were both well overdue for long leave, a six-month home leave that was one of the standard perks of working overseas in those days. Shortly after Donnell Snr had gone to Australia in November 1957 he died of a heart attack. Donnell Jnr headed for London to take his leave and to deal with matters in light of his father's death, leaving Glaskin with the new recruits. Glaskin maintained that within weeks these men conspired to enforce the sale of the firm to themselves and threaten to walk out en masse and set up business under another name.[18]

Following the takeover, Glaskin asserts that those involved received their comeuppance in bizarre ways. 'What poetic justice ensued!' claimed an exasperated and possibly highly imaginative Glaskin. 'Shortly afterwards, one [of the new recruits] decapitated himself in a motor accident, another shot himself, others went off into their own self-chosen oblivions. Only one managed to remain affluent and extricate himself before the market's recent collapse.' While it is not clear who the first three persons were, the last statement is an apparent reference to David Hebdige, who went along with the takeover and emerged at the helm of the new Lyall and Evatt. He stayed with the firm until the mid-1980s and grew extremely wealthy, becoming chairman of the Stock Exchange of Malaysia and Singapore and owner of an estate in England. Ironically, he too died a painful death in 1994 as a result of a prolonged battle with cancer. Hebdige handed over the reins of management to Dr Sheng Nam Chin in 1985, prior to a major financial crisis involving the Pan Electric Company that caused a suspension of the stock market for three market days. Through forward contracts, Lyall and Evatt incurred debts and losses of more than $100 million, which finally led to its closure after more than 150 years of operation.

---

17 Ibid.
18 GMG (1995a, 67).

Another allegation Glaskin made about Lyall and Evatt raised some eyebrows, although it seems that his claims had more substance this time. He maintained that auditors confirmed that three times since he joined the firm, it had been embezzled by an employee's speculations on his own behalf using fictitious names.[19] The third time this happened it involved a very considerable sum, including Glaskin's own capital that he had been accumulating so he could become a full-time writer, as well as send money to his family in Perth. In a letter to Glaskin, Hebdige alluded to two Chinese brokers who disappeared and nearly a year later he had given up hope of recovering anything from them.[20] This was one of several reasons that led Glaskin to resign from the firm, which he did in April 1958.

During the years Glaskin was associated with Lyall and Evatt he kept a busy schedule. Like many local companies in stockbroking and commodities trading, it was forced to work extended hours to keep in synch with markets in New York and London. Australian Bob Dawson, who spent 11 years working as a produce dealer with Harrisons and Crosfield, attests to this. 'The majority of us started very early in the morning. I was in the godowns at 7 am and did not finish until after six at night, when the New York market opened. By comparison, in London an early start on the rubber and produce market was 10 am, followed by a long liquid lunch, then back to the office at 3 pm to sign mail and contracts and dash to the station to catch the four o'clock home.'[21] Dawson also pointed out that dinners and cocktail parties, which were a constant feature of Singaporean life, were part of the workday because they provided an opportunity to mix with competitors and try to gather information without giving any away. Glaskin echoes a similar sentiment. 'I worked 50 to 60 hours a week … My work demanded socialising three nights a week: Wednesdays, Fridays, and Saturdays. The other three I kept faithfully for writing: Mondays, Tuesdays and Thursdays.'[22]

Sometimes the socialising paid off in unexpected ways. On one occasion, Glaskin was attending a party and noticed that a Chinese gentleman appeared to be in severe pain. He went over to him and gently asked what was the matter. 'Terrible toothache', replied the man, holding his jaw. Glaskin suggested to him that even if he did not drink alcohol he should take a glass of brandy and swish it around in his mouth, as this would work as an anaesthetic. The man took Glaskin's advice and it did the trick, at least

---

19 Ibid., 36.
20 Hebdige to GMG, 8 December 1960.
21 Bob Dawson to JB, 18 November 2001.
22 GMG (1995a, 19).

temporarily until he could visit his dentist. He was very grateful and wanted to express his gratitude to Glaskin. A few days later, he invited Glaskin to his office and bought a huge order of shares from him.[23]

While he worked hard, he also played hard. Apart from his regular Sunday water skiing date, Glaskin found time for other social activities. Like many expatriates in Singapore, he was a frequent visitor to the Tanglin Club, that bastion of foreign privilege and power. Replete with swimming pool, tennis courts and squash courts, it was founded in 1865 when 'forty good men and true' met to establish 'a club for the English in Singapore'.[24] The following year the committee purchased a property that was part of an estate that included an orange grove and a nutmeg plantation. It developed a clubhouse with a bowling alley and carriage house. In 1900 more land was acquired and in 1981 a new clubhouse was built. Vera Vaughan Bowden – known as 'Miss Formica' for her efforts to promote that wonder of the modern kitchen in Singapore – has fond memories of the Tanglin Club. 'It was *the* club. Your driver would drop you at the steps, then go and park, and would be radioed to come and fetch you when you were ready to go. We had the Coronation Ball there in 1953. It was a grand affair.'[25] Although it was by no means the only club of its kind – there was the golf club, the swimming club, the cricket club, the yacht club, the polo club, the flying club, and more – it was a cut above the rest. Because single foreign women were in short supply, they were often given complimentary memberships to these clubs, something that the men didn't mind at all, according to Vaughan Bowden who scored several free memberships.

The Tanglin Club was the scene of one of Glaskin's notable remonstrations of outrage over what he perceived to be a social injustice. It centred on his association with the young Dr Elizabeth Comber, better known by her pen name, Han Suyin, for her famous early novel, *A Many-Splendoured Thing*. Glaskin had only met her a few weeks earlier and, as young professionals who wrote novels on the side, they had begun to develop a close friendship. Being Eurasian, Han Suyin was not entitled to membership at the Tanglin and had never been inside it. However, Wednesdays was guest night at the club so Glaskin invited her and her husband, Leonard Comber, to be his guests for dinner one Wednesday night. She consented but preferred to come on her own to absorb the atmosphere of the place, which as Glaskin noted, was something that a writer of fiction might well want to do. She opted for

23 LvdP to JB, personal communication, 22 June 2010.
24 Tanglin Club (2012).
25 Vaughan Bowden to JB, interview, 22 August 2001.

drinks after work instead of dinner. They only spent about half an hour at the club but it was time enough for her to get a feel for the place. Apart from Glaskin, she spoke to no one and no one spoke to her, except the middle-aged Chinese 'boy' who served them drinks by the pool.

A few days later, Glaskin was summoned by the secretary of the club to be informed that a complaint had been lodged that he had brought an Asian guest. Surprised, he replied to the secretary that this Asian guest was actually Eurasian and that it had been guest night. The secretary then pointed out that 'night' starts at 7 pm and what is more, guests and hosts alike were expected to wear formal evening attire.[26] Glaskin was enraged. Did he know who she was, that her books were in the club's library, that she was a physician, the wife of a police officer, a person whose intellect could be matched by few members of the club of either sex? He threatened to resign and demanded that the committee be informed of what had happened and that they change the regulation from guest night to guest day. Eventually, though grudgingly according to Glaskin, this was done. Ironically, in 1985, when perusing the club's magazine, Glaskin came across a remark made by the retiring librarian that the most popular book on their shelves was Glaskin's *A Lion in the Sun*, which he had dedicated to 'two good friends, Wynne and Foster Wearne and to a very great one, Han Suyin'.

This encounter with the encrusted traditions of colonial elitism was one of many that Glaskin experienced during his ten years in Singapore. Coming from Australia's more egalitarian society, he was repulsed and appalled by the unabashed hypocrisy and strident racism of many expatriates, particularly British. Although he shared in their privileged life by dint of his job, his personal life transcended many of the barriers of race, class and sexual orientation with which this powerful minority surrounded itself. His chance to retaliate against the snobbery of the ruling class came when he wrote *A Lion in the Sun* and he used it to the full. Many of the characters in the novel are based on his contemporaries in Singapore. He didn't try terribly hard to disguise them, often giving them names whose initials corresponded to those with whom he lived and worked.[27] John Donnell became John Drake and his father, John Donnell Snr became Old Man Drake. Lyall and Evatt's parent company, Lewis and Peat (later Holiday, Cutler & Bath), appears as Grant, MacCauley and Company. Its managing director, Ernest ('the Egg') Grant bears a close resemblance to Vivian Bath, whom Redhill remembers

---

26 GMG (1995a, 33).
27 GMG even names his protagonist Geoffrey M. Graham, whose initials are the same as his own. See Chapter 3, 'Gerald in Wonderland', footnote 47.

as having the most violent reaction to *A Lion in the Sun* of anyone, hardly surprising given that he was prone to such outbursts and given Glaskin's depiction of him as an impetuous, whisky-drinking autocrat incapable of showing an ounce of empathy, except for his own immature and coddled daughter, the oversexed Vivienne.

But Glaskin saves most of his venom for another of the firm partners whom he portrays as Ian MacCauley, 'perhaps the most brilliant rubber broker in Singapore', a reputation the narrator has trouble reconciling with this 'pathetic parody of a man'.[28] He captures his scathing contempt for MacCauley and all he stands for in one hideous scene at a dinner party at the Grants' home, to which MacCauley arrives stone drunk. By the time the meal is served he is almost apoplectic.

> He managed the soup, but his trembling fingers could grip his knife and fork only with difficulty. When his steak had slid on to the starched tablecloth a second time, he replaced it laboriously with his fingers, then called the boy. He demanded to know 'Had he ordered an underdone steak, or hadn't he? Was this steak underdone? You couldn't even get a knife through it! Take it back! Don't just stand there, boy – take it back!' But the boy only stared at him with confused incomprehension, looking from one to the other of us for some further direction. No one seemed to know what to do. MacCauley's temper mounted, his breath blowing out in sharp rancid explosions from beneath the twitching moustache. Then, before any of us could see what he was going to do, he picked up the plate and tossed its contents into the boy's face. For several moments we sat stunned. It was only when MacCauley burst out into large guffaws that Molly attempted to reprimand him. 'Ian, how could you!' She seemed shocked, though not too deeply. Evidently she was accustomed to such behaviour ... No one made any comment; none of us felt we had the prerogative to do so, except perhaps Grant. I was amazed that his only comment was: 'Pretty good shot, old boy! We'd better put you back in the old rugger team ...'[29]

MacCauley's calling the waiter 'boy' is particularly significant. It is such an unconscious act on MacCauley's part but it is laden with meaning. Glaskin uses it – highly intentionally – throughout the novel and also comments on it in his Han Suyin memoir. Perhaps more than any other term, this

28 GMG (1960a, 138–139).
29 Ibid., 186.

simple word reveals the sense of unmitigated superiority and utter disdain that many in the expatriate community had for Asians. The fact that they, as Europeans, had just suffered a humiliating defeat at the hands of an Asian power never seemed to enter their consciousness. They acted as though a few years in Changi prison was just marking time until they could resume their former positions in society. In *A Lion in the Sun* Glaskin uses his Chinese characters to offer a different perspective. Chief among them are Tan Khai Soo, or 'Open Book', the only Chinese partner in Grant, MacCauley and Company, as well as Khai Soo's attractive and intelligent daughter, Helen, one of his seven children. In the protagonist's first encounter with the charming Chinese gentleman, Khai Soo explains to him the order of Chinese names. Sensing that the recently arrived Australian is different from the rest of his European colleagues, he confides in him, 'It is fashionable amongst some of us Chinese to have a Christian – or rather we call it a European – name. Of course,' and he pulled an earlobe with wry contemplation, 'it does make some of us feel as though we have some sort of human kinship with the European, and are not just some sort of infrahuman species with a mere human resemblance, like apes.'[30]

However, Glaskin points out that not all expatriates exhibited such vulgar manners and had such pretentious misconceptions of their position in the scheme of things. Several of his characters are quite the opposite, including the tragic anti-hero Australian Bradley Chase and the British couple Muriel and Godfrey Braine. The latter have three children, are interested in books and painting and join the local dramatic society in preference to the Tanglin Club. Although Godfrey is the junior partner in Grant, MacCauley and Company, he and his wife are regarded as having broken rank with the cocktail-imbibing, charity-promoting social set of expatriate Singapore. But tragedy strikes when they are inadvertently caught up in a vicious outburst of racial anger known as the Bertha (or Maria) Hertogh riots.[31] Godfrey's

---

30 Ibid., 140.
31 The Bertha or Maria Hertogh riots happened in December 1950. After the Japanese had taken over Java in 1942, and facing internment, a Dutch couple left their five-year-old daughter, Maria Bertha, with one of their servants, Che Aminah bte Mohammad. Aminah took the child to Bandung for safekeeping. Maria was brought up a Muslim and given the name, Nadra. In 1947, because of internal warfare in Indonesia, Aminah took Maria to Malaya. By 1949, when the Hertoghs learned of Maria's whereabouts, she was twelve years old and could only speak Malay. A custody battle ensued as the Dutch parents sought to reclaim their daughter through the Singapore courts. On 11 December 1950, the judge ruled in their favour. Meanwhile, Maria had married a Muslim man under Islamic law. Pending Aminah's appeal, she was placed in a convent, which inflamed Muslim sentiments. In retaliation, Malays in Singapore attacked

bloodied body is found floating face down in a canal and Muriel is brutally raped, only to survive and eventually to take up with a Chinese man in a less-than-salubrious part of town. Is this the kind of fate one can expect for not towing the party line?

Glaskin's depiction of the riots is the one aspect of the book that most of his reviewers admired, both in the original 1960 edition and the 1994 republication by Singapore publisher, Graham Brash. The words 'vivid' and 'vigour' appear in several reviews. Val MacQueen, who reviewed the book for the *New Straits Times,* praised Glaskin's ability to 'carry the reader along as though he were observing them [the riots] in person' and acknowledged not having appreciated the extent of the violence nor the heat of feelings until reading Glaskin's rendition of the riots, despite having lived through them.[32] This aside, many reviewers had trouble with his characters, rejecting them as everything from 'politically naïve' and 'emotionally unstable' to 'paper cut-outs' and 'one-dimensional'. Sylvia Marchant, writing in *The Canberra Times*, dismissed the book as 'lightweight' and 'a bit of a yawn' and wondered why Brash bothered to reissue it after 34 years.[33] Interestingly, both she and MacQueen, writing in the mid-1990s, come down hard on Glaskin's writing style and especially his description of women in the story. A generation earlier, reviewers of his 1960 edition, in both Australia and the UK, were much more lenient on this score.

While Glaskin exhibited strong sympathy for Asians in this divided community and tried hard to represent their perspective in his writing, he nevertheless continued to enjoy the good life that came with being an ex-patriate working for a foreign firm. Besides, he had his battles to fight on another front, albeit more clandestine. He was a member of the Tanglin and other clubs and was often seen in the company of Hazel Nathan, a young Jewish woman – a Jew was higher on the scale of social acceptability than a Eurasian or Asian – who partnered Glaskin in tennis and dancing, swimming and dining. But Glaskin gives no indication that his association with Nathan was anything more than a convenient front for his more genuine attraction to young men. 'Romantically, we each had other impossible interests at the time, which made us "simpatico" with each other', he wrote

---

Europeans or Eurasians and burnt their cars. Riots continued for three days and a 24-hour curfew was imposed for two weeks. Not trusting the Malay-dominated police force to deal with the rioters, the British called in a Gurkha regiment to restore calm. Eighteen people died, 173 were injured and 84 cars destroyed.

32 MacQueen (1994, 29).

33 Marchant (1995, C12).

in his Han Suyin memoir.[34] His relationship with Han may well have served a similar purpose, given that he could easily have run foul of the law since homosexuality was a crime in Singapore. She was well known, extremely articulate and strongly independent. Most of all, she was non-judgemental about his sexual preferences. Even at 85, she reiterated this. 'I thought he was good looking but I didn't have any sexual feelings for him. He was a nice chap, that's all. Maybe that's why he felt safe with me. I wasn't rushing at him. Everybody has a perfect right to the kind of life they like. It's none of my business. During the war in England, many girls went "two by two". I even wrote a novel about it called *Winter Love*.'[35]

Han Suyin and most others who came across Glaskin in Singapore may not have known that he was gay, but there were some who did. Charles Kissane was a flight attendant with Qantas Airways during the 1950s and spent much of that decade on the Sydney to London route, punctuated with four-day stopovers in Singapore. He first met Glaskin – and John Donnell – in a garish, brightly lit bar known as The Criterion on Orchard Road. While nothing like a gay bar today, it was then the place to go if you were looking for a male companion for the evening. A few local Chinese and Malay lads mixing with a handful of Europeans was a clue that normal social barriers didn't operate here. Kissane was in his early twenties and Glaskin in his late twenties. Glaskin's film star looks and alluring charm were too much to pass up. After their initial contact they continued to see each other every time Kissane passed through town and kept in touch throughout their lives.

Gay life in Singapore in the 1950s was a very undercover affair because should word get out that you were 'one of them', chances of losing your job, not to mention your social standing in this fishbowl of a community, were extremely high. 'Most of the guys who frequented The Criterion were scared to death that they would be discovered,' said Kissane, 'but make no mistake about it, no right-minded square would be seen dead in the place.' Most Chinese, on the other hand, didn't suffer the same hang-ups about homosexuality as the British. 'They couldn't have given a rat's arse if you were gay or not', said Kissane. 'You only had to go down to Bugis Street to find transvestites parading up and down every night trying to lure British sailors. It was a great atmosphere.'[36] Kissane was one of a number of sexual partners – both European and local – whom Glaskin had during his time in Singapore. Because gay men had to be so secretive about their behaviour, it

---

34 GMG (1995a, 30).
35 HS to JB, interview by author, 18 August 2001.
36 Kissane to JB, personal communication, 26 April 2001.

was often unclear to an outsider whether two men known to be friends were participating in a sexual relationship or not. This ambiguity probably suited everybody, because as long as nothing could be proven and the established order was maintained things could continue as normal. As Redhill remembered it, 'This was Singapore in the 1950s and you didn't proclaim your sexuality as is done today. If you were discreet and presentable, some wives would have you as a houseguest and some would rather not. I suppose it came to that.'[37]

Occasionally, someone stepped over the line and all hell broke loose. The usual response to such opprobrium was to dispose of the offender as quickly as possible, no questions asked. One such episode concerned another Lyall and Evatt employee, Michael Scott. Scott was a bright, intelligent young man who played the piano and could amuse in any social gathering. He was very fond of the Chinese and learned to speak Cantonese so fluently and idiomatically that on the phone he could pass for a local. He was also gay. At one time, Scott shared a house with Redhill and four other expatriate young men. One morning Redhill received a phone call at six o'clock from a distraught Scott. He had been caught *in flagrante delicto* with a Chinese boy on Orchard Road and arrested by the Malay police, who were at a loss to know what to do with him. Worried that this would become a public scandal, Scott called Redhill because he knew Redhill had been in Singapore and Malaya for many years and spoke Malay well. 'It's going to court and I don't want the publicity', said a nervous Scott. 'The papers will be there. Can you help keep the story quiet?' Redhill agreed to try. He happened to know the editors of both major dailies, so he called them and did a little shuttle diplomacy. Both agreed to quash it if the other did and they stuck by their promises.[38]

Unfortunately, the chief of police, who was a friend of one of the directors of Lyall and Evatt's parent company, got word to him. The directors quickly resolved that the best thing to do was to get Scott out of the colony. The fact that Scott also spent many evenings in an opium den didn't do anything to further his cause in the eyes of his employers. As Redhill said, 'You could get roaring drunk at the Tanglin Club, but an evening smoke, that was bad.' The directors were taking no chances. They put Scott in Redhill's charge until the next boat left for England. They gave Redhill Scott's passport on pain of death and instructed him not to give it to Scott until the gangplank

---

37 Redhill to JB, interview, 2 December 2001.
38 Ibid.

was being lifted. The incident affected Redhill – and no doubt others in Singapore, particularly gay men – deeply. 'I must have been about 24 or 25 at the time. I liked Michael a lot. I felt a loyalty to a friend and I would honour it. When I got back to the office after seeing the gangplank up and throwing Michael his passport, I was feeling bloody bad about the whole affair', he said. Vivian Bath, one of the company directors not known for his social graces, turned to Redhill with a scowl and said, 'And now you're bloody well suspect yourself!' Redhill shrugged his shoulders. Bath was not a man you could argue with. In Redhill's words, 'He had a heart of gold but sometimes it was cold and yellow.'[39]

Glaskin makes no mention of Michael Scott in his correspondence or memoirs, although being employees in the same small company they must have been acquainted. However, another Michael did figure prominently in Glaskin's life – Michael O'Flynn. With sparkling eyes and an impish smile, O'Flynn was popular with the ladies, especially on his visits to Singapore from Malaya where he was a rubber planter. One of the ladies he charmed was Glaskin's mother, Delia, who visited Singapore with her sister, Eileen, and Eileen's daughter, Judy. Delia Glaskin was reputedly very fond of Michael. A photograph taken of the group, which also included John Donnell and Charles Kissane at the Raffles hotel, shows O'Flynn seated, glass in hand, between the honey-blond Eileen and the brunette Judy. Delia is off to the left beneath her son Gerald.[40] From the picture, one could surmise that O'Flynn was, literally, the centre of attention. Without doubt, he claimed Glaskin's attention too. At minimum they were good friends, swam at the Swimming Club in Singapore and shared a drink together. But according to one source, Glaskin and O'Flynn were lovers. When O'Flynn's company wanted to transfer him to Kenya he preferred to stay in Singapore, possibly because of his relationship with Glaskin. But in spite of his affection for O'Flynn, Glaskin persuaded him to stay with his company for the sake of his career. O'Flynn finally moved to Kenya and Glaskin lost touch with him. After a stint there, he visited England and the Continent 'to sort myself out', before returning to Australia. In a letter to Glaskin, he expressed a wish to see him again 'to least [sic] yak over "the follies of youth"'.[41]

One other gay man in Singapore who featured in Glaskin's life didn't attract him. Indeed, Glaskin reputedly couldn't stand the man, as revealed in an encounter that demonstrates Glaskin's propensity to show off and

39 Ibid.
40 See photograph on page 5 of the first block of images.
41 Michael O'Flynn to GMG, 4 January 1961.

humiliate people in public with his sharp tongue and clever intellect. The person on the receiving end of his verbal barbs on this occasion was a fine-featured, disarmingly attractive young man with the frightfully British name of Blythe Falls. Falls struggled to define himself sexually, torn between strong societal imperatives to behave as a heterosexual and deep inner urgings that drew him towards his own sex. Like others who wrestled with such dilemmas, he turned to alcohol to drown the pain when it became too much.

Falls was engaged to Vera Vaughan Bowden, who thought him a pretty good catch and wasn't about to let him go lightly. On one occasion, a party was being given in her honour and Falls was her escort. True to form, he became blind drunk and had to be carried out and sent home. Bowden stayed to the bitter end and Glaskin offered to drive her home, but as soon as she reached his car she collapsed. Glaskin helped her into the car where she passed out. Awoken next morning by an anxious Sikh watchman knocking on the window, her first thought was, 'Oh my God, where am I?' Glaskin was curled up next to her, snoring his head off. Bowden disentangled herself from him and made her way to her friend's apartment where she was staying. She didn't know that her friend's mother had gone out early in the morning and had seen her in the car with Glaskin.

The next day, she and Falls went to a lunch friends had arranged for her. No sooner had they walked in than Glaskin came up to them and announced in a supercilious public voice, 'Hi Blythe, you know Vera and I slept together last night.' Jaws dropped. Silence enveloped the room. Bowden fumed, knowing full well she couldn't deny that she had, however inadvertently and innocently, slept with Glaskin. There were at least two witnesses to prove it. Falls looked murderous but channelled his anger into a drunken stupor, causing him to have to make yet another horizontal exit. Reflecting on the episode more than 40 years later, Bowden summed it up succinctly, if not generously, 'This was Gerry's need to be noticed.' [42]

Perhaps part of this need was behind Glaskin's propensity to associate himself with people who had a high public profile, be they in the arts, business, government or other spheres. One such person was Sir Paul Hasluck. In addition to being a noted journalist, historian, poet and essayist, Hasluck was one of Australia's most distinguished public servants who went on to become Governor-General of Australia (1969-74). He was a long-serving minister in several federal Liberal Party governments and stood for the

---

42 Vaughan Bowden to JB, interview, 22 August 2001.

leadership of the Liberal Party in 1967, following the death by drowning of Prime Minister, Harold Holt, but he narrowly missed election. He was known for his lifelong concern for Australia's indigenous people and was instrumental in Papua-New Guinea's evolution to self-government. Glaskin's connection with Hasluck was through Hasluck's wife, Alexandra, herself a well-known author and historian.

In 1958, as Australia's Minister for Territories, Hasluck made a visit to Christmas Island in the Indian Ocean, which was about to be transferred from Singaporean to Australian mandate. With so many Chinese and Malays working on the island, Singapore resented this move and made its position clear. The Haslucks had to stop in Singapore in order to change ship and had they stayed more than 24 hours, he would have been obliged to present his credentials to the Governor, something he was loath to do before seeing conditions on the island for himself. Having Glaskin's phone number, Hasluck tracked him down at Ulu Tiram, the rubber estate near Johore Bahru in Malaya where Glaskin was staying to finish his manuscript of *A Lion in the Sun,* and explained his predicament to him. Glaskin's host, the convivial Australian Brian Chapple, responded with an invitation to the Haslucks to visit the estate, which the Minister was very glad to accept. Glaskin reported that the visit turned out to be of considerable interest to Hasluck, who had the chance to inspect a large and well-run Malayan rubber plantation that he could compare to those in Papua New Guinea for which his administration was responsible.

Not long after the Haslucks, Ulu Tiram was graced by the visit of the noted British playwright, Terence Rattigan. The author of 23 plays, 22 screenplays and eight others for radio and television, Rattigan was often perceived to be the classic playboy, living a life of luxury and extravagance that success on the stage and in the cinema had brought him. His Rolls Royce with its personalised number plate projected this image. But as biographer Geoffrey Wansell has pointed out, behind this public façade was another man, tormented by fears, pain and suffering. His loneliness and homosexuality were hidden beneath a veneer of relaxation and wit. How Rattigan came to visit Ulu Tiram is not clear but Chapple was an avid reader and presumably a man of many connections. For Glaskin it was another chance to rub shoulders with a successful writer, a label he always strove to claim for himself but which for the most part eluded him.

Rattigan's appearance on the rubber estate was not without its own touch of theatricality. A Singapore tailor had made him a black silk pyjama-like outfit that looked uncannily like the clothes worn by Chinese 'coolie' women, which caused something of a sensation, especially among the Chinese employees on the estate. But, recalled Glaskin, 'even the most ill-concealed titters couldn't induce him to change it for something less provocative.'[43] Rattigan, who was accompanied by a friend, was rather quiet this weekend. His friend put it down to the fact that the movie of his screenplay, *Separate Tables*, had been nominated for several Academy Awards, which were due to be announced that day. During the afternoon, a cablegram was telephoned through announcing that David Niven had won an Oscar for Best Actor and Wendy Hiller for Best Actress. Although Rattigan was overlooked this time for an award, the success of the film lifted his mood and was cause for great celebration that evening at Ulu Tiram.

This encounter with the famous playwright had been a precious moment in Glaskin's life, as he recorded in *A Many-Splendoured Woman*, 'With Terry, I had managed to give both fame and achievement yet another gentle nudge.'[44] But try as he may, Glaskin wasn't able to entice Han Suyin to visit the estate to meet either Rattigan or the Haslucks. The Australians failed to impress her and Glaskin wasn't able to reach her in time for Rattigan. Even if he had, it is doubtful she would have accepted his invitation. Han Suyin never shared Glaskin's strong desire to associate himself with those who had achieved fame and fortune. This was one of a number of differences between them that persisted throughout their close and multifaceted relationship that spanned more than four decades and several continents.

---

43 GMG (1995a, 72–73).
44 Ibid., 74.

Chapter 6

Dear 'Old Thing'

I am speaking as a doctor and writer and as your friend.
A friend who wishes you truly all the best.

Han Suyin

For many years in the front right-hand corner of a glass display cabinet in the home of one of Europe's most renowned couturiers sat a small jade ornament of a frog on a lotus leaf. Although it may not have been worth as much as some of the other items in this exquisite collection, to Gerald Glaskin it was priceless. It came to him at his Singapore office in a box wrapped in raw silk as a gift from his friend, Elizabeth Comber, the day after he had coaxed her into water skiing for the first time. In spite of her initial nervousness at attempting this feat, she had accomplished it, like most things in her long and jam-packed life, with determination and aplomb. Another challenge met, another hurdle cleared. And what better way to show her gratitude to her young Australian friend than to give him a small token of her appreciation that was also a memento of the one great passion in her life, China. Glaskin had taken the fragile ornament with him to Amsterdam when he lived there during the 1960s but declined to bring it back with him to Australia for fear of damaging it. Besides, as its keeper and Glaskin's long-time friend, Edgar Vos, reminded him, as long as the piece remained in his care it would always bring Glaskin back to his favourite city, which it did several times.

As well as keeping alive his Dutch connection, the jade ornament was a tangible reminder of one of the most valued and sustaining relationships in

Glaskin's life. It began on 31 October 1956 when the 32-year-old Glaskin penned a short note to Dr Elizabeth Comber to request a meeting with her and lasted until his death 44 years later. The Eurasian physician, who worked in Singapore and nearby Johore Bahru in Malaya, was six years his senior. Using the pseudonym of Han Suyin, she had attracted international attention with the publication of her second novel, *A Many-Splendoured Thing*, in 1952 and the subsequent Hollywood movie, *Love is a many-splendored thing*, in 1955. She was then married to Leonard Comber, an Englishman who worked for the Malayan Police Force and later in publishing in Singapore and Hong Kong. Like his wife and Glaskin, he wrote part-time while holding down another job. His literary output includes several children's books, Chinese detective stories and an academic study of Chinese secret societies in Malaya. Han, on the other hand, had more than 30 books published in English, French and Chinese – a mixture of autobiographical history, fiction, essays and substantial biographies of the Chinese leaders Mao Tse-Tung and Chou Enlai.

In spite of her prodigious bibliography, Han claimed that she never wanted to be a writer. Even at 85 she was adamant about this. 'I wrote for fun, in my spare time, without any idea of success', she said. 'I only wanted to be a doctor, a good doctor.'[1] She stressed that when she sent her manuscript of *A Many-Splendoured Thing* to Jonathan Cape in London, she told the publishers she didn't want any money for it. Be this as it may, and in spite of it being panned by critics, the book took off and eventually earned her a lot of money. 'Six months later every woman on a London bus had the book under her arm', she told me proudly with a smirk on her face. 'People read it and liked it, even though one critic claimed "it was so easy to put down".'[2] While success may not have been Han's goal in writing, she had achieved enough of a name for herself even at this early point in her life that Glaskin wanted to connect with her. This was a chance too good to miss. In his memoir of her, *A Many-Splendoured Woman*, Glaskin describes how he once passed up the opportunity of meeting his other great literary hero, the British writer Graham Greene, when the two of them happened to appear in the same bar of a Bangkok nightclub. He deeply regretted not having accosted the famed author just because the man appeared worried and grieving, an impression that Glaskin later discovered was normal for Greene. Glaskin was determined to learn from this painful lesson. 'Having

1   HS to JB, interview by author, 18 August 2001.
2   Ibid.

missed my one lion of a lifetime, I managed to persuade myself that I would be foolish indeed to miss the opportunity of my lioness. So I wrote to her.'[3]

Write he did, not once but several times. Five polite notes passed between them in two weeks before they finally met over dinner at her home.[4] The evening is etched in Glaskin's memory in fine detail. The three of them, including Comber, discussed their current literary projects. The young Glaskin proudly announced that he was working on 'a piece of not quite science fiction as fantasy but written in earnest realism'[5] – *A Change of Mind* – while awaiting publication of his second novel, *A Minor Portrait*. The latter he had written in Perth earlier that year while recovering from spinal meningitis he had contracted in Singapore. Han revealed that she was working on her novel set in Nepal, *The Mountain Is Young*, which would later catapult her into the realm of a rich, as well as famous, author, when she sold the film rights for it to Paramount Studios for a hefty US$350,000.

These were heady days for this coterie of young writers and Glaskin left the Comber residence that night on a high note. He had found others who shared his passion for writing and were seriously engaged in the hard slog of producing it. At the same time, they all played other roles as young professionals in a society undergoing radical change as the last days of colonialism ebbed away and the new era of independent nationhood took its place. Driving home along Bukit Timah Road, Glaskin could be forgiven for indulging in a little flight of fantasy. As he recollected Han sitting demurely in her chair, his mind flashed back three years to a hotel in Naples where, as a young man from the antipodes, he had been lapping up a little luxury on his first trip to Europe. One morning as he ran down the stairs, he almost collided with the actress Ingrid Bergman and her three children. She smiled, waved and moved on. Once again, fame had passed Glaskin by but this time it left its mark on him. His close encounter with Bergman convinced him that she had so much of 'the same gentle and charming and essentially feminine allure' as Han that she should have played her in the motion picture *Love is a many-splendored thing*.[6] That wasn't to be. Like most other contacts Glaskin had with the ephemeral and fickle world of motion pictures, this was a fleeting fantasy. In the course of his career, six of his

---

3 GMG (1995a, 12).
4 Ibid., 13–17. With the exception of the first, these notes are reproduced in *A Many-Splendoured Woman*.
5 Ibid., 20.
6 Ibid., 21.

books were optioned for films but only one, *A Waltz through the Hills*, ever made it onto the screen, and then only the television screen.

Their contrasting relationship to publishers and filmmakers was a major difference between Glaskin and Han. She was more thick-skinned and worldly-wise than Glaskin. In a letter to him in 1972, she stressed how film producers and book publishers are three years behind their public, likening them to sharks for which nothing counts but fresh meat.[7] While her imagery was perhaps overly dramatic, her message was one that Glaskin needed to hear, especially during the many down periods in his writing life, which became more frequent as he aged. Like the wise elder sister, Han counselled Glaskin that 'you are all too ready to believe their promises' and 'you must learn to tell them all to go to hell'.[8] Fourteen years later she berated him again, this time over his handling of the publication of his memoir of her. The situation was different but her message was essentially the same – 'May I say that you seem singularly trusting and naïve about all these things.'[9]

Others also noted that Glaskin displayed a trust and naïveté, especially in relation to publishing. His last agent, Christine Nagel, who spoke affectionately of the man and tried valiantly to place a number of his later manuscripts, was one of those. 'Gerry tended to regard publishing as the kind of business it used to be – gentlemanly deals and handshakes, terribly proper – whereas it had changed substantially into a more strictly business affair. He didn't seem to realise this', she said.[10] Unfortunately, Glaskin's typical response to this situation didn't improve matters. Perhaps taking Han's advice a little too literally, he could easily become belligerent, which only aggravated the problem. 'He tended to call up publishers and get stroppy with them if they didn't reply the way he wanted them to', said an exasperated Nagel. 'While I understood his frustration, I eventually ran out of publishers I could approach on his behalf.'[11] In calling up publishers, Glaskin inserted himself between them and his agent, which only irritated both parties.

The one bright spot in Glaskin's relationship with publishers was the long association he had with John Bunting of Barrie Books, later James Barrie and Company and eventually Barrie and Rockliff. Bunting was instrumental in

---

7   HS to GMG, 28 April 1972.
8   Ibid.
9   HS to GMG, 28 April 1986.
10 Christine Nagel to JB, personal communication, 20 September 2001.
11 Christine Nagel to JB, personal communication, 1 January 2001.

getting Glaskin's first novel, *A World of Our Own*, into print and, with the help of some favourable reviews, launched the young Australian writer on the road to recognition, at least in the UK if not in Australia. Bunting went on to publish another 12 of Glaskin's books before he left the company. Glaskin despaired over 'the smart young new men' who replaced Bunting. In a visit to London in 1970, Glaskin was devastated when he discovered Bunting's fate. 'It was goodbye to publishers I had been with since the beginning of my career', he said. Then, in a gloomy note of what turned out to be an accurate prediction, he added, 'I was yet to find out that as well it was almost the end of that career.'[12]

While Han had her fair share of troubles with publishers and film producers, she was able to deal with them in a much more objective and detached way than Glaskin. This no doubt reflects fundamental differences in their personalities and their outlook on life. Born the daughter of a Chinese father and Belgian mother, Han grew up bearing the despised label of 'Eurasian', unacceptable to either side of her dual heritage. She learned quickly that to survive she needed to keep her own conscience and weather that no-man's land between traditions and allegiances. Although she was unequivocal in declaring China to be her 'great and only love',[13] she nevertheless always rejected labels people tried to pin on her, be they communist or capitalist, Asian or European. Her collection of five autobiographical histories is powerful testimony to her multifaceted yet fiercely independent spirit, perhaps no better summed up than in the title of the fourth volume, *My House Has Two Doors*.

In reality, her house had many doors and windows besides, but its foundation was firm and unshakable. While her Belgian and Chinese roots have both contributed to the making of this intriguingly complex woman, her relationships with her father and mother were markedly different. As she portrays with unapologetic honesty in her writing, she had an emotionally distant relationship with her mother, compared to the much closer one she had with her father. She rarely managed to gain her mother's approval and learned not to seek it. This was a capacity she brought with her into adult life and carried over into other relationships. Glaskin, on the other hand, seemed to crave acknowledgment and approval from his youngest days. He was used to being the centre of attention and for his first four years of life he was surrounded by aunts, uncles and grandparents, and developed

---

12 GMG (1995a, 112).
13 HS to GMG, 28 April 1972.

intimate relationships with several of them. In contrast to Han, his ties with his mother were intense and her premature death in 1960 caused him great sorrow and anguish.[14]

Little wonder then that Han should experience in Glaskin a strong desire for acceptance and recognition as a writer. This was one of her strongest recollections of the man, although she passed it off as 'a small defect'. 'He wanted to be accepted, to be popular, to be liked. He wanted to write books that were welcome', she said. Then she added, 'If you're a writer, you can expect on the contrary far more hatred than liking.'[15] This was a message she repeated to Glaskin throughout their long association. She reminded him to expect revilement and incomprehension and that 'all writers have always lived in exile everywhere, including their own countries'.[16] While these warnings may have been extreme and hard for Glaskin to swallow, they were usually accompanied by other, more reassuring comments from Han, who knew how to play the roles of supporter and cheerleader as well. Her letters to him are sprinkled with exhortations to this effect – 'I have faith in you … You have done good work and it shall remain … You've got the stuff in you.'[17] Drawing on her own experience, she sometimes offered advice in a more reflective vein. One such piece that has a distinctly Chinese ring to it probably struck a deep chord in Glaskin: 'I think the art is not to let it – the burden – carve a deep rut into one's soul but to shift it lightly on one's skin and to go on singing.'[18]

This difference in attitude to writing and publishing reveals that theirs was not a relationship of equals. Han was clearly the senior partner who not only provided advice and encouragement to the young Australian, but also arranged invitations to writers' conferences and introductions to people in the book and film world that Glaskin was only too glad to accept. The first such invitation was to a conference of writers in China in late 1957, only eight years after Mao and his fellow Communists had taken over the government. Imagine Glaskin's delight at the opportunity to under-take such a visit, given that China was still largely forbidden territory to most Westerners. Through the University of Malaya in Singapore, China invited a handful of Singapore writers to attend – Han Suyin, Cyril Northcote Parkinson (of Parkinson's Law fame), Leonard Comber and

---

14   See Chapter 2, 'A Touch of Class'.
15   HS to JB, interview, 18 August 2001.
16   HS to GMG, 22 October 1965.
17   HS to GMG, 9 March 1963, 25 March 1996, 28 April 1972.
18   HS to GMG, 24 September 1982.

Glaskin. Apparently, Parkinson had suggested Glaskin, although Glaskin suspected it was not without Han's influence and prompting.

After managing to convince his employers at Lyall and Evatt to give him time off to attend the conference, Glaskin made it all the way to the Canton railway station, only to be told by the Chinese authorities that the Australian government representative in Hong Kong had sent an urgent message demanding that he return to the colony immediately. Assuming it was a death in the family or some equally serious event, Glaskin obeyed, only to discover the next day that he needed permission from the Australian government to enter 'Red China', permission that could only be granted by an Australian High Commission, the nearest of which was in Singapore! Glaskin was devastated. It meant that China would remain forbidden to him, in spite of his having come so close to entering it. It would be nearly 30 years before he would tread on its soil and inhale its air. But it would be only eight more years before he would have another encounter with Australian bureaucracy that would leave him with nothing but contempt and disgust for some of the misguided ways of his native country.

Given her growing fame as a writer, it is little wonder that Han attracted a number of people in the literary and film worlds. After the box office success of *Love is a many-splendored thing*, the film rights to her *The Mountain Is Young* were keenly sought by several Hollywood studios. Paramount finally outbid the others and sent a team of people to check out Nepal as a filming location. En route, they stopped in Singapore to consult with Han, who invited Glaskin to accompany her to several meetings with the visiting delegation, often over lunch or dinner. This gilded group included director Edward Dmytrik, production manager Luigi Luraschi and screenwriter Robert Arthur. Glaskin was in another world, one that he yearned to be a part of as a respected and hopefully wealthy writer but which for the most part led only to heartbreak and despair. His own protracted negotiations with Twentieth Century Fox studios over the film rights to *A Lion in the Sun* finally came to nothing, or more precisely to $1000, but only after an alluring $250,000 had been mentioned at one point. This kind of figure sent Glaskin soaring to new levels of ecstasy – 'I was having heart attacks and too many whisky sodas', he told a reporter – before coming crashing down to earth with a gut-wrenching thud.[19] Paramount never proceeded with filming *The Mountain Is Young* either, but Han's ability to ride out such crashing waves was much greater than Glaskin's. Instead, these occasions

---

19 Lang (1989, 7).

only added to his cynicism about those who controlled the printed word and the silver screen.

While Han denied having been a mentor for Glaskin, she was a valued critic whose comments Glaskin took seriously. His work on *A Lion in the Sun* was a case in point. During the week at Ulu Tiram he would pound out page after page of his 250,000-word manuscript and on his way down to Singapore for the weekend he would stop off at Han's home to deliver his fresh copy and receive her comments on what he had left her the previous week. Somehow, between her duties as a doctor and her own endless writing projects, she managed to find time and interest to devote to Glaskin's work. While she had been effusive in her praise of his earlier books, *A Minor Portrait* ('a miniature masterpiece')[20] and *A Change of Mind* ('much better than *Minor*')[21], she was not reluctant to point out shortcomings and make suggestions for improvement where she thought them warranted.

As relatively new writers they were both still exploring different approaches and developing their craft. Although one gets the impression that Han kept her writing much more to herself than he did, Glaskin would share insights with her about her writing from time to time. On one occasion, they found themselves faced with a similar problem and discovered that each was able to offer the other a workable solution. As a mostly narrative writer, she tended to write from the protagonist's point of view in the first person singular. However, in *The Mountain Is Young* this became unworkable when juggling several characters at once. 'Why not let the protagonist write or think her own thoughts?' suggested Glaskin. A light came on for her. Similarly, he had become caught in a rut of writing in what he called 'the third person empathetic' voice, in which all observations were made by the main protagonist but written in the third person singular, with no omniscient narrator. But in *A Change of Mind*, where his two leading characters swapped minds and bodies, he found himself in a real pickle. 'Why not write in the style of your main character, using the first person singular?' said Han.[22] Of course!

This mutual self-help between the two writers was one of several aspects of their professional lives they shared in common. Another was their joint passion for expanding their vocabularies that often resulted in a kind a treasure hunt for ornate and unusual words. Apart from Han's ability to draw on French and Chinese, her appetite for new English words was insatiable

---

20 GMG (1995a, 40).
21 Ibid., 63.
22 Ibid., 43.

and fed by frequent games of Scrabble®. Glaskin had a similar propensity, which she commented on after reading *A Minor Portrait*. 'The words you use!' she exclaimed, referring in particular to 'mortified', which apparently had heretofore escaped her vast command of English, other than in its strict medical sense.[23] While writers invariably need to enhance their vocabularies, Glaskin's use of more obscure words sometimes seems out of context, if not pretentious. His memoir of Han is peppered with words like 'cicerone' and 'susurrant' and 'amanuensis', which would send the average reader scurrying for his dictionary. Glaskin's desire to impress with rare and unusual words is evident in a number of his books. In *A Lion in the Sun* we are introduced to 'a grey, oleaginous sea', 'plangent speech', and 'matutinal hangovers'. In *Flight to Landfall* Glaskin uses the word 'grandiloquent' several times, as if multiple appearances will add to its power and prestige. Perhaps the repeated use of this word – meaning 'pompous or inflated language' – reveals Glaskin's own weakness for the same.

Another similarity between the two writers was that they both were workhorses but Han took the prize in this department, as in most others. In his memoir to Han, Glaskin notes that during the days when they had to make time to write around their full-time jobs, 'we both pressure-cooked our prose, otherwise nothing at all would be written.'[24] He was perpetually in awe of her capacity to produce and seemed determined to try and at least match her output, but usually found himself not up to the task. Writing to her after reading her *Till Morning Comes*, Glaskin said, 'My god, girl, you can work, and do. I only wish I could do half as much but I'm bone lazy.'[25] Han and her (third) husband Vincent Ruthnaswamy both commented on Glaskin's preoccupation with productivity, a repetitive theme in letters he wrote to them. With tongue slightly in cheek she said, 'Gerry had this habit of really wanting to produce. He would ask me how many words I wrote a day. He took exceptional pride in writing faster than others. It was as though he mixed up writing with horse racing!'[26] Ruthnaswamy added another thought on the matter. 'Gerry was good at producing but there wasn't always that spark in his writing. He was disappointed, naturally, when some of his books didn't catch on. But it was as if because they didn't catch on he had to keep on producing.'[27]

---

23 Ibid., 41.
24 Ibid., 19.
25 GMG to HS, 2 November 1983.
26 HS to JB, interview, 18 August 2001.
27 Vincent Ruthnaswamy to JB, interview by author, 18 August 2001.

For Ruthnaswamy, Glaskin's preoccupation with producing was also linked to his drive for fame and success. While every writer wants people to read his books, some welcome the public spotlight falling on them while others shun it or endure it as a necessary part of their work. But for Glaskin it was something almost always in short supply. Ruthnaswamy liked Glaskin and they got on well together but the Indian engineer regarded the Australian writer's focus on success as a handicap. 'Gerry was a person who desperately wanted success. That was the way he was. In his letters he kept mentioning many things that were going to happen with books and films but so few of them did. I think he should have stuck to stockbroking and done writing in his spare time.'[28] Han echoed these sentiments. But for once in their long relationship Glaskin may have had the last word. Writing in his memoir of her, he quipped, 'Writing, she so frequently proclaimed, was merely a pastime. Pastime? I have never known her to have time to pass.'[29]

Writing is a lonely occupation and the need to have some way of gauging outcome is critical. However, having personal yardsticks is one thing; declaring these frequently to others quite another. In his letters and in his memoir to Han, Glaskin regularly commented on the length of his manuscripts and the time it took him to produce them. While in their correspondence this could be regarded as simply writer's talk, in a book that was meant to honour her it seems unnecessarily self-flattering. Similarly, at the end of most of his novels he used the now antiquated practice of stating when and where the book was written. While this may have been regarded as appropriate etiquette in his day, one wonders what difference it makes to the reader to know how long the author took to write the book and where it was written.

Perhaps more interesting is Glaskin's comment about his being 'lazy'. He makes several references to this, although it doesn't always correspond to the rather hectic life he often led or the difficult circumstances under which he wrote due to his endless and recurrent illnesses. And what could have been perceived as non-productive behaviour could also have been the kind of brooding that many writers indulge in before committing thoughts to paper or computer screen. When Glaskin lived in Amsterdam, his Dutch friend and landlord, Edgar Vos, detected this about his Australian guest but was more inclined to call it procrastination. Himself an avid producer, be it of exquisite clothes and stylish hats, Vos said, 'There was a sense in which

---

28 Ibid.
29 GMG (1995a, 23).

Gerry was lazy. Even though he'd work many hours on a book, it would take a long time before he started. I would urge him to do something else, like typing or learning Dutch. But some writers think a lot before they put anything on paper.'[30]

Indeed, getting something down on paper is often a challenge to writers, but going back over it with an editor's eye and a surgeon's scalpel can be even more so. Once again, Han demonstrated an ability to do this that Glaskin could only envy. As she was working on the draft of her second autobiographical history, *A Mortal Flower*, she wrote, 'Most of the back-breaking work is really the redoing. As you know, I redo some chapters up to 40 times.'[31] While 40 was probably stretching a point in order to make it, she did revise her writing many times, something she observed Glaskin was not so able or willing to do with his. 'The most difficult thing, and sometimes the most important thing for a writer is to edit yourself, which usually means to cut yourself', she told me. 'Gerry couldn't do that.'[32] Although he did a lot of cutting of his earlier manuscripts – at the insistence of his publishers – many of Glaskin's later works don't reflect this. Perhaps, ironically, this has something to do with his decision to take Han's advice and have someone else type and retype his manuscripts. He acknowledged that this meant 'sacrificing a last opportunity to change a word or a phrase, reshape a sentence or even rewrite a whole paragraph before the final version went off to the publisher – polishing'.[33]

Regardless of their differences as writers, one thing they did share was a perceived decline in standards of publishing during the late 1960s and 1970s. Many of their letters contain references to this, more so from Glaskin who was having far greater difficulty getting published in his later years. 'The fashion in fiction lapsed from sincerity and integrity into either escapism or a kind of cerebral titillation', claimed Glaskin.[34] He was angered that writers now had to write certain kinds of books dictated by publishers as commercially saleable. 'Having written 14 books just as I liked, with not one of them the same as any other, I couldn't contemplate writing either to a formula or a fad', he wrote to Han.[35] She responded with even more graphic imagery. 'The "market" for books is almost entirely monopolised by

---

30 Edgar Vos to JB, interview by author, 21 August 2001.
31 HS to GMG, 22 October 1965. In my interview with Han, she repeated this claim but reduced the figure to '16 or 17 times', to which Ruthnaswamy attested.
32 HS to JB, interview, 18 August 2001.
33 GMG (1995a, 45).
34 Ibid., 83.
35 Ibid., 97.

a certain genre without diversity, technical skill, and absolutely no literary value. It is hard to go on pitching in such a quagmire. Books are now known as "the product", which makes me think of defecation.'[36]

In spite of her expressed antipathy towards this market-driven approach to writing and publishing, Han was able to embrace it more easily than Glaskin. Perhaps she was luckier too, to be the right person in the right place at the right time. Given the ignorance, puzzlement and even fear that most Westerners had about China and the massive changes that have taken place there in the last 50 years, those who could speak with authority on the subject and were trusted in the West have found a ready audience. With Han's unique bicultural heritage, as well as her skills as a writer of both fiction and non-fiction, she was able to provide this voice. Writing to Glaskin, she acknowledged this fortuitous turn of events. 'I have been lucky because I got on one wicket, China. This is not because I ever thought China would be popular or acceptable but because it is my great and only love. Everything else takes second place. I never reckoned that suddenly China would become so acceptable and popular, yet it has happened.'[37]

Although their writing careers diverged after their time in Singapore, their friendship remained strong. Glaskin revered Han from those earliest years and continued to do so throughout his life. He was convinced she should have received the Nobel Prize for Literature, something that she brushed aside as 'overvalued' and 'just a matter of knowing the right people'.[38] In comparison, Glaskin's own writing seemed to him insignificant, even puerile. It never quite measured up to the groundbreaking work she seemed to be able to churn out. Glaskin wrote to Han after receiving a copy of her book on Mao Tse-Tung and the Communist revolution, *The Morning Deluge*. He referred to it as 'a tremendous work of scholarship executed in a most masterly style and vocabulary' that 'so easily excels most of what is written by English-speaking writers today ... [It] makes my own efforts seem not only puny but paltry. I'm ashamed to have sent them to you.'[39]

While there is some truth in what Glaskin says, he doesn't give himself credit for the role his writing did play in the context of the place and time in which it was created. He liked to shock, and many of his books would have had this effect on their readers, especially mainstream Australians trying to return to a life of normalcy after the onslaught of the Second World War. At

---

36 HS to GMG, 24 September 1982.
37 HS to GMG, 28 April 1972.
38 HS to JB, interview, 18 August 2001.
39 HS to GMG, 23 May 1975.

very least, his writing opened the eyes and minds of average Australians to the world around them in all its baffling diversity and never-ending change. As author and critic Robert Dessaix noted about Glaskin's homosexual novel, *No End to the Way*, 'it was available to not just the *cognoscenti* or to prowlers in the library stacks, but to fathers of three stopping off at a railway kiosk on the way home from work, to men in the suburbs curious about their own sexual inclinations – in other words, to ordinary Australians.'[40] But perhaps because of his propensity to tackle subjects that pushed people's comfort levels, Glaskin didn't find the waiting market and popular adulation he sought, especially in his native Australia which, in the 1950s and 1960s, still preferred to retreat to the old world with which it was familiar rather than to embrace the new one on its doorstep.

If he never did achieve parity with Han as a writer, Glaskin was still able to relate to her in her capacity of physician, if only as her patient. This began in Singapore in 1956 when Glaskin was suffering from severe headaches and his former doctors had retired or were on leave. While he thought the headaches were most probably related to the attack of spinal meningitis he had suffered a year or so before, she was quick to diagnose that they were more likely the result of a neck injury he incurred during training with the RAAF in Canada during the Second World War. The condition was agg-ravated by vibrations of any sort, including those that came from talking on a telephone, something Glaskin did for much of his day as a stockbroker. Her first recommendation that he give up stockbroking he cast aside as imprac-ticable, given that stockbroking was providing him with a steady and often lucrative income that not only supported him but also his family in Australia. She then insisted that he be more intentional about wearing a cervical collar and doing isometric exercises, which he had been doing off and on for years. Two years later, before Glaskin left Singapore, Han dashed off a handwritten note about his headaches, which years later would prove invaluable in his efforts to secure an increase in his War Disability Pension from the Austral-ian government. He reproduced the letter in his memoir of her.[41]

Headaches remained with Glaskin throughout much of his life, as did complications from neck and spinal injuries. Indeed, Glaskin was plagued by innumerable illnesses (I found references to 39) ranging from vascular malformation of the spine and an infection of the gall bladder to hepatitis and hiatus hernia. At times, his various conditions became so interwoven

---

40 Dessaix (1993, 13).
41 GMG (1995a, 68).

and overlapping that one seemed to spark another. Writing to Han, Glaskin reported that doctors surmised that an attack of giardiasis (or bacillar dysentery) launched a flu virus in the liver, pancreas and intestines, which caused him to spend six weeks in bed that resulted in a relapse in his neck![42] Not surprisingly, he made frequent reference to his health problems in his correspondence with Han, given that she was his personal physician for a period in his life. Most of the time, she was willing to make helpful suggestions but at one point Glaskin's repeated references to his never-ending ailments drove her to refer to his 'recital of woes'.[43] Glaskin was taken aback by Han's reaction and apologised for sounding so pathetic.

One of Glaskin's more serious illnesses that occurred while he was in Singapore led him to go beyond Han for treatment. In 1955, several cases of meningitis were reported in Singapore. According to Glaskin, three people contracted the disease, of which he was one; the other two died. He was sent to recuperate in Perth, where he ran into his friend and mentor John K. Ewers, who promptly asked him what he was going to do. 'As I was told – rest', replied Glaskin. 'On your laurels?' asked Ewers. 'Going to write another book?'[44] Although a little offended at Ewers' persistence, Glaskin knew Ewers was right. If he was to stay a writer and not be just a one-book wonder, write he must. What's more, his 'literary mama', Henrietta Drake-Brockman, said exactly the same thing. He threw himself into the task and produced *A Minor Portrait*. After completing the book, he met up with Ewers again. 'Now what are you going to do?' he asked Glaskin. 'I've been trying to find a job', replied Glaskin, concerned about not just his own welfare but that of his large family as well. 'Well, where did you earn your money before?' persisted Ewers. 'Singapore', said Glaskin. 'Don't they want you back?' asked Ewers. 'Yes. But the doctors say I shouldn't return to the tropics', said an obedient Glaskin. 'They tell me I shouldn't smoke, but I can't do without it', quipped Ewers.[45] Shortly afterwards, Glaskin headed back to Singapore to resume his position as a stockbroker and wrote two more novels.

In spite of Glaskin's frequent references to his bodily complaints, Han was not, like some of his friends and acquaintances, ready to call him a hypochondriac. Instead, she reflected that 'he often became so involved with himself that there was no other world for him', underscoring Glaskin's

---

42 GMG to HS, 10 October 1981.
43 HS to GMG, 24 September 1982.
44 GMG (1978a, 32).
45 Ibid.

narcissitic tendencies.[46] However, his partner, Leo van de Pas, had another view on the subject. 'He was definitely not a hypochondriac. He simply would give an answer to the question, How are you? If people hadn't asked this question he wouldn't have brought up his health.' While van de Pas's logic seems sound, he may have been overly charitable in his comment. However, he was also the one person who lived with and cared for Glaskin more than any other, particularly during Glaskin's latter years when his health problems grew steadily worse. He saw Glaskin live through years of agonising pain, take tens of thousands of analgesics, daily hang upside down in a surgical harness, and endure a number of neck collars while trying to type, drive and even bodysurf. If anyone had reason to complain about his body's malfunctioning it was probably Glaskin, but for much of the time he managed to keep his troubles to himself.[47] This often meant a rising level of stress and frustration that gradually built up and sometimes erupted into angry outbursts or acerbic tirades, even against some of his closest friends and associates.

One of these was Peter Hurford, a lifelong friend from Glaskin's early days in Perth, who went on to become a highly successful marketing executive with British Airways in Europe. During his last visit with Glaskin in Perth, Hurford must have trodden on one of Glaskin's all-too-sensitive corns. 'In the middle of our conversation he suddenly started attacking me. I found it very difficult. I told him that I was one of the last people to come and see him. But he didn't relent.'[48] According to van de Pas, efforts to intervene on such occasions only made things worse. 'When Gerry was on a roll, he could not be stopped. Trying to explain or divert would only make it worse. The only thing to do was to let him spew his fury.'[49] Another stalwart friend of Glaskin's, writer Ethel Webb Bundell, also experienced this belligerent side of Glaskin, but unlike many who took offence to it she was more philosophical about it and offered an explanation for it. 'When they dug up Ivan the Terrible, it was discovered that he had a spinal condition causing constant pain, which may have accounted for his temperament. It's possible that Gerry suffered similarly', she said.[50]

---

46 HS to JB, interview, 18 August 2001.
47 LvdP claims that GMG was in constant pain but forced himself to operate as though that wasn't the case, which made LvdP often forget how much pain GMG had to deal with.
48 Peter Hurford to JB, personal communication, 24 April 2001.
49 LvdP to JB, personal communication, 22 June 2010.
50 Ethel Webb Bundell to JB, personal communication, 18 April 2001.

In the midst of being a writing adviser and general practitioner for Glas-kin, Han was above all a friend. The depth of their friendship is reflected in numerous affectionate references in their letters and in Glaskin's memoir of Han. When he first began the memoir, Glaskin titled it *Love and Letters* but later changed it to *A Many-Splendoured Woman*, when the letters never made it in to the final version. One game they played in writing to each other was to refer to her as 'Old Thing'. This came about in a conversation the two had one day in 1958, between the many trips she was then making abroad as a political commentator on China, as well as an established author. 'I am feeling old', she said. 'I didn't feel old when I turned 40 but now that I'm 41 I feel old.' In response, Glaskin blurted out, 'Oh, you poor old thing!' The next letter Han wrote to him she signed 'Affectionately, Old Thing.'[51] Glaskin picked up on her overture and continued to refer to her with this term of endearment. Sometimes, when feeling a little more buoyant, he elaborated a little. One of his letters began with 'Dear Old and Terribly Attractive and Exceedingly Dangerous Thing'![52]

Beyond this kind of intimate frivolity there is nothing to suggest that the love Glaskin professed for Han was at all sexual. Neither gives any hint of this, although Glaskin was always quick to notice and appreciate beauty in a woman, which he often described in such fine detail that it camouflaged his sexual preferences. While alluding to Han in his memoir as 'one of the most beautiful women in the world',[53] he also referred to her in correspondence as 'my platonic pet'.[54] For her part, Han experienced no sexual attraction to Glaskin. Looking back on their early days in Singapore, Han was very matter-of-fact about Glaskin's initial impact on her. 'I wasn't impressed by his looks. I'm sure he was good looking but I just didn't react that way. Ours was perfectly a writing relationship, and that's all.'[55] She was also seemingly oblivious to his homosexual leanings, even 16 years later when he and Leo stayed with her and Vincent in their Paris apartment. 'I just thought it was quite novel, two young friends', she said.[56] Ruthnaswamy, however, had no doubts about Glaskin's sexual inclinations from the beginning but noted that Glaskin was adept at presenting himself as a straight man in public.[57]

---

51 GMG (1995a, 77).
52 GMG to HS, 19 October 1959.
53 GMG (1995a, 62).
54 GMG to HS, 9 February 1960.
55 HS to JB, interview, 18 August 2001.
56 Ibid.
57 Ruthnaswamy to JB, interview, 18 August 2001.

As good friends, Glaskin and Han offered each other advice on various issues and support in times of crisis. More often it was Han who advised or supported Glaskin but sometimes he reciprocated. She was always quick to respond and often quite creatively. One occasion was Glaskin's run-in with neighbours in 1996 in which Glaskin sustained physical injuries. The case ended up in court and in the press. Sympathising with his plight, she treated it in a light-hearted manner and reminded Glaskin that 'sometimes a bit of theatrical drama is necessary'. She advised him to encase himself in plaster and make his entrance into the courtroom in a wheelchair.[58] On a more serious note, she was able to offer Glaskin a solution to his interminable dilemma of where to live, given his love/hate relationship with Australia and his fondness for Europe, particularly the Netherlands. After Glaskin announced for the third time his intention to leave Australia for good, she asked him in a letter, 'Why not decide that you will never settle, like me, and then you will be spared any further decision?'[59] This came as a brilliant insight to Glaskin, who would have acted upon it if only finances and medical treatment hadn't prevented it. He did travel extensively for the next 25 years, mainly throughout Europe and Indonesia, as well as Egypt, India, and China, but Australia remained his home during most of this time, as much as he often detested it.

Han's friendship with Glaskin was not just a two-person affair. It also included Ruthnaswamy and van de Pas. Glaskin's letters to Han were often addressed to Ruthnaswamy as well, or at least were intended to be read by him, and similarly with hers to Glaskin and van de Pas. Han thought highly of van de Pas from their first meeting and advised Glaskin to take counsel from van de Pas, especially on financial matters, as she did from Ruthnaswamy.[60] But her admiration for van de Pas went beyond his practical skills. Writing to both of them at the end of 1972, Han confessed that 'I may not manifest it very much but I do love you both very dearly.'[61] Fourteen years later, she would repeat the sentiment but with a different emphasis. 'I think you and Leo are a wonderful couple, and your courage in sticking to what you are I always terribly admired.'[62]

One major rupture in Glaskin's relationship with Han occurred in 1986 over a number of statements he made in his memoir of her. Although the

---

58 HS to GMG, 9 April 1996.
59 HS to GMG, 2 March 1969.
60 HS to GMG, 20 November 1970.
61 HS to GMG, 16 December 1972.
62 HS to GMG, 4 April 1986.

book was finally published in 1995, Glaskin first raised the idea of it with Han in 1982 and began writing it in 1985, but because of Han's vehement opposition to parts of the manuscript he put it aside. In a letter to a friend, Glaskin admits he even considered burning the manuscript because of Han's reaction to it.[63] From the beginning Han did not support this book but because of her friendship with Glaskin she didn't overtly try to prevent it being written. She gave numerous subtle hints that she would have preferred him not to write it, which he either never understood or chose to ignore. He seemed equally determined that the book would make it into print, ostensibly to honour her but also to leave a record of their relationship and perhaps, as some have suggested, to allow some of her fame to rub off on him.

Glaskin's initial plan for the book, as he described it to Han's publishers, Jonathan Cape, was to write a 10,000-word memoir to which he would attach about 80,000 words of correspondence between Han and himself. Han was hesitant about the use of her letters but agreed to it as long as she could see those passages Glaskin intended to use. He didn't object to this but said that as far as his letters were concerned, they could stay as they were because after all, 'What would be the value of a book if we didn't?'[64] Glaskin became excited about the book and told Han that it would be his best work.[65] He even proposed to Cape that they pay him £2,000 against royalties and in lieu of an advance so he could go to Han's home in Switzerland to work with her to edit the letters and to interview her. He also applied to the Australia Council for a $4,000 Special Purposes grant for the same purpose but neither took the bait.

As valiantly as Glaskin tried he didn't succeed in interesting anyone in the book. Graham C. Greene (nephew of the well-known writer) of Jonathan Cape was the first to reject it because he didn't see it reaching a wide enough market to justify publication. Glaskin was shattered and wrote Greene a highly emotional letter in which he argued that if Han's own publishers wouldn't publish a memoir to her, then who would?[66] Who indeed? Glaskin scolded Greene for not communicating this sad news directly to Han, whom he claimed would be sorely disappointed 'after so many books and so many years.'[67] Nothing in Han's correspondence with Glaskin suggested she would

---

63 GMG to Helen Sinclair-Wilson, 12 February 1996.
64 GMG to HS, 4 October 1984.
65 GMG to HS, 9 December 1984. LvdP recalled that GMG always regarded his last work as his best.
66 GMG to Graham C. Greene, 29 October 1985.
67 Ibid.

have been in the least disappointed. If anything, she might have been greatly relieved by the news of Cape's rejection. Not to be put down by this slap in the face, Glaskin wrote to Han to tell her that he had decided to proceed with the writing anyhow, even if it never was published, because 'I think I owe you this much.'[68] Han responded by pleading with Glaskin to drop the whole thing because she didn't see the book drawing a big public either in China or Britain, her two main markets. Meanwhile, Glaskin had met a Chinese academic couple, Professors Zhang Taijin and Yang Mingqiu, who were in Perth on a sabbatical. Seemingly oblivious to what Han was saying, Glaskin went ahead and enthused the pair about the project and enlisted their services to translate his book into Mandarin. Glaskin and Han had such different relationships to this book that sooner or later a confrontation was inevitable.

To add to Glaskin's woes, his British agent, David Bolt, gave it the thumbs down. Like Greene, he saw the book having limited appeal to the general public, for several reasons. First, he pointed out that few writers have the household name that guarantees the sale of a collection of letters. Although Bolt acknowledged that Han Suyin was 'a name to conjure with', he pointed out that 'we learn all too little of her comments', a critique several others also made of the book. Second, the book contained too little 'literary gossip' and what there was, was more about Glaskin than Han, with only a passing mention of other writers. Third, Glaskin missed opportunities to attract the reader's attention by ignoring such issues as his own homosexuality and Han's relationship to it, Han's supposed Communism and her marriage to an Indian, and her relationship to her own publishers. Bolt's fourth and perhaps most important point was that the manuscript contained no revelations, which is what sells letters. He stressed that Glaskin's letters were more interesting than Han's but that it would be her name that would sell, not his. In addition, Bolt also sensed a lack of controversy in Han's relationship with Glaskin that made the affection between the two seem 'too flattering'. Not to be put down by his agent's pessimistic response, Glaskin tried another of Han's publishers, Sidgwick and Jackson. They also declined to publish the book because they predicted that too small a percentage of Han's readers would see it as essential reading.

Meanwhile, Glaskin had sent a copy of the manuscript to Han for her comments. Comments he received, but nothing like what he expected. She read the whole thing in one sitting and couldn't believe what it contained.

---

68 GMG to HS, 29 October 1985.

In a torrid letter she accused Glaskin of 'gross, rather astonishing errors of time, people, place and the meaning of what was said' that 'at least in three places completely distort everything, including our relationship.'[69] By the end of the letter she had mellowed a little but was still reeling from her reading of the manuscript. 'How could you, Gerry, misunderstand me so much? I realise you do this as a work of affection and respect. But forgive me for saying that I was also much hurt ... Is it not better to have the whole thing quite sound and correct and reliable instead of unreliable?' Reversing her earlier position, she withheld the right to publish her letters, especially in China, and did not want him to even publish his memoir of her, although she acknowledged his right to do so. A long and tempestuous telephone conversation between the two followed. Van de Pas was with Glaskin during the call and remembered the feisty exchange. 'Han was livid because the book exploded the myth of her great love affair with Ian Morrison. She blasted Gerry for about half an hour about all kinds of details. He listened without interrupting or trying to justify what he had written. At the end he said that friendship was more important to him than a manuscript and he would destroy it. Shocked, Han replied "You wouldn't dare!" This calmed her down, but sadly it took quite a number of years before the book was published.'[70]

Ten days later, Han wrote another letter to Glaskin.[71] She admitted that there are two sides to any dispute but made hers patently clear. Apart from the errors of fact, of which she listed 12, her main concern was the possible publication of the book in China. She forbade publication there unless and until she gave her permission and then only with her own publisher, fearing that to do otherwise would create 'awful confusion' for her in China. Given the large number and varying quality of translators in China, she instructed Glaskin to refer his Chinese translators to her. Han grew more concerned about this when Glaskin revealed that he had received an invitation to come to Dalian University in China to lecture for a year. However, his deteriorating health made this a doubtful prospect. But Han had no doubts on the matter. She wrote to a Chinese government official, with a copy to Professor Zhang Taijin who had issued the invitation, strongly advising against Glaskin coming to China on grounds that he was in extremely poor health and could die any time. She claimed that not enough blood was going to Glaskin's

69 HS to GMG, 18 April 1986.
70 LvdP to JB, personal communication, 13 March 2002.
71 HS to GMG, 28 April 1986.

brain, which was causing him to write false and inaccurate information.[72] While she didn't reveal these details to Glaskin, she did urge him not to go to China because of his wavering health. Glaskin never did spend time in China as a visiting writer/lecturer, only as a tourist with van de Pas in August 1985.

Interestingly, van de Pas's comment that Glaskin had exploded the 'myth' of Han's famous love affair with Ian Morrison did not rate all that highly with Han. Like his well-known father before him, Ian Morrison was an Australian journalist who worked for *The Times* (of London) as an Asian correspondent. He was based in Singapore, where his wife and children lived, and travelled widely throughout the region. During his frequent visits to Hong Kong he struck up a relationship with Han, then a doctor and a single parent to her adopted daughter. Their affair ended tragically after about 15 months when Morrison was killed while covering the Korean War. Using the fictitious name of Mark Elliott for Ian Morrison, Han wrote about their relationship in her highly successful book, *A Many-Splendoured Thing*. In his memoir of Han, Glaskin asserted that as well as having Han as his lover, Morrison had a girl in every port across Asia. His source of information for this was Henrietta Drake-Brockman, whom Glaskin had known from his early days as a writer in Perth and who claimed to be related to Morrison.[73] Her description of the young journalist, as reported by Glaskin, was 'Charming, of course – utterly charming. But quite wicked'.[74] When Drake-Brockman visited Singapore, she told Glaskin she would be interested in meeting Han, since she felt inclined to share this information with her, but Glaskin begged her not to, so she relented. However, when he himself revealed it in *A Many-Splendoured Woman*, Han brushed aside his allegation as 'no revelation to me!' and claimed that it smacked of poor taste.[75]

Nine years later when the book eventually was published, few of Han's original concerns seemed to carry the same weight. This time she mentioned only three matters requiring attention – a joking reference that her marriage to Ruthnaswamy was according to Muslim rites; Glaskin's so-called revelation about Ian Morrison; and a reference to an affair that her second husband, Leonard Comber, had with a young Chinese woman, which ended in tragedy.[76] Glaskin responded to all three but didn't change anything.

72 HS to Xin Jiang, 29 April 1986.
73 See Chapter 7, 'Going Dutch', for details.
74 GMG (1995a, 58).
75 HS to GMG, 28 April 1986.
76 HS to GMG, 28 February 1995.

Finally, Han relented and declared that even though there were mistakes, 'it may only add spice to the book.'[77] It seemed that her friendship with Glaskin had triumphed over her concerns for accuracy or her need to protect her own reputation. However, the intervening years hadn't diminished Glaskin's yearning to have the manuscript published. In December 1994, in the process of moving house, Glaskin found the manuscript in the bottom of a case of linen. Apparently he had buried it there, not quite being able to burn it as he once threatened. He resolved to give it one more try and this time he was lucky. A small Singapore publisher, Graham Brash, was in the process of reprinting *A Lion in the Sun* and *The Beach of Passionate Love* and given Han's former Singapore connections, Glaskin convinced them to take his memoir of her as well. However, the book was now vastly shortened to about 40,000 words without the letters. It finally appeared in November 1995.

After the many battles Glaskin had fought with agents, publishers and Han herself, he still found the book 'compulsive reading'.[78] Regrettably, he seems to be one of the few people who did. Robin Yee of *8 Days*, a Singapore media magazine, called it 'an excuse for self-aggrandisement' that unashamedly glorified its author at the expense of its subject. 'Correspondence between the two writers and photos provided are too few to satisfy anyone who wants to know more about the doctor who stunned the world with her novel, *Love is* [sic] *A Many-Splendored Thing*', Yee wrote.[79] Glaskin knew he had set himself up for this kind of accusation and slipped in his own defence in advance. In the epilogue he concedes that, 'There will be some, I know, who will say I have written as much of myself as I have of you.' He then adds a curious justification for this claim. 'Without knowing why, they will be right, of course, if perhaps for the wrong reason. Of *course* I had to write about me. With your medicine as well as your writing, so much of that "me" was formed entirely by you. To have omitted the "me" would have been to have omitted all too much of the "you".'[80] Yee also discounted Glaskin's prolegomena about his missed opportunity to meet his literary hero Graham H. Greene as 'pretentious and marginally relevant'. Most of Yee's criticisms ring true but Glaskin didn't see them that way. He dismissed them offhandedly as coming from 'just another of those silly ambitious ladies (of either sex) with a non-gender name like "Robin".'[81]

---

77 HS to Angela Yeo (Graham Brash), 14 July 1995.
78 GMG to Mosman Ishmail (Graham Brash), 19 November 1995.
79 Yee (1996).
80 GMG (1995a, 137–138).
81 GMG to Gaël Lee (Graham Brash), 9 January 1996.

Yee's comments echo those of another reader from an Australian publisher to whom he had sent the manuscript five years before. The publisher declined publication for a number of reasons, primarily because not much was revealed about Han Suyin. The reader referred to Han as 'the passive, if not reluctant, partner in the correspondence'. She noted that much of the letters and the memoir related to the health of the two writers and to their mutual disdain for publishers and their representatives, subjects that do not have wide appeal. She also pointed out that Glaskin's frequent denigratory remarks about Australia would go down better in Europe or Asia than in Australia, which was their market and one to which Han had only tenuous connections.[82] Undeterred by this rejection, Glaskin continued to press his agents in the United States and Europe to take up the book and kept trying to have the book published in China despite Han's wishes. It never happened.

Why Glaskin should have been so insistent on publishing his memoir of Han is not clear but it lends itself to the accusation that he wanted to ride on her coattails. She herself hinted at this in her letter advising against Glaskin's proposed visit to China. 'This Australian writer, whom I know [sic] for over 35 years, is only trying to "climb on my fame" in some ways,' she said, 'although of course, he is also, at least he says so, very friendly to me.'[83] Others have suggested similarly. Several of Glaskin's friends commented on how much he paraded his relationship with Han in front of them. Although van de Pas disagrees that Glaskin flaunted his acquaintance with Han, Glaskin himself was quite open about it, especially if it appeared to enhance his own reputation, as one incident makes plain. On his ill-fated attempt to enter China in 1957, he struck up a conversation with a young Chinese businessman on the train between Hong Kong and Canton. Their exchanges were very pedestrian until Glaskin revealed that he was a writer and a friend of Han. 'My prestige became almost immeasurable once I let slip that I did indeed know the famous Han Suyin', he said.[84]

The desire to ally himself with fame and fortune persisted throughout Glaskin's life and his relationship with Han was an important part of that desire. But it went beyond that. For Glaskin it had a special significance, even mystique, about it. He leaves the reader with the impression that their coming together was not just chance but something that was meant to be, as incongruous as it may seem given their diverse upbringings in such vastly different countries – the little girl from Peking (Beijing) and the little boy

82 University of Western Australia Press to GMG, 24 April 1990.
83 HS to Xin Jiang, 29 April 1986.
84 GMG (1995a, 47).

from Perth. In the epilogue to the memoir, Glaskin states that Han's expressed love for China helped him to understand his own love/hate relationship with Australia. Then, in a reference to the Chinese understanding of ying-yang and with an intriguing twist of logic, Glaskin remarks, 'Our opposites are so similar that it is no wonder we found ourselves to be so much alike'.[85] While Han might not have shared his conclusion, she no doubt would have agreed with his next statement. In a final acknowledgement to 'dear Old Thing', then in her late seventies, he alludes to their mutual love and confesses that he is 'still toddling along behind' her. Whatever else may have changed, the nature of their relationship clearly had not.

---

85 Ibid., 138).

Chapter 7

Going Dutch

I had not the slightest idea that the years I was to spend in Amsterdam
would be among the happiest – yet also the unhappiest – in all my life.

Gerald Glaskin
A Bird in My Hands

On a bitterly cold Sunday morning in January 1964 Gerald Glaskin stood at the window of his friend's fourth-storey Amsterdam apartment. As he glanced down he tried to imagine how his body would disfigure the concrete squares of the pavement below. Across the street he noticed his light brown Renault Floride in which he had travelled over 100,000 kilometres around Europe. It was parked in the same place it had been for the last two months ever since he had been stricken with a strange illness. Summoning what little strength he had left, he pushed up the window and a blast of frigid winter air rushed in to meet him. Anticipating this, he had turned up the gas heater to protect the two canaries that would remain behind in their cages after he had made his exit from this world. He was especially concerned about Swee, the female, who had taken ill not long after he had and had lain listless for days in her nest. As he sat on the window ledge, fingers pressed on the inside of the window and thumbs on the outside, Glaskin breathed out.

At that moment a wild screech came from behind. He knew it was Swee but couldn't imagine what was the matter. He swung his legs back inside the room and struggled over to her cage. Her wings flapped wildly as she hung upside down with one foot caught in the wire of her nest. Apparently, she had tried to lift herself from her nest to eat from her seed container but had slipped and become trapped. Glaskin went to her cage and freed her. As her warm body lay limply in his hands he looked at her with profound gratitude. This pathetic little creature had saved him from committing the ultimate sin and had given him the most precious gift he could ever expect. Reflecting on this epiphanous moment in *A Bird in My Hands* he said, 'For the first time that day I could bring myself to pray. Not for myself ... but for the sick helpless creature lying so passively, so trusting, in the palm of my hand ... And I knew then, that – the moment of madness having come, and passed – I should never suffer from it again.'[1]

For the fourth time in his life, Gerald Glaskin had been given a reprieve from death. For that ultimate experience, he would have to wait another 36 years.

Glaskin's attempt to end his life was not an impulsive act of a rash man. Rather, it was the carefully planned and premeditated act of a severely depressed man for whom life's promises and possibilities had all but disappeared. Since arriving in Europe in 1961, Glaskin had wanted to change his growing reputation as a writer from one who wrote 'purely a story' to one who produced 'novels of importance'.[2] With seven published books to his name and film rights to a number of those already optioned he had proven his ability to write and attract an audience. He now wanted his work to have an impact in society, not merely to pander to his readers' desire for titillating entertainment. With typical Sagittarian abandon he threw himself into the task. He intended to write one book with three stories, a trilogy of novellas on sexualities. However, Glaskin's choice of subject matter – prostitution, sex with a minor, incest and homosexuality – did not initially excite his publishers, Barrie and Rockliff. They told him bluntly they had no desire to publish such material as it would tarnish his image. 'I considered [these stories] the best I had written', said a despondent Glaskin. 'Fortunately, so far as the novellas were concerned, so did my agent.'[3] However, no other publisher his agent approached would touch them. Glaskin began to doubt both his skill as a writer and his critical judgement. He had wasted a whole

---

1 GMG (1967a, 189).
2 Ibid., 107.
3 Ibid.

year's work and generated no income. On top of this, three film options – for *A Change of Mind*, *A Lion in the Sun* and *The Beach of Passionate Love* – had been dropped. He was not only discouraged but also scared. He was nearly 18,000 kilometres from home and his funds were beginning to run dangerously low.

Then, just before Christmas 1963, Glaskin was out drinking and dancing with friends one Saturday in an Amsterdam nightclub when suddenly he started to shake violently. He turned ash-grey and passed out. When he revived 15 minutes later his friends were frightened and wanted to take him to a doctor right away but Glaskin insisted it could wait until morning. The next day Dr Joop Broekman visited him and first thought Glaskin might be suffering from malaria or grippe. He finally decided that Glaskin's symptoms indicated jaundice but pointed out that this was a cover for the real culprit, which could only be detected once the jaundice had been dealt with. He prescribed a strict diet of steamed or boiled vegetables, buttermilk, sugar and black tea.

Glaskin began to feel his grasp on life loosen and it worried him. Although he had undergone several near-death experiences – in the navy and in a car accident – this was an entirely different matter. It brought with it a depression that he described as 'settling heavily like the cold and thick slush in the street outside ... almost a fear'.[4] One day, he looked in the mirror and noticed he was about as yellow as his friend's two canaries. His hair, which had grown nearly down to his shoulders, turned greyer by the day; his urine was as black as coffee and his excrement as white as plaster. The first week had been sheer agony but as his six-week sentence of convalescence came and went with no signs of recovery his spirits sank to an all-time low. This young writer who sometimes spent 12- to 14-hour days at his typewriter now couldn't care less about writing. He tried writing in an exercise book, but to his dismay found he couldn't even hold the pen. What is more, not a single word would come. He frequently wept and felt certain he was going to die. 'Nothing mattered ... Nothing had meaning ... Death seemed so much the closer, and perhaps the more preferable to life', he later wrote.[5]

Throughout this torment Glaskin was blessed with one thing – the unremitting kindness and generosity of friends, Dutch friends, and one in particular, Edgar Vos. Vos was one of the Netherlands', if not Europe's, most renowned couturiers. His clientele included royalty and leading society

4   Ibid., 124.
5   Ibid., 170–171.

figures across the Continent. He was written up in almost every prominent style and fashion magazine and his business expanded from the Netherlands to include operations in the United States and Hong Kong. In his younger days, his boyish good looks helped him get work as a model and some minor film roles. But success and fame did not come to Vos without a price. As a 10-year-old boy, he was living in what was then the Dutch East Indies when the Japanese invaded the country. His father, a captain with the Dutch merchant shipping line KPM, was away at sea. The Japanese separated Vos and his 13-year-old brother from their mother, whom they put in a different concentration camp. Vos survived four years of untold brutality and hardship, and at one point collapsed and was given up for dead. When his captors killed his brother, as well as his favourite dog, he had little reason to want to go on living.

Scouring the innermost recesses of his being, this young teenage boy managed to find the will to overcome such horrific odds. Perhaps his Friesian ancestry, with its reputation for persistence and determination, had something to do with it. But the struggle didn't end with the defeat of the Japanese. After the war, Indonesian sentiment against the Dutch began to surface, so for their own protection Dutch civilians were interned in camps once again. Vos was separated from his mother a second time, but they were later reunited in the same camp. One day, Gurkha troops came and loaded all the inmates of their camp into trucks and took them to the port of Surabaya. Angry crowds threw hand grenades at the convoy but Vos's truck reached the harbour where they boarded a ship for Singapore. On the way, the ship stopped in Jakarta, where they met with Vos's father, who, knowing nothing of the fate of his wife and two sons, had remarried. Although his parents came back together for a time, they eventually divorced and Vos returned with his mother to the Netherlands, where he picked up the threads of a tattered education and graduated from the Dutch Academy of Arts.

Glaskin uses these tragic events from Vos's life in two of his books, *The Man Who Didn't Count* and *Flight to Landfall*. In *Count*, Australian writer Morton Thomas finds himself being followed by two strange men and when he becomes the target of several attacks on his life he makes a hasty exit from his home in London to the Netherlands. Sitting on a park bench in Amsterdam's lush Vondelpark, he strikes up an acquaintance with an attractive young Dutchwoman, Anneke Vos. A hat maker by trade, Anneke was born in Indonesia, her father was a sea captain with KPM, and she was captured and imprisoned by the Japanese with her older sister, Ria. Before the Japanese torture and kill Ria, they kill not only Ria's dog but also her monkey and pigeons. Like Edgar Vos, Anneke returns to the Netherlands and begins her education late in life. Vos was not particularly impressed with Glaskin's use of poetic licence. 'If he had wanted to talk about me, he should have just called the character Edgar and let me be a boy', he said.[6]

Although Glaskin's connection with Vos goes back to his Singapore days, he never met the young Dutchman until he arrived in the Netherlands. Interestingly, Glaskin and Vos give entirely different accounts of how they met. While the truth may lie somewhere between the two, this also could be another instance of Glaskin, the storyteller, embellishing the facts to hook his reader.[7] According to him, he met Vos through Vos's father when he was the captain of the KPM ship, *Maetsuycker*, on which Glaskin travelled on one of his many trips back and forth between Singapore and Fremantle. Vos's father suggested to Glaskin that if he ever visited the Netherlands, he should look up his son, Edgar. When Glaskin first arrived there in 1961 he became lost wandering around Amsterdam's maze of semi-circular streets and canals as he tried to find his hotel. Finally, he plucked up the courage to approach a stranger on the street and ask directions. Writing in a book dedicated to Vos's quarter century in fashion, Glaskin wrote, 'It took only a few sentences for me to guess him to be Edgar Vos, of all the Amsterdammers I could have asked.'[8] Coincidental? Synchronistic? Too good to be true? For Vos it was all that and more.

> Gerry didn't tell me then or ever that he knew my father. I only found that out from things he wrote. My father hated gays. He didn't speak to me for 12 years because I was gay, so he would hardly have told Gerry to look me up when he came to Holland. I first met Gerry in a gay bar. He was with two other friends, travelling around Europe and visiting Amsterdam for a short time. Gerry started flirting with me and I just giggled. Then I went to another place and met them all again. This time he asked me to dance. Afterwards, I took him home and he didn't want to leave. His two other friends went on but he stayed in Amsterdam.[9]

A more likely scenario for sure, but whatever the precise circumstances of their meeting Vos fell for the young Australian whom he found to be

---

6   Edgar Vos to JB, interview by author, 21 August 2001.
7   According to LvdP, it was Vos who liked to embellish his stories, rather than GMG, so much so that GMG often referred to them as 'Vossen verhalen' – fox tales.
8   Eijsbouts (1986, 28).
9   Vos to JB, interview, 21 August 2001.

'very beautiful, very handsome, a film star type'.[10] The attraction was mutual and the two became lovers for about half a year until the initial lustre wore off and they changed their status to good friends, which they remained throughout Glaskin's life. But how much Vos's early feelings for Glaskin were related to the fact that Vos was on the rebound from the painful demise of his relationship with another Dutchman, Cor van Mourik, is a moot point. Mischa de Vreede raises this question in her memoir of Vos, *Maak me Mooi* [*Make Me Beautiful*]. Not long after they met, Vos and Glaskin went on a holiday to Riccione on the Adriatic coast of Italy. They were sitting on the beach late one day when a brilliant sunset filled the sky. Instinctively, Vos cried out, 'Cor, come and look at this beautiful sunset.' Glaskin responded 'Sorry, Edgar, this is Gerry, not Cor. You say his name every time something nice or pleasant happens.'[11] Vos didn't attempt to argue or pretend. He confessed that in spite of his break-up with van Mourik, he was still in love with him and not Glaskin.

Although Glaskin didn't win Vos's heart, he did gain at least two things out of their affair. First, Glaskin borrowed the name Cor, and possibly other details from the man's life, for one of his two protagonists in *No End to the Way*. Glaskin had a strong propensity to use his own life and those of friends and acquaintances to mould his characters. Vos believed Glaskin used Cor van Mourik in this way. Like the protagonist Cor, van Mourik was married to a woman yet professed to love another man – in this case, Vos – as well. In *Maak me Mooi*, de Vreede recounts an episode in which van Mourik had just returned from his honeymoon and begged Vos to be his lover. Tired of being used in this way, a tearful but insistent Vos retorted, 'I still love you but only if you get a divorce and live with me properly.' For the next 48 hours, van Mourik sat sulking on the step at the entrance to Vos's apartment. When Vos appeared with Glaskin and introduced him to van Mourik, the latter was confronted by his rival's stunning good looks and persuasive charm. Only then did he reluctantly accept that he was the sorry loser in this love triangle.[12]

However, there is another strong contender for the person on whom Glaskin based his character Cor. Glaskin dedicated the book to 'John and Joop', the former being an allusion to his Singapore flatmate, stockbroking colleague and one-time lover, John Donnell, while the latter is a reference to one of Glaskin's earlier lovers in Perth, another Dutchman, Joop van Gijn.

---

10 Ibid.
11 De Vreede (1999, 125).
12 Ibid.

Glaskin's record for falling in love with Dutchmen is impressive. It began with van Gijn, continued with Vos and numerous other short-term liaisons during his stay in Amsterdam and was cemented in his 32-year relationship with Leo van de Pas. Van de Pas is of the opinion that *No End to the Way* is strongly autobiographical, although it precedes his first contact with Glaskin by several years.[13] He believes that the character Cor is closely based on van Gijn. Like his fictitious counterpart, van Gijn worked as a barman in a Perth hotel and, van de Pas thinks, was married before he met Glaskin. After Glaskin and van Gijn split up, the Dutchman went to Queensland where it is rumoured he remarried, just as Cor does in the novel.

The second thing Vos gave Glaskin was a place to live, something he desperately needed if he were to stay in the Netherlands for an extended period of time. An apartment became vacant in Vos's building so he arranged for Glaskin to take it. Situated immediately beneath Vos's own attic apartment in the fashionable Pieter Corneliszoon Hooftstraat in South Amsterdam, it was compact in typical Dutch minimalist style yet had everything he needed to live and work. Moreover, it was only a few blocks from the popular Vondelpark, an artfully designed agglomeration of gardens, lakes, walkways and cycleways named after the 17th century Dutch poet and dramatist, Joost van den Vondel. By day it is a place of ambling pedestrians and bustling bicycles but towards evening it is a favourite haunt for romantic couples of all kinds, not least gay men. Wim Vreedevoogd, one of Glaskin's good friends and occupant of the apartment below him, remembered Glaskin's delight in joking about the name of the park. 'Gerry had a fantastic sense of humour. He claimed he knew why Vondelpark was given that name – "Oh, to fondle in Vondelpark!" he would say.'[14]

The proximity of Glaskin's apartment to Vos's own proved fortuitous when Glaskin fell ill and descended into deep depression. Ever the carer, Vos suggested that Glaskin move in with him during his convalescence. It would be easier for Vos to look after him in his own place, apart from the fact that his apartment had a phone in it and Glaskin's did not. If Glaskin needed anything, he would only have to call downstairs to Vos's shop. Besides, Vos argued, his attic apartment offered views of the sky and neighbouring rooftops, something his own studio did not. Besides running two shops – he had another in the city of Laren – Vos attended to Glaskin's every need, including preparing meals and making conversation in order to keep his

13 LvdP to JB, personal communication, 24 April 2001.
14 Wim Vreedevoogd to JB, interview by author, 20 August 2001.

guest's spirits from flagging. He also arranged for friends of his to drop in from time to time to add a little variety to Glaskin's sedentary and routine life, while being careful not to overburden his patient.

Apart from Vos and his friends, Glaskin had two other companions throughout his ordeal with jaundice. They were the canaries, Piet and Swee, whose strikingly different personalities Glaskin depicts with affection and detail in *A Bird in My Hands*. There are actually three birds; the first Piet died from an inability to moult, so a replacement mate was found for Swee. Glaskin's description of the impact of the bird's death on the two men is a touching portrayal of male emotion.

> Need I tell you that two grown men could not confront each other for the sight of each other's face? I had to leave the room to weep for this unbelievable sorrow, this dual sorrow, that so overwhelmed me: one for the loss of Piet and the other for Edgar's loss. It took him several hours before he could bring himself to bury the sad, stiff, cold little corpse in the garden at the back of the building.[15]

Thirty-four years later, Vos was more matter-of-fact about the loss of the canaries.

> I liked the canaries but they didn't mean the same to me as Gerry makes out they did. It was difficult because, like with dogs, you cannot go away for long without having to arrange for someone else to feed them. When my present partner came to live with me, he didn't want them so he opened the window and they flew away. I didn't really miss them.[16]

Given the life-threatening traumas Vos had suffered as a boy and young man, it is hardly surprising that he might have taken this attitude to the birds. For Glaskin, on the other hand, they were one of his last reasons for living in the midst of some of his darkest days. More intriguing is Vos's response to Glaskin's attempted suicide. While he admitted that he may have been partly responsible for Glaskin's condition because of his rejection of him as a lover, Vos was also sceptical about the way Glaskin wrote the episode in *A Bird in My Hands*. 'I don't think Gerry seriously contemplated suicide. It sounded more like a special effect. We had recently broken up and at first I thought he was just saying he was ill because he wanted to come back to me. I really didn't believe him.'[17]

---

15 GMG (1967a, 99).
16 Vos to JB, interview, 21 August 2001.
17 Ibid.

Delia Glaskin with son Gerald
– an unusually close bond.

Photographer unknown. Photo
courtesy Leo van de Pas.

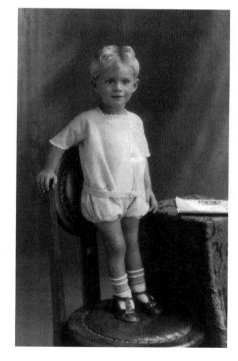

A charmer from his earliest days.

Photographer unknown. Photo
courtesy Leo van de Pas.

The managing elder brother:
Glaskin (centre) with siblings
Dixie (left) and Loris (right).

Photographer unknown.
Photo courtesy Leo van de Pas.

Glaskin at 17, a young
naval recruit

Photographer unknown.
Photo courtesy Leo van de Pas.

Glaskin at 17 – the Indian prince.

Photographer unknown. Photo courtesy Leo van de Pas.

Sjoerd Steunebrink, penpal and longtime friend, age 17.

Photographer unknown. Reproduced from *One Way to Wonderland*, courtesy Fremantle Press.

A sun-tanned, beer-drinking Aussie.

Photographer unknown. Photo courtesy of Leo van de Pas.

The Glaskin family, left to right: Hilary, Myree, Roland, Llewellyn, Loris, Dixie, Gerald, Delia and Gilbert, circa 1955.

Photographer unknown. Photo courtesy Leo van de Pas.

Raffles Hotel, Singapore. Standing: Glaskin, Charles Kissane. Seated, left to right: Delia Glaskin (mother), Judy Preston (cousin), Michael O'Flynn, Eileen Preston (aunt), unknown and John Donnell.

Photographer unknown. Photo courtesy of Leo van de Pas.

Water-skiing friends in Singapore. Left to right: Harold Tay, Sieuw Mee and Glaskin.

Photographer unknown. Photo courtesy Leo van de Pas.

The Rock Hudson look.

Dust jacket of *The Land That Sleeps*.
Photographer: George Britnell.
Photo courtesy Leo van de Pas.

Writing companion.

Photographer unknown. Photo
courtesy Jo Darbyshire.

Glaskin's 'literary mama', Henrietta Drake-Brockman.

Photographer unknown. Photo courtesy Geoffrey Drake-Brockman.

John K. Ewers, Glaskin's mentor and friend.

Photographer uknown. Photo courtesy Trisha Kotai-Ewers.

Vincent Ruthnaswamy and Han Suyin at Keukenhof, the Netherlands, April 1966.
Photographer: Gerald Glaskin. Photo courtesy Leo van de Pas.

Glaskin with friend and former lover Edgar Vos in Amsterdam.
Photographer unknown. Photo courtesy Edgar Vos.

Glaskin may well have enhanced the story of his attempted suicide for dramatic effect, but his writing of the memoir was strangely prophetic of two other suicides that took place in Amsterdam in the late 1960s and were indirectly related to Glaskin. In her memoir of Vos, de Vreede recounts the sad events surrounding the death of the doctor who attended Glaskin, Joop Broekman. Broekman was gay and had a number of gay patients. Although this was the Netherlands in the '60s – the place many gay men around the world regarded as the most open-minded and accepting of same-sex relationships – it was not always like that for men who lived there. De Vreede's husband was an architect who had designed a structure to join Broekman's house with that of his lover – a married man with children – so the two could have easy access to each other. Finally, the strain of living a dual existence became too much for the man and he committed suicide. When the police asked Broekman to come to the station for interrogation, he pretended he needed to lock his apartment, but went to his surgery, opened a glass cupboard and took a quick poison. Two funerals were held that week instead of one.

While his six and a half years in the Netherlands plunged Glaskin into the depths of despair and taunted him with death, they also showered him with some moments of bliss. His Dutch sojourn not only allowed him to cultivate new friendships and explore new places in the Netherlands, it was a springboard to discovering other parts of Europe as well, especially southern Europe where he revelled in a summer climate reminiscent of his native south-western Australia. In July and August 1963, he spent six weeks travelling through France, Spain and Portugal with Jackie Markus, a young gay man with whom Vos did business in Amsterdam. Glaskin was a prolific writer of postcards and this trip proved no exception. From Seville he wrote to Vos, 'This is the fourth card I've written to you today and altogether the 14th in one day, so I think that's more than enough!'[18] While the content of the cards contains no great revelations, they did offer Glaskin a chance to practise his elementary Dutch, usually just words and phrases but sometimes complete sentences and occasionally a whole card.

One memorable trip occurred in the spring of 1962. Glaskin and Vos were travelling through Catalonia in north-eastern Spain when they came upon the little village of Port Lligat near Cadaqués, home of the renowned artist Salvador Dali. Vos was trying to photograph Dali's house when the artist spotted him. He approached Vos and asked if he could paint a picture

---

18 GMG to Vos, postcard, 13 August 1963.

of him. Vos was flattered and modelled for the famous painter. Although he never obtained his own portrait, he did succeed in getting two other Dali originals. Glaskin was enraptured by the chance to rub shoulders with such a celebrated artist, though no doubt a little peeved that Dali didn't want to paint him instead. Part of Glaskin's fascination with the man was their shared interest in the workings of the human mind. Dali's obsession with surrealism and Glaskin's preoccupation with mind travel, out-of-body experiences and lucid dreaming were a perfect match. Far from the eccentric that Dali has often been perceived to be, Vos and Glaskin found him to be quite an ordinary, albeit extraordinarily creative, person. When Glaskin returned to Australia in 1966, Vos presented him with a copy of Robert Descharne's book *The World of Salvador Dali*. With a hint of one-upmanship Vos wrote, 'A very good journey and may you soon sell a movie so that you can return to Europe and also buy an original Dali.' From this book Glaskin later quoted Dali to Vos: 'The absence of a loved person leaves us in a sentimental vacuum.'[19]

During his time in Europe, Glaskin often found himself hosting friends and acquaintances, particularly from Australia. One of those was the author Henrietta Drake-Brockman and her husband, Geoffrey, a brigadier in the Australian Army and a writer of sorts himself.[20] Drake-Brockman had a special place in Glaskin's life as a writer. He referred to her as 'my literary mama' and wrote a short essay in her honour with the same title.[21] The Drake-Brockmans lived in the prestigious Perth riverside suburb of Peppermint Grove, a stone's throw from the house in Mosman Park where the Glaskins resided for a period. When his grandmother, Nan, told the young Glaskin this news, he couldn't resist trying to make the acquaintance of this 'real live authoress, one of those unbelievable creatures I thought existed only overseas'.[22] So much in awe of Drake-Brockman was he that it took him weeks to muster the courage to call on her. He would walk past her front gate, hovering up and down on the footpath, hoping to see and perhaps even meet this goddess.

A few days before Christmas 1937, Drake-Brockman looked out of her study window and noticed a young lad lurking suspiciously outside her

---

19 LvdP to JB, personal communication, 24 April 2001.
20 Henrietta Drake-Brockman was a foundation member and honorary life member of the Fellowship of Australian Writers (WA), as well as a long-serving member of the advisory committee of the literary journal *Westerly*. Her writing credits include short fiction, novels and plays. She died in 1968.
21 GMG (1994–1999).
22 Ibid., 3.

house. 'Do you want something?' she called out. This was the invitation he had been waiting for. Taking a deep breath, he unlatched the gate and walked up the path to the front door. First contact must not have been easy, for Drake-Brockman had an imperious air that caused even some adult men to cringe.[23] She also had a high-pitched, quavering voice that may have been the result of an accident she suffered. Glaskin once summed her up as 'a bit like Queen Mary, stiff-necked'.[24] This depiction of her was engendered by her 'wryly ironic smile ... the poised carriage, the tilt of her head as she spoke, her stately walk'.[25] She presented a daunting picture to her nervous young visitor. In fear and trepidation, the 14-year-old Glaskin ventured inside and made himself known. In answer to her question, he told her there were three things he wanted: her autograph in his copy of her novel *Blue North* that he had recently received as a birthday gift; her advice on whether he should apply to work as a journalist with *The West Australian* newspaper; and her opinion on his first short story, 'The Parrot', a fantasy set in South America about the transmigration of souls between a dead woman and a parrot.

She obliged on all three counts in her typical businesslike yet gracious way. She dashed off her signature with its usual flourish and she strongly advised him against working for a paper because, she warned, authors and journalists are a totally different kettle of fish. 'Work at anything else you like, but not on a newspaper if you want to write books', she said.[26] After reading his story, she cautioned Glaskin about setting his stories in exotic locales about which he knew very little. She admitted having made the same mistake herself as a 14-year-old writer, although her published works were all based on more familiar places and the people who inhabited them. Clearly, the Australian propensity to devalue one's own country was alive and well in those days.[27] Glaskin took her advice to heart. Even his flights into fantasy and science-fiction are set in places with which he was familiar, be that Perth, Amsterdam or London, as his novels *A Change of Mind* and *The Man Who Didn't Count* and his short story 'The Inheritors' attest. So much did Glaskin value this advice from his 'literary mama' that he refers

---

23 Quoting fellow author Jack Harvey, GMG reported, 'I simply don't know how you get on so well with that Henrietta woman. She terrifies me.' Glaskin was mystified by this reaction coming from a person who had been in the merchant navy, survived a disastrous shipwreck and spent more than six weeks in a lifeboat. Kotai-Ewers (1996).
24 Ibid.
25 GMG (1994–1999, 3).
26 Ibid., 4.
27 See Chapter 13, 'Don't Go West, Young Man', for elaboration of this mindset.

to it at the front of his collection of short stories, *A Small Selection*, which he dedicates to Drake-Brockman.[28]

From this tentative beginning, Drake-Brockman and Glaskin developed a firm and enduring friendship. She acted as a mentor to the young writer and whenever he achieved success she would be the first to praise him. She did this with his first novel, *A World of Our Own*, and included an excerpt from it in the anthology *West Coast Stories*, which she edited as a fund-raising project for the Fellowship of Australian Writers (WA). Earlier she had included his short story 'Uncle Tom's Funeral' in another anthology she edited, *Coast To Coast*, which Glaskin cherished as his first time in print in hard cover. 'She was always so proud of me, prouder than anyone else I can think of, even in my own family, and she was not at all shy of displaying her pride.'[29] It was almost a motherly pride, as Glaskin remembered it. 'I think she looked upon me as her son', he said, even though she had a son and daughter of her own. Indeed, when his own mother died in March 1960 after her horrendous ordeal with uraemic poisoning, Glaskin spent a lot of time with the Drake-Brockmans, who by this time had moved to a city apartment. But although she was always eager to applaud his accomplishments, Drake-Brockman was not averse to critiquing his work when she thought it demanded it. She told him bluntly on more than one occasion that he overdid the italics in *A Lion in the Sun*. He maintained that she made too much use of italics too, not in her writing but in her histrionic speech. As their relationship developed, it became clear that it was reciprocal and at times Glaskin was able to take the lead.

One way in which he did this was acting as their host when the Drake-Brockmans visited the Netherlands in 1962, where Glaskin had become firmly ensconced in his beloved Amsterdam. She was researching the story of Dutch ship *Batavia*, wrecked on the Western Australian coast in 1629, which she chronicled in two books, the fictitious *The Wicked and the Fair* and non-fictional *Voyage to Disaster: The Life of Francisco Pelsaert*.[30]

---

28 GMG dedicates his anthology of short stories, *A Small Selection* (also published in paperback as *Sometimes It Wasn't So Nice*), to Henrietta Drake-Brockman with this note: 'who, after reading my first attempt at a short story when I was only fourteen, said: "Gerry, when I was fourteen I wrote a wonderful short story about Venice. You've chosen South America – " And now both of us write about the places we know...'

29 GMG (1994–1999, 1).

30 Drake-Brockman spent 10 years researching the *Batavia* story, including diving on the wreck herself. Quoting his Chinese academic friends, Professors Zhang Taijin and his wife Yang Mingqiu, Glaskin boasted that Drake-Brockman had the unique distinction in English literature of having written and published both a fictional and non-fictional account of the same event.

Glaskin delighted in playing the 'cicerone' – one of his favourite words – driving his guests to museums, archives and even the 350-year-old home of his literary mama's protagonist, Lucretia Jancz. In addition, they took in concerts, operas, art galleries and restaurants. One of Glaskin's fondest memories of the Drake-Brockman's visit to Amsterdam was the night they ventured into the city's red-light district, Zeedijk. Not surprisingly, Geoffrey Drake-Brockman found the expedition a lot more tantalising than his wife. The 60-plus-year-old army brigadier was having the time of his life but Henrietta clearly wasn't. She couldn't wait to get back to their hotel. To Glaskin, this was not due to any sense of prudery or outraged modesty on her part. He wrote, 'I wasn't merely amused; I could hardly have been more deeply touched. For it was plain for anyone to see that she not only still deeply loved him, but was still "in love" with him. It was the most wonderful thing she had ever taught me.'[31]

Drake-Brockman's influence on Glaskin encompassed more than advice on writing and publishing; the bond between them matured into some-thing much more intense. When he left for Singapore in 1949, he went to say goodbye to his beloved mentor, to find her almost in tears at his departure, which only caused his own eyes to water as well. Six years later when Glaskin was back in Perth recovering from spinal meningitis, she strongly encouraged him to keep writing. He did and produced his second novel, *A Minor Portrait*. Interestingly, this is a story about a relationship between a young 14-year-old boy and a much older, genteel Frenchwoman who paints water colours and travels in a chauffeur-driven car. It begins when the woman espies the fast-maturing youth frolicking naked at his secret swimming hole on a lonely stretch of beach and moves on to include a sexual relationship between them that sends the young man's life into a tailspin. While there is nothing to suggest that Glaskin's relationship with Drake-Brockman followed this course, Glaskin may well have used this early encounter with a woman of class and distinction to create his work of fiction. Their relationship was undoubtedly more restrained and governed by rules of social etiquette acceptable to Perth society of the day but it did mellow over time. After Glaskin's return from Singapore, she insisted he call her Henrietta, a small but significant gesture in the context of the world in which they lived. Glaskin and she often took in films together, especially at the annual film festival for which she was a reviewer and which did not particularly interest her husband. Of her many

31 GMG (1994–1999, 9).

qualities that impressed Glaskin, one that stood out was her application to writing – always work first and no interruptions until it was finished. Her chaste approach to the task no doubt rubbed off on Glaskin, although with his many health problems and his love of the beach he sometimes found it difficult to emulate.

While the Drake-Brockmans may have demonstrated to Glaskin what a committed, loving relationship was all about, he was soon to discover it for himself. Many remember 1968 for student riots in Paris and other European cities, the Soviet invasion of Czechoslovakia that ended 'Prague Spring', and the twin assassinations of Dr Martin Luther King and Robert Kennedy in the United States. But for Gerald Glaskin, these cataclysmic global events were merely the backdrop to his own personal drama of far greater proportions. This was the year he met his life partner Leo van de Pas. Like many significant events in life, this one happened because something else didn't. It was a balmy July evening and Glaskin had driven 30 kilometres to Laren to have dinner with friends but took his time because he didn't need to be back in Amsterdam until around midnight. He was expecting his good friend Rupert Schieder, a professor of English at the University of Toronto, to arrive that day, but knowing how trans-Atlantic travel would take its toll, suggested to Schieder to sleep on arrival and meet him at a nightclub between midnight and 2 am.

Glaskin arrived at their rendezvous shortly after midnight but there was no sign of Schieder. He waited and waited but his guest never turned up. Not knowing where Schieder was staying, Glaskin had no way of contacting him. The next day when they met, Schieder apologised and explained that he had asked the hotel staff to wake him up in good time but they had failed to do so. While waiting for Schieder to appear, Glaskin noticed another Dutch friend, Meindert de Back, at the bar so he joined him. As they sipped drinks, Glaskin's attention was diverted by a couple on the crowded dance floor. A tall young man with blond hair was dancing with a girl who had tears streaming down her face. The young man looked deeply concerned about his partner. They were so absorbed in each other that when the music changed from a slow, moody rhythm to a more frenetic beat, they carried on as they were. When de Back noticed that Glaskin seemed entranced by the couple, he said, 'That's Leo, a friend of mine. Cheering up someone again, by the look of it – when he could do with a bit of it himself.'[32]

---

32 GMG (1978b, 36).

De Back also explained to Glaskin that his friend and the girl were simply good friends. The girl had a lover who was away in Germany and when her family discovered the relationship they threw her out of the house. She had no money and nowhere to go. She was waiting for other friends to take her to their place. Glaskin was struck by the young man's compassion for his friend and asked de Back to invite him over to their table for a drink. Before van de Pas joined them he collected his coat from the cloakroom and put it on, despite the fact that he was sweating profusely. He was suffering from a bad cold and told his companions that he wouldn't have been at the club at all had it not been for the girl's predicament. When Schieder hadn't arrived by 2 am and de Back had found other company for the rest of the evening, Glaskin offered to walk home with his new acquaintance. After all, he lived in the same direction as Glaskin. What had been a long day and an eventful night was just the beginning of a whole new chapter in Glaskin's life.

Leo van de Pas was 25 years old, 19 years younger than Glaskin. Tall with blond hair and broad shoulders, he exuded a kind of soft masculinity that Glaskin found attractive. He was the third of five children and second son of the Dutch author, teacher, journalist and film critic Willem van de Pas, who was tragically killed while crossing the street when Leo was 17. His siblings had married and dispersed throughout the Netherlands, while his mother continued to live alone in the family home in De Bilt near Utrecht. Van de Pas had a yearning to become a genealogist but this required a university education, which, owing to his father's early demise, was not within his financial reach. In addition, like all young Dutchmen of his generation, he participated in national service and at 19 found himself conscripted into the army and sent to New Guinea. Back in the Netherlands, he was offered a job by an Irish antique dealer in England and jumped at the opportunity, not only to indulge his passion for historical memorabilia but also to improve his English and earn his keep. Alas, these dreams soon evaporated as van de Pas found himself duped. The dealer was doing little business and had a strong aversion to paying him. Returning home penniless and humiliated, van de Pas took a meagre-paying job as a bank clerk in Amsterdam and lived in a damp and mouldy attic apartment, accessible only by ladder and with one tiny window.

Within hours of meeting van de Pas, Glaskin found himself entranced by the young Dutchman. He was enamoured by the compassion van de Pas had shown his friend on the dance floor and quickly felt a strong empathy with his new acquaintance. The more he inquired about him, the more he found they had in common. Both had a number of siblings, both had been denied a university education, both had served in their country's military, and both shared a passion for writing. And of course, both were attracted to men, although each had many women friends. Before they parted that first night Glaskin turned to van de Pas and asked him a question that would change the course of van de Pas's life: Would he care to accompany Glaskin back to Australia and work part-time as his assistant? He would mostly type Glaskin's manuscripts but could pursue his own genealogical interests the rest of the time.

Always more cautious than the impulsive Glaskin, van de Pas was not ready to answer right away. He would go to bed and sleep on it. The next day they arranged to meet at the royal palace on The Dam. He would give Glaskin his answer then. However, as with Schieder the night before, Glaskin found himself stood up once again. Knowing van de Pas's address, Glaskin decided to go to see what had happened to him. It turned out that van de Pas's cold had grown worse and his doctor strongly recommended he stay in bed for several more days. They sat and chatted and after a while Glaskin suggested they go to the popular American Hotel in Leidseplein for coffee. Ignoring medical advice, van de Pas accepted Glaskin's invitation. As they sat at a table overlooking this busy square, van de Pas agreed to give Australia a try. However, there were a number of things he had to attend to first, so he would not accompany Glaskin when he left by ship in two weeks' time. He would come later by air.

Glaskin's invitation was not altogether altruistic. Having to wear a neck brace and daily insert himself into a harness to help alleviate his spine and neck pain, he needed assistance. Also, if he had someone to retype his manuscripts it would save him hours of sitting at a typewriter, which was often a burden. He anticipated that his small income would support them both, as long as he could continue to write and sell books as he had been doing. He offered to pay van de Pas's airfare to Australia and, should van de Pas find either Australia or him disagreeable, Glaskin would pay his return fare to the Netherlands. He also promised free board and lodging, insurance payments, medical costs, clothes and a small monthly stipend of $50. While by no means lavish it was a reasonable offer, assuming that Glaskin could keep his end of the bargain. Meanwhile, Dennis Winterbottom, a friend of Glaskin's who headed the Immigration Department at the Australian Embassy in The Hague, pointed out that van de Pas would be eligible to migrate in his own right under Australia's Assisted Passage Scheme for only

100 guilders.[33] Van de Pas readily agreed to this, thinking it only reasonable to give his new country a two-year trial before deciding on its fate.

When Glaskin left the Netherlands at the end of July he understood that van de Pas would follow in a couple of months. But Glaskin had serious misgivings that van de Pas might have second thoughts about his decision. Glaskin's intuitions were correct. Van de Pas never caught the plane on which he had been scheduled to fly. He had nagging doubts about leaving the security of a job, home and familiar country for an unknown part of the world so far away. He decided to talk over the decision with several friends. One of those was Wim Vreedevoogd, whose optimism knew no bounds. 'I told him I thought Gerry was a wonderful man and that Australia was a fantastic country. This was a once-in-a-lifetime opportunity and he should take it.'[34] Dennis Winterbottom, whom van de Pas went to see to explain why he missed his plane, was more reserved in his opinion. While trying to be reassuring, he reminded van de Pas that the decision was entirely his. Mulling over the advice he had received, van de Pas finally decided to make the trip. After the gruelling flight from Amsterdam and a stopover in Sydney, he arrived in Perth exhausted and disoriented on 4 October 1968. It was one of the hottest October days for years, only to be followed by a week of unseasonably cold temperatures. Ten days later, Perth experienced an earthquake that registered 6.9 on the Richter scale. His life had been literally, as well as figuratively, shaken up.

This was the beginning of a fallow period in Glaskin's writing career. Although he had two books published in 1967 – the volume of short stories, *The Road to Nowhere*, and the memoir of his illness and attempted suicide, *A Bird in My Hands* – it would be another seven years before a book would appear under his name. Money trickled in at odd intervals but it was never dependable. An American publisher bought the pocketbook rights to his controversial novel, *No End to the Way*, but the first advance of US$1,000 dwindled to A$608 after commissions and exchange rates intervened. It was

---

33 The Assisted Passage Scheme was instituted by the Australian government in the aftermath of the Second World War in an effort to attract new immigrants to the country. It offered to bring prospective immigrants to Australia for the equivalent of GB£10, providing they stayed at least two years. If they reneged on this agreement and returned home before that time, they would have to repay the Australian Government the full fare. Initially limited to British ex-servicemen and their dependents, the scheme was later extended to include immigrants from Western, Central and Eastern Europe.

34 Vreedevoogd to JB, interview, 20 August 2001.

just enough to pay van de Pas's stipend for one year. Then in February 1968 Hollywood film producer Leslie Green wrote to Glaskin to ask if *A Change of Mind* was available for a film option. Green had met Glaskin in the late 1950s and they shared a mutual acquaintance with the well-known Japanese writer Yukio Mishima. Since earlier rights to the film taken out by a British producer had reverted to Glaskin after three years of inactivity, Glaskin was able to offer them to Green, who paid him US$445. There were rumours that Australian actor Peter Finch was interested in directing, producing and even acting in *Flight to Landfall* and *The Road to Nowhere*, but like many such rumours they never materialised. Said a despondent Glaskin, 'It seemed as though I was always on the verge of the "breakthrough" that my various agents said they were expecting to happen any day. Undoubtedly I was – but I just never quite made it.'[35]

Then, as so often in his life, his Dutch connections came to Glaskin's aid. His old Dutch publisher, Succes, bought the Dutch translation rights to *The Beach of Passionate Love* and gave him his third Netherlands Book Club edition and an advance of just under $1000. The other piece of good news came in the form of a parcel from his Dutch boyhood penfriend, Sjoerd Steunebrink, now a successful anaesthesiologist in the United States. Along with a selection of stylish American clothes, he sent Glaskin and van de Pas a cheque for US$500. For a while, it appeared that life was smiling kindly on the two of them. But Glaskin hadn't been able to produce books as he used to. Isometric exercises and use of a neck harness did little to ease his pain. He reverted to more conventional physiotherapy and massage and his usual regimen of drugs, which had the deleterious effect of blurring his vision and sapping his incentive to write. Even his collars no longer worked as well, especially in the summer heat. There was nothing for van de Pas to type and finances were increasingly precarious. He decided he must find a job. He opted for one as a draftsman with the state government but by the time he completed the three-month training and was about to sign a two-year bond, Glaskin had managed to generate a new load of work for him to do, so van de Pas decided to forego the job.

It was on the cusp of the 1970s and, thanks in part to significantly increased government support for the arts, Australia was experiencing a revival of its long-dormant motion picture industry. Glaskin decided it was time to convert some of his books into screenplays. He threw himself into the task with renewed vigour and application, attending films, studying

---

35 GMG (1978b, 46).

scripts and reading books on the subject. For his first attempt he chose to tackle *A Change of Mind*, shifting the setting from Perth to London to the United States to accommodate the varying demands of the film's producers. However, Green wasn't able to get the backing he sought on a paperback edition of the book to accompany the film and he dropped his option.[36] But not before a peculiar incident occurred that Glaskin referred to as 'one of the most shattering things I have had happen to me in a lifetime'.[37]

Green first alerted Glaskin to the fact that the New York-based Sagittarius Productions, Inc. had started filming a movie titled *Change of mind*, starring the African American actor Raymond St. Jacques. According to Glaskin, the plot concerned the interchange of personalities between a middle-aged married man with children and a young, single athletic male, the ethnicity of the latter being the only essential difference between this film and Glaskin's book – in addition to the dropping of the indefinite article from the title. Glaskin's initial anger at this 'coincidence' was soured by the ironical fact that not only was he a Sagittarian but that Sagittarius Productions announced the making of the film on 16 December (1968), his birthday. What's more, the company claimed that their film was based on an original screenplay written by Seelig Lester and Richard Wesson, who were also the film's producers. In a submission to the Academy of Motion Picture Arts and Sciences they also listed themselves as the writers of the original story.[38]

Green made enquiries and protests, as did Glaskin's British and American agents, but to no avail. Letters among all parties began to billow out of Glaskin's files. After Green obtained a copy of the synopsis of the script from the producers he became more ambivalent about their chances of proving it had been plagiarised from Glaskin's book. 'It was hastily written but I was less concerned with doing justice to the screenplay than conveying the story', he wrote. 'As you can see, there is no similarity at all. However ... I think you may have a good case in the title.'[39] Green was speaking from his knowledge of American copyright law. However, in the UK, where the book had been published, it was another matter. Glaskin's British agent, Hilton Ambler, clarified this for him. 'You may want to ask [Glaskin's US agent] Marianne McNamara to brief an American lawyer on your behalf to see

---

36 Other parties also expressed interest in the film rights to *A Change of Mind*. These included the British producer Leslie Elliott, who had purchased the film rights to *The Man Who Didn't Count*, and the French producer Edouard Luntz. Neither made good on their initial expressions of interest.

37 GMG (1978b, 51).

38 Library of the Academy of Motion Picture Arts and Sciences to JB, 22 October 2001.

39 Leslie Green to GMG, 28 February 1969.

what can be done about an injunction preventing Sagittarius Productions using the title "Change of Mind" … we don't think that there is a case for an injunction because there is no copyright in titles … in this country.[40] As usual, Glaskin did not concede defeat without putting up a good fight but eventually he had to acknowledge he had little basis on which to make a case. As he noted in *Never Again*, 'Numerous books have the same titles and countless more almost the same plots; but apart from an obvious transcription from a well-known book to a film, nothing could be done. Certainly there was no protection against titles and basic plots being used from one medium to another.'[41] As a final desperate effort he wrote to Sagittarius Productions himself, sending them a copy of the original Barrie edition of the book with its British Book Club Recommendation and listing its various translations and pocketbook editions. He never received a reply.[42]

Glaskin's only consolation in this sad saga was that when the film was made it attracted little acclaim. Glaskin himself was given a private viewing, thanks to his friend Colin Nicholas, a cinema manager in Perth. Nicholas said Glaskin left the theatre fuming. In a letter to Green shortly afterwards, he wrote, 'There were some scenes … which smacked more than somewhat of my novel. But then it passed on to – what? What a hybrid plot it is! One third change of body, the rest racialism. Not a bad film, certainly not a good one. You should be able to make a far better one.'[43] Six months later, Green wrote to Glaskin, 'their picture turned out so badly and came and went so fast, that if we were to do the picture now I'd be tempted to use the book title and the hell with them.'[44] But Green himself had no intention of making the movie. He was unable to put together a financial package and even if he had he would not have used Glaskin's screenplay. Green admitted as much in an earlier, frank assessment of Glaskin's script. 'While it is indeed interesting and has a great many merits, we both feel it is of less dramatic treatment

40 Hilton Ambler to GMG, 7 March 1969. In an earlier letter to GMG on 10 February Ambler had quoted research done by McNamara with the US Copyright Office. She had discovered four properties listed with the title '(A) Change of Mind'. As well as GMG's novel there was another novel, a radio play and a dramatic play in seven scenes. The latter was registered in 1950 by Arnold Sondregger who, according to the Library of the Academy of Motion Picture Arts and Sciences, tried to sue Lester and Wesson in 1971 for using the same name as his play.
41 GMG (1978b, 51).
42 Neither did I. When I tried to investigate this matter in 2001, I learned that Wesson had died but that Lester was alive and a member of the Writers Guild of America. The Guild would not divulge his contact information but offered to forward a fax to him from me, which I sent but to which I never received a reply.
43 GMG to Leslie Green, 20 May 1970.
44 Green to GMG, 11 March 1971.

than we have in mind. You have written an exciting book to read and I think the film can and should be just as exciting an experience. I hope you won't feel put off by my candid response but I think you will not appreciate a less than honest view. I know from experience how difficult it is to adapt fiction to the screen. It often requires a special set of tools to wrest a dramatic film from equally dramatic literature.[45]

Although Green may not have thought Glaskin had sufficient dexterity with those tools, other producers did. One was the UK-based, South African actor-turned-producer Rex Sheldon who, after having read Glaskin's script of *O Love*, also wanted him to write a screenplay for *No End to the Way*, with the intention of shooting both films back-to-back to save costs. He dangled the figure of A\$7,000 for each film option in front of Glaskin. Sheldon wanted Glaskin to come to London to work on the script. Payments were discussed and contracts would be signed on his arrival in the UK. Thanks to a windfall profit Glaskin made on shares he had bought 'on spec' and an ongoing trickle of royalties from a number of his books, Glaskin was able to afford the sea passage to England for van de Pas and himself. Upon arrival in London they were fortunate to be offered accommodation in a friend's flat and set to work on the film script of *No End to the Way*. This could be 'the big one' that would spread Glaskin's name far and wide, given the controversy the novel had already stirred after it was banned in Australia. For six weeks they slaved away at separate desks and produced two scripts for Sheldon. Glaskin had a sense of exhilaration as he and van de Pas drove down to Cornwall to stay with a millionaire stockbroker friend from Glaskin's Singapore days to celebrate their labours. Returning to London, Glaskin wrote to his brother Llew, 'I found Sheldon madly on the phone saying that an Australian syndicate of financiers want him to make films out there and my agent has given him three of my properties, and if he can get them he wants all three.'[46]

The euphoria was short-lived. What appeared to be the verge of a break-through turned out to be just another cresting on Glaskin's roller-coaster ride with film producers and book publishers. Sheldon wasn't able to find a backer for his joint film project and the only director he interested in the film, Basil Dearden, was killed in a car accident while filming on location near London's Heathrow airport – ironically, Glaskin noted, while shooting a scene about a character killed in a car accident near Heathrow.[47] Were

---

45 Green to GMG, n.d.
46 GMG to Llew Glaskin, 29 September 1970.
47 Ibid.

the gods laughing at Glaskin or telling him to let go of his dream of script writing and get back to other writing that he might have a better chance selling? But there was one more blow to come. Returning to Australia, Glaskin discovered that Sheldon had played a trick on him, as deceptive as anything that might appear in a movie. He claimed that Sheldon had signed the contract in vanishing ink![48] On top of this, he had used a British postal strike as an excuse for not issuing promised payments from his Swiss financiers to Glaskin's Amsterdam bank account. If this wasn't disheartening enough, the screenplay Glaskin wrote for *A Waltz through the Hills* on his return voyage to Australia was also rejected by an American producer.

Not to be deterred by these setbacks, Glaskin ploughed ahead with other scripts. Interest expressed by the Australian actor Michael Pate in the novella *The Road to Nowhere* led Glaskin to try his hand at a script for that, followed by another for *O Love*. At one point, agents were circulating film scripts from five of his books throughout Australia, the UK and the USA. All the time, van de Pas was kept busy typing and retyping page after page of film script. His ability to type in English had improved markedly since he first arrived in Australia, thanks in part to an intensive touch-typing course he took. He and Glaskin were developing into a well-oiled team. But alas, no one bought any of their work. Still not defeated, Glaskin was determined to write not only 'the best book I had ever written' but 'one such as had never been written before'.[49] It was time for the magnum opus, appropriately titled, *At the End of It All*. Life was too short to be frittered away on such trivia as fantasies and thrillers. It was time to make a statement. But a statement about what? Well … everything, almost. With fire in his belly, Glaskin wrote:

> I wanted it to portray life with all its realities harsh and gentle: suffering and happiness, misery and mysticism, cruelty and charity, vice and virtue, love and loathing, cult and occult. Moreover, I wanted to use techniques that would present all this material as briefly and compactly as possible, and all in a perhaps bewildering juxtaposition as in life itself. I practised the techniques, planned the ostensibly simple yet complex plot, delineated the characters to be involved, and drove with Leo over the various settings. I watched, listened, felt, smelled. I was determined to be as different from any other writer, including my previous self, as had been Faulkner and Joyce, yet also different from them again. The

---

48 GMG (1995a, 112).
49 GMG (1978b, 73).

[surfing] accident had given me a new self; I wanted it also to give me a new writer.[50]

Such visions of grandeur weren't to be realised. Excruciating neck pain prevented Glaskin from sitting for any length of time at the typewriter. In six months, he had completed just two hundred pages, about a third of the intended book. At that rate it would take another year at least to finish it and what would they live on in the meantime? Suddenly, an advertisement for fellowships from the Australian Commonwealth Literary Fund looked extremely enticing. Glaskin had received a grant in 1957, so why not again in 1972? After all, he had produced 13 books in the interim, so surely he would be a likely candidate for a fellowship. Meanwhile, feeling fairly satisfied with what he had written, Glaskin decided to send off the first third of his book to Macmillan publishers in Australia. After several months he received a negative reply that he deemed disagreeable and pretentious.

This time the Australian government came to his rescue. Glaskin was awarded a $6000 grant to complete *At the End of It All* and to research another story that he had tried several times to start, *Alicia*. With his bank balance looking a little healthier, it was time for another trip to Europe for him and van de Pas. They travelled on the Italian liner *Achille Lauro*, from Fremantle via the Pacific, Cape Horn, Buenos Aires, Rio de Janeiro and Madeira. But not before Glaskin had an operation to remove his gall bladder. While convalescing from the operation, Glaskin worked hand in glove with van de Pas transcribing and editing tapes from interviews with his maternal grandmother, Nan Gugeri. These would become the memoir *The Eaves of Night*, published three years later in *Two Women*, along with his adaptation of his play about the last night in the life of Marilyn Monroe, *Turn on the Heat*. While the sea journey was a welcome respite from routines and interruptions, it was also a period of concentrated work for Glaskin and van de Pas. By the time the ship berthed at Rotterdam the second section of *At the End of It All* had been written, corrected, retyped and corrected again. Said a proud Glaskin, 'If I could afford it, I would spend my life on ships, for I have always found them by far the best places in the world for me to work.'[51]

Using van de Pas's mother's home in De Bilt as their base, Glaskin and he set about completing the third and final part of the now burgeoning trilogy of a book. They were beginning to wish they too would soon arrive

---

50 Ibid.
51 Ibid., 80.

'at the end of it all'. But Dutch hospitality being what it is, they found themselves deluged with visitors and reciprocating visits with family and friends, with little opportunity to work at the pace and intensity they wished. The answer to their dilemma was a five-week package tour from Amsterdam to Mallorca for only 500 guilders each. It was too good to pass up. In spite of nearly coming to blows with a hotel owner over a broken toilet seat and having to use the beds as desks, Glaskin and van de Pas applied themselves to the task and completed the third section of the book. What is more, when the hotel owner discovered that his obnoxious guest was an international writer who received telephone calls from London and New York, the incident over the toilet seat shrivelled into insignificance and peace was restored.

Since the night they first met in Amsterdam and Glaskin raised the question of van de Pas becoming his assistant, Glaskin had come to rely on his Dutch friend more and more. Without his assistance, both as a typist and a live-in carer, he never could have managed. He was aware of this and was reminded of it when van de Pas and he visited Han Suyin and Vincent Ruthnaswamy in Paris in the early 1970s. A retired colonel and engineer from the Indian Army, Ruthnaswamy played a similar role for Han as van de Pas did for Glaskin. She noted this in a letter to Glaskin. 'You have a wonderful asset and that is Leo. I'm glad that you and Leo are together because I think that he is complementary in some ways to you. We all need such complements. Vincent is such a complement to me, bless his soul. But … he has had to give up so much for me and what does he get for it but the sound of typewriters cracking away and having to retype manuscripts when I am hurried and all sorts of nauseating stuff about contracts.'[52] Glaskin expressed a similar sentiment in *Never Again*. 'We are both blessed with the good fortune of having such marvellous assistance, she and I, as are numerous other authors I know – and it seems to me that the assistants are invariably much nicer people than us writers.'[53]

On a scale of niceness, van de Pas would easily come out ahead of Glaskin. His malleable manner and willingness to stand by Glaskin through thick and thin have been noted by many. Yet it must not always have been easy for van de Pas to show such unflinching loyalty. Several close friends commented on the way Glaskin was prone to be dismissive of van de Pas and even treat him with disrespect. One of those was Edgar Vos. 'In Holland,

---

52 HS to GMG, 28 April 1972.
53 GMG (1978b, 84).

Gerry would never introduce Leo to friends, not even my mother, and Gerry was very close to my mother. It was as though he was ashamed of him.'[54] When Vera Vaughan Bowden visited Glaskin in Perth she noticed a similar pattern. 'Gerry first introduced Leo to me as his secretary but I soon realised that he was more than a secretary', she said.[55] Even van de Pas's sister, Riet, admitted that Glaskin was prone to treat her brother 'a bit like a servant at times.'[56] But long-time friend of both men, Rae Kean, had a different take on the matter. 'Gerry bullied Leo mercilessly,' she said, 'but it was only superficial. He had a very deep respect for Leo as a person. And Gerry was Leo's world. It was the sort of relationship they both got a great deal from. The last thing Gerry asked me to do before he died was to look after Leo.'[57]

Glaskin and van de Pas were lovers from their earliest meetings in Amsterdam but they never flaunted their relationship publicly. Nowhere in numerous references that Glaskin makes to van de Pas does the word 'lover', 'partner' or other such term occur. It is always 'assistant', 'secretary', or in latter years, 'carer' and even 'nurse'. Although this is probably symptomatic of the places and times in which Glaskin lived, nevertheless it suggests that Glaskin wished the true nature of their relationship to remain hidden from public view. While it is understandable that they should want to protect their privacy, they did not live a closeted life. They participated in social functions together, be they public or private. Soon after he arrived in Australia, van de Pas attended gatherings of the Fellowship of Australian Writers with Glaskin. This was the year that Glaskin was president of the Western Australian branch of the Fellowship and found he had taken on more than he had bargained for. Although Glaskin resigned halfway through his term as president, he may not have lasted this long had it not been for van de Pas's support, whether it be typing minutes or helping Glaskin dispose of putrid lemons that had dropped from the tree outside the Fellowship's headquarters at Tom Collins House.

Van de Pas may well have joined the Fellowship as a writer in his own right, albeit in a very different field. All the time he worked for Glaskin, van de Pas was beavering away on his beloved genealogical projects. He compiled two enormous manuscripts on the descendants of William the Silent (William of Orange) the German-born, 16th century leader of the

---

54   Vos to JB, interview, 21 August 2001.
55   Vera Vaughan Bowden to JB, interview by author, 22 August 2001.
56   Riet van de Pas to JB, 23 August 2001.
57   Rae Kean to JB, personal communication, 13 September 2001.

Dutch struggle for independence from Spain. He sent one volume in Dutch on Dutch descendants to Elsevier publishers in Holland and the other on British descendants in English to Burke's Peerage in London. Unfortunately, both publishers turned down his work. However, in 1977 van de Pas was offered a job in London by Debretts, the prestigious British publisher of biographical reference books. Once van de Pas realised he could earn more and live more cheaply in Australia, he declined the position. Moreover, the thought of uprooting his life once again and relocating to England was not one he cared to contemplate.

Van de Pas's reputation as a genealogist grew over the years. His work became recognised for its comprehensiveness, quality and reliability. A number of prominent persons have consulted him, including HRH Princess Michael of Kent for the historical volume *Cupid and the King* and subsequent books. Among his many published works are genealogies of the House of Orange, the Habsburgs and Prince William of Wales. His bestseller has been his volume on Lady Diana Spencer but perhaps more impressive is his *Royal Ancestor*, which traces eight generations of descendants of King Edward III and sells in the UK for £100. Closer to home, the late Australian business magnate and philanthropist Robert Holmes à Court contracted van de Pas to produce a book on his ancestors. Today, van de Pas's compilations and monographs include over 2000 biographies of notable persons, as well as articles in numerous publications. According to leading British genealogist, Tim Powys-Lybbe, 'Leo has one of the best compendiums of genealogy I know of. His knowledge of European and European-origin families is unrivalled. He has an excellent and extensive collection of genealogy reference books in all languages – and here his skill as a linguist is so vital.'[58]

But like other forms of writing, genealogy didn't provide the financial anchor that van de Pas and Glaskin needed. That eventually came from a radically different source. After working full-time for Glaskin for five years, van de Pas took a job as a reservations officer with MacRobertson Miller Airlines, later Ansett Airlines of Western Australia. He worked with the company for 23 years before being given an invalid pension at age 52. During this time he not only provided a steady stream of income for Glaskin and himself but also was able to take advantage of highly discounted airfares to make trips back to the Netherlands, the cost of which he otherwise would have found prohibitive. While van de Pas put in regular hours with the airline,

58 Tim Powys-Lybbe to JB, 6 June 2002.

Glaskin did the shopping and cooking, in addition to whatever writing he could manage with his neck collar, body pains and other persistent ailments. With a steady pay packet coming into their household they were able to afford a cleaning lady, one of whom faithfully served them for 25 years.

Whatever its ups and downs, van de Pas and Glaskin created a relationship that lasted more than three decades. If anything, it only became more intense in the last few years when van de Pas found himself increasingly having to tend to his partner's needs as Glaskin's body began to fail. Like so many aspects of Glaskin's life, this relationship had a strong Dutch connection woven through it. Perhaps Glaskin was acting out of some deep, unfathomable intuition when, as a 14-year-old student at Perth Modern School, he begged to be chosen as a pen pal for the Dutch boy, Sjoerd Steunebrink.[59] Glaskin, who never believed in coincidence, probably would have called the choice prophetic, or at minimum, synchronistic. So often, the Netherlands provided the kind of political and social safety net, as well as personal care and attention, which Glaskin so much craved but which Australia so rarely afforded him. 'How much kinder, how much more considerate than my own fellow-countrymen, were the Dutch … I shall never understand why I haven't written a book called *Happiness Is a Place Called Holland*.'[60] His love affair with the Dutch that began with this boyhood correspondence and continued until his death was a defining theme in Glaskin's life.

---

59 See Chapter 2, 'A Touch of Class'.
60 GMG (1978b, 22 and 30).

Chapter 8

Writer in Search of a Cause

I believe it is the destiny of Australian writers, through their writings, to assist Australians to an awareness of themselves and of their country.

John K. Ewers

Glaskin wrote when he felt compelled to and he wrote about what he knew, often with little effort to disguise the real-life people and situations from which he drew inspiration. Not only was he moved to write books and short stories, but articles, essays, even letters-to-the-editor on a range of issues that crossed his path and tickled his fancy or, more likely, got his goat. His name frequently appeared in Perth newspapers, be it for the atrocious state of the men's changing rooms at Cottesloe Beach or Western Australia's outdated drinking laws or the antiquated, inefficient and outright dangerous practice of giving way to the right when driving on the left side of the road in Australia. Glaskin had opinions on almost every subject and was not at all reluctant to vent them. Interestingly, he did not take up the cudgel in the name of gay rights but chose to do that through some of his novels instead. Indeed, a number of Glaskin's books reflect themes that were close to his heart. Not only did Glaskin write on a diversity of subjects, he also prided himself on the variety of genres and writing styles he tackled. He wrote fiction and non-fiction, for adults and children, novels, short stories, novellas, memoirs, plays for stage and television, film scripts, even a musical. He revelled in this mélange of writing forms. In an interview with playwright, novelist and poet Dorothy Hewett, Glaskin proudly boasted that he never wrote the same kind of book twice. Referring to his play *Turn on the Heat*, a fictionalised account of the last night in the life of Marilyn Monroe written for one actress, he asserted that 'I wanted to write something that was totally different, even for theatre.'[1]

'Different' seemed to be the operative word for Glaskin, much to the chagrin of his long-time British agent, David Bolt. In their prolific correspondence over the years, Bolt made numerous pleas to Glaskin to stick to the kind of writing he did best which, in Bolt's estimation, was basic storytelling. Tiring of Glaskin's potpourri approach to writing, Bolt pleaded with him, 'Please give some thought to a new full-length novel like *Flight to Landfall* … your forte is as a straight novelist and I should very much like to get that side going again. At your best – dangerous phrase – you are above all a first-rate storyteller and first-rate storytellers are scarce on the ground. Publishers really are constantly looking for them.'[2] Four years later, Bolt was still despairing that Glaskin had not heeded his advice. Glaskin had sent his agent the manuscript of his short novel about a young boy and a kangaroo, *Do Animals Go to Heaven?* When he read it, Bolt was most disappointed. 'I'm tremendously sad except that it's mercifully short and presumably didn't take too long to write. Here we have your superb *Flight to Landfall* and I'm at a loss to know why this hasn't spurred you to continuing up that path, instead of getting sidetracked like this. It is your forte, it's what you do well, better than almost anybody I can think of. It's basically the adventure with the additional depth and characterisation which brings it into the category of serious novel.'[3]

Whether it was an innate urge to always be conquering new frontiers, a Sagittarian drive to ever expand his intellectual horizons, or just a deep revulsion to the idea of writing to please someone else, Glaskin didn't follow Bolt's advice. Perhaps we get a clue to this riddle in another statement he made in his interview with Hewett. When she asked him, 'Do you see yourself as a completely unconventional writer?' he replied, 'I don't have an image of myself as a writer at all. I don't know what kind of status I have. I still think that I'm not a literary writer but I'm not purely a commercial writer either. A theme interests me, I spend months and months thinking it out, and then I put it down on paper. Once it's done it's over and done with.'[4] This reveals several things about Glaskin's approach to writing. First, his

---

1   Hewett (1967, 35).
2   David Bolt to GMG, 14 January 1975.
3   Bolt to GMG, December 1979.
4   Hewett (1967, 41).

claim to being neither a literary writer nor a purely commercial writer rings true. He never had pretensions about the former and he despised the latter. If he sought to emulate anyone, it was his literary god, Graham Greene, whom he praised as having depth but who wrote in a straightforward, entertaining manner. Although he always strove to write as powerfully as he could in whatever genre he tackled, Glaskin was also aware of his own limitations as a writer. Reflecting on the demise of another local writer who became frustrated because his literary capabilities didn't match up to those of great writers, Glaskin wrote,

> It has taught me a great lesson – always to write. Use the material that I have to the best of my ability and as much as I can – never be satisfied with the standard I have reached but always strive to improve – but at the same time, never to lay down the pen because I feel that I cannot wield it as well as others have done. I must accept the limits of whatever talent I have, if any, and write as much as I can with the material I have acquired. After all, it is better to be a bad writer, if writing is the craving of the soul, than to be a successful solicitor, bank clerk, doctor, teacher, unskilled labourer (!) if the heart and spirit are not in these works.[5]

Second, Glaskin's statement of his self-image as a writer reveals a compulsion to get something down on paper – once the gestation period has run its course – as well as a certain detachment from his work once a project was completed. From his frequent references to how many words he wrote per day or how many hours he spent on a chapter or weeks or months on a book, it seems that the quantity and pace of his writing were at least as important to him as the quality. Cousin David Buchanan encountered this when he phoned Glaskin one day just as Glaskin was in the final throes of writing *The Way You Went*, his story about the tragic death of one of his young neighbours. Not waiting to ask why Buchanan called, Glaskin announced, 'I can't talk. I'm dictating … Leo says that we're up to page 96. I've only got a few pages left. Remember the boy who killed himself? I've nearly finished his book. Got to go, darling. Bye.'[6] Buchanan recalled that Glaskin wrote the whole book in two weeks, dictating to van de Pas who typed the manuscript. At the end of the manuscript, Glaskin wrote: 'Written, and rewritten several times. Mosman Park. Western Australia. 3 pm, 24 June – 3 pm, 7 July 1989", as though he had had a stopwatch ticking the whole time.

---

5 Note in a ledger detailing his attempts to sell his short stories. GMG (1949b, 2 January).
6 David Buchanan to JB, interview by author, 12 November 2002.

In similar vein Glaskin wrote to David Bolt of his Bali-based novel, *Carnal Assault*, 'I don't think I've ever worked so hard and fast on a book before, especially with no help of any kind, not even for fair copies. I have it down to 120,000 words, 340 pages.'[7]

But once Glaskin completed a project he seemingly had little trouble letting go of it and moving on to something else, almost in a 'been there-done that-what's next?' kind of way. This approach to his writing may have contributed to Glaskin's growing number of unpublished manuscripts in the latter 25 years of his life. In 1984 he updated a list of these he had compiled five years before – 19 in all, encompassing novels, short stories, memoirs, dramas, musical plays, television plays and film scripts. In addition, he listed at the bottom of the page another 12 'projects in mind' that were still simmering in his consciousness.

Perhaps most revealing in Glaskin's response to Hewett's question is his statement that his writing is essentially theme driven. While this propensity he shared with many writers, in Glaskin's case it seemed more intense and personal than most. His themes have a ring about them of causes he espoused or issues he felt deeply about, at least in his more serious works, both published and unpublished. They included Australia's phobias in dealing with Asia and Asians; its responsibility to develop the country's vast untapped resources, especially in the north and interior; its poor record in acknowledging its Aboriginal citizens as full human beings; the increasing prevalence of youth suicide in Australian society; the inability of Australians to embrace diverse sexual orientation and homosexuality in particular; the dangers of incest in family life; and perhaps most of all, the loneliness of so many people today.

Glaskin's first encounter with Asia happened in his own backyard when he was about five years old. Horse-drawn carts were still seen in the streets of suburban Perth in those days, their hawkers selling everything from bread and milk to pharmaceuticals and household items. One whom Glaskin remembered above all others was a Chinese greengrocer called 'John'. His straw coolie hat shaded the wrinkled skin of his aging face and his loose-fitting, western-style clothes. As soon as she heard the ring of his horses' hooves coming down the road, Glaskin's mother would head for the front gate and the cart laden with fruit and vegetables. Once she had made her purchases, John would carry them for her around to the back door of the house. One day, as he lugged the load behind Delia, he was surprised to

---

7   GMG to Bolt, December 1978.

see a young boy wrapped in a blanket and sitting on a cane chair in a sunny spot in the garden. Glaskin, who was home from school recovering from whooping cough, was equally surprised by this stranger who had entered his world. John mimicked a gesture of sympathy towards the young boy before depositing the goods and returning to his cart. The following week the same scenario repeated itself, but this time the squat little Chinese man brought Glaskin two gifts – a small green jar of preserved ginger and a paper bag full of used postage stamps from China. The expression of delight and fascination on the young boy's face was more reward than the old man could have asked for.

But for Glaskin it was not just the unexpected gifts he received that made him so happy and allowed him to forget his illness for a while. It was John's smile – 'the kindest smile of encouragement I had ever experienced'[8] – that made a lasting impression on him. Whereas other children may have re-coiled in fear at 'the brown stain of his smile and the twin wing-lines of … his eyes', Glaskin associated them with friendship and kindness, gentle-ness and reassurance. Moreover, the stamps formed the beginning of a collection that absorbed him for years to come and introduced him to a world of differences beyond the familiar Australia he knew. Little did he know then that he would count several Chinese men and women among his most cherished friends throughout his life. Little wonder, too, that the mysterious otherness of Asia would not be the threat to him that it was to many Australians of his generation and several to follow.

It is not difficult to understand why Anglo-Australia felt so threatened by the presence of so many people of such different cultural roots and economic standing just to its north. Much has been written and spoken on the subject and many films have captured aspects of this part of Australia's past. The Second World War helped to inflame these feelings and reinforce stereo-types of 'the yellow peril' and 'conquering hordes from the north' eagerly awaiting their chance to take over this vast, underpopulated continent. With the demise of colonialism following the war, Australians felt more vulner-able to the forces of change impinging on them. At the same time, the war and its aftermath opened eyes and windows on a world that once seen, felt, heard, touched and tasted, Australians couldn't ignore. Some were fascinated by the diversity and complexity of peoples and cultures at their doorstep, especially in the nearer countries of Southeast Asia, and felt compelled to try to understand them and become enmeshed in them. For Asians who

---

8   GMG (1995b, 2–3).

chose – or dared – to come to Australia in the early post-war period, either for education, employment or permanent residence, it was not an easy time. Multiculturalism was years away from seeping into the consciousness of mainstream Australia and, coupled with the phobia of communism that swept across the country during the Cold War years, Asians in Australia often took the brunt of a blatant racism born out of fear and ignorance.

One who experienced this scourge was a young Chinese Malay, Paul Lee (Lee Kwok Poh), who came to Australia in 1952 to study dentistry. During his time as a student in Adelaide, Lee had his first encounter with Australian racism. When looking for boarding houses, he would find a vacancy in the newspaper but when he showed up on the doorstep he would invariably be told the place was taken. Given his determination to be the first to check out advertisements, Lee knew there was little chance someone else had reached there first. Even among fellow students, Lee felt very much the outsider. As the only Chinese student in his year, he was often the butt of jokes like 'Don't wake up the sleeping dragon!' and 'Look under your bed!'. But he also had to contend with an Australian mindset that equated Asian, or 'yellow', with communism, which was to be at least as much feared and eradicated. In his student days in Adelaide, Lee recalled the night a friend asked him home to dinner with his family. Keen to meet an Australian family, he gladly accepted the invitation. After dinner he thought he would do the right thing and help with the washing up. He was standing behind his friend's mother, tea towel in hand, when she turned around and said, 'I understand that you're a communist, Paul.' To counteract these stereotypical responses, Lee would sometimes try to inject humour into the situation. While doing lab work, he enjoyed being a little provocative. 'What's wrong with communism?' he would ask. 'I was brought up in very communist environment – a Catholic school. You give Brother Joseph a cake and you share it among all the other brothers. That's real communism.' Telling this tale 50 years later, he added wryly, 'God, the look I used to get from them!'[9]

When he finished his training in Adelaide, Lee was unable to get a job in the South Australian Public Service so chose to go to Queenstown on Tasmania's remote west coast instead. It was either that or New Guinea. When he arrived there he realised why Queenstown had vacancies for a dentist. It was isolated and wet. Lee found himself working 'eight days a week' but when he had time off and the rain stopped, he revelled in bushwalking through the stunning terrain and indulging in his favourite hobby of

---

9   Paul Lee to JB, interview by author, 12 November 2002.

photography. While in Tasmania, he came to realise that Chinese weren't the lowest rung on the ladder of Australian racism. An Indian student from Malaya who also hadn't been able to get a job in Adelaide came to Tasmania with Lee. When they went into a shop together, Lee noticed that he was treated quite well but that his darker-skinned friend was often mistaken for an Aboriginal and dealt with in a much more demeaning way. Eventually, it wasn't racism as much as the rain that wore him down in Tasmania and when a position opened up at the Perth Dental Hospital Lee headed west.

One of the first people he met at the hospital was a young dental nurse, Myree Glaskin. She told Lee that her brother had spent quite a few years in Singapore and Malaya and asked if he would like to meet him. Having tired of the monoculture of mainstream Australia, Lee jumped at the opportunity. From the moment they first met, Lee and Glaskin clicked. They found they had much in common, be it a passion for spicy Asian food, practising Bahasa Malay on each other or dabbling in photography, something Glaskin enjoyed but which, in Lee's estimation, he didn't have enough patience for. Glaskin always had to be on the move and kept suggesting places they might go on holidays together. His first thought was to go back to Malaya but Lee protested, 'But that's just where I came from! I want to go somewhere different.' Glaskin relented. 'How about the Australian outback then?' he asked. Having seen slides of the brilliant iridescent colours around Alice Springs that fellow dental students had brought back from field trips to the area, Lee eagerly agreed. Glaskin was entranced by the notion of exploring those parts of his country in which only a handful of people lived and not many ventured into. Moreover, he was acutely aware of the stark contrast between Southeast Asia crammed with people and intense vegetation and Australia with vast unpopulated stretches of arid or semi-arid land. The irony of the situation was not lost on him. He wanted to see it for himself, then write about it, both as non-fiction and as grist for his novels and short stories.

As they began plotting their trip, it became clear that Lee envisaged accomplishing a lot more than Glaskin had in mind. He wanted to travel the entire length of Western Australia north from Perth, across to Darwin, south down the Stuart Highway to Alice Springs and back to Perth across the Nullabor Plain via Adelaide. Although the latter 3200 kilometres could be done by train, that still left 11,300 kilometres by car – Glaskin's 1959-model FC Holden station wagon. And Lee had six weeks leave in which to do the whole thing. Not only was it an ambitious plan, it was also costly. Although Lee would contribute to the expenses, they still needed more. Glaskin then struck upon the idea of having a publisher commission him to write a book about the experience. Since American interest in Australia was on the rise, Glaskin tried the US publisher Doubleday.[10] They agreed to fund the trip but their initial offer of US$500 plus royalties did not excite Glaskin so he light-heartedly wrote to them that he would be happier if the sum were three times as much. When he arrived at Broome, a cable from Doubleday advised that his higher figure had been accepted.[11] Now he felt more obligated than ever to complete his end of the bargain. The result was *The Land That Sleeps*, a travelogue book-ended with mini-essays that preach to an Anglo-American-Australian audience on the challenge confronting the 'sleeping giant down under' that 'waits to be awakened'.[12] It is the familiar call to 'populate or perish', a kind of 1960s reminder that the old 'yellow hordes from the north' were still yapping at the heels of what was then essentially White Australia. The book attracted little critical interest, but provided grist for the mill for both *Flight to Landfall* and *The Road to Nowhere*.[13] Fifty years after it was written, it is an intriguing and possibly important historical record of a part of Australia that has not only awoken from sleep but has become the driving force behind one of the world's most resurgent economies.

Lee, and this trip with him in particular, was an important bridge in Glaskin's life. It helped to close the gap between his love/hate relationship with his native Australia and his urge to connect with the peoples of the newly emerging post-colonial Asia. His ten years in Singapore had already established a firm foundation for the latter. His personal relationships with Han Suyin and water skiing friends like Harold Tay, and his sexual escapades with men of many different hues, were the pillars that built on this foundation. The willingness of his Asian friends to embrace his homosexuality was an important factor in these relationships and no doubt a blessing compared to the adverse treatment he might expect as a gay man at the hands of his own countrymen. According to Lee, Glaskin's homosexuality was never an issue with him. 'When I found out that he was gay, it took me a little while to accept him because I came from a Catholic school where we

---

10 Two examples of this interest were the use of trace elements to extend agricultural and pastoral land around Esperance in southeast Western Australia and the Humpty Doo rice project in the Northern Territory.

11 No author listed. *The West Australian*, 24 September 1960.

12 GMG (1961c, 630).

13 One Australian reviewer suggested Glaskin would have been better off confining himself to sharing his own experiences, rather than taking on the broader and more controversial subject of 'northern development'. Graham (1962). *The Times Literary Supplement* found it 'readable, but not memorable'. No author listed (1962, 589).

were brainwashed about homosexuality. But I couldn't have cared less. He was such an interesting person to talk to. Not many Australians in the '50s and '60s were as widely travelled as Gerry.'[14] Nevertheless, rumours spread around Perth that because of his association with Glaskin, especially after their outback safari, he must be 'one of those' too. Lee denied that Glaskin ever made any sexual overtures to him during their time together.

Glaskin's decade in Singapore built on a pro-Asian sentiment that was already embedded in him from his earliest years. Although he rarely engaged in political debate on the issue, Australia's relationship to Asia was always close to the surface with Glaskin. In 1971, he wrote a short note to the premier of South Australia, Donald Dunstan, congratulating him on the courage, wisdom and vision of his public statement on Asian immigration to Australia. Glaskin described it as 'one of the few statements, and therefor [sic] attitudes, to have revived at least some hope for enlightenment.'[15] Glaskin revealed his attitudes to Asia and Asians in his writing, most notably in his three novels set in Southeast Asia, *A Lion in the Sun*, *The Beach of Passionate Love* and *Flight to Landfall*, the latter in part only.

All three books touch on different aspects of Australia's attempts to come to terms with its Asian neighbours. An unabashed indictment against the overt elitism and racism of a fading colonial power in Asia, *A Lion in the Sun* focuses heavily on the plight of the Chinese at the hands of their British overlords.[16] *The Beach of Passionate Love*, which began as a travel article then grew into a short story and finally evolved into a novel, gets more beneath the skin of the nuances of Malay culture. The main British character in the book, Harry Lee, comes off second best, while the Australian, George Cransden, is portrayed in a more sympathetic and understanding light. But the native Malays are clearly the winners. Wanting to reconnect with the young Malay woman, Maimunah, who risked her life to help him escape from the occupying Japanese in the Second World War, Cransden returns to Kelantan on Malaya's east coast. In Singapore, he meets the precocious young Lee who wants to go to Kelantan to establish a commercial fishing industry. Cransden offers him a lift but as the journey unfolds it becomes clear that Lee has another mission. He wants to marry the exquisite Malay princess Zaraniah, a desire she doesn't reciprocate. Lee won't take no for an answer and in the course of his repeated efforts to woo her, becomes entangled in a series of cultural faux pas and personal blunders, culminating

---

14   Lee to JB, interview, 12 November 2002.
15   GMG to The Rt. Hon. Mr Donald Dunstan, 14 January 1971.
16   See Chapter 5, 'A Singapore Fling', for more detail on *A Lion in the Sun*.

in a final confrontation with Zaraniah's Malay suitor and Lee's eventual mysterious disappearance. Cransden is enmeshed in this unravelling drama, wedged between the bumbling ineptitude and senseless bravado of his British travelling companion and his affection for Maimunah, her two sons and all Malays. He finally returns to Australia, taking with him Maimunah's eldest son, Hamid, to study economics at university there. Cransden is portrayed as the benevolent Australian, a sort of one-man Colombo Plan,[17] doing his bit for Australian-Asian relations. Glaskin paints a sharp and poignant contrast between Lee and Hamid, as the following musing of Cransden depicts.

> He spoke as though he was certain of every detail of his future career, and he had an air of purpose that once again reminded me strongly of Harry Lee. But Hamid's purposefulness was very different from Lee's. Although both were striving for material gain in the world, Lee's driving force was obviously more for his own personal accomplishment, an obsession amounting more to a kind of megalomania. Hamid's ambition, I sensed, was just as tenacious as Lee's, but without the slightest tinge of selfishness or vanity.[18]

Towards the end of the book, Glaskin reveals his own vision of a multi-racial world living in harmony, if only by necessity rather than design. In a dialogue with Hamid, Cransden spells out an apartheid-like notion of humankind, with its different races all purposefully evolved to suit different climatic conditions and made to appear repulsive enough to one another so as not to intrude on one another's territory. Hamid swallows Cransden's fanciful theory, but notes that as barriers between people break down, differences appear less fearsome. However, he has one gnawing question. 'Why is it that there are always some people, like yourself for instance, who are not repelled by this difference in physical appearance – so that they become attracted to some other race, and even come to love it?' The noble Cransden replies, 'There must always be exceptions to everything, I suppose … Even if it's only for those very few, who see no difference beneath the colour of a skin, to lead the way to a *real* civilization of having all the different species come to live peaceably with each other. The world is shrinking so fast, my boy, that already we find that we *have* to live peaceably with each other, if we're to survive at all. And that sounds to me as good

---

17 Established in 1950, the Colombo Plan is an inter-governmental program designed to strengthen the economic and social development of Asian-Pacific countries through human resources development. Australia was one of the original seven member nations.

18 GMG (1961b, 210).

a reason as any.'[19] Hamid has one final question for Cransden – 'If all the races eventually intermarry, what skin colour should we become?' Revealing Glaskin's own preoccupation with physical beauty and a predilection for Asian hues, Cransden replies 'A gorgeous golden brown … the colour of you Kelantanese!'[20]

Glaskin uses *The Beach of Passionate Love* to paint a flattering, almost idyllic, picture of traditional Malay life. In the Author's Note he admits to having delved into a number of academic texts on Malay culture and society, in addition to his own experiences of it during the time he lived in Singapore. Glaskin was fascinated, and no doubt attracted, by Kelantan and its people. He was fortunate to be there for the fishermen's drum contest and the Puja Pantai (beach worship) thanksgiving festival, which is held every four or five years. He was particularly lucky to be invited by Sultan Ibrahim of Kelantan to his birthday celebration, which lasts three days and nights and is attended by more than a thousand people.[21] The book is peppered with Malay expressions and detailed references to Malay customs, so much so that Glaskin's writer friend David Hough jokingly suggested to him that he might be better suited writing for *National Geographic*. Hough intended the comment as a compliment to Glaskin's powers of description and Glaskin never forgot it.[22] The book's reviewer in *The West Australian* wasn't so enamoured by this aspect of Glaskin's writing. He noted that 'with a plot slow in movement, one has the sensation sometimes of reading a travel book rather than a novel'. He suggested Glaskin could have concentrated the story into 'the long-short form'.[23]

The Beach of Passionate Love was translated from English into five other languages. Not surprisingly, given their long association and fascination with the region, the Dutch loved it, as did the Germans. Book club editions in both countries became bestsellers. The Americans weren't so inclined. Three publishers rejected it. As Doubleday pointed out, it lacked the action and pacing American readers demand. Negotiations began for filming the story, but like most of Glaskin's other film options this one never eventuated. Riding on the book's success, Glaskin wrote to the Malaysian Director of Tourism, suggesting his department might like to bring out a special

19 Ibid., 311–312.
20 Ibid., 312. Correspondence between GMG and several young Malay men suggest that he found the 'gorgeous golden brown skin' very attractive indeed, and that the attraction was mutual.
21 No author listed. *The West Australian*, 25 November 1959.
22 David Hough to JB, interview by author, 19 November 2002.
23 Kornweibel (1961).

paperback edition to help publicise this part of Malaysia. Given that 'The Beach of Passionate Love' is a direct translation of the Malay name Pantai Cinta Berahi, there was reason to think it might have a tourist lure. But the director told Glaskin that the beach was being developed by the Kelantan State Development Corporation and a private developer and suggested he might like to contact them with his proposal.

The third book in Glaskin's Asian triad, *Flight to Landfall*, is the confluence of three geographic streams in Glaskin's life – the Netherlands, Southeast Asia and Australia. While the heart of the story takes place in a remote corner of the Kimberley region of Western Australia, it originates in Perth, moves to Singapore and from there to the Dutch East Indies (Indonesia). Its characters are primarily British and Dutch expatriates fleeing the Japanese invasion on the last Dutch plane out of Surabaya, only to make a crash landing in the harsh terrain of the Great Sandy Desert. Seven of the 20 passengers and crew survive the 'landfall' but only two live to tell their almost unbelievable tale to the visiting author from the south, who has been asked by the Western Australian government to investigate rumours of diamonds in the area. Glaskin draws on his visit to the magnificent Dale's Gorge further south in the Hamersley Range in the Pilbara region to describe the stunning landscape into which the survivors stumble and make their home. While *Flight* may be the kind of classic adventure story made to order for Reader's Digest Condensed Books and highly favoured by Glaskin's agent, David Bolt, it doesn't add much new insight into Glaskin's perspective on Australian-Asian relations. However, it does reveal how the Japanese invasion of Southeast Asia made many Australians suddenly aware that they did at least share something in common with their immediate neighbours to the north, even if it be only a revulsion of and resistance to a common enemy.

Glaskin used historical events as the backdrop for one other story set in Southeast Asia, although it was never published. Perhaps it was written 25 years too soon, or perhaps it was, as David Bolt found it, overwritten and too detached in style.[24] Whatever the reasons for its failure commercially, *Carnal Assault* was another attempt by Glaskin to tackle sexuality in one of its varied forms – sexual violence perpetrated against women. A famous Australian actress who is holidaying in Bali with her invalid husband is taken hostage by terrorists and subjected to repeated rape. While in detention, she falls in love with another hostage, an African American violinist with whom

---

24 Bolt to GMG, 12 January 1979.

she becomes sexually involved as well. Somewhat reminiscent of the Patty Hearst saga, the woman finds that, to her horror, she eventually becomes accepting of her situation to the point of feeling compassion, perhaps even love, for her oppressors. Glaskin wrote the story in 1978 but publishers in the UK, USA and Australia rejected it. It languished in his files until 1995 when he tried reviving it in light of the changed political situation in Indonesia. Writing to his new British agent, Bob Tanner, Glaskin tried in vain to convince him of the book's timeliness. 'It's still not too late for the East Timor situation. Indeed, that seems worse than ever, along with the events in Bali making the book even more plausible.' Were he alive today, Glaskin may have had an even stronger case, given more recent events in the region.

If diverse forms of sexuality and a passion for Asia were two of Glaskin's major preoccupations, several others also emerge in his work. One of those was youth suicide. It wasn't just a distaste for the notion of suicide that affected Glaskin but a quite visceral grasp of the emotional devastation associated with it. Glaskin was no stranger to suicide. Apart from his own attempted suicide in Amsterdam, there were two suicides in his own family during his lifetime.[25] Both involved young men, one on the Gugeri side and the other a Glaskin nephew. The most shocking and potentially destructive to him personally was that of his Uncle Alan, second youngest brother of his mother Delia. Glaskin never forgot the way he discovered the awful truth of Alan Gugeri's death. It was Easter 1932 and Glaskin's grandparents took his parents, himself, his younger brother Dixie and baby Loris with them to visit the family property, Acacia Springs, in the Darling Ranges east of Perth.[26] Gugeri's friends, George and Lewis, also accompanied them in another car. As they drove down the gravel track to the little wooden house, the eight-year-old Glaskin couldn't wait to fling himself into the arms of his favourite uncle, with whom he'd stayed on other occasions. Racing from the car as fast as his legs could carry him, he suddenly came to an abrupt halt. Staring up at him from the ground was his uncle's decaying body 'lying on the rough blood-soaked gravel with his mouth open and hideous from more congealed blood; ants in his mouth, eyes and nostrils, even his ears; his rifle alongside him and also one boot, his toe still in the trigger guard, and the back of his head blown clean off his skull.'[27]

---

25 See Chapter 7, 'Going Dutch'.
26 'Acacia Springs' was the actual name of the place but the Glaskin family referred to it as 'Cacia Springs'.
27 GMG (1975, 101).

Although Nan always referred to her son's death as an accident and others debated whether it was, Glaskin had no doubt it was suicide.[28] His aunt Eileen confirmed this for him when she reminded Glaskin of several aspects of Gugeri's life. As a child, he was dyslexic and at school was regarded as a slow learner, which would have done little to enhance his self-esteem. With the onset of the Depression, he quickly found himself out of work and went to look after Acacia Springs. Although he loved nature – he would observe ants for hours and use their behaviour to forecast the weather – it was a horribly lonely life for a young man, just looking after chooks and tending fruit trees. His social life was limited to his friends, George and Lewis, and amateur road cycling, at which he excelled. Ironically, both may have contributed to his death. As a cyclist, he was knocked unconscious in an accident with another rider. He should have been hospitalised but instead had brandy poured down his throat to revive him. When he arrived home he vomited as soon as he staggered out of the car, his face still covered with gravel from the fall. According to Eileen, 'All you could see were his eyes. Staring. And already with a funny look in them.'[29] Not long afterwards, Gugeri fell in love with a young woman, Violet, who lived on a neighbouring property. But when Violet switched allegiance to Gugeri's best friend, George, Gugeri began acting strangely. Eileen was so concerned about her brother that she recommended to her mother that he be taken to hospital, but Nan adamantly refused. Not long after, the handsome, athletic, 22-year-old was dead. Glaskin had lost 'one of the most beautiful-looking men, as well as the kindest, I have encountered in a lifetime.'[30]

Another tragic suicide of a young man was to leave its mark on Glaskin's life nearly 40 years later. Griffith Watkins – 'Griff' to friends – was a promising novelist and poet, as well as a popular art teacher at a Perth high school. He won his first literary prize at 14 while still at school. He went on to win local and national prizes for his short stories and poetry. One of those prizes Glaskin was partly responsible for awarding. Along with two other Perth literary figures, he was asked to be a judge in a short story competition run by *The Weekend News* in 1961. All three judges were astonished by the 200 entries submitted but they were particularly impressed by one of Watkins'

---

28 The coroner's report on his death certificate simply states that 'the evidence is not conclusive as to whether accident or design.' There is no mention of the accident or the inquest held afterwards in either of the two Perth daily papers or the local *Swan Express*.

29 GMG (1975, 112).

30 Ibid., 102.

12 stories, 'God in the Afternoon'. According to Glaskin, it 'stood out from all the rest like the dog-star in the sky'. It was the one he wished he could have written himself.[31]

But it also had a ring of premonition about it for Glaskin. It tells of a young man who is recovering from a motorcycle accident in which it is implied that his fellow passenger died, while he himself is suffering from a bone disease. But most of all, he is depressed and angry and wants to withdraw from the world. He wants to rid himself of all those trying to 'smother him with their duteous love and sympathy' – his bickering parents, the platitudinous priest, the overly cheerful nurses. His black Labrador in tow, he heads for the beach where he comes across his friend's dinghy, into which he manages to drag himself and row out from the shore. With much trepidation, he finally takes the plunge and half jumps, half falls into the water. Gradually, exhilaration replaces apprehension as he moves around the boat in the water and feels that he has 'returned to his belonging'. Unlike the humans in his life, the water is something he can trust and respect. Reluctantly, he returns to the boat and rows sadly back to the shore.

Eight and a half years after this story was published, Watkins' body was found floating in a pen at the Claremont Yacht Club in Perth's Swan River. A heavy belt pulley with a two-foot axle attached was fastened to a chain around his waist. He had been missing for 13 days, during which time police and friends – including Glaskin and van de Pas – had been searching Cottesloe and Swanbourne beaches, since his car and a bundle of clothes had been found parked nearby. Theories sprang up that he had drowned in the ocean or that he had run into trouble in the sand dunes north of Swanbourne that border on a military barracks and were a favourite haunt for nude bathers and gay men. Like many others, Glaskin was devastated at the news of Watkins' death, for which he partly blamed himself.

Immediately after the short story competition results were announced in April 1961, Glaskin contacted Watkins at his parents' home. He couldn't wait to meet this young man whose writing had made such an impression on him. When he saw Watkins' lean body and smiling face with its alert eyes, wavy dark hair and made-to-order white teeth, he may have been impressed in other ways too. After all, Watkins was 31, single and still living at home. Glaskin was just seven years older than Watkins, who no doubt struck him as a sensitive, caring and creative soul. Not only did Watkins shine as a

---

31 An essay GMG wrote about Watkins for inclusion in a collection compiled by Peter Jeffrey. GMG to Jeffrey, 19 October 1989.

short story writer, but also as a poet, novelist, painter and potter. He in turn was probably delighted to find a published author of the stature of Glaskin willing to assist him navigate the maze of the publishing world.

Accepting Glaskin's invitation to visit him, Watkins arrived on his doorstep laden with four manuscripts for him to read. Glaskin declined, but offered to give him an introduction to his literary agent in London, Sheila Watson, who had a reputation for launching new writers. True to form, she placed Watkins' *The Pleasure Bird* with Longmans. Whatever gratification Watkins received from this was short-lived, because when Longmans rejected his other manuscripts he became dejected. Glaskin tried reassuring him that this was par for the course in the writing game and that 'the only joy was in the writing itself, no matter what agony it might seem at the time.'[32] But apparently Watkins didn't see it this way. There was little joy for him any more, from writing or any endeavour. In a scrawled message to a friend that his mother found 19 years after his death, Watkins had written, 'It is no use to stretch out my hand, for the mists that separate us swallow up my arm.'[33]

While the deaths of Alan Gugeri and Griffith Watkins affected Glaskin deeply, one other young death in which he was intimately involved also left a permanent imprint on his psyche. In the early 1950s, when Glaskin was riding high as a young stockbroker in Singapore, Han Suyin introduced him to one of the richest businessmen in the city, Loke Wan Tho. Wan Tho was a highly anglified Chinese who owned theatres and hotels and lived in the penthouse suite at the top of the Cathay Building, then Singapore's tallest. He admired Glaskin's writing and read much of it while still in manuscript form. Glaskin was favoured in return by invitations to lavish parties for which Wan Tho was renowned. At one function he found himself being eyed by a young American who was little more than 20 years old and new to the colony. Glaskin had watched him playing tennis at the Tanglin Club and found his athletic body most alluring.

But this night Glaskin had his eyes set on a young woman whom he considered potential marriage material. When she disappeared into the ladies' room, Glaskin headed to the balcony for fresh air. The American followed, sipping his *stengah* and sucking at his cigarette. He perched himself on the railing, back against the wall at the end of the balcony, his eyes all the time fixated on Glaskin with unmistakable intent. Glaskin broke the ice. 'Please don't sit there like that. You could so easily fall', he begged his admirer. But

---

32 Ibid., 3.
33 Moran (1990).

the young man merely shrugged his shoulders and continued his salacious gaze. When he didn't move, Glaskin turned and walked back inside. As he did so, he thought he heard the American move also, no doubt intending to follow him. Then came a horrendous high-pitched scream, hideously loud at first but quickly fading until it came to an abrupt halt, leaving a numbing silence. Glaskin was paralysed. 'If only I had …' he kept saying to himself. 'I will never know how it happened, but I will always know that it did', he said.[34]

Over the years, the rising rate of teen suicides in Australia appalled him and began to consume him. Glaskin cut out articles on the subject from local papers. One article underscored that as many as 60,000 young Australians tried to take their lives each year, giving Australia the dubious distinction on having one of the highest youth suicide rates in the Western world. Young men were four to five times more likely than young women to take their lives.[35] Glaskin lamented this situation in an article he wrote in 1994, in which he contrasted the lot of youth in Australia then compared to his era. He described the depressed state of young people in the '90s, living in small, often single-parent nuclear families, faced with increasing difficulty of finding employment and constantly bombarded by media and marketing forces that glorify an acquisition-based lifestyle. 'I see the dismay, even despair, on their faces in almost every street I walk', wrote Glaskin. 'Or worse, that frantic grasping for some kind of enjoyment writhing in discos to ear-blasting music that boxes them in even further into their encapsulated loneliness. In the last two months alone, I have known, to my astonishment, two who just opted out of a life they no longer wanted. And I miss them. I mourn them. I just wish I could have got to know them far more than I did, so that perhaps I might have been able to help.'[36]

One young man Glaskin did get to know and whose premature death he deeply mourned was a neighbour in his Mosman Park flat. Sixteen-year-old Paul (Pawel) Rabuszko died when he fell from the sixth-storey balcony of a block of flats in the Perth suburb of Highgate in March 1989. Although the coroner's report concluded that the cause of death was multiple fractures to the back of the skull and there were no suspicious circumstances, not everyone was convinced.[37] A friend of Glaskin's who had access to the

---

34 GMG (1989a, 55).
35 No author listed. *The West Australian*, 11 August 1998.
36 GMG (1994, 3–4).
37 Since there was no inquest into Rabuszko's death, details of the coroner's report were not made public.

autopsy report told him that Rabuszko's body was filled with heroin. In his novella *The Way You Went*, which Glaskin refers to as a roman à clef, he plays out a number of possible scenarios about the last moments of Rabuszko's life. After spelling out these possibilities, Glaskin is left with the question he started with: Once you are gone, does it matter the way you went? He doesn't answer the question directly but he creates his own miracle ending to this tragically short life in which Rabuszko was 'flying like an angel, flying to the stars so firm in their firmament.'[38]

Glaskin's sensitivity to the plight of the less fortunate in society extended beyond young people to other groups. One of those was Aboriginal Australians, who feature prominently in his writing and throughout his life. From his earliest days in Carnamah where Aboriginal children where his first playmates to his writing of the life of Daisy Bates in his play *Woman of the Dreaming*, Glaskin exhibited a strong empathy for Aboriginals. One of his early short stories, *Birthright*, describes two young Aboriginal girls being abused on a bus on a wet night in the middle of winter.[39] As disturbing and poignant as this story is, it was only a passing reference to a subject that other Australian writers of his day pursued in much greater depth. One of the most notable in this respect was his friend Mary Durack, who spent much of her early life living on Kimberley cattle stations and who portrayed Aboriginal Australians in her novels as unique and intricate individuals. Glaskin honoured Aboriginals in his writing in a less personal way, yet with sympathy and realism. He made a determined bid to acquaint himself with Aboriginal culture – often using Durack as his mentor – and frequently condemned the blatant, and occasionally more subtle, racism that prevailed in Australia at the time. Glaskin's two books that best exemplify this are *A Waltz through the Hills* and *Flight to Landfall*.

In *A Waltz through the Hills*, one of the central characters is the Aboriginal Frank Smith. Smith chances upon Andy Dean and his sister Sammy, who have run away from their small wheatbelt town after the death of their only remaining parent to escape being sent to different orphanages. They plan to walk more than 200 kilometres to Fremantle and stow away on a ship bound for England, where their grandparents would care for them. Their first encounter, in which Smith catches Andy trying to steal his rabbits, has overtones of much larger issues. 'You white kids think you can do

---

38 GMG (1989a, 116).
39 GMG (1956). As well as being published in the local newspaper *The Countryman*, the story also appears in his short story collection *A Small Selection* (GMG, 1962b)/ *Sometimes It Wasn't So Nice* (GMG, 1968b).

whatever you like, don'tchers! You reckon you can come and take anything from off of us, don'tcher!' says an angry Smith.[40] But Smith breaks out in uncontrollable laughter when Andy protests that he stop swearing in front of his young sister, Sammy. Glaskin then depicts another side of Smith, and by extension, of his race, seen through Andy's young and discerning eyes. 'There was a look of youth all over him. And yet, when he again looked into those dark and deeply sequestered eyes, the eyes were older somehow than anyone's he had ever seen … These eyes somehow had an agelessness about them, as though they would never die.[41] During their trek to the city, a close bond develops between Smith and the two children. The travails of living off the land and being alert to avoid the growing search party looking for them push Andy and Sammy to their limits. But Smith is their guardian angel, supporting them, teaching them, feeding them, leading them to their destination. He even steers them through the onslaught of a savage bushfire before they finally reach the city and the massive publicity their story has generated.

As the children prepare to fly out of Perth to England emotions reach a climax. While government representatives make a last desperate effort to convince Andy and his sister to remain in Australia and become adopted by one of the dozens of families who have offered to take them, Frank whispers in Andy's ear a piece of age-old wisdom from his own ancestors. 'You go, young 'un. You'll be with your *own* people, then.' Andy doesn't know how to respond. Then it comes to him. 'But he felt sure Frank would be right. He'd been so right with everything before. He wanted to tell this to Frank but he didn't know how to say it. And then, even though he knew it was a funny thing for a boy to do, to a man, he put his arms around Frank's neck as he was stooped there, on the gangway, and he kissed him. But Frank wasn't surprised. He looked very happy. Then Sammy kissed him too.'[42]

It is a touching story and one that struck a chord with many people in many countries. It was one of Glaskin's most successful books, being translated into Danish, Dutch, French, German, Norwegian, Russian and Swedish, as well as being issued in English in both hard and soft covers, including as a Heinemann New Windmill Classic edition with multiple reprints. The BBC broadcast it twice and it was serialised in a number of English-speaking countries and throughout Europe. When it finally appeared as a television movie 27 years after the book was published, the story gained

---

40 GMG (1961a, 144).
41 Ibid., 146.
42 Ibid., 251.

even more exposure, both in Australia and abroad. In spite of it having a very similar plot, the appearance of the 1971 film *Walkabout* didn't seem to affect the success of *A Waltz through the Hills*.[43] The joint production of Western Australia's Barron Films, Britain's Primetime Films and America's Wonderworks gave it strong global coverage. The string of prizes the film picked up only added to its prestige and popularity that indirectly reflected on Glaskin.[44] Before he died Glaskin saw at least one of his books appear on the screen. Although he had his differences with producer Paul Barron over terms of payment and his choice of Englishman John Goldsmith as scriptwriter, Glaskin was delighted with the result and with Ernie Dingo's performance in particular. He brought out the qualities Glaskin wanted to imbue in his lead Aboriginal character – humour, depth, compassion and more. Said an enthusiastic, almost fawning, Glaskin, 'I think he is Australia's best male actor, and he just happens to be an Aboriginal.'[45]

An interesting and telling footnote to *A Waltz through the Hills* occurred during Glaskin's research for the book. He had come to know an Aboriginal footballer in Perth, Bruce Williams. Williams agreed to accompany Glaskin on a trip throughout the southwest of the state to check out the route he was to use for the children's trek to the city. One experience stayed with him forever. It happened in Katanning, a town on the Great Southern Highway 280 kilometres southeast of Perth. Presumably Williams was familiar with the Aboriginal community in the district, even though it was a little farther south of the area in which Glaskin set *A Waltz through the Hills*. When they arrived in town, they headed straight for the Aboriginal reserve, which Glaskin was surprised to find he wasn't permitted to enter. But as if to balance the scales, when he tried to book the two of them into a hotel for

---

43 In August 1969, GMG was shocked when he learnt that work was underway to film *Walkabout*, adapted from a novel of the same name by James Vance Marshall. The story involves a 14-year-old girl and her six-year-old brother lost in the Australian bush. They are discovered and aided by a young Aboriginal who is undergoing his rite of passage to adulthood. GMG immediately notified contacts in London and asked them to check on the information. He acted as if he had never heard of the film or the book, even though the latter was published in the mid-1950s. GMG claimed that his idea for *A Waltz through the Hills* came from a newspaper article about two children lost in the bush that family friend Ruby Weatherall gave him. She typed the manuscript and GMG dedicated the book to her. LvdP to JB, personal communication, 23 June 2010.

44 The prizes included the 1988 Australian Bicentennial PATER Award for Best Children's Drama, the 1988 Chicago International Festival of Children's Films First Prize for Children's Drama, the 1989 Australian Penguin Award for Excellence (Children's Drama), as well as Ernie Dingo's award for Best Actor in a Telefeature for his role as Frank Smith.

45 Lenton (1988, 41).

the night, the licensee made it clear that Williams was not welcome in his establishment. Ironically, Glaskin himself received similar treatment when he trekked around the north of Australia with Paul Lee. He had developed such a dark tan that he could have been taken for an Aboriginal. When he and Lee stopped at a pub near Tennant Creek, the barman wouldn't talk to him because he thought Glaskin was an Aboriginal. Said Lee with a smile. 'But they would talk to me, a Chinese. I couldn't believe it!'[46]

The poignancy of these experiences was not lost on Glaskin, who included several instances of racial discrimination in his novel. In one incident, in answer to one of Andy's numerous and persistent questions, Smith explains why he had been incarcerated on several occasions. One of these occurred when he and his sister, Daisy, had just arrived in Perth and were looking for a place to stay. A white man started harassing Daisy. He wouldn't take no for an answer, so Smith delivered a few well-placed blows that left the man with two black eyes and a broken nose. Smith received a six-month gaol sentence for his efforts while his opponent scored just one week. The injustice of the situation riles the young boy. 'It's not fair! It's just not fair!' he rages.[47]

Glaskin's other novel with significant Aboriginal content is *Flight to Landfall*. Although none of the main characters is Aboriginal, they appear at many points in the story and are pivotal in the eventual rescue of those who survive their agonising ordeal. Glaskin goes out of his way to emphasise aspects of Aboriginal culture in this book, adopting a rather didactic tone in places, as though he is trying to teach the reader as much as he can about Aboriginal traditions. He does this largely through the central character of Dirk van Dooren and his wife Fiona. Van Dooren is the Dutch pilot who takes the party to Australia, survives the crash and eventually marries his first wife's old school friend, the young Englishwoman Fiona Scott-Fraser, the other remaining survivor. They settle down, build a home and raise a family in the very place that was their refuge after the crash. Aware that they owe their lives to a group of Aboriginal people who appeared at the moment they were most desperate, the van Doorens have become firm believers in Aboriginal mythology, folklore and bushcraft. In so doing, they display a remarkably enlightened attitude towards indigenous Australians for their time.

When Harry, the one Aboriginal who speaks some English, goes off with van Dooren to the nearest station for help, Fiona is left in the company

---

46 Lee to JB, interview, 12 November 2002.
47 GMG (1961a, 185).

of the remaining Aboriginals. She is terrified of them, both because she thinks they might be dangerous and because she might catch some terrible disease from them. She is beside herself and fears losing her sanity. Just as she is about to commit suicide by jumping from the top of the gorge, an Aboriginal woman rescues her. The woman is accompanied by a young girl with a dislocated shoulder, which the woman indicates she wants Fiona to fix. Pulled back from the brink of death, Fiona finds a purpose in life as she tends to the child's needs. Over time she comes to regard the old woman as her mother, a far cry from the day she first encountered her as 'a filthy, disgusting, subhuman species of creature.'[48] And not just a surrogate mother to replace her cold, distant and deceased English mother, but her 'spirit mother'. Just before her spirit mother dies, she foretells her death by announcing to Fiona that the rainbow serpent is coming to take her spirit away. As she predicted, death claims the old woman, with a rainbow signalling her demise. Amid incessant wailing of mourning relatives Fiona goes to be with her 'mother', who is still dressed in filthy rags crawling with flies. In a simple but symbolic gesture, Fiona takes the old woman's 'dirty claw of a hand' and presses it to her cheek. Once again, the chasm between black and white has been bridged.

Dirk van Dooren is equally sensitive to the presence of Aboriginal people in this place he calls a sanctuary, which he has come to regard as home. But not his home in the usual sense of the word. He politely explains to a visiting writer, 'I hope you will understand me, but we consider this as their home, not ours. In a way, we are really just guests here ourselves.' In similar vein, his young daughter says of her garden, 'I didn't plant it myself. It's always been there. It's just that I look after it so I call it mine.'[49] The Aboriginal notion of not possessing the land but being guardians of it and all it contains is a message Glaskin repeats throughout the book. But, as van Dooren points out, if anyone were deemed to be owners of the land it would be the original inhabitants, not more recent arrivals like himself. Furthermore, in a reference to Aboriginal spirituality, van Dooren says, 'they have something so few of us whites ever have – an instinctive knowledge of truth. They don't have to make themselves believe in a god. They don't need an act of faith. The reason is simple; they never doubt or forget it for a moment … They just know, everything from a star to a grain of sand – which are perhaps the same things. This is something most of us are unable to learn, with all

48 GMG (1963, 372 UK edition; 1980, 320 US edition).
49 Ibid. (1963, 69 UK edition; 1980, 39 US edition).

our so-called intelligence.'[50] Van Dooren has mixed feelings about attempts by missionaries and educators to change the Aboriginal way of life, but he makes a strong case for honouring their traditions and trying as much as possible to incorporate them into the present.

Given that Glaskin wrote this in the early 1960s, when Aboriginal assimilation into mainstream Australia was still an accepted goal by many, and before the emergence of a mature Aboriginal land rights movement, it was plain where his sympathies lay on the questions of Aboriginal self-determination and cultural integrity. But his propensity to lecture his readers on these issues meant that Glaskin wrote more than he needed, at least in the eyes of some of his critics and even his admirers. One of those was Hope Dellon, an editor at St. Martin's Press in New York, which republished *Flight to Landfall* in 1980, 17 years after its original British publication. Although Dellon praised the book as having some of the most mesmerising story telling she had ever read, she found the first two sections a bit slow and old-fashioned and offered to help Glaskin rework them.[51] Dellon pruned a lot of Glaskin's colloquialisms, historical data not directly relevant to the plot, extraneous diversions, and references to Aboriginal culture and its adaptation to station life. The result was the US edition is 44 pages shorter than the UK edition. Glaskin appreciated her editing skills and acknowledged these in the book.

Dellon's interest in the book was no doubt triggered by the success of its publication by Reader's Digest Condensed Books (RDCB) in a number of European and Commonwealth countries. St. Martin's in turn sold the American rights to RDCB (USA) for $20,000, half of which went to Glaskin. Although he had to endure having his book condensed from 450 to 100 pages, Glaskin acknowledged that this allowed him to reach an entirely different public who otherwise might never have read the book. What's more, *Flight to Landfall* became a windfall at a time in his life when he was in financial straits, due to the aggravation of his war injuries by his surfing accident, which severely restricted his ability to write. The RDCB version sold in 14 editions in 10 languages and although he only earned a few cents per copy this resulted in a healthy sum over a period of several years, given that at least 850,000 copies were published. Combine this with advances and royalties he received from the original British edition, St. Martin's payment, translations into Dutch and French, reprints, Public Lending Rights and

---

50   Ibid. (1963, 67 UK edition and 1980, 39 US edition).
51   Hope Dellon to David Bolt, n.d.

five film options, *Flight* may well have been his most commercially successful book.[52]

Dellon wasn't the only American who sniffed a winner for the US market. *Kirkus Reviews* singled it out as a particularly noteworthy book with 'lots of ripe, hot description, even more satisfying character development … a sweet, scary, earthy saga' and *Publishers Weekly* described it as 'haunting'.[53] The film producer, Edward Meyers, was in raptures over it – 'brilliantly written … a compelling and sensitive story … a novel for all times and all seasons' – although he never managed to find the funding for making it into a film.[54] The British press accorded the original version similar accolades. *Books and Bookmen* stamped it with the cliché 'unputdownable' and lauded Glaskin for stepping 'right into Nevil Shute's shoes'.[55] But local critics weren't so kind. One in particular, Tom Hungerford, didn't buy it at all, not least because of the association with Shute, whose writing he despised. Hungerford likened Glaskin's descriptive prose to chestnuts borrowed from fourth-grade composition and accused him of plagiarising a phrase from Randolph Stow's *To the Islands*.[56] He maintained 'There is no humour and little drama which one has not encountered a dozen times before, and the characters have barely one dimension.'[57]

This marked divergence of opinion between foreign and local critics was typical of the reception Glaskin received for many of his books. Generally, the former praised his work and the latter were much less enthusiastic about it. In this case, the strong Australian content seemed to find favour with foreign readers, possibly because it fulfilled the fantasies many foreigners had about Australia. As harsh as Hungerford's critique is, it is the only one I could find from Australian sources. Perhaps if the book had been published in Australia as well as in the UK and the USA it may have attracted more local attention. This was an issue Glaskin faced with most of his 20 publications.

---

52 The 850,000 figure is a conservative estimate of the total sales of the RDCB editions of *Flight* based on GMG's notes and letters. I suspect the actual number is quite higher. I estimate his gross income from *Flight* to be approximately A$50,000.

53 No author listed, *Kirkus Reviews* (1980) and Bannon (1980, 43).

54 Edward Meyers to Douglas Rae (GMG's London-based film agent), 31 October 1977.

55 N.B. (1964, 32).

56 In the original UK version of *Flight to Landfall*, GMG wrote 'a soul is a strange, strange country' (114) and in the later US edition he changed it to 'And I thought to myself, as had Rilke, a soul is indeed a strange country' (65). In *To the Islands* Stow wrote 'My soul,' he whispered, over the sea-surge, 'my soul is a strange country.' In GMG's copy of Stow's book, he underlined these words and wrote beneath them 'Aber mein [sic] Seele ist ein fremder [sic] Land. Erik Maria Rilke? Schiller?' So it seems that Stow himself may have borrowed it.

57 Hungerford (1964, 21).

One other piece of writing displays Glaskin's interest in Australia's relationship to its Aboriginal people. The not-so-short short story *The Road to Nowhere*, included in his anthology of the same name, fictionalises an episode that he and Paul Lee experienced in their overland journey chronicled in *The Land That Sleeps*. Lee recalled that moment with a glint of terror in his eye. 'We were going around in circles. We kept saying, "That's the same windmill we just saw". Eventually we found our way back to the main road. I think we reached Brooking Springs station about half past six. They were expecting us late morning and had already sent out a search party.'[58] In like fashion, a Perth couple becomes lost in a maze of tracks on a Kimberley station property. They are running low on petrol and water and encounter the usual hazards of outback driving – bulldust, massive potholes, irritating flies, searing day heat and night cold. At the previous town they are advised to take the back road rather than the high road because of cattle movement, but this proves their undoing. Their last sight of humans is Aboriginal people at Quongdong station. Their situation becomes perilous and they are about to take their own lives when they notice a piece of paper stuck on a board at a windmill. They discover they have been caught in a triangular maze and are at the abandoned Maggie's Hope, a lot closer to Quongdong than they had imagined. They make it to the top of a rise, see the station, a puff of smoke and a lone Aboriginal. The husband fires his rifle to attract the attention of the Aboriginal and their torment is over.

The story feeds on the familiar themes of 'lost in the outback' and 'saved by Aboriginals' and projects attitudes and stereotypes of that time by many white Australians towards Aboriginal people. 'You should see your face! I couldn't tell you now from a flaming nigger, if one were to come along', said the wife to her husband.[59] And, in an inference of implied hostility by Aboriginals towards whites, she says, 'What I don't understand is why some of those damned gins at that last homestead didn't stop us from going on, if we were taking the wrong road. They just sat there, all gabbing in a circle. And even if they couldn't speak any English at all, which I think all abos can these days, then they could have at least made a sign.'[60] Given that this book was published in 1967, the year of the referendum that ensured the rights of Aboriginal Australians were protected under federal laws, Glaskin accurately mirrored the dismal state of race relations in Australia at the

---

58 Lee to JB, interview, 12 November 2002.
59 GMG (1967b, 239).
60 Ibid., 236.

time.[61] Perhaps he had been affected by the murmurings of an indigenous movement for equal rights symbolised in the strike on Wave Hill Station in the Northern Territory by the Gurindji people in 1966. Perhaps, too, as a gay man, he identified in an indirect way with Aboriginal people. The two groups both knew what it was to be marginalised and regarded as less than human by mainstream Australia.

Throughout his career, Glaskin distinguished between his purely enter-tainment novels – such as *A Change of Mind* and *The Man Who Didn't Count*, which lent towards fantasy and romanticism – and his more serious works. With him, it was usually either 'just a story' or 'a book of importance'. However, his Asian triad seem to fit somewhere in between, which maybe is one reason why the books sold so well. Like most of Glaskin's works, they exude an undercurrent of a message as well as tell a good tale. He espoused many themes, but his greatest passion he reserved for two that were close to his heart and all-pervading in his life – love, particularly same-sex love, and loneliness.

---

61 The 1967 referendum did two things – granted the Commonwealth Government the power to legislate with respect to Aboriginal people, and included them in all censuses. The right of Aboriginal people to vote had been accorded in legislation enacted in 1962 (1965 for Queensland). However, many of the rights assumed by citizenship were denied Aboriginal people and in some states legislated against.

Chapter 9

Love

Perhaps his most brilliant and touching book was O, Love.

David Bolt

If Chapter Six in *No End to the Way* is any kind of clue, Glaskin's earliest introduction to the mysterious world of male sexuality was brutally frank yet couched in a caring, perhaps even loving, relationship. In retrospect, he was probably lucky. It could have been a lot worse and for many young boys growing up in 1920s Australia it undoubtedly was. Sex was something you didn't talk about in general conversation; only behind the back of the school toilet or late at night in camp tents in sniggers and lurid jokes. Usually, it was older boys passing on their worldly wisdom – invariably lacking in accuracy but heavily laced with bravado – to the naïve younger ones. More often than not, it was a neighbourhood friend or visiting relative who performed the act of initiation on the gullible and unsuspecting young male.

Glaskin's fictionalised account of his own dawning of sexual consciousness is a classic example.[1] Uncle Kev, the 16-year-old younger brother of his father, lures his innocent nephew behind the grapevines in the backyard of Grandma's house, undoes his trouser buttons and shows 'it' to him. The five-year-old is awestruck at the size of his uncle's member and wonders if his will ever grow that large. Uncle Kev begs him to touch it, hold it, move it up and down. He knows something is wrong about all this but he can't resist. Suddenly, Uncle Kev gasps and his throbbing appendage erupts

---

1   LvdP recollects GMG telling him that his first sexual encounter was with an older boy, but not a relative. LvdP to JB, personal communication, 23 June 2010.

like a volcano, leaving a gooey white mess for him to clean up with his handkerchief. This was the beginning of a long series of such moments, secret moments just between the two of them. Uncle Kev commands his nephew not to tell anyone and his accomplice swears not to do so. God only knows what might happen if anyone ever finds out. The two become a familiar site in the backyard, digging, gardening and doing you-know-what.

Then one weekend when his parents go away and leave him with Grandma things take an unexpected turn. Uncle Kev invites him into his bed and cuddles and kisses the young boy, more than his own mother and father ever do. He relishes this affection until Uncle Kev starts doing something to him that hurts so badly he wants to cry out. But it's no use. Grandma is deaf and sleeping on the other side of the house. Uncle Kev relents for a while and then tries again. Eventually, his nephew submits to the pain and ceases to struggle. 'You've got to do it to become a man', Uncle Kev tells him, and he believes it. Over time, as the invitations to stay with Uncle Kev increase and as the boy matures into a young man, his bond with his uncle solidifies into what he calls 'love'. When Uncle Kev is killed in a motor cycle accident, the boy cries his heart out, night after night, week after week. He vows never to tell anyone about his special secret with Uncle Kev. There will never be anyone else to replace him. Well, at least not for a while.

Somewhere in the midst of this graphic, if familiar, tale is a kernel of truth extracted from the life of Gerald Glaskin. He reportedly did have a sexual encounter with a relative at a very early age and no doubt with other boys as he journeyed through primary and high school, in addition to his own admitted experiences at Boy Scout camps and later in the navy.[2] Glaskin's fascination with sexuality and his own struggle to define himself as homosexual, bisexual, or more humorously and perhaps more aptly, trisexual – try anything at least twice in case you don't like it the first time – led him to attempt a trilogy of books on sexuality. The first of these was the novella, *O Love*, which relates an affair between Ralph Thompson, a successful, well-to-do, 40-year-old Perth lawyer who lives alone and 13-year-old Connie Williams, recently arrived from the eastern states. Connie is extremely childlike – she cuts out paper dolls – except when it comes to sex. They soon quarrel and Connie spurns Ralph, who goes to her residence and chances upon Connie having it off with Derek, whom she had told Ralph was her 'husband' but later confesses is her brother. Thompson quickly realises that he can never compete with 'this young Greek-god of a youth' and backs

2   See Chapter 3, 'Gerald in Wonderland'.

off. But when Derek is apprehended and beaten by the police on an assault charge, Thompson comes to his aid. Meanwhile, Connie becomes pregnant and wants to keep the child but is forced to give it up for adoption. She ends up in a welfare home and is forced to attend school, while Derek is imprisoned for two years.

Incest, prostitution, sexual exploitation of minors, dysfunctional families and poverty – they are all part of this 85-page novella. They are also all part of a vicious cycle that reflects society's lack of social compassion and pre-occupation with commercialism and personal gratification. This is Glaskin the preacher once again, delivering one of his sermons through the vehicle of short fiction. While refraining from judging Thompson's personal morality and behaviour, Glaskin heaps coals on a society that breeds situations such as this. 'But it was an environment concocted for them by the commercial avarice of that very generation which condemned them. Perverse humanity!'[3] This is the same environment whose threat of nuclear war and annihilation of the human race may be heightening a sense of insecurity in teenagers, causing them to have more sex and produce children at an earlier age than ever before – a doomsday scenario spelt out by a nurse friend of Thompson whom he persuades to assist Connie.

In the midst of this mess, Thompson has an epiphany about his relation-ship to Connie. 'But with me she was still a child, even if I were her lover. But such an elderly lover. I had long since realised this, and knew the role I was intended to play – that of a father.'[4] This dramatic change of gear on Thompson's part emanates a sense of compassion that was absent in his earlier dealings with Connie. Then it was uninhibited lust and an infatuation with her girlish habits that drove him to pursue her. He didn't even pretend to call it love. 'I had long ago learned that I lacked the capacity to love. I may have had it once but not any more. Not any more, for a long time now. This has long been my regret; a maladjustment which I recognize and to which, over the years, I have had laboriously to adjust myself.'[5]

O Love reveals a longing for the lost glory of youth and Glaskin's obses-sion with the physical beauty of the human form, both male and female. It is titillating yet depressing. As with many of Glaskin's books, it is written in a rather didactic, forceful style, as if he wants to make sure that the reader really understands what he is driving at. He wrote it in May 1961 on the high seas between Fremantle and London. Glaskin enjoyed writing on board ship

3   GMG (1964, 90).
4   Ibid., 65.
5   Ibid., 29.

and did much of it on his many voyages between Australia and Europe. Perhaps it was something about being set free from the ceaseless demands of daily life that allowed his mind to cast adrift and float to places it would otherwise not venture. The novella was published three years later in 1964 together with its complementary story, *O Loneliness*. Some have likened it to Nabokov's *Lolita*, which was first published in France in 1955. Nabokov was one of Glaskin's favourite writers but Glaskin did not try to emulate Nabokov's aesthetic style of prose, nor did he share Nabokov's passionate rejection of the idea of fiction as a vehicle for social and moral comment. *O Love* is a case in point.

While Glaskin had no pretensions that *O Love* was a work of genius, it did win praise from some quarters. His British agent, David Bolt, described it as 'perhaps his most brilliant and touching book'.[6] David Martin, reviewing it in *The Bulletin*, found it to be the strongest fiction he had read in months. He was especially impressed with Glaskin's portrayal of Connie, which he described as 'outlined with remarkable economy'. He contrasts her character with Nabokov's Lolita, in that though she behaves like a child, she is a woman who has a profound effect on the man who seduces her and thus avoids becoming a psychological cliché. Martin's only regret is that the story is too short — he would have liked Glaskin to project Ralph into more varied conflict situations. But this aside, he found the story had 'a beautiful unity and a powerful after-swing … written with poise and inner conviction'. Then, with a comment that could not be made about much of Glaskin's writing, he noted, 'It is a tale that takes sides without labouring its background'.[7]

O Love also attracted considerable attention in the film world in the UK, the USA and Australia. First to show interest was British producer Ronnie Shedlo, but when Jonathan Cape published *Baby Love* by Tina Chad Christian, which has a similar story line, Shedlo lost interest. In an attempt to entice other producers, Glaskin wrote his own screenplay of the book but he never seemed to be able to crack the winning formula as a scriptwriter. However, through a serendipitous series of events, things began to fall into place. In England, a young technical director, Roy Stevens, who had worked in Australia with director Fred Schepisi on filming *The chant of Jimmy Blacksmith*, decided to try his hand as producer/director for the first time. Steven's wife had found a copy of *O Love, O Loneliness* on a market stall and

---

6   David Bolt to JB, personal communication, 6 December 2001.
7   Martin (1965, 40).

he wanted to film it. Stevens convinced the Australian Film Development Corporation (AFDC) to give him a grant, most of which went to the then London-based Australian Alan Seymour to write the script.

Seymour was a highly successful writer, producer and editor for both radio and television, as well as novelist, playwright and theatre critic. He worked for both the Australian Broadcasting Commission (now Corporation) and the BBC for many years, and is perhaps best known in Australia for his controversial play, *The One Day of the Year*.[8] Seymour also knew Glaskin from days of yore in Perth. Their connection went back to Perth Modern School, which both Seymour and his partner, Ron Baddeley, attended. They later crossed paths with Glaskin in Perth's intimate gay community in the 1940s and 1950s, and connected again when Glaskin moved to Amsterdam in the early 1960s and would visit London. Seymour remembered with delight one winter's day when Glaskin favoured them with his presence at their small Chelsea flat. 'He wore a long black overcoat and a black Russian-style fur cap and looked fantastically glamorous. He happened to lob for coffee one morning just as our old Cockney cleaner-lady was leaving. As I saw her off down the stairs she whispered to me, 'Your friend is so 'andsome. Is 'e a fillum star?' I said, 'No, he is a writer.' She nodded sagely and said, 'I knew 'e was sumfink like that.'[9]

Seymour set to work on the script, using as much of Glaskin's dialogue as he could, a practice he always tried to follow when converting novels to film scripts. Although he drew mainly from *O Love*, he incorporated slight references from *O Loneliness* as well. Stevens, confident that this was going to be a winner, offered Glaskin £500 for two years against a purchase price of £6000 for the film rights. Although Glaskin's agent, David Bolt, thought this a rather paltry sum, Glaskin wasn't about to turn it down in light of his experience with film producers and signed a contract with Stevens in December 1980. Optimism was running high and there was talk of having the accomplished British actor Alan Bates in the lead. But once again Glaskin's hopes were dashed. When script assessors read what Seymour had written they had conflicting opinions about the dialogue. The AFDC decided not to proceed with the project and Stevens was not willing to risk any of his own money. Seymour was as sorry as Glaskin. 'It was a pity it was

---

8   The play premiered in Adelaide 20 July 1960. It had been chosen for inclusion in the inaugural Adelaide Arts Festival but was rejected by the Board of Governors for fear that it might cause offence to armed forces personnel for its treatment of Anzac Day commemorations. It won an Awgie Award for best television drama in 1962.

9   Alan Seymour to JB, personal communication, 24 May 2001.

never made', he said. 'It could have been a strong dramatic piece and a nice study in people, all of whom were outside mainstream Australian suburban life.'[10]

Seymour later conjectured another reason why the project was dropped. Before he started writing the script, he had lunch with a prominent member of the AFDC who made it plain to him that while female nudity was permissible, male nudity was not. Seymour was puzzled at this sexist distinction, but he could envisage how it would lead its promoter to have trouble with his script. 'He may well have found it too confronting, the queasy relationship of a very young girl, precociously mature-*looking*, thought to be 18 but turning out to be 13, in a fairly obviously exploitative sexual relationship with an older man and then a nice case of incest on top of it', said Seymour. 'If he'd read the book he should have known all that but it is quite possible he never had.'[11] Either way, the AFDC did not follow through with a second grant, and once again the film ground to a resounding halt. There was still a flicker of light at the end of the tunnel when, in 1984, the Perth-based Shepherd Baker film company renewed their film option for *O Love*. This time it was Barry Humphries who was rumoured to be favourite for the role of Ralph Thompson. While Humphries went on to become the superstar his Dame Edna persona professes to be, Glaskin and his *O Love* characters remained tucked away on dusty bookshelves, unknown and unsung.

O Love was only one part of Glaskin's proposed trilogy on sexuality. *O Loneliness*, about intergenerational incest, was another; *O Life*, about a gay relationship, was to be the third. The latter, originally titled *The Way In*, caused grave problems for his British publishers, Barrie and Rockliff. From today's vantage point, it is hard to reconcile that incest and heterosexual exploitation of minors was perfectly printable subject matter but that homosexuality was off limits. It is easy to forget that half a century ago homosexuality was still such a taboo subject in British society. Although the Wolfenden Report recommended the legalisation of homosexual relations between consenting adults in private in 1957, it was another 10 years before the Sexual Offences Act was passed to give effect to the report's proposals.

Glaskin and his publishers had a good tussle over the third member of the trilogy and in the end Barrie and Rockliff prevailed. They published *O Love, O Loneliness* as twin novellas under one cover. Glaskin wrote a second part to *The Way In* and called it *The Way Out*, titles that in themselves might

---

10   Alan Seymour to JB, personal communication, 4 September 2002.
11   Ibid.

have been a little too suggestive for some of Barrie's board members. The resulting full-length novel was retitled the rather innocuous *No End to the Way*, implying a kind of inevitable endlessness to life's journeying but giving little hint of what lay between the covers of this disarmingly honest book.[12] It is a moot point whether this title was an improvement on Barrie and Rockliff's earlier suggestion of *You Can't Get Away from It*. But even with its change of name, the book still nearly didn't make it into print. All but one of the directors did not want to publish it. However, that one director, presumably Glaskin's faithful advocate, John Bunting, exercised his power of veto and overruled the others.[13]

However, there was one caveat. Barrie and Rockliff insisted that Glaskin use a pseudonym for this book. He was reluctant to do so and equivocated for some time but finally agreed. Ostensibly, Barrie and Rockliff were concerned that a book dealing so overtly with homosexuality would tarnish Glaskin's emerging reputation as a writer. What exactly this tarnishable reputation was puzzled Glaskin. It seemed that Barrie and Rockliff were more concerned about preserving their own image than his. This was the only one of his 20 published books in which he used a pen name and he deeply regretted his decision. The notoriety *No End to the Way* achieved when it was banned in Australia might have helped sales of his other books significantly. On a more emotional note, the decision broke Glaskin's heart because he was so proud of the book.[14] However, with the benefit of hindsight he reconciled himself to the final outcome. In a 1994 interview he declared, 'if it had been *O Love, O Life, O Loneliness*, it wouldn't have sold anywhere near as much as what either one of them did altogether. And yet, both of them, *O Love, O Loneliness*, complemented themselves, focussed as stories or studies, and in reader appeal. *No End to the Way* needed to be by itself, once I had written its second half.'[15] One thing was certain. He was glad he didn't pursue the tongue-in-cheek suggestion of one Barrie and Rockliff director who said, 'Why don't you write a fourth, and then we could call it *O Love, O Life, O Loneliness, O Hell?*'[16]

---

12 GMG also uses this phrase in *Flight to Landfall*. When Fiona is called back from the brink of suicide by her Aboriginal 'mother' to care for the young girl with a dislocated shoulder, she rediscovers her vocation as a carer and is reminded that there is 'no end to the journey, no end of the way'. GMG (1963, 433 UK edition; 1980, 381 US edition).

13 Cover (1994a, 6).

14 Ibid.

15 Ibid., 10.

16 Willett (1999).

Glaskin's choice of pseudonym is intriguing as well as ambiguous. It was commonly believed that he coined the name 'Neville Jackson' to seek revenge on the legal system in Western Australia, with which he had several unpleasant encounters, and one particularly embarrassing one, in the course of his lifetime. Both Nevile (correct spelling) and Jackson were judges of the Supreme Court in Western Australia, the former from 1955 to 1970 and the latter from 1949 until 1969, when he became Chief Justice, a position he held until 1977. Although neither man was involved in Glaskin's several court appearances, they provided the symbolic face of a system Glaskin had grown to despise and a convenient target on which to vent his anger. Glaskin, however, gave an alternative explanation for his choice of name, perhaps to protect himself from possible legal repercussions. He claimed to have taken Jackson from his great-great-grandfather, Captain William Dockwary Jackson, Superintendent of Rottnest Island from 1866 to 1883.[17] As convenient as this explanation may have been, it doesn't account for Glaskin's use of 'Neville'. The former rationale would seem more in keeping with Glaskin's sharp wit and pugnacious nature.[18]

The pride Glaskin professed in *No End to the Way* is understandable. It is not pride in a finely honed piece of artistic writing with immaculate turns-of-phrase and evocative imagery; Glaskin could rarely be accused of that. Nor is it profound in the sense of exploring in depth some of life's great truths. It is Glaskin being his honest, blatant self, seeking to draw attention to something that infused his life with emotion and meaning and, simultaneously, to put the spotlight on an aspect of Australian society where the espoused principles of justice and fairness to all were all but unheard of. As Robert Hughes made plain in his epic *The Fatal Shore*, three groups in Australian society had been marginalised and dehumanised since the earliest days of convict settlement – women, Aboriginals and homosexuals.[19] More than a century and a half later, they were still relegated to second-class status in Australia. Each would make major strides in ridding themselves of their position at the bottom of the heap in the decades to come, but at the beginning of the 1960s when Glaskin was writing *No End to the Way*, inklings of self-consciousness and self-organising within these three groups were still embryonic. As far as homosexuals were concerned, things were

---

17 Cover (1994a, 9) and GMG (1975, 141).
18 Cover noted that GMG 'was far too clever to let an opportunity to target the legal system slip'. Cover to JB, personal communication, 30 October 2002.
19 Hughes (1987). See particularly Chapter Eight, 'Bunters, Mollies and Sable Brethren', 244–281.

quite bleak. It would still be 10 years before the pioneering Australian gay rights organisation Campaign Against Moral Persecution, Incorporated (CAMP, Inc.) opened its doors, and 18 years before the first Gay and Lesbian Mardi Gras was held in Sydney.

Into this arena strode Gerald Glaskin, head high and no holds barred. Once again, from the comfortable if cramped berth of an ocean liner heading west across the Indian Ocean, he started tapping out on his portable typewriter the first part of what would become *No End to the Way*. Drawing on his imagination and his own experiences, Glaskin churned out the story. When Ray Wharton, a successful Perth advertising executive, meets fair-skinned, blond-haired Dutchman Cor van Gelder in the downstairs bar of the Palais Hotel, the attraction is mutual and electric. Things seem to be going swimmingly, with regular doses of sex in the office, as well as at Cor's flat, until a friend reveals to Ray that Cor is married and his wife, Mia, is pregnant. Even worse, Cor has a sugar-daddy relationship with influential businessman Rob Hamilton. Out to destroy Cor's relationship with Ray, the jealous Hamilton offers the married couple money to return to the Netherlands, a ploy that pleases Mia and which Cor seemingly accepts. But at the last minute Cor eludes Mia and the departing ship at Fremantle. Not to be outdone, Hamilton blackmails Ray, ruining his business and his health. Cor slides into a morass of drinking, promiscuity and violence, which results in both of them being hospitalised, Ray for physical injuries inflicted on him by his Dutch lover and Cor for psychological problems. The psychiatrist treating Ray advises him that for his own safety they have bought a one-way train ticket for Cor to Sydney. Ray and Cor have a final blissful 20 minutes together at a friend's flat before parting forever. After dabbling in another unsuccessful gay relationship Cor moves to Queensland, where he marries a woman 'who understands' and whose father owns a string of chain stores, one of which Cor will manage. Ray goes to Hong Kong, where he finds a 'little Chinese friend' who reads his palm and tells him he will live a long life.

This graphic – but not pornographic – portrayal of a gay relationship in 1960s Perth captures a time and place with which many gay men from that era easily identify. The Palais Hotel is a makeover of the once-famous Palace Hotel, whose downstairs bar was the premier watering hole and gathering node of Perth's gay fraternity for decades. Although the hotel no longer exists, its façade remains today as part of the Bankwest tower, one of Perth's tallest buildings on the corner of William Street and St Georges Terrace. But during the 1940s and 1950s, it wasn't up but down that gay men looked as they entered the Palace. As if symbolic of their place in the social order, they would descend from the main saloon bar down the staircase to the basement with its horseshoe-shaped bar, the 'gay' bar. Other hotels such as the Savoy and the Shaftesbury sometimes attracted gay clientele but none rivalled the Palace. As one regular put it, 'If you didn't go to the Palace Hotel, you didn't exist.'[20]

Friday and Saturday nights were prime time at The Palace and with early closing hours the bar served as a place for men to meet, survey the crowd, maybe pick up someone for the evening or make plans to go on to a private home for an impromptu party. A peculiarity of The Palace was that it attracted men from a wide cross-section of Perth society – as well as interstate and overseas travellers – from workmen with dirt under their fingernails to double-breasted suiters from jarrah-pannelled offices on the Terrace. Sexual attraction knows no borders and The Palace was no exception. The toilets at the rear of the hotel, affectionately known as 'the bog', were notorious for the frenzied activity that took place within their four walls. Police raids were not unknown and it was rumoured that police even took out the lights and replaced them with infrared cameras to record the goings-on. More than one man ran foul of the law there but one in particular caused gossip to fly around the downstairs bar for months afterwards. He was a member of the Senate of the University of Western Australia, a high-profile philanthropist, an artist of renown with a gallery that bore his name, and had a knighthood to boot. Not to mention that he was respectably married. Because of his stature and connections in Perth society, his embarrassing arrest was hushed up.

Not only locations but many of Glaskins characters in *No End to the Way* were also drawn from real life. The few changes of name he used required little imagination to decode, especially if the reader happened to be familiar with Perth's close-knit gay community in the 1950s and 1960s. It is no wonder that the book caused quite a stir in the city when it was released. As one of Glaskin's friends so delicately put it, 'There were some people in Perth who would like to have seen Gerry's body washed up in the river because of that book.'[21] One of those would have been Sidney Davis. A government draftsman and theatre set designer-cum-director, Sidney Davis was by all accounts a competent and intelligent man, but his personal style left something to be desired. He was convinced that with the right amount

20 Murray Mason to JB, personal communication, 19 September 2001.
21 Ibid.

of charm and persuasion, he could entice any man to have sex with him. As one of his contemporaries reflected, 'nobody was safe because it was the lure of the conquest with him.' On the fourth page of the book, using the barely disguised name of Sid Needham, Glaskin paints a portrait of the man that could only be described as unflattering at best.

> So back to the bars you look, and almost straight away you see Sid Needham, squashed – or rather squashing himself – in between two groups where it's easy to see he's got a prospect in each, and hasn't yet made up his mind on which to pounce ... he still looks the same as ever, dapper under his wavy hair, forever grinning those intimidating leers of his, his eyes skidding and plundering around the room all the time ... Impossible to think that he was the first one to seduce you, when you were just 18 ... But Sid is nearly always the first to seduce everyone. It's his specialty. Takes 'em once – or maybe twice or a few times, just to make sure they're so far gone in the game they'll never get out of it again – and then tosses them into the circle.[22]

Although Glaskin acknowledged that his characters were often drawn from real life, he maintained that invariably they were composites of two or more people. However, in this case there was a strong consensus among gay men in Perth at the time that the character of Needham was Davis. The likenesses were too numerous and too close fitting to be anyone else. When asked to describe their recollections of Davis, his contemporaries didn't hesitate to spew venom on the man. 'Poisonous', 'wicked', 'vicious', 'dangerous', 'backstabber' came rolling off their tongues. Said one observer, 'If he could say an ill word about somebody, he would.'[23] If anyone had doubts about the Needham-Davis connection, Davis himself did not. When the book hit Perth, an acquaintance tipped off Davis that a pen portrait of him was in it. Davis read it and was enraged. When Davis met Glaskin sparks flew. But Davis' vehemence was more than matched by Glaskin's eloquence and wit.

It happened early one afternoon as Glaskin was coming out of the fashionable Luis restaurant down by the Esplanade where he had been lunching with friends. Davis decided to start small and work up. 'Been writing any good books lately?' he inquired. To which Glaskin replied with a smirk, 'Sidney, have you been trying on caps and find they fit?'[24] They

22 Jackson (1965, 15).
23 James Glance to JB, personal communication, 20 November 2002.
24 LvdP to JB, personal communication, 27 April 2003.

fitted all too well and Davis threatened to sue Glaskin. But Davis was caught in a bind. If he dared take legal action, he would be admitting to being the abominable, lecherous seducer of young men and boys that Glaskin painted him to be in the book. Glaskin relished the Catch-22 situation in which Davis found himself. Recalling it later to a friend he said, 'Can you imagine the court case? "How do you know this is you?" Davis would be asked to prove. "Well, it says that I seduce young boys and I've got beady eyes and ..."' Glaskin roared with laughter.[25] What's more, Glaskin had history on his side. Davis had few others he could appeal to in the gay community to support him in the matter. As an acquaintance of both Glaskin and Davis pointed out, 'We've got to remember that this was the early '60s and the gay movement wasn't a movement and we didn't even use the word gay'.[26]

Surprisingly, the person who probably had most reason to hold a grudge against Glaskin for using him as the basis for a character in the novel was fairly blasé about it, at least 35 years later. In the 1960s, Ken Sutherland had the unique distinction of being a professor of dentistry at the University of Western Australia and a maker of chocolates, a rare and somewhat puzzling combination of talents. In justifying his twin passions, Sutherland commented wryly, 'It would have been immoral of me not to make work for my students when they graduate!' Sutherland was alerted to the fact that he appeared in *No End to the Way* when a friend called one morning to say, 'Neil and I have been reading a book and we think you're in it!'[27]

Sutherland didn't even have to read the book because he knew what was coming. But as he turned page after page, he found his life staring back at him under the Ocker-sounding name of Bruce Farnham, familiarly referred to as 'Old Bruce', a professor of biochemistry at the University of Western Australia. Farnham is a buoyant soul who can always be relied on to come to Ray's aid. He first revealed Cor's marital situation to Ray and is there at the end when Ray and Cor part after a violent interlude. Old Bruce is the glue that holds the story together. Ever the gentleman, Sutherland's reaction to the news was one of polite protest. 'I had no problem with Gerry using me in the book, except the reference to chocolate making. I was the new dean of the science faculty and on a number of committees. There was no mistaking this professor who made chocolates! I even made them for the

25 Kevin Pearce to JB, interview by author, 21 November 2002.
26 David Hough to JB, interview by author, 19 November 2002.
27 Ken Sutherland to JB, personal communication, 20 September 2001.

governor and his wife, who were good friends of mine. Fortunately, there were no repercussions for me as a result of the book being published.'[28]

It was fortunate indeed, because he had much to lose if his cover had been blown by this book. Sutherland came to Perth from Melbourne in 1953 to occupy the chair of dentistry at the University of Western Australia. He came with some reluctance since he had to give up a lucrative partnership in facial surgery he had just begun in Collins Street. He had been in Western Australia during the war as a dentist with the Royal Australian Air Force, so he had an inkling of what he was coming to. He was not only skilled at his profession but amiable and diplomatic as well. He soon found himself chairing committees and taking on more and more responsibilities outside of teaching and research. By the time he retired, his qualifications looked like a string of computer code after his name – MBBS, MDSC, LDS, FDSRCSED, FDSRCS, FRACDS, FACD, FICD. Not only was he busy running the dental school, he was on a hospital board of management, president of the Dental Board for 16 years, inaugural chairman of the Australian Dental Examining Council and president of the International College of Dentists. Even after retiring, Sutherland continued lecturing for two years because his successor was hospitalised. Outside academia, he became the founding Grand Master of the local chapter of Delta Sigma Delta, an alumni organisation of dentists loosely based on the principles of Freemasonry.[29] The chapter established the annual Sutherland Oration in his honour. It was little surprise then that in 1979 Sutherland was awarded the Member of the Order of Australia. The person who presented him with the award was his friend Sir Wallace Kyle, Governor of Western Australia. When Sutherland first came to Perth from Melbourne, he was warned about the difference between the two cities by Malcolm Kosh, a gay journalist from Perth whom he had met in Melbourne. His advice seemed sound. 'You've got a big job in a small community where everybody talks to everybody', said Kosh. 'You've got to be very, very careful. Don't try and do anything except through direct contacts.'[30] In 1956 Sutherland mentioned to Kosh that he was planning

---

28 Ibid.
29 According to Sutherland, Delta Sigma Delta has little to do with Freemasonry. It started in Ann Arbor, Michigan, USA, in 1882. The name was a transposition of the letters DDS, Doctor of Dental Surgery. In 1927 Australian Bill Tuckfield, who had been introduced to fraternities while doing post-graduate work in the United States, established the first chapter in Victoria. Chapters eventually formed in all Australian states. Membership is by invitation only by secret ballot of existing members. Although it has its own rituals, it is not religious or sectarian. It is an honour bestowed on a member by his peers.
30 Sutherland to JB, interview by author, 14 November 2002.

to go to Singapore during the Christmas holidays. Kosh said he had a good friend from Perth who worked there and could give him some useful contacts. His friend was planning to come down towards the end of the year, so Kosh promised to introduce Sutherland to him.

The occasion for their meeting was one of the regular Saturday night parties held at the magnificent riverside home of one of Perth's well-known gay couples, Eddy and Claude. Kosh arranged for Sutherland to meet Glaskin first at a nearby hotel for a drink and from there they would proceed to the party. 'Gerry was very professional and extremely businesslike about everything and I began to wonder what was going on', said Sutherland. 'But once we arrived at the party and he'd had a few drinks, he didn't pull any punches. He was doing all sorts of naughty things. He was a lovely-looking man and chasing after whatever he could get.'[31]

Evidently Glaskin was getting quite a bit, especially in Singapore, since he furnished Sutherland with plentiful contacts and helpful tips for his three-week splurge. One of the most memorable of Glaskin's referrals was to Lim Yew Hin, the attractive young manager of the Cathay Hotel, of whom Glaskin said, 'If you don't want to go to bed with him the first night, there's something wrong with you.' Sutherland was not disappointed, not only with Lim but with the hotel itself, which had a backdoor entrance that made late night returns wonderfully inconspicuous. Like Glaskin, Sutherland loved Singapore at that time. It was not the clinical, modern glass and steel city it has become. Bazaars and outdoor markets thronged its myriad alleyways and the tantalising aromas of sizzling satay and pungent stir-fries enveloped you at every turn. Moreover, for the gay tourist it was paradise. You could walk down Brasbasah Road or wander around the Padang and take your pick from the array of willing young men of many different hues – Malay, Chinese, Indian or Arab. It was a feast for the senses in the fullest sense of the term.

After this initial introduction, Sutherland didn't have a lot of contact with Glaskin over the years. However, when they lived in neighbouring suburbs Glaskin would sometimes invite Sutherland over for a cup of coffee. Glaskin wouldn't say a lot but let Sutherland do most of the talking. He later realised that Glaskin was using these occasions as grist for his mill in writing *No End to the Way*. When Sutherland read the book he was astonished how much of his speech was in there word for word. 'My god, I used to say those things!' he said. 'For example, I used to travel quite a lot to the eastern states because

---

31 Ibid.

of my work, which was unusual in those days. I would often say "I get into a plane like catching a bus to Fremantle". That ended up in that damn book.'[32] But Sutherland didn't begrudge Glaskin using him in this way. He enjoyed his company and found him highly intelligent and well read.

However, there was one occasion when Glaskin didn't impress Sutherland. It was not due to his presence but rather his absence. Sutherland had invited about seven or eight people for dinner. All had arrived except Glaskin. He didn't phone either. Sutherland was perplexed. Eventually, he decided to start dinner, thinking Glaskin would show up at any minute. They wound their way through several courses and came to dessert. Still no Glaskin. The party ebbed to a close and the guests left. Then, in the early hours of the morning the telephone rang. Glaskin and his lover, Joop, had had a huge argument that had developed into a brawl on the street. Glaskin had been injured and couldn't come to the party. Joop, however, was feeling like some company so Sutherland invited him over to spend the night. This episode formed the basis of the final knock-down-drag-out scene in *No End to the Way* between Ray and Cor, embroidered as the story demanded but essentially transposed from real life to the printed page. Glaskin was doing what he did best as a novelist and Sutherland was his willing, if unconscious, helper.

Contrary to what its title implies, *No End to the Way* does have an ending and a significant one at that. Both Ray and Cor go on to rebuild their lives in other places and with other people. It may be a sad ending of the relationship between the two that seemed so idyllic in its earlier stages but it isn't the traditional tragic ending that became the hallmark of many gay novels of its time and before. Just in case the reader didn't perceive this for himself, Glaskin makes a point of telling him so. 'Most gays you know *don't* finish up on guillotines or getting hung or shooting themselves or jumping off cliffs … What does happen, and what's almost as bad, is that they no sooner get started on an affair than it gets broken up, somehow or other, and they just drift out of it again … No guillotines or anything – just drift – and everything such a waste.' But to ensure that he doesn't give the impression that all gay relationships end up this way either, Glaskin notes that there are some couples who stay together for decades. They are the lucky ones or those who have the fortitude to see them through the long haul. To round up his little sermon he writes, 'it takes a good deal of character to be a decent homosexual.'[33]

---

32 Ibid.
33 Jackson (1965, 231).

His insistence on a non-tragic ending to this novel was not just a reaction to a trend in gay fiction to which Glaskin objected. He also claimed it was his way of defying the British Home Office that delayed the publication of the book due to the 'absence of the obligatory tragic ending by death of the main protagonist'.[34] This statement, which sounds quite puzzling, even absurd, to modern ears, shows just how deeply Britain was still mired in Victorian mores when it came to acceptance of homosexuality. Since homosexuality between consenting adults in private was still a crime in Britain, any story that failed to punish its characters for committing this illegal act was deemed to be glorifying and promoting it and hence breaking the law.

Glaskin wasn't the only author to run into this brick wall. The celebrated English writer E. M. Forster was faced with the same situation with his gay masterpiece *Maurice*. He was so emphatic that *Maurice* have a happy ending that he was prepared to wait until after his death and until Britain had legalised homosexuality – 57 years as it turned out – to have his book published as he wrote it, not as others would dictate he should write it. In a 'Terminal Note' that Forster added in 1960 to the original manuscript of *Maurice* he made this clear.

A happy ending was imperative. I shouldn't have bothered to write otherwise. I was determined that in fiction anyway two men should fall in love and remain in it for the ever and ever that fiction allows, and in this sense Maurice and Alec still roam the greenwood. I dedicated it 'To a Happier Year' and not altogether vainly. Happiness is its keynote – which by the way has had an unexpected result: it has made the book more difficult to publish. Unless the Wolfenden report becomes law [it did in 1967], it will probably have to remain in manuscript. If it ended unhappily, with a lad dangling from a noose or with a suicide pact, all would be well, for there is no pornography or seduction of minors. But the lovers get away unpunished and consequently recommend crime. Mr Borenius [the perceiving clergyman] is too incompetent to catch them, and the only penalty society exacts is an exile they gladly embrace.[35]

But if Glaskin and his publishers thought they had problems with the British censors, it was Australia that presented a tougher obstacle for them. The hardcover edition was unveiled in the UK on 25 February 1965. Within

---

34 Entry on Neville Jackson in the Ozlit@Vicnet Database of Australian Writers, which GMG probably wrote himself. Schmidt (1996).
35 Forster (1971, 246).

weeks, the Australian Department of Customs and Excise had declared the book a prohibited import.[36] Copies were seized and destroyed. Journalist Max Harris took up Glaskin's cause with ferocity. In an article in *The Australian*, he referred to the incident as 'one of the most nauseating episodes in recent Australian literary history'. Pointing out that *No End to the Way* was not in the least pornographic and that homosexuality had become commonplace as a theme in modern literature, Harris deemed the ban 'just one more example of the stupidity and capriciousness of Australian censorship'.[37] Glaskin wrote to the Minister of Customs and Excise in July to protest the ban. At the end of the following January, he received a reply from the minister who advised Glaskin that he had accepted the advice of the Literature Censorship Board and was lifting the ban. Glaskin immediately wrote to Barrie and Rockliff, advising them of the good news and suggesting that 'with the right kind of publicity, you should be able to get pretty high sales.'[38]

Unfortunately for Glaskin, sales of the hardcover edition didn't soar. By the end of 1966 total sales for the UK and export markets were only 3500 copies. Six American publishers and seven French publishers turned it down and somewhat surprisingly it was one of Glaskin's few major titles that didn't make it into Dutch. However, the numbers improved significantly with the sale of paperback rights to Corgi Books in the UK, who did an initial print run of 30,000 copies in January 1967, followed by an additional 20,000 in September 1968. A number of these were flown to Australia and appeared in airport and railway station bookstalls across the country, giving the book widespread public access. The attendant publicity that this was 'a banned book' wouldn't have hurt sales either. And for the thousands of closeted gay men, not to mention curious straight men and women throughout Australia, the alluring cover of a sexy young man in his trim bathing trunks would have been enough to make them at least snatch a copy to glance through and quite possibly buy. Strangely, the figure on the cover bore a striking resemblance to Glaskin. Glaskin once met the model used on the cover at a party in London and both were stunned by their striking similarity. Anyone eyeing them together could have mistaken them for twins.

---

36 There seems to be a difference of opinion about date the ban was imposed. In a letter to John Pattison, Barrie and Rockliff, 2 February 1966, GMG quotes the Minister for Customs and Excise saying the ban was imposed in December 1964, two months before the book was published. But writing in *The Australian* journalist Max Harris (1965) says the book was declared a prohibited import three weeks ago, i.e. early March 1965.
37 Harris (1965).
38 GMG to John Pattison, Barrie and Rockliff, 2 February 1966.

The American publisher MacFadden-Bartell also issued a paperback edition in September 1969. Two and a half years later it had sold more than 29,000 copies, not too disappointing although they were anticipating better because they printed more than 100,000. Then, in January 1985, Corgi reprinted 10,000 more paperback copies, of which 2000 went to Australia. Twenty years after its initial appearance *No End to the Way* was still finding readers. By this time gay-themed novels were commonplace. Gay fiction had become a hot seller, with the likes of Edmund White's *A Boy's Own Story* and Armistead Maupin's *Tales of the City* series in the US. Ironically, the UK-based Gay Men's Press, which brought out a series of modern gay classics, declined to accept *No End to the Way* because they considered its ending too depressing for young gay readers battling with the onslaught of AIDS and the flood of literature that came in its wake. Two decades can make a lot of difference in reader taste.

The importance of *No End to the Way* cannot be underestimated. It was significant in several ways. First, although Glaskin did appear before the Royal Commission on Homosexuality in Western Australia in 1974 and was a card-carrying member of the local chapter of CAMP, Inc., he rarely entered the political arena as a gay rights campaigner.[39] He preferred to wage war with his pen instead. He used *No End to the Way* to make a statement about the injustices suffered by gay men in Australian society of the day, especially the lack of legal recognition of their relationships – a battle still being waged nearly 50 years later on some fronts. On the last page, in a letter Cor writes to Ray in London, he says, 'But just think, if we'd been able to go *there* [to Holland] to live, we would have been *legal* and not just a kind of *criminal*.'[40]

Second, for thousands of closeted gay men in Australia and elsewhere, beset by doubts and fears about their socially unacceptable sexual orientation, it opened a window on a part of life that had been denied them for so long. Letters poured in from all corners of the globe to attest to this, whether from the Anglican priest in London who was both 'moved and harrowed' by the book, the young man in Warsaw who was 'delighted that there are still writers in the world who can write about all human feelings and publishers who may want to print such work', or the desperately lonely gay man in the

---

39 On one occasion, he was asked to chair a panel for CAMP and agreed to do so but withdrew at the last minute because of illness. He had done substantial preparation for the meeting and willingly gave his notes to the person who filled in for him, for which the organisers of the event were most grateful.

40 Jackson (1965, 240).

small town of North Platte, Nebraska, who wanted to know where the novel was set and how he could pick up men. One of the most poignant pieces of fan mail came from Lancashire in England.

> To have tackled such a subject is a courageous thing and to have succeeded so well shows your skill as a writer. It shows too your depth of understanding for those men that must out of necessity lead, if not unhappily, at least lead lonelier lives. You have shown through your treatment of the subject an awareness and tolerance of what such individuals as Cor and Ray have to suffer because of their condition. I thank you for writing a book that seeks not to glorify homosexuality but rather to show that it is a very real problem and one that affects many men to whom a normal way of life is denied through no fault of their own. Such people have a right to lead their own lives in their way. Many folk would do well to recall the words 'There but for the grace of God go I.' I write from experience for I too suffered as do your characters ...[41]

Closer to home but on the other side of the country a young man from Sydney had a similar response. Stopping off in the southern Queensland town of Gympie on a journey north with his boyfriend in 1974, Jeremy Fisher wandered into a newsagent and found his eyes pulling him to a paperback copy of *No End to the Way*. 'It was the lurid cover ... that attracted me, the naked torso of the blond on the cover', wrote Fisher.[42] He stuffed the book under a magazine and nervously paid for it. He had grown up in a country town like this and knew that it wasn't smart to be identified as different, especially as 'one of them'. Even as a university student in cosmopolitan Sydney he had been the victim of a vicious homophobic attack by conservative members of the Anglican Church.[43] But the risk of being outed on this occasion turned out to be well worth it. As soon as he started reading the book and realised it was set in Australia he was elated. It was

---

41 H. Hargraves to GMG, April 1970.
42 Fisher (2003, 21).
43 As an 18-year-old student at Macquarie University, Fisher lived at the Anglican-run Robert Menzies college. Feeling lonely and depressed, he attempted suicide and nearly succeeded. The master of the college, who found a Chinese mask (a gift from his father) and gay liberation materials in his room, demanded that he reject both homosexuality and Satanic practices (which the master deemed the mask implied) if he wished to stay in the college. Not being willing to comply with these conditions, Fisher was effectively expelled and welcomed the support of his parents to set him up in his own flat away from the college. Once his story reached the ears of fellow students, it became a *cause célèbre*. Members of the Builders Labourers Federation placed work bans on a number of university buildings and Fisher found himself the subject of a morning television show.

'the first book I read of which I could say "this has a homosexual point of view". That is, I – me, this person, the odd thing inside my head – could identify with it as a reader because there was an acceptance of same-sex love which seemed entirely natural to me, despite a universe and millions of voices which proclaimed the opposite.'[44]

Several aspects of the book particularly impressed Fisher, although he was not fully conscious of why until years later when he took a much deeper look at it and his experience of reading it as part of a doctoral thesis he was writing. One aspect was the way Glaskin kept his narrator 'proudly, determinedly gay'.[45] That Fisher identified so strongly with this was due, he deduced, to Glaskin writing it in the second person and the present tense, devices that give both a sense of intimacy and collusion with the reader. Another aspect of the novel that impressed Fisher was its ending, in which Ray Wharton doesn't renounce his sexuality but surmounts the difficulties and fears of living as a gay man and determines to continue doing so. Finally, Glaskin met one of Fisher's primary criteria for writing from a homosexual point of view – that the writer, as opposed to the narrator, identify himself as homosexual, something that Fisher perceived the more celebrated Patrick White was reluctant to do.

While *No End to the Way* affirmed the integrity of gay men and drew attention to their plight as second-class citizens, it was important for another reason. Although Glaskin never sought the dubious label of being 'a gay writer', he did want to be a provocative writer. He liked to shock and jolt people out of their smug, middle-class lethargy and innocent naïveté. In face-to-face encounters he was a master of this art, especially when it came to dealing with homophobia, a condition he was convinced was suffered by repressed homosexuals who thrived on taking out their illness on gay men. 'I like to challenge people', said Glaskin. 'I don't know whether this is me as a person or me as a writer. I want to draw them out in many ways.' Several of those ways he perfected over the years. If someone said to him, 'I hear you're gay' he would respond, 'Oh shit, you're the last one I would have thought would be interested!' Another of his favourite tactics was to outdo them at their own game and use the word 'poofter' as effortlessly and frequently as its homophobic proponents did. Once during a very nasty scene a guy said to him, 'You can't be a poofter because fuckin' poofters don't say poofter!'[46]

---

44 Fisher (2003, 22).
45 Ibid., 23.
46 Cover (1994a, 4).

His practice of drawing out his opponents so they had to confront their own weakness invariably worked. In *No End to the Way* Glaskin used the same kind of directness in his characters. It went much further than most other Australian novels published up to that time in telling it like it was from the perspective of a gay man. Jon Rose's *At the Cross* and Stuart Lauder's *Winger's Landfall* were tame by comparison, not to mention Kenneth (Seaforth) Mackenzie's *The Young Desire It*, first published in Australia in 1963 although initially published in the UK in 1937. Like Glaskin, Mackenzie grew up in Perth but a decade earlier than Glaskin. He exhibits a much more subtle, lyrical style than Glaskin in this his first novel, based on his own experiences as a boarder at one of Perth's prestigious private schools. Although *The Young Desire It* has much to recommend it as a novel, it was not the book that many gay men in Perth in the 1950s and 1960s could easily relate to unless they had attended a boarding school. The story could well have taken place in an English public school, as novels such as Michael Campbell's *Lord Dismiss Us* have successfully portrayed.

In this sense *No End to the Way* filled a gap in the lives of gay men. In Adelaide, Brisbane or Hobart in the 1950s and 1960s, they could turn to the larger cities of Melbourne and Sydney for respite and relaxation if their home towns became too unbearable, but Perth was a different kettle of fish. Its gaping distance from the larger urban metropolises of the east coast made travel unthinkable for all but the most affluent. Geoffrey Blainey's 'tyranny of distance' was an undeniable reality for those Australians who grew up on the shores of the Indian Ocean rather than the Pacific.[47] So, as in many other aspects of Perth life, its gay community developed in its own way and on its own terms. In his novel, Glaskin gave a public face to this. While not everyone thanked him for his efforts, many were able to say an affirmative 'This is me!' for the first time. Finally, someone wrote about the place they knew and the kind of life they lived there in an open and unapologetic manner. For Western Australians, perhaps more than other Australians, this was a rare and welcome experience. It was the same kind of grateful acknowledgement that Tim Winton made of fellow Western Australian writer Randolph Stow when he said, 'Stow was the first writer I read who actually wrote about the place I came from. He's hugely neglected at the expense of other writers, particularly Patrick White.'[48]

---

47   Reference to Geoffrey Blainey's popular book *The Tyranny of Distance: How Distance Shaped Australia's History*.
48   JB (1995, 3).

Perth had a vibrant gay life in the years following the Second World War, but in common with many other parts of Australia it was largely a private affair, conducted mostly behind closed doors at parties, in the sand hills at the farthest end of any beach or in the toilets and parks that were the beats. It would fit closely with historian Graham Willett's description of 1950s Australian gay life as 'a scene of the night and ... very largely invisible to the rest of society. Its members hoped for nothing more than to be left alone. It eschewed – indeed, never seriously imagined – political action and what underpinned its apolitical stance was fear, a deep and abiding fear of mainstream society.'[49] According to one astute observer of the times who lived in both Perth and Melbourne, such fear was rooted in a more fundamental struggle with authority. 'The one overriding problem for gay people was authority. Not only gay society, but society in general. Authority of the police, the law, the church, your boss, older people – authority had to be respected and never, ever questioned. And if you were told something was morally wrong and shouldn't be done, well that was that. There was no argument, no debate, no discussion. Nevertheless, despite all this, there was a very secret, very cautious gay society there.'[50]

Secret, cautious, gay and a whole lot of fun. When early closing hours at The Palace forced the crowd to evacuate the downstairs bar, they would disperse to private homes to continue partying. Not many gay men had places large enough to host sizable parties but some of the older and wealthier did and these became known venues in the Perth gay scene, if only by invitation. One of these was the Wintercourt Flats in Adelaide Terrace, a respectable two-storey block of brick-and-tile flats that was home to a number of gay men, including some of Perth's gay elite, one of whom was a prominent broadcaster with the Australian Broadcasting Commission (now Corporation). Wintercourt was the scene of many a wild party, where bedazzling peacock feathers and tightly-fitting pants were par for the course. Liquor flowed, the latest Broadway LPs blared in the background and one-liners whipped back and forth like a feisty exchange in a fencing match. As one participant of those halcyon days summed them up, 'Everybody drank and smoked as if there was no tomorrow. Every whim was indulged in.'[51] The chance to throw off the shackles that mainstream society clamped on gay men and to be outrageous – or just simply themselves without having to be eternally on guard – was such a welcome relief.

---

49 Willett (2000, 9).
50 King (1996b).
51 King (1996a).

Popular events such as the annual Halloween Ball at the Embassy Ballroom that gave abundant opportunity for the more florid members of the gay scene to strut their stuff, and later on the elaborate drag cabarets at the North Perth Town Hall that attracted sell-out crowds provided occasions to let off steam. There was The Convent, a boarding house in the university suburb of Hollywood, whose flamboyant owner, The Reverend Mother Priscilla, insisted in dressing up as a nun and whose parties attracted a wide cross-section of Perth society. There was also the bar at His Majesty's Theatre and the two 'hope and grope' underground theatrettes in Hay Street that boasted more activity in the seats than on the screen. Meanwhile, downriver in the port city of Fremantle another node for gay men had come into its own. The Cleopatra – 'one of the roughest pubs in the southern hemisphere' – was a magnet for visiting sailors and locals who delighted in servicing their every need. Before container ships, cargo vessels frequently called at Fremantle and their sex-starved crews were always out for a good time. Swinging parties were often held on board and many a visitor stayed overnight. One particular local was famous for overstaying the night. 'She' would invariably have to get a ride back to land on the Fremantle Harbour pilot boat the next day.[52]

By and large police were not repressive but sometimes festivities got a little out of hand and gay men found themselves entangled with the law. One such occasion occurred in April 1954, when a Swanbourne man known for his lavish parties had thrown open his home to his gay friends. A few weeks before he had had an altercation with a neighbour, who, out to exact revenge, called the police to have them investigate the party this Saturday night. Around half past nine, just as the laughter was bouncing off the walls and the music was romping along, the front door was flung open. In stormed plain-clothes detectives armed with cameras flashing in every direction. 'Don't move. Stay where you are!' they yelled at the horrified gathering, who were all photographed like animals in a zoo before being subjected to a humiliating search. The detectives went through everything, examining ashtrays for traces of marijuana to bed sheets for evidence of illegal sexual activity. They found nothing incriminating but left in their wake a fear that terrorised gay men in Perth for a long time to come. One who was present has never forgotten that horrific night.

> The consequences of that police raid were enormous. I was 21 at the time and I was very nervous. I had a good job and an office ... I heard that others had been visited at their places of employment by the police,

---

52 Ibid.

particularly those guys who worked at Boans ... Somebody had given a false name and they were trying to track this person down. This particular boy ... packed his bags and raced back to the farm where his parents were, because he was so terrified – as we all were – of being exposed. I was frightened that my parents in Bunbury would be quizzed about this and it would get into the papers with our names. It was sheer terror. It went on for weeks and weeks ... there would be another interview; somebody else would be dragged into a police station and quizzed. 'What really went on at those parties?' they wanted to know. Fortunately, I was never dragged in there but the boy who went up to his parents' farm in the country shot himself dead.[53]

There were fewer parties for gay men in Perth for quite some time after this incident but eventually the circuits began flowing again. For all its small-town parochialism and English manners, Perth was a surprisingly gay-friendly city in the '50s and '60s. As one gay man put it 'Every toilet was a beat and Swanbourne was "our beach".'[54] Swanbourne, just north of Glaskin's favourite Cottesloe Beach, was situated at the foot of a major military barracks with a range of low sand hills immediately behind it. Randy soldiers joined civilians in cruising the dunes in search of quick sexual gratification. On weekends it became a hive of activity. Gay men who liked to indulge in the finer things of life would arrive with picnic baskets under their arms. Out came the pressed tablecloth, polished silverware, and for those with more discerning taste, a candelabra and Russian coleslaw. All served with a glass of sparkling Porphyry Pearl or chilled Chablis and, of course, naked. Who needed to go to Greece or San Francisco or even Sydney to have a gay time? For all its isolation, Perth did have its delights. Because this area was Commonwealth Government land, local police tended to stay away, which made it a relatively safe area for gay men. However, this wasn't always the case, as some discovered to their regret. On one occasion, under pressure from residents in the surrounding area, police sent in helicopters and officers on foot equipped with walkie-talkies to 'clean up' the area. The story was splashed over several pages of *The Daily News*, replete with photographs. But such moments were the exception rather than the rule and eventually Swanbourne's popularity extended far beyond the confines of the gay community. It attracted men and women of all sexual persuasions,

---

53 King (1996b).
54 Ibid. (1996a).

especially nude bathers, until the local authorities finally relented and demarcated a section of the beach as 'clothing optional'.

Using his skills as a writer and drawing on his own experiences, Glaskin dared to put a face on all this. In so doing, he was making a public statement about his own sexuality – although masked by the Neville Jackson pseudonym – and giving other gay men permission to do the same. When he wrote *No End to the Way*, Glaskin probably had little idea of the impact it would have on the lives of gay men in Perth or throughout Australia or around the world. He may not have even been aware of the disproportionately large numbers of gay men whom one anthropologist claimed earned Perth the reputation of being Australia's 'top homosexual city'.[55] But he did know that in thousands of homes of suburban Australia were young men who, like himself, were struggling to reconcile competing and conflicting parts of themselves that never seemed to fit together. There was the good son or brother, intelligent, perhaps good looking, brought up to be obedient to his parents and polite to others and contribute usefully to society. At the same time, there was this other strange person who, while expected to court and marry women, found himself quite oblivious to the attractions of the opposite sex and inexplicably drawn to his own. And in between was the silent no man's land where the subjects of sexuality and feelings were totally taboo. As one gay man remembered it, 'the times we lived in did not encourage any of us to express our thoughts. We were too middle-class in our values. I suppose too "nice", and "nice" people didn't give expression to such "filthy" thoughts.'[56] Glaskin helped fill this void and helped bring wholeness to the lives of many who had only known fragmentation and despair. In this respect *No End to the Way* may well have been his most important book.[57]

---

55 Giving evidence at a Royal Commission into Homosexuality in Perth, anthropologist G. T. Tillett said there were at least 25,000 men in the metropolitan area whose sexual outlet was totally homosexual. This figure did not include married men who practised homosexuality, bisexuals and those who did not engage in homosexual activities. Tillett said that informants were almost unanimous in stating that Perth's homosexual population was more extensive and involved more people proportionately for the size of the city than elsewhere in Australia. No author listed. *The West Australian* (1974).

56 Davis (2002, 1).

57 *No End to the Way* may have also been important in a completely different context. GMG's London-based Australian friend, Peter Hurford, reported that the book was once used in Cold War espionage in which he had been recruited by MI6 to play a role. Orchestrated by Basil Stores (nephew of the Sir Ronald Stores, well known for his work in the Middle East at the time of T. E. Lawrence), the activity involved Hurford and a Russian employee of UNESCO who was being set up for future homosexual encounters in which he could be compromised. Hurford was given instructions to be in Paris at a rendezvous point at 4 pm on a particular day. A car picked him up and took him to

As significant as it may have been, *No End to the Way* was not Glaskin's favourite piece of writing containing gay characters. That was another much shorter piece also set in suburban Perth. 'The Asking Price' was a short story about two gay men who move into the highly fashionable suburb of The Heights, which could easily be Mosman Park or Peppermint Grove, Dalkeith or Nedlands. Steinberg is a wealthy older Jewish man – and an ex-champion Aussie Rules footballer no less – whose dashingly good-looking young partner, Henderson, is a brilliant pianist. Neighbour Amy Johnson decides that their arrival in The Heights is a catastrophe that needs to be dealt with once and for all. Full of zeal, she organises the neighbours to try to oust the couple by having people refuse to socialise with them, excluding them from all the local clubs, persuading the local children to practise their musical instruments loudly, littering over their fence and letting dogs loose on them. But one by one all her tactics fail. The men ingratiate themselves with everyone in the area. Finally, even Amy herself succumbs when the two men invite her to join them for dinner along with the governor and his wife, an invitation she cannot possibly refuse. To make matters worse, her husband will be away on the day of the dinner so Steinberg suggests she bring her dishy 19-year-old son instead. It is a cutting satire in the Oscar Wilde mould. Prejudices are laid bare for all to see and money overrides all other considerations. In a moment of 'I-told-you-so' mixed with 'Oh my God!' Johnson declares, 'There was talk of some rather weird stag parties. Well, they'd expected it, hadn't they? She'd warned them, hadn't she? The absolutely awful thing about it was: it seemed to have drawn a fair number of participants from the district itself, people no one would have dreamed of. The golf pro for one, the Adams boy for another, that house-termite sprayer and even the Reverend Reggie Baker. She *hoped* it was only talk. But one never knew ...'[58] When the University of Western Australia literary journal, *Westerly*, published the story in 1968 it raised a number of academic eyebrows but it was praised for its 'concinnity and compelling pace'.[59]

If 'The Asking Price' has any message it is perhaps that wealth and power can outmanoeuvre the most ingrained prejudices. Many of Perth's gay men who were part of the city's social and economic elite knew this. The number of prominent gay men who were on friendly terms with the longstanding

---

meet the Russian in the presence of one other person. Hurford had his copy of *No End to the Way* with him and was instructed to show the book to his contact in an attempt to whet his sexual appetite. Peter Hurford to JB, interview by author, 29 August 2001.

58 GMG (1968a, 5–11).

59 Mareya and Peter Schmidt (1996).

state premier, Sir Charles Court – never one known for reaching out publicly to gay men – was quite remarkable. Glaskin himself was in this category, although his connection with Court was not by way of wealth but more his impressive public persona, articulateness and family connections.[60] However, when Glaskin tried to get Court to intervene on a censorship issue, the premier refused to oblige. There were lines over which he would not step.

While Glaskin accrued a certain amount of public recognition for his artistic endeavours, it was nowhere near what he thought he deserved, especially from those close to home. But he did not attempt to use his reputation as a writer to gain acceptance as a gay man. He never assumed he needed to. His homosexuality was part of who he was and others could take it or leave it. If they had an issue with it that was their problem, not his. As close friend and fellow writer Ethel Webb Bundell put it, 'He didn't try to please anyone, win them over, soften his approach. What you saw was what you got.'[61] But as a gay man and a writer, he did know what it meant to experience loneliness. Perhaps this was the price one must pay for loving one's own sex or committing one's life to the solitary discipline of being a writer. Glaskin was intensely conscious of loneliness and its impact on his own life and the lives of those around him. Along with the yearning to love, loneliness occupied a primary place among themes in his writing.

---

60 GMG's second-youngest sister, Myree, married the son of one of Court's ministers, Ross Hutchinson.
61 Ethel Webb Bundell to JB, personal communication, 18 April 2001.

Chapter 10

Loneliness

Our classic Australian writers have produced
a 'literature of loneliness'.

Mary Durack

When the young Gerald Glaskin found his revered Uncle Alan lying in a pool of his own blood he was speechless. The horror and meaningless of what he observed was too much for his eight-year-old mind to grasp. He didn't cry, at least not then. He just stood and stared. The crying came later when he witnessed the consuming sorrow that enveloped his maternal grandmother who mourned her son's death in a darkened room for almost a year. Over time, as his searching mind frantically sought to make sense out of this tragic event one thing became painfully clear. 'After that, I knew for the rest of my life what loneliness and the absence of love – almost any kind of love – can do to a man, not only to a woman,' wrote Glaskin, 'and I have always tried to safeguard myself, and others, against the insupportable agony of it ever since.'[1] Perhaps it was the raw shock of this brutal encounter with death that seared itself into Glaskin's soul at such an early age, but throughout his life he found himself besieged by the awful notion of loneliness, especially the loneliness of men. According to popular mythology of his day, Australian men shunned emotion and stoically endured whatever lot life cast their way, even if it meant a life of unbearable solitude, as his mother's younger brother had experienced so acutely at such an early age. Loneliness was a fate worse

---

1   GMG (1975, 102).

than death and, as Glaskin intimated, something to be guarded against at all costs. Members of his own extended family provided abundant reminders of the need to do this.

One day in 1948, while working at the Ford Motor Company in North Fremantle, the 24-year-old Glaskin was informed that he had a visitor. He was surprised and puzzled who it could be. When he first laid eyes on the man in the grey suit pacing up and down by the receptionist's desk he blinked a couple of times because he thought it was his maternal grandfather, whom he affectionately called 'Pop'. Why he should be paying him a visit at work? On second glance, he realised it was a smaller, younger version of Pop. Holding out his hand to greet the man, Glaskin discovered he was making the acquaintance of his maternal great-uncle, Francis, Pop's brother. He had come from Melbourne to visit the family and expected to find Glaskin's parents and siblings in Perth. He was sorely disappointed to learn that they were in Japan, owing to Gilbert's tenure with the British Commonwealth Occupational Force there. He had only a few days left in Perth so this morning he had come especially to see the eldest son of one of his favourite nieces. After Glaskin asked his boss's permission to speak with Francis, he began chatting with his great-uncle, inquiring about this one and that. But Glaskin soon found they had little to say to each other. Since he had never known the man it was like meeting a stranger on a bus and striking up conversation. However, Glaskin did find they shared one thing in common. 'I think we shared loneliness', he reflected to himself afterwards. Then, as if thanking his lucky stars, he mused, 'But of course he never found writing to eschew it as I did.'[2] Shortly afterwards Francis Gugeri returned to Melbourne and to his rooms, where they later found his body. He died a natural death – alone – as he had been throughout his life.

Francis wasn't unique among Glaskin's relatives in this way. In 1963, while living in Amsterdam, Glaskin made a visit to the home of his maternal ancestors in Vacallo in the Italian border region of Switzerland, just above Chiasso in the canton of Ticino. It is where the Gugeris (originally spelt Guggeri) have their roots and being more partial to his mother's side of the family than his father's, Glaskin was keen to connect with this part of his history. He brought with him photographs and documents from 1851 taken by his great-grandfather, Peter Anthony Gugeri, before he left for England and Australia. But when Glaskin arrived there in the spring of 1963 he was surprised by what he found. Although the village and the *Palazzo del*

---

2   Ibid., 154.

Residencia were almost identical to how they looked in the photograph taken 112 years before, the way the building was being used had radically changed. Only four of the 23 rooms of the palazzo were occupied and a garish neon sign proclaimed Restorante Rizza on the side of the building. Like the near-empty palazzo, the family itself was crumbling and in danger of going out of existence. Glaskin discovered only one male heir who had recently married and was the sole hope of continuing the family name. However, he did make acquaintance with 'numerous unmarried and very elderly Senori Guggeri, all little bald and fat, if rather more peasant-looking replicas of my grandfather, Pop, and poor Uncle Francis'.[3]

On this trip, Glaskin was accompanied by his lifelong friend George Britnell. They had been schoolmates and grown up together in Perth, both discovering a mutual interest in members of their own sex, although their relationship reputedly was platonic. Britnell was a prize-winning photographer and took several excellent portrait shots of Glaskin that appear on the dust jackets of some of his early books. Britnell also wrote lyrics to music Glaskin played on the piano. They connected at many levels and each held a deep appreciation of the other. Three years after their European sojourn, Glaskin wrote to Britnell to share the emptiness his life had become, both personally and professionally. Glaskin was struggling with the decision whether to return to Australia or not. Britnell responded in a brotherly but blunt fashion, addressing Glaskin by one of his popular nicknames, Jo. He referred to loneliness as that 'killer in our make-up' and, in order to deal with it as a writer, recommended that Glaskin knuckle down and apply himself to the task. Keeping busy was Britnell's way of staving off the twin demons of the loss of creativity and the onset of loneliness that Glaskin found himself grappling with. Although Britnell's solution to Glaskin's dilemma seems simplistic and schoolmasterish, it may have been just the kind of adrenalin shot Glaskin needed at this point in his life.[4]

But it was probably the second half of Britnell's aerogramme that had the greatest impact on Glaskin. Alluding to the plight of the gay man, Britnell counselled Glaskin to move on from the lure of the hunt that drives many men to seek refuge in a promiscuous lifestyle and try to find someone with whom he could share his life. It is something many gay men desire but not all are granted. This was particularly true at this time when living together in an openly gay relationship was fraught with difficulty in a heavily

3   Ibid., 159.
4   George Britnell to GMG, 29 September 1966.

homophobic Australia, although much more possible in the Netherlands. Britnell continued:

> Undoubtedly, personal loneliness is our greatest problem and fear. We all need, and will always need, someone close; we must feel we are wanted by someone – this is our breed. And – again – this is something you MUST do … find somebody and find them soon. But do not aim for the skies, Jo. I feel that at our age, one must make many sacrifices in this regard, that the deed must be revealed only as an expression of deep feeling and not as a deed of need, or for the fun of it. I believe we must make all allowances for the other party, even first thoughts as to the other's wishes about all things before one makes one's mind up. Yes, I know this brings about a certain loss of one's own individuality, but I feel it is necessary at our age.

And referring to the person Britnell had found to share his life with, he wrote:

> You say you 'envy' my circumstances … you must realise that this expression gives me a close insight into your own feelings. I tell you straight – I thank God for allowing me the untold joys I have experienced these past two years. I know only too well that this has been the only 'living' part of my life. But I have had to wait a lifetime to reach it … and now one may say that it is almost too late! But I have no qualms about it. I have to live with the realisation that it will end, or break, through one cause or another. In the meantime, no sacrifice is too great … and many have to be made, as you will realise. It is not just one big 'Ball' … but I am not complaining in the least. It has been wonderful … it is wonderful … and if and when the time comes, I am prepared for it with other things.[5]

Strangely, both Britnell's advice to Glaskin to find a partner and his caution about the possible fleeting nature of such relationships came to pass. Regretfully, the circumstances in which they did were not quite as anyone anticipated or would have wished. Less than two years after he received this letter, Glaskin met van de Pas in the Netherlands and within a few months, the Dutchman was on his way to join Glaskin in Australia.[6] When van de Pas arrived in Perth, not only was Glaskin there to meet him but Britnell as well. Van de Pas saw a great deal of Britnell during his first six months

---

5   Ibid.
6   See Chapter 7, 'Going Dutch', for details of this period.

in Perth but the following Easter, at just 49, Britnell died of a heart attack. Australia had lost a fine photographer and Glaskin a very dear friend. Glaskin mourned his loss almost as much as that of his mother who had died nine years before. But he had gained someone to assuage his loneliness and to help him through the endless work of typing and retyping manuscripts, as well as the painful days of caring for his ailing body that would be with him for another 32 years. Britnell was right; life isn't one big ball. It is a journey of many ups and downs but right until he drew his last breath Glaskin had someone he could count on to be there and hold loneliness at bay.

While Glaskin seemed concerned about the way loneliness affects men, and gay men in particular, he was not deluding himself that loneliness is unique to the male of the species. Indeed, a number of women in his extended family bore testimony to that. One of those was his Great Aunt Grace, who epitomised the loneliness that comes with age.[7] For Glaskin, she raised many troubling questions. 'Poor Grace – she had never cooked. How ever did she feed herself? Out of tins and bottles I believe. How did she survive? On a pension, till that was cut off until such time as a small inheritance from her sister May had been absorbed. How did she cope with her loneliness? She didn't marry, although I understood she could have several times.' Then in a moment of speculation Glaskin alluded to the lengths some will go to prevent loneliness swallowing up their lives. 'Someone once suggested that Fan discouraged all of Grace's suitors so that she herself wouldn't be left alone. I never saw this possibly selfish and, I believe, sometimes spiteful side of Fan; she had always been so loving and lovable to me. But more than likely this was so.'[8]

Glaskin's concern for those who experience loneliness in their latter years was probably not just an altruistic one. It was undoubtedly related to premonitions about his own approaching days as a senior citizen. As one who had grown up in a large family surrounded by loving relatives on both sides, he was used to, and perhaps even dependent upon, the presence of others, even if he were separated from them and felt neglected by them much of the time. With some of them he had no association at all, either by his choosing or theirs. Unlike many gay men, Glaskin's homosexuality didn't cause his immediate family to disown him but it did mean that he had no offspring to look to as a source of support and companionship as he grew older. This could explain the unusually strong interest he took in many of his

7   See Chapter 2, 'A Touch of Class', for details about Grace Jecks.
8   GMG (1975, 164).

nephews and nieces, often to the point of insinuating himself into their lives much more than their parents, or they, felt comfortable with.[9]

Just as loneliness was not peculiar to men, neither was it unique to the aged. 'Lonely indeed are the aged, as I recounted in *Eaves*. Lonely indeed are the young', said Glaskin.[10] The plight of the young in modern society, reflected in the mounting number of youth suicides in Australia, greatly distressed Glaskin. Behind this growing alienation of the young he saw a much broader, more insidious force at work. 'The Great Australian Loneliness no longer applies only to the Outback; it moved into the cities and suburbs some time ago. One has only to look down an Australian street ... to find solitude its main ingredient. Australians have gravitated into the weirdest and dreariest existence I have known anywhere in the world.'[11] He bemoaned the loss of the large, multi-layered family that he had known and loved as a boy. It had disappeared along with many other aspects of a slower paced, more interconnected lifestyle as Australia embraced suburban sprawl and scattered nuclear families as the norm.

For Glaskin, these sociological shifts were all the more alarming when he compared them to what he experienced in living in other parts of the world. In Singapore and Malaya, even though the forces of change were on the move, cultural tradition had kept family ties from unravelling to a much greater extent than in Australia. In the Netherlands the sheer proximity of so many people living within such limited space meant that friends and family were never more than a couple of hours' drive away. Consequently, as Glaskin experienced when he was seriously ill in Amsterdam, people would frequently drop in to chat or check on one another. That familiar, welcoming phrase, 'Come in and I'll put the kettle on' had all but disappeared from the lexicon of modern Australia and it bothered him immensely. In a fit of Glaskinesque pique, he wrote, 'The Australian way of life; the Australian way of death.'[12]

One other kind of loneliness Glaskin couldn't resist commenting on was one he knew intimately – the loneliness of the writer. He had experienced this from his earliest days of writing short stories but more emphatically once he embarked on the gruelling task of writing longer works. In an interview with the noted playwright, poet and novelist Dorothy Hewett, in which he discussed his play *Turn on the Heat*, Glaskin made this plain. 'I think I've

---

9   See Chapter 4, 'The Managing Elder Brother'.
10   GMG (1978b, 18).
11   Ibid.
12   Ibid.

written too many bloody books and I've got sick of writing books because of the loneliness. I wanted to depict the loneliness as a major theme so that theatre could start to understand the loneliness of the novelist, or working alone, acting alone, and so forth.'[13] In a later reference in the interview to his own experience of working in the Netherlands he added, 'I should have chosen the theme of the writer himself [instead of Marilyn Monroe], I suppose, who gets up out of his bed, especially if he is living alone in a foreign country with a foreign language spoken all around him, and then just goes to his typewriter, works alone all day till at the end of that day he is almost a screaming idiot and he wants to rush out and just look at faces.'[14]

While the time Glaskin spent in the Netherlands contained some of the peak experiences of his life, it also included some of his lowest moments. The two went hand in hand, as so often seems the case. Commenting on his close friend, Edgar Vos, Glaskin wrote, 'Look beyond the apparent spontaneity in his eyes and not far beneath you can see his loneliness.' But Glaskin could not resist adding, 'He didn't know the awful loneliness of a writer, as I do."[15] Glaskin underscores this point in *The Man Who Didn't Count*, when he says of Morton Thomas, the London-based Australian writer who is pondering his precarious situation, 'But hadn't he known he would be committing himself to a lifetime of loneliness when he had chosen the isolation of a writer?'[16]

As a writer, Glaskin had to learn to make peace with loneliness because it came with the territory of his chosen profession. But this inescapable fact only accentuated the loneliness he experienced in the rest of his life and de-manded a response from him. One way he did this was through his writing, which contains numerous references to loneliness. The most prominent and overt of these is his novella *O Loneliness*. Based on the supposed true story of a Perth family, Glaskin lets his imagination roam in creating this complex and at times confusing story about intergenerational incest. He also slips in a hint of homosexuality and references to suicide for good measure, as if to ensure that his reputation for shocking his reader is kept intact. Ben Laidlaw, a wealthy Perth lawyer, father of five boys and an adopted daughter, Celia Jnr, drives his friend and client, Geoffrey, to a house in the hills outside Perth where Celia Jnr and her son, Robert Stobel Jnr, are living. The pair are about to take off for Europe and Geoffrey is going to house sit in their

---

13 Hewett (1967, 35).
14 Ibid., 44.
15 GMG (1967a, 24).
16 GMG (1965a, 41).

absence. On the way Ben chides Geoffrey, a writer and narrator of this story, about how writers are prone to make their characters too simple, instead of the complex, devious and unexpected people they really are. He drops hints with phrases like 'a capacity for loneliness' and 'an affinity for incest'. As the story unravels, it is clear that the Stobel-Laidlaw families share both traits and that Ben himself is as much a part of this vicious circle as the other members of the family he describes to Geoffrey.

The phrase 'the plot thickens' must have been invented for this story. Within its 113 pages the following story unfolds. Celia's mother, Celia Snr, the daughter of the wealthy owners of a Western Australian department store, married Robert Stobel Snr, a schoolboy friend of Ben Laidlaw and the son of an incestuous relationship between his mother and her brother. Imbecilic and childlike, Celia Snr was obsessed with dolls and Roman Catholicism. She went insane after consummating her marriage with Stobel Snr and died in childbirth. Stobel Snr was an accomplished concert pianist who spent 20 years performing in Europe and North America. Not only was he the father of Celia Jnr but he was also her lover. Before he died of a heart attack at 44 he impregnated his daughter who gave birth to a son, Robert Stobel Jnr. The latter inherits his father's gift for piano playing and also his physical features, making him almost a replica of the man. However, Robert Jnr's interest in Nick, the Greek gardener, is where he parts company with his father. The story abounds with doubles and repeated scenes, even to the point of two different characters wearing the same clothes 20 years apart. It would be a filmmaker's challenge, if not nightmare. The fact that Robert Stobel Jnr is about to go to London to make his concert debut, just as his father had done at age 18, has shades of David Helfgott about it.[17]

This is a story where the setting itself has the stature of a character and an intriguing and resplendent one at that. It seems likely that Glaskin fused two locations in the Perth hills to create the setting for this novella. One was the Gugeri family property of Acacia Springs at Glen Forrest and the other a house in Gooseberry Hill that itself is the stuff of legend. According to Glaskin's fictional account, 'Francisco's Folly' had been built 75 years

---

17   David Helfgott, the brilliant young Australian pianist whose life was portrayed in the motion picture, *Shine*. Helfgott went from Perth to London on a scholarship to the Royal College of Music, where he suffered a mental breakdown that led him to return to Perth to spend many years in a mental hospital. Although he eventually regained the ability to play the piano and perform publicly, he never fully recovered from his ordeal.

before by a crazy monk who was the original owner of the property. Over 30 years, he had created many of its special features, including a grotto, stained glass windows, cloistered rooms, arched doorways and an unusual world map hewn out of rock. When Celia Snr arrived on the scene, she had the cloisters torn down and a Roman bath built. The house symbolises loneliness and destruction and, as an old gardener-caretaker noted, 'had a habit of eventually claiming most people who lived there.'[18]

The actual structure that fed Glaskin's imagination in this instance was known as McLarty's Folly, situated on Gooseberry Hill's 'Knoll' above Helena Valley with unrestricted views of Perth and the coastal plain. Work was begun on the building in the 1920s by John Mitchell McLarty, a schoolmaster who toiled on weekends with the help of his students for over 10 years. They built walls, arches and doorways from local ruddy ironstone and brick. Italian stained glass windows, Swedish-like macramé bell pulls and the Spanish-style columned courtyard were imported touches that still stand today. McLarty died of cancer before the roof went on and hence the name, McLarty's Folly. Lindsay Gordon Colebatch, son of the one-time Western Australian premier, Hal Colebatch, finished the house, which became part of 'the crazy cultural life of Gooseberry Hill', known for its colourful parties and improvisational theatre.[19] When the ebullient Gordon Colebatch died in 1955 at 56 of a heart attack, his death came as a great shock. Overcome by smoke and exhaustion, he collapsed while helping other residents fight a bushfire that swept up the valley and threatened their properties. Horrified and distressed friends brought in his body and laid it out on the kitchen table. The Folly had claimed yet another victim, which only added to the sinister reputation that Glaskin attributed to it in his novella.

According to the house's present owner, there is little in Glaskin's descriptions of the place that correspond to the house that she bought and shares with her son. The one exception might be the area surrounding the house that Glaskin delighted in describing in some of his most florid prose, imbuing the natural landscape with anthropomorphic qualities. 'Here and there, great tumescent boulders sprouted, like huge and unseemly warts, from the aged, time-ravaged face of the land.'[20] And looking west to the Indian Ocean coastline he painted a picture of 'one of the loveliest views

18 GMG (1964, 191).
19 Mary Durack quoted in an advertisement for the auction of 'MacLarty's [sic] Folly' in March 1995, produced by the real estate firm Blundell's Pty Ltd.
20 GMG (1964, 113).

anywhere in the world'.[21] 'Beyond the garden, the earth fell away steeply to the plain below, the dwarfed and placid city, and the sea. Flecks of cloud were germinating in the afternoon sky, filtering the long slanting rays of the sun dazzling the eye both directly and from the splintered glitter it reflected from diminutive house-roofs and from the distant thin gleam of the sea. It was breathtaking.'[22] For one critic this 'atmospheric innuendo' exuded shades of Henry James and Randolph Stow.[23]

However, it wasn't the exterior landscape Glaskin was aiming at in this book; it was the interior – the parched, hollow landscape of our lives viewed through the lens of a family ridden with incest and loneliness. Glaskin gives the impression that he is testing a theory in this book, stating a hypothesis then laying out the proof of its validity. Typically, he approaches the subject head on, speaking boldly through the voice of his characters and Ben Laidlaw in particular. Early in the story he presents his thesis, using Laidlaw as his mouthpiece.

> I always thought of loneliness as a negative quality, a lack of something. But now I think it's something very positive. In fact, I think it's really a surfeit of something. A surfeit of a capacity or a propensity, for loneliness … I now believe that it's as much a positive attribute, or characteristic as I call it, as a talent for any of the creative arts, or a gift for figures. It's as positive a quality as a leg or an arm. To a person who has this capacity, ridding himself of it would involve a form of amputation. And then he would no longer be his real, or whole, self. It is so positive that I believe it can not only be passed to successive generations, but can also infect other people.[24]

Further on Laidlaw picks up on the same theme and pushes it to its logical conclusion. In describing Robert Stobel Snr, he drops a pearl of wisdom that nobody can deny.

> He had built his loneliness around him as solidly as a wall of steel … This loneliness was no mere condition of circumstance … It was something positive, as positive as the granite in a pillar. It was as though the living flesh had been stripped from him, leaving only the bare bones of his loneliness … You became not only aware of his

21 Ibid., 117.
22 Ibid., 121.
23 Martin (1965, 40).
24 GMG (1964, 110).

loneliness, but, no matter how congenial your own life might be, there was something in the mere sight of him that wrenched at you, and you became immediately aware of those moments in your own life when, as I suppose everyone does at some time or other, you realise, in the end, you are always alone. No matter even how compatible a marriage may be, there are always times, inevitably, when you are reminded that you depart from this life one at a time, and at any given time.[25]

Glaskin worked hard to make his case for the passage of loneliness and incest from one generation to the next. Speaking of Stobel Snr's own mother, Laidlaw commented, 'there was something of his mother's expression in his face, too. And it was this that reminded me of what a lonely woman she must have been, for in all the world, she could find only her own brother to mate with. You can say what you like, Geoffrey, but I swear that she not only passed that look of hers on to him, but also a capacity for loneliness.'[26] But Laidlaw himself was not immune to such propensities. As Geoffrey noted with some alarm, 'Now I could see the loneliness of Ben Laidlaw ... his hidden and perhaps hideous affection [for his own adopted daughter]'.[27] The gleam in Laidlaw's eyes as they followed Celia Jnr around the room was nothing less than 'obscene'. Could it be that the incestuous drive not only followed bloodlines but in the case of adopted children, actually crossed them?

Glaskin revelled in dangling such extraordinary possibilities in front of his readers. There is no lack of them in this book. Describing an exchange between Celia Jnr and Stobel Jnr, Geoffrey reflects, 'She seemed to gaze at him with a certain solicitude, almost flirtatiousness, so that, had I not known them to be mother and son, I might almost have thought them lovers.'[28] As if this weren't enough, Geoffrey hints at yet another relationship in this multigenerational sexual potpourri. This time Nick, the gardener, is the suspect. 'It seemed preposterous that Celia could be his mistress, but again, upon further consideration, especially of her own childish air which she so frequently adopted, it occurred to me that the possibility was not entirely to be discounted.'[29] O Loneliness raises more questions than it answers and it abounds in speculation. 'Was it all really so infectious, so contagious?' asks Geoffrey, who, like the rest of us, cannot quite believe this astonishing

---

25 Ibid., 186.
26 Ibid., 187.
27 Ibid., 210.
28 Ibid., 176.
29 Ibid., 178.

psychodrama he has been privy to. In the same vein, we are left to marvel at the two-edged sword that genius can be, as it simultaneously breeds both artistic talent and mental retardation. Glaskin leaves the reader with plenty to ponder but to give the story some sense of completion, he kills off the last remaining members of this twisted family in an aircraft crash. In the end, we are left with just the house and 'its natural companion', loneliness.

One other aspect of this book deserves attention. Once again, we see Glaskin playing with voice and point of view to tell his tale — 'the technique of narration through a secondary participant by way of an outsider', as critic David Martin described it. Martin found this led to 'a rather doughy piling up of data which obscures the characters'. He felt as if he were reading a potted saga or play instead of a true novella. This caused him to rate *O Loneliness* as more ambitious but less successful than its companion story, *O Love*. It is a fair comment and one that might lead most readers to agree with his image of the latter story as 'a hard gem' while the former is 'like a chandelier out of its proper hall'.[30]

While *O Loneliness* stands out as Glaskin's most prominent attempt to address the question of loneliness, some of his other novels and short stories grapple with it as well. Indeed, in his first novel, *A World of Our Own*, loneliness is a major theme, reflecting Glaskin's own preoccupation with it as a young man in his mid-20s. His original title for the book, *One Man Alone*, suggests this. The central character, Alan Ross, comes back to Perth after serving in the air force during the Second World War and like other returned servicemen he struggles to create a life for himself in this strange new world. He gains a reputation for being a socialite, attending and hosting parties and barbecues with abandon. But all this frenzied activity cannot fill up the emptiness that is at the core of his life. What is causing this is not clear and when he becomes engaged to the pretty Dorothy Reeves it seems that all might be rectified. This isn't to be. In a confessional outpouring to his mate, Bill de Grancie, Ross explains why he has decided to terminate his relationship with Dorothy and head overseas. At the heart of the matter is a war injury that has left him sexually impotent. In a two-and-a-half-page homily, Ross reveals the pain in his life and how this illuminates the meaning of it.

> There's nothing to feel. That's the whole thing about it. Nothing has any meaning. There's no meaning to my staying here – or going away for that matter. I suppose the thing that really hurts most is the loneliness,

---

30 Martin (1965, 40).

and the emptiness, and what seems futility in whatever life I have left. There's nothing much in life, once that's gone. There's no possibility of a wife, of love and love returned, or a family growing up around you, in your own home. And they're the main things of life; they have always been and always will be. It doesn't matter how much the world itself may change with the passing of time, these are the things that make up a world of one's own. And isn't that what people live in, a little world of their own? That little world is the secret of life ... and the meaning of it. Without it, you're completely alone.[31]

In a moment of existential musing, Ross admits that each of us enters this world and departs from it as a solitary being, but then dismisses this 'consciousness of loneliness' as a passing thing that we can keep at arm's length by immersing ourselves in the people and life around us. But the more Ross tries to do this the more acutely alone he finds himself to be, and the more he comes to despise the power-hungering, materialistic way of life he observes all around him. He resolves that only two things finally matter in this life – the knowledge that the greatest possession is life itself and the need to continually strive to improve the lot of all humanity, not just oneself and those who constitute 'a world of one's own'. Furthermore, Ross asserts that a person should find contentment with what he has, absorb himself in what he does and understand that what he does is of the greatest importance. With these as his guiding principles, Ross decides to cut ties with home and go abroad, where he anticipates he will discover his calling, even if it means giving up the one life he has known.

These pronouncements sound like the grand vision of a young man seeking to infuse his life with direction and meaning, to articulate a philosophy that will keep him in good stead amid a world of conflicting values and changing circumstances. Such was the situation of Glaskin at 25 when he wrote these words. He had been back from the war nearly four years, tried a handful of unfulfilling and demeaning jobs, and decided to risk and try his lot at writing a novel. A number of his friends getting married and his own sexual ambivalence didn't help matters. His diary entry for Monday 31 January 1949 reflects the state of abasement and self-doubt to which he had succumbed. 'I cannot sink to any lower standards – driven to desperation with loneliness and semi-impotency – my reason for being 'One Man Alone' (ever since the Air Force accident) and a writer (if a writer) at all, realizing

---

31 GMG (1955, 391).

so painfully how different I am from other men.'[32] He needed a radical shift in his life to raise himself up from this morass. With a job offer in Singapore and the first draft of *A World of Our Own* complete he was up and off. Over the next decade he did indeed create a world of his own, with his high-earning job as a stockbroker, the writing of four more novels, a gay social life in the most literal sense of the term and expanded horizons that travel to Europe and Asia brought him.

But loneliness would still thwart him over his next 40 years and he would keep coming back to it in his writing. One book where it rears its familiar head is *No End to the Way*. In the second last paragraph, Ray, the narrator, has just received a letter from Cor, his former lover who has married – a woman, no less – and is heading for north Queensland. When you come from Perth that is about as far away as you can imagine living in Australia. But is it far enough? Will it help erase the past and dispel the one thing that Cor fears more than anything else – loneliness? Says Ray, 'If there's one thing he can't face, he says, it's loneliness; just the mere prospect of it frightens him to death. And he can't see anything but loneliness ahead of you [sic] in the *gay* life, not these days.'[33] Ray is giving voice to a familiar subject among gay men – the fear of aging and dying alone. He articulates it even more forcefully earlier in the book when he says, 'one day you wake up to find yourself 50, no longer attractive, just a sad old aunty still trying to put on the brave young bright act, but can't any longer, and so you're stuck with your loneliness.'[34] But clearly, loneliness is not just the province of gay men. In *O Love* middle-aged Ralph Thompson, listening to the tragic story of how his 13-year-old lover, Connie, suffered at the hands of her demented father, declares, 'These prosaic if sturdy walls of mine seemed to ache with the horror and loneliness of it all, and all I could do was to hold her the more closely in my arms, and feel her, suddenly, shaking and crying against me.'[35] And when Connie is comforting Thompson, he reflects, 'I had never in my life felt so humble, so humiliated and so ashamed – but above all, so lonely and left out of things.'[36]

Glaskin's Cold War espionage novel, *The Man Who Didn't Count*, provides a clue to how we might escape, even if only temporarily, the terror of loneliness. It comes in the form of dreams, a fascination of Glaskin's that he

---

32 GMG (1949a, 31 January).
33 Jackson (1965, 240).
34 Ibid., 231.
35 GMG (1964, 61).
36 Ibid., 51.

pursued in his later work on lucid dreaming and the Christos Experiment.[37] In this novel, he lays out a kind of worldview focused on the significance of dreams and death. He does this through the character of Anneke Vos, the attractive young Dutch milliner with whom the protagonist Morton Thomas has an affair. Ever since she watched her sister tortured to death by their captors in a Japanese concentration camp, Vos has come to value every living moment as a gift. She has seen through what someone like Thomas takes as the limitations of life. During a bicycle ride into the Dutch countryside, Vos explains to her Australian writer friend that loneliness comes from a feeling of detachment from life, which we only experience in our waking hours. Dreams, which are timeless, offer us the possibility of overcoming loneliness because we are never detached or bored in our dreams. Death is our only fear and without death and fear there is no time. When time and fear are removed in dreams, we are left with only a wondrous awareness of this world and sometimes we are privileged to glimpse other worlds. Glaskin elaborates on these themes in his Christos trilogy and his unpublished magnum opus *At the End of It All*. Here we get a preview of what is to come.

On a more earthly plane – a little too earthly for some more conservative theatre goers in 1960s Perth – Glaskin pulled no punches in addressing the loneliness inherit in the lives of many celebrities and artists. He did this in his one-act play *Turn on the Heat*, which he declared was only loosely based on the last night in the tragic life of Marilyn Monroe. However, when interviewed by Dorothy Hewett, Glaskin stated quite explicitly that he felt Monroe had died in desperation from loneliness more than anything else and wanted to convey this in this monologue by using one actress and one set for the entire play.[38] The play ran for three weeks at Perth's Hole in the Wall theatre in June 1967 and the actress who played the protagonist, Marion Marlow, was Eileen Colocott, wife of the theatre's and the play's director, Frank Baden-Powell. Colocott, who received high praise for her intense solo performance, felt a strong kinship with Monroe and with Glaskin's fictional depiction of her in the play. In the same interview with Hewett, Colocott declared, 'I always felt terrific sympathy for [Monroe], and just as written, as a person. I felt there was so much of it any woman could understand, particularly the loneliness thing, so many women have come to me and said, "O! I can so much understand the loneliness." Most women at some time in

---

37 See Chapter 12, 'An Egyptian Nomarch'.
38 Hewett (1967, 35).

their lives have felt this terrible loneliness and desperation that she felt, the terrible sadness and waste of it all. Emotionally it just got me *there*.'[39]

But not everyone identified so strongly with Glaskin's character and two felt so antagonised by his efforts that they made their feelings known. One was a woman in the audience who was so outraged by the rape scene that she filed obscenity charges. When Glaskin answered a knock at his door one morning he came face to face with a CIB detective who said he needed a copy of the manuscript so that the Crown Law Department could decide whether or not the charge was justified. Glaskin obliged, but writing to his old Amsterdam friend Margaret Walker, he confided, 'if there is a court case, not only I but many others intend to make it a *cause célèbre*.'[40] Alas, the opportunity for Glaskin to display his theatrical skills yet again in a Perth courtroom never came about. It took six months of agonising waiting for the local authorities to make a ruling on the case but when they finally did they dismissed it on a technicality, according to Glaskin – he did not write the script in Western Australia. He had dashed it off while holed up in a hotel room in Lebanon during riots in Beirut.[41] Saved by geography, but he was no doubt disappointed he couldn't have used the anticipated courtroom drama to help publicise the play. Unfortunately, the obscenity charges had the opposite effect. Plans to run the play in Adelaide, Melbourne and Sydney were cancelled. Its 13 performances in Perth were the only ones it would ever have. It grossed $1111, of which Glaskin was paid a royalty of $83.40.

In his interview with Hewett, Glaskin vigorously defended himself against the obscenity charge. 'I did the rape scene particularly to show that you can talk about ANYthing at all, even in the public audience of theatre, provided it is done with sensitivity and compassion, and to try and explain a point of view. To me, the play cannot be the play at all without the rape scene, because it shows the reasons for the disintegration of her entire personality.'[42] Whether it was because of this scene or other aspects of the play is not clear, but on the other side of the world another person was troubled by the play also. This was Monroe's one-time husband, playwright Arthur Miller. Miller was the new president of P.E.N. International when Glaskin attended the organisation's international congress in New York in

---

39   Ibid., 36.
40   GMG to Margaret Walker, 31 August 1967.
41   Whether this was the reason given for dropping the case is not clear because in Western Australia at the time documentation relating to this type of complaint was only required to be retained for 10 years before being destroyed. Current police records contain no reference to it.
42   Hewett (1967, 39).

1966, along with his friend, Henrietta Drake-Brockman, and Elizabeth Durack, artist and sister of Mary Durack. In his interview with Hewett, Glaskin declared, 'After being with Arthur Miller for about four weeks … I realised how one-sided his whole attitude was to Marilyn Monroe, and I thought I'd like to depict the other side of the coin even if it's only a fictitious thing.'[43] When Miller heard about the play, he threatened Glaskin with legal action, which only reinforced the unwillingness of other theatres, not only in Australia but in Paris and Amsterdam as well, to produce the play. Although his first performed play had an exceptionally short run, Glaskin managed to use it to provoke a number of people and make yet another statement about loneliness.

Glaskin was not alone in writing about loneliness. It is a perennial theme many writers have used and developed in different ways. Australian writers especially seemed to have exhibited a penchant for it. Writing in 1968 in the literary journal *Westerly*, Mary Durack referred to Australian writing as 'a literature of loneliness'. Reviewing the anthology *On Native Grounds: Australian Writing from Meanjin Quarterly*, selected by C. B. Christensen, she wrote, 'No longer can it be said that Australian writers are limited to themes relating to the bush, the landscape, mateship and narrow nationalism. Nonetheless the outback continues to loom as a psychological factor in our literary consciousness, its exploration seen less as a physical challenge than as the individual's search for his own soul in a pitiless void.' Quoting the literary scholar H. P. Heseltine, she pointed out that 'classic Australian writers have produced a "literature of loneliness", their understanding of an isolated environment leading naturally enough to a concern for the essential loneliness of the individual. In whatever other respects modern Australian writers may differ from their literary forebears this tendency would seem to be as strong today as it ever was …'[44] Much of Glaskin's writing would seem to bear this out. Not only in his novels but in many of his short stories he touches on the 'the essential loneliness of the individual'. Stories such as 'Small World', 'The Road to Nowhere' and 'The Ice Yacht' are cases in point.

It is not surprising that loneliness occurs as a theme so frequently in Glaskin's writing. As one who had deliberately moved away from his roots and dared to place himself in unfamiliar environments, he would have come to expect loneliness as inevitable. As a gay man growing up in a homophobic country, he would have experienced the loneliness that comes with being

---

43 Ibid., 35.
44 Durack (1968).

in but not of his society's mainstream. As a writer, who spent weeks and months sitting at a typewriter, searching the inner reaches of his soul and scouring his imagination to evoke a mood and tell a tale, he would surely have known loneliness as his constant companion. And, as one who dared to boldly confront those whom he thought had slighted him, he must have realised that loneliness would be the price he would pay for his words and actions. But it seemed to be a price he was willing to pay, as in one skirmish after another he drew the line in the sand and disassociated himself from individuals and institutions.

Chapter 11

Tilting at Windmills

Pain is a treacherous master that can rob people
of the softer part of their nature.

Rae Kean

In spite of repeated threats to do so, and several dramatic episodes in which he did destroy some of his literary and personal archives, Gerald Glaskin left behind him a paper trail that would make even the most earnest researcher gasp for air. In ploughing through this plethora of documents, letters, press cuttings and more, it is impossible not to be struck by one thing – Glaskin's consistent attempts to fight for what he believed to be right, to redress injustices, especially those suffered by writers, and not to let slide any slight, perceived or real, to himself. Often he had a legitimate concern, a valid complaint or a justifiable axe to grind. But invariably, the way he went about pressing his case, aggressively tackling anyone who dared challenge him and relentlessly pursuing his adversaries reduced his effectiveness, lost him possible supporters and diminished his stature in the eyes of many. His acerbic tongue, his demeaning remarks directed at others for incompetence and rudeness and his propensity to tell people how they should be doing their job never earned him any points.

A number of his letters are testimony to this. Written on the spur of a heated moment, they are laced with vitriolic language poured forth in a stream-of-consciousness style and conclude with the flourish of a flamboyant signature. If only he had let them sit a couple of days and come back to them with a cooler head and more strategic focus he might have saved himself much trouble and notched up a few victories for his cause. But that would have been quite a different Gerald Glaskin from the one who is the subject of this book. With this Glaskin, few organisations and individuals he dealt with escaped his wrath. Writers' associations, agents, publishers, libraries, neighbours, politicians, police officers, building managers – even young women at check-out counters in supermarkets – were on the receiving end of Glaskin's verbal and written volleys. Letters of resignation by Glaskin or declarations of termination of their relationship by the other party abound in his files.

What gave rise to this combative streak in Glaskin's character is the stuff that psychologists, physicians and academics could debate at some length and still might not come to firm conclusions about. Several have speculated about possible contributing or related factors but nothing conclusive has emerged. One hypothesis was that he might have suffered from Asperger's Syndrome, a neurobiological disorder characterised by autistic-like behaviour and marked deficiencies in social and communication skills.[1] Those suffering from it have difficulty with transitions or changes and are often given to obsessive routines and a preoccupation with a particular subject of interest. While many have normal IQs, some have exceptional skills or talent in a specific field. Although they are not usually combative, they do have difficulty in grasping another person's point of view and lack an ability to respond with emotional reciprocity. Among those who are said to have suffered from Asperger's Syndrome are the Irish poet W. B. Yeats and the Canadian pianist Glenn Gould. Glaskin's long-time physician, Dr Alex Cohen, dismissed the idea that Glaskin was in this select company. 'It's easy to bring that [syndrome] into the equation. It both vindicates and makes interesting the topic. Gerry was just an angry man', he said.[2]

Another attempt to explain Glaskin's aggressive behaviour concerns the training he received in the RAAF in Canada. Glaskin and his cohorts were taught to resist extreme stress, should their aircraft be shot down and they find themselves in enemy hands. At one point they were given earphones and programmed for 24 hours non-stop. After the war those who had undergone this training were deprogrammed, but by the time this took place Glaskin was in Singapore and missed out. According to some who knew him, he was very different when he came out of the air force from when he went in. Van de Pas attributed Glaskin's aggressive outbursts to this experience.

---

1   Van Langenberg (2002).
2   Alex Cohen to JB, interview by author, 11 November 2002.

One incident would seem to support this theory. Shortly after Glaskin had taken possession of his flat in Warnham Road, Cottesloe, he came home one evening to find three men ransacking the place. He immediately grabbed several liquor bottles and started hurling them at the intruders who made for the nearest open windows and rushed to their car. Fortunately, the car behind theirs turned on its lights so Glaskin was able to take down the number plate of his assailants' vehicle and they were eventually caught. However, when the police interviewed Glaskin they warned him that had he hurt any of the offenders he could have been charged with assault. Glaskin was flabbergasted.

Others have doubted there was a direct connection between the programming and Glaskin's aggression. Alex Cohen was sceptical. 'Obviously, that emotion [to hate the enemy] is engendered in troops. It has to be. And also a very strong capacity to resist torture and privation. If a person doesn't have those ingredients in their make-up and in their soul they wither.' But extrapolating Glaskin's belligerence over a wider range of situations, Cohen added, 'The people and institutions on whom Gerry's anger was visited very rarely posed a threat to him. I can understand pursuing the theory if he were programmed to respond with violence to a threat. But for the most part, Gerry got upset when he perceived a threat. It was more like the Black Prince's motto – *noli me tangere* [touch me not] – no one touches me with impunity.'[3]

Glaskin's cousin and playwright, David Buchanan, who did a doctoral thesis on pain medicine and literature, had a different interpretation. 'Anyone with the slightest background in psychology or psychiatry would tell you that if *only* those debriefing programs were that effective. This was part of Glaskinitis, as I call it.'[4] At most it would seem that Glaskin's military programming merely reinforced a pre-existing psychological condition. If Glaskin's stories about his altercations with some of his earliest teachers are to be believed, it is clear that he was never one to cower before authority or take lightly to being provoked. Early in life he also became conscious of his ability to use words with much greater dexterity and more profusely than his peers. He soon learned that words could be an effective weapon against those who would try to rough him up or taunt him, and he used them to his advantage.

---

3   Ibid.
4   David Buchanan to JB, interview by author, 12 November 2002. For more on 'Glaskinits', see Chapter 4, 'The Managing Elder Brother'.

One group of people who experienced Glaskin's anger and pointed penmanship was his agents. Throughout his life, no fewer than 20 agents represented him in the UK, Europe, the USA and Australia. In addition, he approached several others, some of whom refused him point-blank. That the majority of these agents were in Europe is no mere chance. It reflects the state of publishing in the 1950s through the 1970s, where British publishers had a gentlemen's agreement with American publishers that divided the English-speaking world into territorial markets. 'Empire' (later Commonwealth) rights for countries like Australia tended to go to British publishers. It also reflects the limited state of publishing in Australia in the post-war years, as well as the widespread custom of translating books written in English into multiple European languages. From the beginning, Glaskin's relationship with his agents was fraught with difficulty. The first agency was A. M. Heath and Company in London, to whom he sent a copy of his manuscript of *A World of Our Own*. Like most others who read it, they saw no chance of publishing it because of its excessive length and its outspoken sexual references. Bitterly disappointed, Glaskin asked if they would consider sending it out to publishers if he promised to 'both cut and tone it down', but they declined.[5]

For a short time, Glaskin had the good fortune of having as his agent the novelist Paul Scott, who for many years worked for the firm of Pearn, Pollinger and Higham (PP&H). Later known for his highly successful *The Raj Quartet*, Scott was much admired by many writers – M. M. Kaye and Morris West among them – for his unfailing service to them.[6] Unfortunately for Glaskin and others, Scott gave up being an agent to undertake full-time writing in early 1960. Shortly before Scott left PP&H, David Higham and Laurence Pollinger had a parting of ways. Pollinger left to set up his own agency, taking his son with him.[7] Scott sided with Higham. Within agencies such schisms occurred, with author allegiance a matter of great concern. In contrast to the short-lived experiences Glaskin had with his early agents, those that followed would be more lasting. David Bolt and Sheila Watson, originally with David Higham and Associates, became Glaskin's agents off and on and under different guises for a quarter century. Glaskin's relationship with Bolt and Watson was not easy for either them or him; he terminated his

---

5   GMG to A. M. Heath & Co Ltd, 30 October 1952.
6   In her biography of Paul Scott, Hilary Spurling titles one of her chapters 'A prince among agents'. Spurling (1990).
7   Ibid., 231.

association with each of them at different points and shifed back and forth between the two. Bolt and Watson eventually had differences with Higham and broke ranks to form their own firm, which later still they split into two separate entities, although on amicable terms. Amid all these changes it was the relationship between Glaskin and Bolt that stood out and weathered the test of time.

Bolt was born and educated in England, served in the Indian Army and the Malayan police and lived in South Africa for a time, all of which gave him a perspective on the world that would have gone beyond that of many other agents. He also authored several novels, so could empathise with the plight of the writer. Glaskin and Bolt had a regular and voluminous correspondence, mostly via aerogrammes. Between 1975 and 1985 Glaskin wrote 214 letters to Bolt, an average of 19 per year or more than one a month. One year he wrote 36. Bolt simply couldn't keep up. He would be part way through replying to one letter when two of three more would arrive. Out of desperation he complained to Glaskin that he was swamping him with information. Glaskin wrote back, justifying his actions by saying that he wanted to keep Bolt up to date by sending him copies of everything he sent to everyone else.

His reply is revealing of one of Glaskin's habits that tended to alienate him from agents, publishers and others. Impatient at the slowness, incompleteness or inadequacy of their responses to his overtures, Glaskin would take matters into his own hands and write directly to the party concerned, often bypassing his agent while berating him for not doing enough. Writing to his friend Alan Seymour in 1986, Glaskin fumed, 'I have such a bum agent in David Bolt, I have to see to the republishing arrangements [for *A Waltz through the Hills*] between Heinemann and Penguin and also between Australia and the UK with both myself. But I have just sacked Bolt for various other reasons as well and will negotiate most everything from Australia.'[8] Bolt admitted he didn't have an insider's knowledge of the Australian publishing scene and was prepared to let Glaskin have a freer hand in taking initiative in that market. But such forbearance on Bolt's part may not have been prudent. In some cases, due to Glaskin's inexperience, ineptness or impatience, it backfired. Discussing the film option for *O Love*, one of Glaskin's books that most impressed Bolt, he wrote despondently, 'I'm less happy about *O Love* because although the terms for the renewal

---

8   GMG to Alan Seymour, 4 May 1986.

option are unexciting, it was you who agreed to them and if Douglas [Rae] has confirmed them we can't back out.'[9]

During Glaskin's earlier years as a writer, when words were flowing out and money flowing in, Glaskin and Bolt seemed to get along reasonably well. Barries were eager recipients of much of Glaskin's work – thanks in large part to Glaskin's inside advocate in John Bunting – and Bolt managed to find homes for some of Glaskin's short stories and negotiate translation rights for much of Western Europe. Glaskin and he exchanged news of their personal lives via Christmas cards or friendly references in their letters to each other's health or holiday plans. But from the early 1970s onwards, when Glaskin's love affair with Barries had run its course and other publishers were rejecting his manuscripts with increasing frequency, things between Glaskin and Bolt began to sour. Bolt persisted in sending out Glaskin's manuscripts, often against his better judgement but under pressure from Glaskin to keep at it. In May 1975 Bolt reported that nine publishers had declined *At the End of It All* and 15 had turned down *Small World*. He commiserated with him and tried to offer a glimmer of hope. 'Cheer up. These are boringly difficult times everywhere but England isn't altogether finished, whatever the Australian press may think, and publishing is still very much alive and kicking. And so are we. At the top end of the scale, very high prices are still being fetched. I would positively rejoice to get you in among them, even if it is to our financial advantage.'[10] Bolt urged Glaskin, as he so often did, to return to the kind of writing he considered Glaskin did best – straight-forward storytelling exemplified by *Flight to Landfall*, the sort of writing publishers favoured in their shift away from literary novels to more commercially saleable material.

But Glaskin did not heed Bolt's advice. Instead, he kept feeding him manuscripts like *Carnal Assault* and *Do Animals Go to Heaven?*, both of which Glaskin maintained were among the best writing he had ever done. Bolt strongly disagreed. He was extremely critical of *Animals*, accusing Glaskin of bad writing and inserting himself unnecessarily into the story. When three other readers of the manuscript made similar remarks, Glaskin backed down and rewrote the opening chapter, eliminating all references to himself, publishers and agents. But the rest of it he left untouched. Determined to prove Bolt wrong, Glaskin took matters into his own hands and sent the manuscript to other publishers, including Penguin Books Australia, who, while acknowledging that the book's story elements were fundamentally

9   David Bolt to GMG, January 1981.
10   David Bolt to GMG, 14 January 1975.

Playing the fool.

Photographer: Edgar Vos.
Photo courtesy Edgar Vos.

Glaskin 'on the rocks' in southern Europe.

Photographer unknown. Photo courtesy Leo van de Pas.

Han Suyin in Australia, 1970.

Photographer: Leo van de Pas.
Photo courtesy Leo van de Pas.

Glaskin delving into
parapsychology.

Publicity photo for *Windows of
the Mind*.
Photographer unknown. Photo
courtesy Leo van de Pas.

A mature Glaskin.

Dust jacket photo for *Flight to Landfall* (US) and *One Way to Wonderland*.
Photographer: Leo van de Pas.
Photo courtesy Leo van de Pas.

Doing a 'run' in the Christos Experience.

Photographer: D'Arcy Ryan. Photo courtesy Penny Sutherland.

Leo van de Pas, Glaskin's
life partner for 32 years.

Photographer: Coral Newman.
Photo courtesy Rae Kean.

Glaskin [left] and Leo van de Pas
[right] at the wedding of friends Rae
and Peter Kean, 29 March 1986.

Photographer: Coral Newman. Photo
courtesy Rae Kean.

Glaskin with neck brace, which he wore for much of the time from 1967 until his death in 2000.

Photographer: Leo van de Pas. Photo courtesy Leo van de Pas.

Glaskin at 72.

Photographer: Leo van de Pas. Photo courtesy Leo van de Pas.

achter-
volging in
amsterdam

roman van G.M. GLASKIN

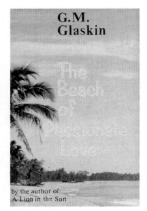

G.M.
Glaskin

The
Beach
of
Passionate
Love

by the author of
A Lion in the Sun

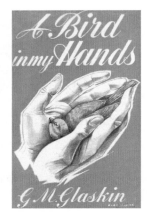

A Bird
in my Hands

G.M.Glaskin

"Contains profound reflection on the relation
of physical beauty to love and sex"
DAILY EXPRESS

ACE
BOOKS
2/6

A
CHANGE
OF
MIND

A startling novel by the author of
THE BEACH OF PASSIONATE LOVE
G. M. GLASKIN

MAYFLOWER 11343

The Man Who
Didn't Count

G. M. Glaskin

The electrifying novel of a man who
swapped boredom for sheer terror.

A DOOR
TO INFINITY

PROVING THE
'CHRISTOS TECHNIQUE'
OF MIND TRAVEL

G.M. GLASKIN

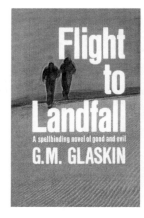

Flight
to
Landfall

A spellbinding novel of good and evil
G. M. GLASKIN

G. M. GLASKIN

FUITE VERS LA CÔTE

THE
LAND
THAT
SLEEPS

Travel and Adventure
in the Virgin West of Australia

G.M. Glaskin

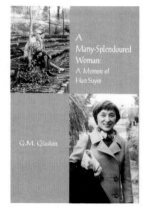

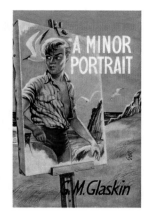

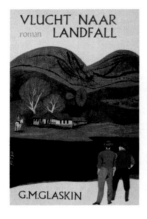

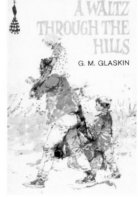

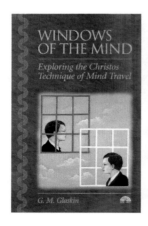

sound, reiterated Bolt's criticisms almost word for word – too much extraneous material, especially personalising, reminiscing, moralising and repetition. *Carnal Assault* proved to be just as much a stumbling block for Bolt. He went to some lengths to explain to Glaskin that the reasons for his critique had nothing to do with the story's sex and violence but with its presentation, which he described as 'clogged with overmuch background only marginally relevant to the plot, and it's (to some extent I guess necessarily) static, and without the sort of 3D characters you usually provide. Too cerebral, perhaps, for the type of story.'[11]

The verbal sparring matches continued back and forth between Perth and London, aerogramme by aerogramme. Usually it was Glaskin throwing the punches and Bolt defending, but sometimes roles were reversed. In a moment of exasperation, Bolt started one of his letters to Glaskin with, 'It's really like being in the stocks, the way the brickbats come hurtling across from Australia.'[12] However, there were occasions in which Bolt confessed he had slipped up, such as when he forgot to send Glaskin copies of the 1985 edition of *No End to the Way*, though he was quick to apologise for such oversights and ready to move on. But Glaskin's persistent tirades of alternating anger and despair didn't relent. The number of underlinings and exclamation marks in both their letters increased. At one point, so concerned had Bolt become about the tone of Glaskin's endless carping and negativity that his opening sentence-cum-paragraph was, 'Are you feeling all right?'[13]

Around the same time, Bolt's pessimism and sharp critique of Glaskin's memoir of Han Suyin, which Glaskin so fervently wanted to see published, only added to the growing schism between the two. In a letter to Han Glaskin claimed that 'I've always had to sell everything myself and just let him rubber stamp the contracts'.[14] By January 1987 Glaskin's patience with Bolt had run out. Glaskin wrote to Bolt, indicating that their relationship was about to terminate. He began, 'I am not surprised that yours of 13 January, just received in reply to mine of the 5th, contains your usual querulous self-justifications and counter-accusations, but I had expected at least some responsible and possibly productive content for once.' He listed the various publishers and film producers he had written to because of Bolt's indolence and laxity and threatened to report Bolt to the Society of Authors

---

11 David Bolt to GMG, 11 May 1981
12 David Bolt to GMG, 13 April 1967.
13 David Bolt to GMG, 25 September 1985.
14 GMG to HS, 3 December 1985.

in Britain and Australia. Signed 'Yours regretfully', a familiar ending to many of Glaskin's letters, it was the warning shot across the bows. Ten days later Glaskin cut ties with Bolt and asked him to transfer all his materials to Bolt's former partner, Sheila Watson. Watson agreed to take him on and Bolt obliged, no doubt with a sigh of relief.

Watson was familiar with Glaskin from earlier dealings with him and her willingness to include him in her stable of writers was not without some reservations.[15] She told him bluntly that his current love affair with the novella was not a commercially viable proposition. Whatever Glaskin thought of this advice, he presented Watson with detailed instructions on what to do for many of his languishing manuscripts and books, beginning with the Christos trilogy and his troubled memoir of Han Suyin. But before 18 months had passed, Glaskin had written to the Australian Society of Authors, with a copy to the Society of Authors UK, advising both bodies that he had had terminated his relationship with both agencies – Bolt's and Watson's – because of negligence and incompetence. Justifying his claim, Glaskin listed numerous faults in their representation, from ignoring his repeated requests to advise him of submissions in the UK to not having submitted manuscripts because the agent found the subject matter distasteful or not having opened manuscripts at all. Watson apparently took Glaskin's termination statement seriously but in November 1990, nearly two and a half years later, Glaskin wrote to Watson saying that Bolt had just told him that the reason he hadn't heard from her in over a year was due to the fact that she was no longer representing him. Glaskin appeared shocked at this revelation and promptly terminated his relationship with Watson (again), calling her behaviour 'odd', 'unethical' and 'unprofessional'. Given his letter to the two authors societies in June 1988, Watson may well have used the same adjectives to describe Glaskin's behaviour.

The upshot of this debacle was that Bolt again took up the reins of being Glaskin's agent, although a letter from Bolt to Glaskin in April 1990 suggests that Glaskin had been continuing to send him manuscripts and Bolt had been willing to pass them along to publishers, so 'termination' seems

---

15 When Bolt and Watson broke ranks with David Higham, GMG wrote to Higham (4 April 1971), 'I've asked Sheila Watson to continue to represent me at Bolt and Watson and should be grateful for you to pass over to her any material you have.' However, it appears that in the ensuing years, Bolt took GMG under his wing. Then, in December 1981, GMG wrote to Watson, asking her to take over from Bolt (while Bolt and she were still working together) because he didn't feel that Bolt had confidence in his ability to write. Shortly afterwards, GMG apologised to Bolt and resumed his relationship with him, at least for another six years.

to have been a rather vague and elastic term.[16] In spite of the often-heated exchanges between them, Bolt and Glaskin did manage to retain a certain respect, possibly affection, for each other. Even after his 1987 termination as agent, Bolt wrote, 'Sorry to part on a sour note (honestly, yours not mine) ... I very genuinely wish you well'.[17] To say that Glaskin was not the easiest of writers to deal with would be an understatement. He never did write another *Flight to Landfall* that Bolt so earnestly urged Glaskin to do and he never did blossom into 'the new Howard Spring' that Bolt and his colleagues at David Higham and Associates once hoped he might.[18]

In his angry letter to the Australian Society of Authors in June 1988, Glaskin concluded that 'it is better for Australian authors not to be represented by British agents, except through an Australian agent or publisher who acts on his behalf.'[19] There may well have been some truth in this, but if there was Glaskin failed to capitalise on it. He had relatively little, if anything, to do with Australian agents early in his life and by the time he did seek them out there probably wasn't much they could do for him, even though they tried.[20] Apart from those agents with whom he fell out of favour, Glaskin's own dealings with Australian publishers, several of which turned into nasty confrontations, no doubt sullied his reputation and made it doubly difficult for agents to represent him. Two relationships that soured stand out from the rest. One involved the Sydney-based agent and entrepreneur, Anthony Williams, and the other was with the Australian actor/director/producer, Michael Pate.

Glaskin first met Williams in the early 1960s in London. Williams' agency was in association with the international William Morris Agency. Glaskin had sent Williams copies of 10 of his screenplays, stage plays, television plays and his musical of *A Waltz through the Hills* but Williams had not succeeded in finding homes for any of them. Anxious to know what their status was, Glaskin phoned Williams' office but repeatedly was told that Mr Williams was in the proverbial meeting. When he could not stomach this

---

16 Bolt to GMG, 25 April 1990.
17 Bolt to GMG, 6 February 1987.
18 Bolt to JB, personal communication, 12 June 2001.
19 GMG to the Executive Secretary and Management Committee, The Australian Society of Authors, Inc., 9 June 1988.
20 His last agent, Christine Nagel, submitted GMG titles to numerous publishers but did not receive a single promising reply. In a report to GMG in September 1997, Nagel listed 10 titles sent to 21 publishers. She observed that GMG's intervention and stroppiness with publishers made her task even more difficult than it already was. Nagel to JB, personal communication, 1 January 2001.

treatment any longer, Glaskin began upping the rhetoric with Williams' office staff. The tactic backfired. He received a curt reply from Williams, indicating that he had in fact been out of the office a lot of the time. But it was Glaskin's dealings with his staff that drew Williams' ire. 'I find it difficult to comment temperately on your behaviour on the telephone to my staff who are doing their job in a manner about which no one has ever complained. If you think that a hectoring and unpleasant attitude will get you anywhere, it won't ... You can be assured that we will not accept any further communication from you as I am not prepared to allow my staff to be subject to abusive telephone calls.'[21] Glaskin scribbled at the bottom of the letter, 'What a shit!' In his reply to Williams' 'quite vituperative letter' Glaskin defended his actions, claiming he wasn't aware of having made any abusive telephone calls to Williams' staff. And in a last-ditched effort to regain the ascendancy, he declared he had decided to terminate his use of the agency. He suggested that Williams reacquaint himself with the legal obligations of an agent to his client and as a parting blow noted that he not only deplored Williams' professional failings but regretted their personal acquaintance as well.[22]

Glaskin was approaching 70 when he wrote this letter and his compounding health problems were not letting up. He hadn't had a book published in nine years and the last one, *One Way to Wonderland*, was a commercial failure. The only bright spot on his literary horizon had been the success of the 1988 television film of *A Waltz through the Hills*, which reflected in part on him as the author of the novel on which the film was based. It was over an earlier attempt at filming *A Waltz through the Hills* that Glaskin had yet another of his unfortunate skirmishes. This involved Michael Pate.[23] In January 1969, Glaskin wrote excitedly to Pate about possible film adaptations of three of his books set in Western Australia – *Flight to Landfall*, *A Waltz through the Hills* and *The Road to Nowhere*. Glaskin was buoyed by what seemed to be the imminent possibility of the filming of two of his other novels, *The Man Who*

---

21 Anthony Williams to GMG, 4 June 1993.

22 GMG to Williams, 12 June 1993.

23 Involved in Australian radio and stage productions since childhood, Sydney-born Michael Pate moved to Hollywood in the early 1950s, where he became known for his roles in John Wayne's *Hondo* (1953), the 1954 television adaptation of *Casino Royale* and *PT 109* (1963). During his time in Hollywood, Pate also tried his hand at screenwriting. In 1968 he returned to Australia where audiences knew him for his role in the television series, *Matlock Police*. He made his debut as a feature-film director with the television movie *Tim* (1979), for which his adapted screenplay won Best Screenplay Award from the Australian Writers Guild. In later years, he has concentrated on producing, writing and directing. He died in 2008.

Didn't Count and *A Change of Mind*. Pate was enmeshed in the production of the television series *Matlock Police* and didn't bite the carrot Glaskin dangled in front of him until March 1975, when his son Christopher, who was an up-and-coming actor, became enthralled with *A Waltz through the Hills*, as Pate admitted he himself was. When Pate suggested the two of them get together to talk about the possibility of filming *A Waltz through the Hills*, Glaskin responded enthusiastically. His enthusiasm was enhanced by the fact that since he had first mooted to Pate the idea of filming *A Waltz through the Hills*, the American ABC Pictures Corporation had taken out an option to film the story but had finally given up when Australian unions objected to their bringing American actors and crew to Australia to film the production.[24]

However, in the ensuing four years this mood of high anticipation and geniality evaporated into what finally became an ugly showdown between Glaskin and Pate, with the Australian Writers Guild (AWG) caught in the middle. Early on, Pate's interest in making *A Waltz through the Hills* led him to apply to both the Australian Film Commission (AFC) and the Western Australian Film Council for grants and to spend a significant amount of time on editing down Glaskin's 'vastly overlong' script to a workable length. A contract was drawn up between the two parties and being a member of the AWG Glaskin claimed that he was obliged to have the contract vetted by the guild, of which he was a committee member in Western Australia. The vetting, which was done by the Guild's WA president, Paul Kehoe, found numerous faults with the contract and stated them unapologetically. Glaskin sent Kehoe's comments to Pate, who found them offensive. Glaskin wrote to Pate expressing regret at his response to the vetting and pointed out that Kehoe's comments were not his own and that he had gone to some lengths to compromise between the two.

But Glaskin felt he had been wronged and referred his case to the Disputes Sub-committee of the AWG, whose four volunteer members spent an enormous amount of time and voluminous correspondence working on the case. The outcome of their work was not as Glaskin had hoped. Glaskin's claim that Pate pay him $1250 for work on a brochure, supposedly covered by the $4000 to be provided by the AFC grant, they deemed invalid because Pate never received the grant. To Glaskin's suggestion that Pate's letter detailing his intentions regarding script fees and percentage of profits was

---

24 Ironically, when the Western Australian company Barron Films eventually made a television movie of *A Waltz through the Hills* they used US-based Irish actor Dan O'Herlihy in one of the lead roles.

a 'legally binding letter of intent to contract' they replied, 'as the intention to contract was followed up by a contract which was never negotiated and all dealings terminated, your prospects would appear to be slim.'[25] The only thing the sub-committee thought Glaskin might have a possible claim upon would be $500 for an option to rights. They strongly advised Glaskin not to proceed with adapting his book for film without first arranging a contract for the rights to the original work and not to work speculatively on preparing a screenplay without a legal contract to cover it.

Glaskin wrote many screenplays based on someone's expressed interest in them and none was ever taken up. He no doubt assumed that since he already had a significant track record as a published author, film producers would automatically welcome him taking the initiative on writing screenplays to his works. But this wasn't the case, as Glaskin found out by hard experience. Apparently, others shared Glaskin's fate. In his final letter to Glaskin, the chairman of the AWG Disputes Sub-committee, Hugh Stuckey, wrote, 'The major point which arises from your experience is that writers should not speculate with their work. We appreciate your own particular difficulty, not having an agent to represent you, but when tackling a major work such as a feature film, every precaution must be taken to protect the author. We will draw the attention of all our members to this problem via the Bulletin and do our best to eliminate this kind of dispute in the future.'[26]

Stuckey's reference to Glaskin's lack of an agent was an astute comment, although it is not quite accurate. At this time, he still employed David Bolt in London but given Bolt's distance from Australia and his unfamiliarity with the antipodean publishing world, Bolt tended to defer to Glaskin on these matters. Once again, this proved detrimental and ultimately disastrous for Glaskin. Although he was intelligent, competent with financial affairs and capable of writing grammatically correct – if overly emotional and provocative – letters, he was his own worst enemy when it came to conducting matters of this sort, which called for tact and diplomacy as well as legal smarts. As Stuckey wrote politely but pointedly, 'we feel that a mature approach would have resulted in professional negotiation.'[27] For Glaskin, this dressing down must have seemed the last straw. A few weeks before, he had written to David Bolt, 'What a sorry state of affairs. With all these failures on hand, would you believe 16 of them, as against 18 publications, I still can't even

25 Hugh Stuckey, Chairman, AWG Disputes Sub-committee to GMG, n.d. but received by GMG 25 October 1979.
26 Ibid.
27 Ibid.

contemplate starting something else, except perhaps something else for children."[28]

Compared to the difficulties Glaskin had with agents throughout his career, his dealings with publishers would seem to be significantly better. After all, J. M. Barrie – later James Barrie Books Limited, Barrie Books Limited, Barrie & Rockliff and Barrie & Jenkins – published 14 of his books, and the Singapore publisher Graham Brash published three, although two were reprints. Other publishers included Doubleday, Delacorte, Heinemann Windmill Classics, Reader's Digest Condensed Books, St. Martin's Press, Wildwood House and a slough of paperback imprints – Ace, Arrow, Corgi, Four Square, McFadden-Bartell, Mayflower, Panther, Penguin/Peacock, Prism and Unity. His only Australian publications came from Ure Smith, which published *Two Women*, and Fremantle Arts Centre Press (now Fremantle Press), which published *One Way to Wonderland*, two relatively minor and financially unsuccessful books in the context of his total output. In addition, numerous European publishers printed foreign translations of his works. While this number of publishers might look impressive on a listing or résumé, it doesn't reveal the extent to which Glaskin struggled with the state of publishing in his day and with particular publishers, some of whom found themselves in the same kind of acrimonious confrontation with Glaskin as did several of his agents.

To probe the nature of these disputes, it is helpful to understand the state of publishing at the time, especially as it affected Australia.[29] Until the early 1960s, the Australian book marketplace was dominated by British publishers and British books.[30] Shortly after the Second World War, British and American publishers signed an agreement to protect what was an important export market for British publishers and an insignificant one for US publishers. Known as the British Traditional Market Agreement (BTMA), it allowed British publishers to demand full Commonwealth rights for a book (except educational books) or not at all. This state of affairs led many Australians to refer to the 'US/UK publishing cartel'.[31] However, by the mid-1970s, the BTMA had begun to be dismantled. Two events in particular contributed to this. One was the signing of a Consent Decree by

---

28 GMG to Bolt, 6 October 1979.
29 Two articles were helpful in this regard – Patricia Holt's 'Publishing in Australia' (1978) and Robin Bromby's 'Brought to Book: The Ills of Australian Publishing' (1989).
30 Holt (1978, 54). By 1960, as many as 75 per cent of all books sold in Australia were imports and most of those were from the UK.
31 Ibid., 44.

21 US publishers in 1976 and the other was the publication in Australia of *The Thorn Birds*, whose 75,000-copy hardcover sales astonished everyone, Australians included.[32]

These developments caused American publishers to rethink their attitude towards Australia as a market for books. They also spelt doom for the era of 'Britain's literary colonialism', in which British publishers regarded Australia as their own backyard.[33] But this was the era in which Glaskin came of age as a writer and produced the bulk of his published work. It is therefore not surprising that he and many other Australian writers sought British publishers to print and distribute their work. There was a firmly held belief that a British publisher's name on a book's title page added to its authority and appeal in Australia.[34] Indeed, as Glaskin's mentor and friend John K. Ewers declared, 'To have a novel published in London made me someone to be treated with a kind of awesome respect.'[35]

Ewers' comment illuminates another key aspect of the time and place in which Glaskin emerged as a writer. Australia was still struggling to throw off the shackles of a national inferiority complex – which some have traced back to convict days – that added negative connotations to the term 'Down Under'.[36] The rest of the world, the world that mattered, was 'up over'; it was Europe, particularly the UK, and to a lesser extent North America, or more specifically the United States. In order to make it in many fields, but especially the arts, one had to prove oneself 'up over' and then return 'down under' and hope that recognition came your way. Glaskin put much of the blame for this attitude at the feet of Australian journalists and publishers. The former he accused of harbouring resentment against authors, based on his assumption that every journalist at heart was an author manqué, in whose bottom drawer was 'an uncompleted, or an unpublished, or an unpublishable novel'. Such resentment is greatest, he feared, when the successful author happened to be Australian.[37] Publishers were equally guilty, as he proclaimed in a 1962 article that appeared in the Hong Kong journal *Eastern Horizon*.

> Because of the very fact that an author happens to be Australian, [an Australian] publisher assumes him to be inferior and vastly prefers

---

32 Ibid., 42. Until that time, Australian publishers considered a 5000-copy sale very good and an 8000-copy sale excellent.

33 Bromby (1989, 25).

34 Holt (1978, 43).

35 Ewers (1983, 177).

36 Holt (1978, 42).

37 GMG (1962a, 42).

to publish ... the superior and 'safer' works from established authors overseas. Admittedly, some Australian authors are (unfortunately for them) published by Australian publishers, but seldom if ever with the publicity and réclame accorded to their overseas colleagues.

This, naturally, compels the Australian writer to seek publication overseas, usually in Britain where he finds himself infinitely better off for both remuneration and réclame ... Indeed, it seems to me that the best of Australian writers are invariably published overseas.[38]

This Australian reluctance to recognise its own best and brightest may have affected Glaskin in another way. He went abroad and proved himself both as a stockbroker and a writer, but on his return to Australia he never received recognition on his home turf. His combative nature and the way in which he inflicted it on agents and publishers in particular no doubt contributed to this. But there were also practical difficulties getting his books into Australian bookshops once they were published abroad. Glaskin often harped on this stumbling block in his letters to friends and acquaintances. It was a legitimate complaint. Said Edward Coffey of Hodder and Stoughton, 'If we publish a book [in Australia] our first printing will be 5,000 copies; if we bring it in from the UK, we may take 500.'[39] Glaskin no doubt fared better with paperback editions of his books, given the fact that traditionally Australia has been a strong paperback market.[40]

Glaskin's differences with publishers were many and caused him much anguish. His correspondence with David Bolt and Han Suyin is littered with disparaging remarks about the state of the trade.[41] So incensed did he become about this matter that in 1978 he attempted to write a book about it, which he titled *Never Again*. Not surprisingly, no publisher took it up but it did allow Glaskin to vent his feelings on this subject and other matters as well. When it came to the state of publishing today he pulled no punches. 'The world of books was already deteriorating to a degree that what in the '70s might be regarded as the cream had only as recently as the '60s been merely the scum, even from those survivors previously the cream of writers',

---

38 Ibid., 42–43.
39 Holt (1978, 66).
40 At the top of the list of best-selling Australian paperbacks up to this time were books like *The Power of One* by Bryce Courtney, *The Thorn Birds* by Colleen McCullough and *Jaws* by Peter Benchley, the latter selling 750,000 copies, an enormous figure given the relatively small population of Australia.
41 See Chapter 6, 'Dear Old Thing', for Glaskin's exchanges with Han Suyin.

he wrote.[42] But he reserved most of his venom for those in the industry who demanded higher returns and fewer risks. 'Multi-million [dollar] publishing houses … are determined to stay that way, multi-millioned. Few now publish work unless it is going to "make money" and even then with the further proviso of "and plenty of it". Mostly it is small publishers – indeed, the very smallest – which keep up any standards the publishing trade may still have. All too many, growing richer but almost indistinguishable from each other, have become mere assemblers for printers. Publishing in its former true sense is fast disappearing – just how fast we were very soon to find out.'[43]

These dual peeves – the growing greed of large-scale publishers and the declining standards of what they printed – were a litany for Glaskin. As he perceived it, the two were enmeshed in a kind of Catch-22 situation. He maintained that because (hardcover) books were too expensive for the average person, publishers instead favoured cheap, softcover editions. For Glaskin, 'softcover' was a euphemism for 'robust' or 'lurid' books which, because of their popularity, were what writers were persuaded to write.[44]

Glaskin was not alone in waging this campaign on behalf of downtrodden and impoverished writers. John K. Ewers echoed similar sentiments in describing the fate of his *Money Street*, published by Hodder and Stoughton in 1933 and which sold 3412 copies in the first nine months, then considered very good for a first novel. But as Ewers pointed out the returns on these sales were minimal, due to a royalty system that favoured books sold in the UK at the expense of those sold outside. Only the 509 copies sold in the UK received the full 10 per cent royalty (nine pence a copy). The remaining 2903 that were sold outside the UK (most of them in Australia presumably) were regarded as 'colonial sales' on which a royalty of three pence a copy was paid. 'This iniquitous system of treating sales in one's own country as "colonial" and subject to a reduced royalty was then normal practice for books published in England and continued for many years to come', wrote an irate Ewers.[45] To add fuel to his fire, Ewers also noted that:

> people go into bookshops and see hundreds of books with customers poring over them and a few actually buying some, and envy authors for the fortunes they make. And what makes them really envious is to think that, well, writing isn't work anyhow, and there are all those authors

---

42 GMG (1978b, 74).
43 Ibid., 85.
44 GMG (1960b, 29).
45 Ewers (1983, 231).

making pots of money just sitting on their bottoms doing nothing! ... Even some booksellers have similar ideas. They resent authors receiving the ten percent royalty on retail sales when they have put no money into producing or selling them, while they, the booksellers, receive a miserable thirty to forty percent on the retail price. Sometimes, in these days when the retail price can be varied at will, they can make fifty percent or even more![46]

The economic plight of the writer was not the only concern Glaskin had about the publishing trade. There were other issues that rankled him and specific publishers with whom he crossed swords over these issues. One issue was the retention of manuscripts by publishers for what Glaskin considered were unduly long periods of time. He had this grievance with a number of publishers, including the Australian subsidiaries of the British publishers Heinemann, Thomas Nelson and Macmillan. When Heinemann kept his manuscript of *Carnal Assault* for nearly a year Glaskin was exasperated. He wrote an angry letter to Nicholas Hudson, the managing director, who replied apologetically. Glaskin thanked Hudson for his letter but pointed out that it explained nothing. Glaskin maintained, quite rightly no doubt, that it would have helped to have the reason for their rejection of his work, even their reader report(s), rather than an apology. Along with *Carnal Assault*, Hudson also turned down *Do Animals Go to Heaven?*, both of which Glaskin described as 'top-rate books'. He let Hudson have his standard spiel on the deplorable state of publishing in Australia, claiming that it made him no longer want to write. But trying to maintain the upper hand in this dispute, Glaskin finished off the letter with a touch of humour and a prophetic voice that a quarter century later does not sound as far-fetched as it probably did at the time. He wrote, 'There is still a reading public. Authors might need to find some other way to get to them, circumnavigating publishers. Word processors linked to pay-computers with print-outs might be much closer than you think.'[47]

This tangle with Heinemann resembled an earlier one in which Glaskin became embroiled with Macmillan in 1971. At issue was the fact that Macmillan had held some of his manuscripts for more than nine months, especially his voluminous *At the End of It All*. In the interim, Glaskin interpreted correspondence between himself and the publisher to imply acceptance, which prevented him from taking it to other publishers. Part of

Glaskin's correspondence was with the parent company of Macmillan in London, who eventually apologised for the 'shockingly long time' they took to reach a decision, laying the blame at the feet of their Australian colleagues from whom they were unable to get a firm decision. When the manuscript was finally turned down Glaskin felt misled. Brian Stonier, Manager of Macmillan Australia, tried to explain to Glaskin the reason for the length of time they kept his manuscripts. 'From your correspondence it appears that you require a rapid decision on your work and such a decision must always be negative in the field of fiction. Anyone can give you a negative answer promptly but a publisher who is making a determined effort to establish a market and a viable print run for a new fiction manuscript will always take quite some time to do it. You are able to reject a manuscript in six weeks; seldom can we accept one in that time. This has been the position in your case and the time taken (and effort spent) had been much longer than usual because the manuscripts were better than usual.'[48]

For Glaskin this was not an adequate reply. He took his dispute to the Australian Society of Authors (ASA), with whom he was becoming a familiar name. The Society essentially reiterated Stonier's comments. Naturally, this did not satisfy Glaskin nor enamour the ASA to him. For help he turned to the ASA's British counterpart, The Society of Authors, of which Glaskin was a member from 1959 to 1979. He thought that the UK body had established a policy on the retention of manuscripts that made it mandatory for a publisher either to return a manuscript within six weeks of receiving it or to ask for an extension of another six weeks to come to a decision. However, when Glaskin wrote to the Society he was told they did not have such a thing. The secretary concluded that Glaskin must have been thinking of a code of practice prepared by the Publishers' Association, a copy of which he sent Glaskin. The secretary explained that outside a contractual relationship between an author and a publisher there was no way to enforce that kind of timeline on a publisher. The ASA agreed. It would seem that Glaskin didn't have a case. But that didn't deter him from trying at least one more time to press his claim. This time it was much closer to home, with the Fremantle Arts Centre Press.

Fremantle Arts Centre Press Press (FACP) (now Fremantle Press) is a small but successful publishing house established in 1976 to promote the work of Western Australian writers. Among its more notable authors are

---

48 Brian Stonier to GMG, 28 September 1971. The manuscripts were *At the End of It All*, *Turn on the Heat*, *The Two Dollar Miracle* and *One Way to Wonderland*.

Tim Winton, Sally Morgan and Elizabeth Jolley. In 1977, Glaskin tried to get FACP to publish *One Way to Wonderland* but they declined. Glaskin wrote to the Chief Executive, Ian Templeman, berating him and his colleagues for their inordinate delay in replying and queried the competence of their reader. He pointed out that FACP's rejection of his manuscript came on the heels of his own inclusion as an author in the American publication, *Who's Who in the World*. He decried the fact that such authorship was 'acceptable by international standards but not by those in Western Australia'. Lamenting that 'achievement overseas incurs only resentment and treatment like this', he vowed that 'there can be no further offers to your press'.[49] But this proved not to be the case. In 1984, FACP did eventually publish *One Way to Wonderland* but prior to that Glaskin had submitted his manuscript of *Do Animals Go to Heaven?* Again he lambasted them for retaining it for an unreasonably long period of time. A reader's report had recommended *Animals* for publication in September 1982. Glaskin was advised of this in February 1983 but in December that year FACP advised him of the imminent publication of *One Way to Wonderland* and stated that *Do Animals Go to Heaven?* would be deferred until 1985. Glaskin couldn't take it any longer. He wrote angry letters to Templeman, the ASA and the state Minister and Shadow Minister for the Arts to call a stop to this 'despicable and unethical' method of dealing with manuscripts. In his defence Templeman pointed out that upon assessment, Glaskin's manuscript was placed on a provisional list for possible publication at a later date and that he could either leave it there in hope of future publication or remove it.

In the course of these and several other episodes, Glaskin's dealings with the ASA became legendary. His position was: I am a member of this organisation, the organisation is meant to advocate on behalf of authors; therefore, I will demand they do everything in their power to defend my position. Theoretically, he was within his rights but given his relentless pursuit of his adversaries, his dictatorial tone in writing and on the telephone and his high-handed manner of dealing with people of all ranks in the organisation, the ASA, like several other organisations Glaskin belonged to, finally tired of him and he of them. Matters came to a head when Glaskin wrote to the Chairman of the ASA, Ken Methold, complaining of the ineffective leadership of the Western Australian representative Brian Dibble and of his dissatisfaction with the poor service the ASA had rendered him over the years. Methold wrote back strongly defending Dibble for his

---

49 GMG to Ian Templeman, 16 April 1977.

contribution to the ASA, both in WA and nationally. He also pointed out that the ASA correspondence with Glaskin went back to 1973, and from the beginning of 1984 to September 1985 alone they had received 15 to 20 letters from him, to which they had responded by phone or letter. 'We have attempted to provide you with more service – good, bad or indifferent, in your view – than probably any other ASA member', wrote Methold. And, as a last resort, he added, 'If it has not been adequate in your opinion, then perhaps you should discontinue your membership.'[50] Glaskin did in 1989, but not before hauling over the coals the editor of the Society's publication, *The Australian Author*, for producing 'a retrograde publication if ever I have seen one'.[51] While his critique may have had some validity, Glaskin's constant carping and impossible demands had worn thin his welcome at the ASA. In resigning his membership, he had lost a potential ally in his fight for the plight of the writer, but it was one membership that many at the ASA doubtless would not miss.

Intriguingly, this was not the first time Glaskin had resigned from the ASA, although it was the last. In 1971, he had resigned over the refusal of the then editor of *The Australian Author*, Nancy Keesing, to publish his somewhat satirical article, 'Publishers' Bloomers?', which he wrote in response to another article, 'The Publisher's Side', by Michael Page, publishing manager of Rigby Limited and another ASA member. Page laid out how publishing was an economically precarious industry that depends upon that fickle and intangible reality called 'public taste'. He enumerated the key questions publishers need to ask when deciding whether to risk going with a book and cautioned writers to tailor their work to the parameters within which particular publishers worked. This latter point infuriated Glaskin, even if he misconstrued its intent. In retaliation he made a mockery of Page's arguments, writing in a hyperbolic style that begs to be read aloud. The journal's then editor, Barrie Ovenden, accepted the article for publication as a way of presenting the author's case but indicated that it may have to wait an issue or two to find space. Shortly after, Ovenden moved on and Keesing became editor. The article didn't appear in the next issue.

Some time later Keesing returned the article to Glaskin, saying it had been temporarily lost in the handover of editors. Furthermore, she declined to publish it now for two reasons – it was nine months after Page's article had been published and readers would have forgotten the original piece by then,

---

50 Ken Methold to GMG, 18 September 1985.
51 GMG to Robert Pullan, May 1985.

and they needed space for obituaries in the next edition. Glaskin dismissed both arguments. He appealed to the ASA's Management Committee to back him up, but they chose to go with Keesing instead and asked Glaskin to withdraw the article. Reluctantly, and against his better judgement, he did. Not long afterwards, Keesing was appointed to the Literature Board of the Australia Council and was one of three people whom Glaskin would blame for his repeated failures to be awarded grants by the Council for the rest of his life.[52] Whether there was any truth in this or not, Glaskin never did receive further grants from the Board, in spite of appeals from Mary Durack and John K. Ewers on his behalf.

But at this moment Ewers went on the offensive and took Glaskin to task for his resignation from the ASA on the basis of this incident and particularly his denigration of Keesing, whom he praised as 'sound' and 'admirable' and 'my friend for many years ... [who] would not willingly hurt you or anyone else'. Ewers reminded Glaskin that 'publishers do have a different point of view' and recalled an instance in Glaskin's younger days when Ewers had told him what the writer, Arthur Upfield, thought about publishers: That every publisher was a bastard. 'You drew yourself up and said your [sic] didn't find yours like that', said an amused Ewers. 'You know that you are inclined to regard anyone who crosses you as a bastard.'[53] This kind of blunt feedback from one of his trusted mentors must have been hard for Glaskin to stomach. But two days earlier, in another letter, Ewers had laid the groundwork for it. Describing his regret over Glaskin's resignation from the ASA, Ewers, then the ASA's Regional Vice-President for Western Australia, spelt out his position on the matter.

> It follows that any organisation may from time to time decide to do something with which not all members may agree. I am inclined to agree with you that lengthy obituaries of members should not be published in the society's journal, but I do not see that as a reason to resign from it. If every member of any organisation acted on personal impulse in this way there would soon be no organisations of any kind left.

---

52 GMG claimed that Vic Williams, Western Australia's representative on the Literature Board, conveyed verbally Nancy Keesing's message that as long as she and Richard Walsh were on the Board GMG could not hope for the grant he has asked for. Keesing served as a member of the Board from 1973 to 1974 and as its chair from 1974 to 1977. Walsh was a member of the Board from 1973 to 1976.
53 Ewers to GMG, 29 July 1971.

You may remember that you resigned from your position as President of the local FAW [Fellowship of Australian Writers] in a similar moment of impulse before your term of office expired, and at the same time made your resignation cover also membership of the FAW. Surely, the only way to help to mould an organization nearer to your heart's desire is to remain a member and work diligently to that end.[54]

The last sentence reflects a major difference in character between the two men. Ever the gentleman, Ewers was known for 'the dignity with which he made his pronouncements, the same kindliness he showed to everyone and the esteem in which he was held in every part of the writing world in Australia'.[55] Mary Durack praised his 'selfless and unflagging contribution to the literary life of his state', noting his formidable knowledge of Australian writers and his infective enthusiasm.[56] Jean Lang (Crowe) commented that Ewers was 'generous always with help and encouragement to fellow writers, especially beginners, in an environment that was not kind to writers.'[57] While Glaskin, too, showed a willingness to assist young writers – in which may well have been influenced by Ewers' example – he often lacked the tact, humility and patience of his elder mentor in dealing with people. He also did not exhibit the same degree of vision or spiritual conviction in his writing that caused one local writer to refer to Ewers as 'the elder statesman of writing'.[58] In his inaugural presidential address to the FAWWA, which he titled 'The Great Australian Paradox', Ewers called on Australians to have large hearts, broad minds and indomitable courage, and he urged Australian writers to assist their fellow countrymen to strive for an awareness of themselves and of their country.[59]

When Ewers died in 1978 aged 74, Glaskin wrote a small article about him in the journal of the Australian Society of Authors. Like Glaskin's memoir of Han Suyin, this article tended to focus heavily on Glaskin and lightly on its avowed subject, other than those episodes in Glaskin's life in which Ewers featured. Out of the anecdotes emerges a clear sense that Ewers played an important role in Glaskin's life, especially at pivotal points when Glaskin needed guidance and direction. Glaskin acknowledged this when he conceded that 'with all his faults and his frailties – and Lord knows we

---

54 Ewers to GMG, 27 July 1971.
55 Buddee (1982, 25).
56 Durack (1982, 21).
57 Lang (1982, 57).
58 Buddee (1982, 25).
59 Greenwood, (1982, 46).

all have them – [Ewers] had been right so often'. Glaskin mourned his loss, but it was not so much the grievous loss of a dear friend and trusted advisor as it was the sad departure of a fellow campaigner on behalf of countless unpublished authors who had suffered at the hands of inconsiderate, out-of-touch literary boards and self-styled, profit-driven publishers. He wrote, 'But perhaps now someone will do something about these unpublished works, just as you yourself tried so much to do something about them, and for so many others.'[60]

Ewers' reference to Glaskin's resignation from the FAW illuminated an incident that was not only significant in itself but was to become symptomatic of a pattern in the years to follow. In 1946, Ewers and Henrietta Drake-Brockman had convinced Glaskin to join the local branch of the Fellowship. The organisation, which had formed eight years earlier following the visit to Perth of the American literary agent, Hartley Grattan, brought together a number of prominent Western Australian writers of the day, including Katharine Susannah Prichard, Mary Durack, Walter Murdoch, Mollie Skinner and Gavin Casey. Ewers was the Foundation President of FAWWA and excelled at giving the annual presidential address. When Glaskin returned to Perth from Amsterdam in 1968, the author of 15 books, he was asked to take over the reins of the organisation. Although he had serious misgivings, he felt obliged to give back to the FAW something in return for the encouragement, support and practical help a number of its members had given him in his younger days as a writer. In addition, he had strong feelings about the plight of writers in Australia and saw this as a platform to right many of the wrongs they suffered. Glaskin took the position seriously and threw himself into it with his usual passion. He reinstituted the Round Table, at which aspiring writers and poets read aloud their work for critiquing, but found himself taking home entire manuscripts to review, at no cost to their authors but considerably consuming of his own time.

Glaskin soon discovered that this was not the job he thought it would be. First, little things niggled him, like the way many able-bodied members promptly left at the end of meetings, leaving him in his neck collar and Leo van de Pas to clean up and reset the room. Irritation soon spilled over into resentment and anger that came to a head over the issue of a memorial to honour the life of Henrietta Drake-Brockman. Glaskin referred

---

60 GMG (1978a, 33).

to the episode as 'the most tasteless squabble I have known anywhere'.[61] After consulting with Henrietta's husband, Glaskin recommended to the appropriate committee that a granite garden bench inscribed with her name would be a fitting memorial. The committee approved and asked Glaskin and Mary Durack to arrange for its construction and erection. But when news of the decision was shared with the wider fellowship, some members – whom Glaskin referred to disparagingly as 'mostly women poets' – opposed it. In a letter to the Fellowship they underscored their objection to the granite bench by asserting that 'Henrietta had never been sat upon in her life'.[62] Glaskin was startled and shocked that a small group would dare challenge the committee's decision and by default his leadership on the matter.

Not given to backing down in the face of confrontation, Glaskin proceeded with plans for the bench. He even prevailed upon Alexandra Hasluck, then Lady Hasluck, wife of the Governor-General and close friend of Henrietta Drake-Brockman, to travel from Canberra to Perth to unveil the memorial. But the dissenting ladies were not put off by such high-handed tactics. They gathered more signatures and circulated a letter in which they threatened to boycott the ceremony and even resign if the memorial remained a bench. Glaskin had had enough. Instead of the opponents of the bench boycotting the ceremony, he himself did, using as his excuse that he had suddenly been called to Sydney on business. On 10 September 1969, less than a year after taking office, Glaskin wrote a letter of resignation to Bert Vickers, Senior Vice-President of the Fellowship in WA. 'I can see no reason for continuing in what has become an onerous situation through behaviour I consider not only out of order but tasteless.'[63] Glaskin later wrote that the Fellowship of Australian Writers was 'a fellowship I could well do without'.[64]

The FAW, the ASA and the AWG were three organisations with which Glaskin had his differences that led to a falling out and ended in his resignation. One other organisation with which Glaskin found himself offside was the Australia Council's Literature Board. Ever since he was awarded a Commonwealth Literary Fund Fellowship in 1956/57, Glaskin made repeated applications for grants and fellowships to assist him with his writing. He was relatively successful, receiving six totalling $18,450 – two fellowships from the Commonwealth Literary Fund (predecessor to the

---

61 GMG (1978b, 61).
62 Ibid., 63. According to LvdP, Henrietta Drake-Brockman had told GMG that she missed not having a place to sit in the garden of Tom Collins House.
63 GMG to F. B. Vickers, 10 September 1969.
64 GMG (1978b, 65).

Literature Board), one grant from the Literature Board, two grants from the Film, Radio and Television Board of the Australia Council (formerly known as the Film and Television Board), and one bursary from the Western Australian Arts Council.[65] But from the early 1970s onwards he was singularly unsuccessful in convincing funding bodies to support his projects. Ironically, it was during this period that government expenditure on the arts took a quantum leap forward, catapulted by the generous funding initiatives of the newly elected federal Labor Party government headed by Gough Whitlam.[66] The Whitlam government not only increased the number of fellowships awarded but extended them to three years for senior writers, instituted a three-year guaranteed annual income of $6000 for 'established writers of talent' and created writer-in-residence programs at universities and other tertiary institutions.

Glaskin argued that given his incontestable status as an established writer he was deserving of such support. Apparently, the 'of talent' requirement was where he ran into trouble, although Glaskin suspected fouler motives at play. He made application but was refused repeatedly. In 1973 he accused members of the Board of being prejudiced against him in denying him a grant. He wrote to the Prime Minister, Gough Whitlam, as well as to the chairman, Professor Geoffrey Blainey, and members of the Board. Van de Pas also wrote Blainey a letter in which he reiterated that Glaskin had been unjustly treated. Blainey denied this, maintaining that the long manuscript Glaskin had submitted – *At the End of It All* – received unfavourable reports from the Board's readers. What piqued Glaskin was that two other Western Australian writers, whom he deemed unworthy, had received three-year grants.[67] Blainey then stated that after a decision had been tentatively made not to award Glaskin a fellowship the Board reconsidered the matter and, in light of Glaskin's long experience as a writer, they decided to ask two

---

65 His first grant was £1000 ($2000). I have included this amount in calculating the total of $18,450, although there is some question whether GMG actually received it. Australia Council records show that he relinquished the grant because of his non-resident status and their refusal to postpone it another year. GMG claims that the Literature Board later changed it from a grant for future work to an award for his work on *A World of Our Own*. This seems unlikely but I have not been able to verify whether it happened or not.

66 In its last year (1972), the Commonwealth Literary Fund had a budget of $250,000. The following year (1973–1974) the newly established Literature Board's budget was just over one million dollars. Shapcott (1988, 2).

67 Western Australian writers who received three-year Guaranteed Income awards in 1973–1974 were Richard Beilby, Donald Stuart and Mary Durack. Randolph Stow received a three-year Fellowship ($9000 per year) but relinquished his grant before its term expired. Ibid., 31.

more readers to assess his latest manuscript. Alas, they turned it down too. However, Blainey made still another concession to Glaskin. Should his longer manuscript be firmly accepted by a publisher, they would again consider his claim for a grant before the next round of fellowship applications were called. All these gestures led Blainey to declare that, far from being discriminated against, Glaskin had been given preferential treatment and that the Board did not usually enter into correspondence about reasons for the rejection of applications.[68]

Blainey's letter did little to quell the rising tide of anger and resentment in Glaskin towards the Australia Council. Indeed, it seemed to have the opposite effect. The following April, in response to an advertisement for nominations to the new Australia Council Literature Board and/or Film and Television Board, Glaskin nominated himself. He listed among his references Sir Paul Hasluck, Government House, Canberra and Sir Charles Court, Parliament House, Perth. But even with such lofty names to endorse him he failed to gain a seat on the board. So firmly did Glaskin believe that he was entitled to a fellowship that he doggedly pressed on with his claim. In December 1974 he wrote to the ASA's Management Committee chairman, G. C. O'Donnell, 'I am unable to continue writing because of exhaustion from the mere daily chores of looking after myself, instead of being able to afford to have a woman come in to perform my domestic requirements. Both Literature Boards of 1973 and 1974 were informed of this, yet still denied me what, with 16 volume publications, I consider as a right: the guarantee of income for established writers …'[69]

Ever committed to his cause, Glaskin ploughed on throughout the 1970s, submitting applications for Senior Fellowships year after year but to no avail. In 1977 he tried to use his inclusion in *Who's Who in the World* (for authorship) to add weight to his case, but Glaskin's own fascination with his listing in such volumes – he was included in at least nine in his lifetime – didn't impress the Literature Board.[70] Bemoaning his fate, Glaskin wrote to the Board's secretary saying that he now had to abandon authorship. Not being able to solicit sympathy for his plight, in 1980 he tried another tactic –

---

68 Geoffrey Blainey to GMG, 9 January 1974.
69 GMG to G.C. O'Donnell, 27 December 1974.
70 Although inclusion in such volumes happens for a variety of reasons, GMG seemed to believe that they underscored, if not enhanced, his prowess as a writer. However, he did appear to have some distance on the matter. When he received an announcement describing his 'exclusive inaugural invitation to the board of governors of the American Biographical Institute Research Association', he scribbled on it 'What a load of new codswallop!'

submitting two applications in different names. One came from Mr Neville Jackson, Battle Street – the former name for Murray Avenue and somewhat appropriate in the circumstances – Mosman Park and another with the same date from Mr Glaskin, of Warnham Heights, Warnham Road, Cottesloe. Alas, even this did not do the trick.

Perhaps there was some truth to Glaskin's assertion that certain members of the Literature Board did not wish to see him receive grants. Certainly, three people who were on the 11-member Board had all had run-ins with him over other matters – the aforementioned Nancy Keesing, Geoffrey Blainey regarding a proposed project by Western Mining Corporation in which both he and Glaskin were involved, and Richard Walsh, managing director of Angus and Robertson, over the possible publication of *At the End of It All*, whose manuscript was the substance of debate in Glaskin's application for a grant in 1973.[71] One of the many people to whom Glaskin turned for assistance in his plight was his member of federal parliament and Minister for Education, Kim Beazley Snr. After listening to Glaskin's pleas, Beazley surmised that Glaskin must have trodden on some corns as, 'unfortunately, so often happened in this country – even, he said, in matters of justice and other public service.'[72]

One of those corns may well have belonged to Richard Walsh. In 1972, when Glaskin finished his three-part, catchall novel *At the End of It All*, he tried in vain to interest publishers in it. Although David Bolt expressed little enthusiasm for it, he did send it out to numerous publishers, none of whom showed any interest in it.[73] But new hope sprang up when the Australian publisher Angus & Robertson (A&R) decided to open an office in London. The thought of being published in the UK and Australia – and possibly the USA too with A&R's affiliations there – seemed too good to be true. From the Netherlands, Glaskin zipped off his manuscript to A&R's Fisher Street office post-haste. Shortly afterwards, he received a phone call from a Felix Brenner, asking him to come to London to discuss publishing the book. Glaskin was elated. Brenner stood in stark contrast to most publishing executives Glaskin had dealt with. He was young, American and 'startlingly

---

71 Board members were appointed by the Federal Minister for the Arts for a three-year term. In 1973 and 1974 the board consisted of 11 members, with Nancy Keesing as chairman. Geoffrey Blainey was not a member at that time but was the founding chairman. In 1975, the Board introduced outside assessors to enlarge their pool of resources and opinions.

72 GMG (1978b, 116).

73 In a summary sheet GMG updated in 1976 *At the End of It All* had been sent to 15 publishers and *Small World* to 24.

high camp'. Above all, he was friendly, brushing aside standard publisher-author keep-your-distance etiquette in favour of dramatic flair, alternating outbursts of high energy and apparent exhaustion, and displays of limp-wristed, eye-rolling behaviour that Glaskin suspected were directed at his assistant editor with 'the rather compromising name of Ian Dear'.[74] Brenner's behaviour may well have been equally directed to Glaskin himself, whose highly attractive figure, quick tongue and imposing style would not have gone unnoticed by the young American.

According to Glaskin, Brenner swept him off his feet. Not only did Brenner want to publish *At the End of It All*, he also expressed interest in Glaskin's Christos book, *Windows of the Mind* and his short novel, *Small World*. Before long, Brenner was asking for everything Glaskin had written and two of van de Pas's genealogical volumes as well. He promised that contracts would be drawn up and ready to sign in no time. Of Glaskin's and van de Pas's output, he claimed 'They're a factory. A veritable factory.'[75] However, when Glaskin went to sign contracts, Brenner's mood was much more sober. He apologised that the contracts had been held up. He then introduced Glaskin to 'two slim figures, one taller than the other, blue denimed, looking for all the world like two penurious authors asking for an advance to keep them going.'[76] One of them was Gordon Barton, the Australian millionaire who had just acquired Angus & Robertson and the other was Richard Walsh, the company's new publisher, both of whom gave Glaskin a rather cool reception. Taking Glaskin aside, Brenner then confessed they had already published several books with contracts unsigned. Moreover, advance and royalty figures were frequently filled in only once the initial sales had been ascertained.[77] Glaskin was dumbstruck. Nevertheless, Brenner assured him that his contracts would be awaiting his arrival in Sydney. He promised to arrange for John Abernathy from A&R to meet him on the day stopover his ship had in Sydney. This didn't happen and at least for one good reason: Abernathy had died shortly before. Glaskin telephoned the company and asked for Walsh but he wasn't available. When he arrived back in Perth, a letter from Bolt informed him that A&R in London still hadn't signed a contract.

Fed up with A&R's procrastination, Glaskin referred the matter to the Society of Authors in London, thinking this action would call the

---

74 GMG (1978b, 90).
75 Ibid., 92.
76 Ibid., 93.
77 Ibid., 94.

publisher's bluff and induce him to sign contracts. The ruse didn't work. Brenner's response was to switch the first contract from *Small World* to *Windows of the Mind*. Glaskin refused and insisted on all contracts being signed. Brenner promptly returned all manuscripts to Bolt. Glaskin tried appealing to Walsh but to no avail. The Society of Authors instituted legal proceedings against A&R, using *Windows of the Mind* as the book for which A&R had defaulted, since this was the only one for which they had written evidence of the company's intent to publish, and this only in a telegram. But even this tenuous argument became invalid when Glaskin's US agent sold *Windows of the Mind* to Delacorte, since any sale of this book meant that Glaskin had suffered no damages. Walsh visited London again while the case against A&R was being prepared and Phillipa MacLiesh from the Society of Authors took the opportunity to discuss the affair with him, hoping to persuade him that Glaskin had been badly treated and deserved at very least an *ex gratia* offer of compensation. Walsh refused. MacLiesh was sorely disappointed; Glaskin was crestfallen. Dejectedly, he wrote, 'The power of the publisher had outweighed the rights of a lone author. It was an exercise in futility if ever I have known one, for not only was nothing gained but a great deal was lost. So much for standing up for one's rights.'[78] To add insult to injury, A&R's office in Sydney could not find any of the manuscripts Brenner reputedly had sent them from London and worse, as far as Glaskin was concerned, Walsh was elected to the Literature Board of the Australia Council.

Glaskin's trials and tribulations with publishers did not end there. Neither was he alone among authors in their disputes with publishers. But his determination to stand up and fight for what he believed was his right, whatever it took, marked him off from most others. In the process, he left behind him a trail of bruised and battered psyches. No doubt this took its toll on his fragile, deteriorating and complicated health. He may have been wise to take counsel from his old mentor, John K. Ewers, although at times Ewers had suffered Glaskin's anger and disdain as much as many others. Ewers knew what it meant to struggle for what he believed, but his tactics and strategies were more indirect and his attitude more philosophical than Glaskin's. Writing in his autobiography, Ewers said:

> It is timely perhaps to sound a warning against the practice too commonly followed in western countries of equating the value of any artistic form – literary, graphic art, music or whatever – with financial

---

78 Ibid., 101.

returns ... Literary success can only be measured in one's own personal satisfaction, or perhaps in the recognition of the truly discerning reader. It is at best an ephemeral achievement ... Perhaps when all is said and done, it is the striving for expression that is the only worthwhile aspect of any kind of writing.[79]

---

79 Ewers (1983, 268).

Chapter 12

An Egyptian Nomarch

Dreams have always had an importance for me:
'the finest entertainment known and given rag cheap'.

Graham Greene
A Sort of Life

After the chilly, moonlit night he spent camping at Dale's Gorge in Western Australia's Pilbara region in July 1960, Gerald Glaskin was most reluctant to leave. 'I had a ridiculous but nevertheless undeniable temptation to want to live there for the rest of my life' he wrote in *The Land That Sleeps*.[1] It wasn't just the awesome beauty of nature's artistry in the Hamersley Range that had seduced him. It was also the strange dream that had come to him in such vivid imagery that he was compelled to jump out of his sleeping bag and write it down. His sudden burst of activity awoke his companion, Paul Lee. 'What on earth are you doing?' inquired Lee. 'Surely not note-taking now. It's two o'clock in the morning!' A little embarrassed, Glaskin confessed, 'I dreamt of a poem, a strange little poem, with the title written vertically down the side of the page. I had to get it down.' Perplexed but intrigued, Lee asked to see what Glaskin had written. 'It's like a scripture, isn't it? You mustn't lose it', he said. Glaskin took Lee's advice to heart and included the poem in his book just as it had appeared to him in the dream.[2]

---

1   GMG (1961c, 69).
2   The poem, titled 'To Popes and Politicians' reads: Do not, on Earth, to make this Heaven Hell!/But do, on Earth, as you would in Heaven/as you should in Heaven/as you could on Earth, and you will do well. Ibid., 68–69.

This was not the first time in his life that Glaskin had been conscious of the potency of dreams and it would not be the last. But it was, perhaps, a precursor of things to come, in which Glaskin would not only discover the power of naturally occurring dreams but the vast, untapped potential of induced or lucid dreams for revealing hidden layers of human consciousness. As his life came to an unravelling and dispiriting close, it was his work with dreams that gave Glaskin a much needed sense of purpose and unity and a conviction of the existence of a supreme being that allowed him to write, 'So I can now believe.'[3]

Glaskin's intense fascination with dreams began nearly a decade after the above episode. In May 1971 he was at the home of friends Jill and Ragnar Haabjoern, with whom he was to go out for the evening. While waiting in their living room for his hosts to appear, he glanced at the pile of magazines on their coffee table and found his eye drawn to one titled *The Christos Experiment – Introductory Principles*. Idly leafing through this homespun publication, he was about to discard it as another of those pseudo-religious rags put out by some weird group when a heading – A Method to Remember Past Lives – leapt out at him. At that moment his friends appeared and noticed his interest in the publication, albeit suffused with a high degree of scepticism. 'I'd like you to read that', said Jill. 'A friend of mine tried it and says that it not only works, it's incredible.' Glaskin asked if he knew this friend, which it turned out he did. It was a person whom he respected greatly and so felt impelled to not only read the publication but, in his inimitable feet-first style, try the experiment himself to see if it was all it was made out to be. This he did a few evenings later in the company of this same couple, Jill acting as the practitioner or guide on this occasion. The result was something so extraordinary that Glaskin eventually wrote three books on the Christos Experience[4] and its relationship to regular dreaming, one of which was heralded as a 'a classic in parapsychology'.[5]

---

3   GMG (1989b, 177).

4   The terms 'Christos Experiment', 'Christos Experience', 'Christos Technique' and 'Christos Procedure' are used throughout material written on the subject. The initiator of the term, Jacqueline Parkhurst, used both 'technique' and 'experiment'. GMG favoured 'experience' to denote the particular method described in the magazine and 'experiment' to refer to the broader work by Parkhurst and others who used the 'technique' or 'experience' as one tool among many in their counselling and psychotherapy.

5   This claim, made by the publisher Prism Press, is a reference is to *Windows of the Mind*, the first of the trilogy GMG wrote on the Christos Experiment. It was initially

The Christos Experiment, as described in the magazine, was so named by Perth psychologist Jacqueline Parkhurst. In the late 1960s, Parkhurst began investigating ways to bring about changes in consciousness without the use of drugs, such as LSD, which had become popular among researchers as well as the wider youth culture around this time.[6] Parkhurst's then husband had learned the technique – known as Multi-Level Awareness – from American William Swygard, who claimed it could 'bring into your physical consciousness your entire past'.[7] She saw the technique as a means of inducing symbolic imagery in a client while allowing the person greater freedom of expression than is usually the case with guided imagery and hypnotherapy. Parkhurst chose the word 'Christos' (from the Greek *Kristos*) because of its original meaning of 'anointed' or 'enlightened' one. She regarded it as a humanistic or developmental psychology technique in the Jungian tradition, similar to Jung's Active Imagination method. She stressed the importance of using it in a counselling relationship between therapist and client, and not as a party game or the latest mind-tickling fad. In a paper she wrote in 1982 in which she asked 'Which therapy for which client?', Parkhurst advocated an eclectic approach to therapy. She enumerated dozens of therapeutic approaches of which the Christos Technique was one, which could be used mainly as an intuitional tool but also as an emotional, mental and even transpersonal technique.[8]

The Christos Technique consists of four stages. First, the practitioner – called the 'runner', sometimes with the help of another person – massages the ankles and 'third eye' position of the forehead of the subject who lies supine on the floor, a cushion under his head, shoes off and eyes closed. This is designed to relax the subject and is sometimes enhanced by playing background music. Second, the runner begins a series of mental exercises intended to free the mind from 'conditioned certainties' and to shift perception from its usual state to one of heightened awareness. The runner asks the subject to visualise himself growing five or six centimetres longer through the bottom of his feet. Once the subject has achieved this, the runner asks him to return to normal size, a sequence repeated several times. The same process is done with the head, followed by a return to the feet but this time the subject visualises himself growing 60 centimetres. When the

---

published in 1974, another edition appeared in 1986 and a reprint in 1999. Despite this, sales figures for the book did not live up to the marketing hype.

6   See Masters and Houston (1966).
7   Swygard (1971).
8   Parkhurst (1982).

subject has successfully accomplished these tasks, the runner asks him to imagine himself expanding in all directions like a giant inflated balloon. Throughout these movements and the entire experiment the runner keeps asking questions of the subject to encourage him to describe his experience as it happens and record it. Third, the runner asks the subject to visualise and describe his front door, followed by the scene from his roof, then float up 500 metres and relate what he sees. Finally, the subject is asked whether it is night or day, and whatever his response he is asked to change it to the opposite, thereby being reminded that he has control over what he is doing. These initial exercises, which can be varied according to individual need, familiarise the subject with image making, inducing a void that he can then fill with his own images.

The fourth and critical stage is guiding the subject back to land, in daylight and feet first. If the subject merely returns to where he came from, the runner tries again to have the subject rise up higher than before and then return. Once the subject has landed, the runner plies him with questions about his environment, beginning with what he is wearing and extending from there to include the nature of the land, any inhabitants and whatever experiences the subject encounters. After a while, usually about 45 minutes, the runner asks the subject if he has seen all he wishes to and if so the runner concludes the experiment. At any time throughout the procedure, the subject is conscious of activity in the room around him and is able to 'return' if he chooses to. Usually the subject is astonished at the time taken for the experiment, imagining it to have been only about a quarter of the actual. In contrast to the subject, who is encouraged to totally immerse himself in the experience, the practitioner should be the objective guide, moving the process along by asking open-ended, non-leading questions. His job is to help the subject still his objective mind and allow him to proceed however he chooses. The practitioner only intervenes when the client has come to a standstill or is blocked. However, as Parkhurst pointed out, the practitioner is also important because people are used to silently watching what appears rather than working with it to extract its meaning.

The types of experiences subjects have with the Christos Technique vary considerably. From clients with whom she worked, Parkhurst identified personal problems, general and archetypal symbols, psychic dramas of historical events and past-life regressions, peak experiences of joy and bliss, developmental individuation of future plans and goals, body image and sensory perception change, awareness of the unconscious processes of others, non-human experiences and death experiences. She stressed the need for the subject to identify what he wished to gain from the experience before commencing it, although cautioned that it appears to 'produce its own experience regardless of the individual's conscious choice'.[9] Furthermore, as a therapeutic tool, Parkhurst insisted that the Christos Technique does not end with one 'run'. Like any behavioural change, it requires practice, discussion and follow-up. She found best results came from working with subjects over several months, sometimes longer, with one run every three weeks or so. For her it went beyond psychotherapy to preventive health care. 'I see the Christos as a means of sanctioning fantasy, creativity and non-logical processes in the individual's mind ... We can give the person the courage and the seal of approval to become greater than he is, to branch out in new ways and discover previously unsuspected creative talents.'[10]

Parkhurst also enumerated indications calling for the Christos Technique and contraindications suggesting when not to use it. She found it a useful device for those suffering from stress or mild depression, working through a mid-life crisis, bereaving the death of a family member, enhancing confidence and self-image, resolving personal conflicts, promoting creativity and finishing dream analysis. She found it unsuited to those with minimal verbal skills, those with a highly logical or rational mind, the exceedingly extrovert and those who have difficulty with visual imagery. This latter category Glaskin referred to as 'haptic', from the Greek *haptikos*, able to lay hold of. These are people whose primary sensation is touch, not sight. In contrast to 'visuals', they take their cues from body sensations, not the surrounding environment, they tend to see the parts and not the whole, and are strongly inclined to participate rather than observe. In an early study undertaken with a sample of more than 1100 subjects, 47 per cent were found to be strongly visual, 23 per cent strongly haptic and the remaining 30 per cent neither clearly one nor the other.[11] Glaskin came across several people in his use of the Christos Technique who were haptic to varying degrees. These included his partner, Leo van de Pas, and another close friend, the highly regarded artist Bryant McDiven. Like the better known Marc Chagall, McDiven had no trouble projecting images on a canvas but considerable difficulty in inducing images in his own mind. It was hardly surprising that the visualisation stage of the Christos Technique posed a formidable barrier to him, as it did to van de Pas. After van de Pas's fourth attempt, and notwithstanding his initial apprehension to undergo the experiment,

9   Ibid., 2.
10   Ibid., 25.
11   Lowerfeld and Brittain (1947).

Glaskin likened his being haptic to 'actual blindness that prevented him from "seeing" ... a wall though which he couldn't penetrate'.[12]

But Glaskin faced no such challenges. In fact, the first time he used the technique he found himself leapfrogging the step of visualising his front door and experienced himself standing in front of a very different kind of door – tall, wooden double doors bonded with metal and embedded in a massive stone wall hewn from a cliff face. Gazing around, he was confronted by a rocky escarpment that rose up from a tawny, brilliantly lit plateau through which a river flowed towards the sea and a distant coastline. Looking down, he saw himself with dark skin and long thin limbs. He was well over 180 centimetres tall, in his thirties and dressed in a loose-fitting, knee-length garment and headband. Before entering through the doors, which were surprisingly easy to open, he took off his leather thongs. As he proceeded he found himself in a kind of mausoleum containing stone sarcophagi in which one day he would be buried like his mummified ancestors around him. The circular building rose to a dome, from which moisture dripped to a hole in the floor and exited via a channel in the floor.

Below the mausoleum was a small settlement of white-domed houses over which he ruled as its elected leader and historical recorder. His own house was larger than the others, with two stories and an antechamber in which he worked with his metal and stone tools etching and painting a stone tablet. Glaskin's 'self' regretted that he had only such primitive instruments with which to work but knew that the time would come when this would change. As he pondered this eventuality, light streamed in through an unpaned window onto the colourfully tiled floor. He suddenly floated free of this self and looked down at this body sitting there like Rodin's 'thinker' gazing at the tablet. At the same time, his actual self observed both figures. Life was pleasant enough and he was determined to enjoy what he had left of it, before dying at a ripe old age of about 35.

After 'returning' from this journey, Glaskin was amazed at what he had experienced. The brilliance and clarity of the images were unlike anything he had known before and he only wished they could have continued. Although he was equivocal that he had actually regressed to a past life, he was sure that his adventure – which he was convinced had taken place in ancient Egypt – contained a message about a struggle he was facing in his present life. In typical Glaskin fashion, he was categorical about its interpretation. For some years now, and especially since his 1967 surfing accident in which his neck

---

12 GMG (1976, 164).

injuries severely curtailed his productivity as a writer, he had found himself increasingly the victim of writer's block. It wasn't just that he found the muse eluding him. He was also overcome by a feeling of futility about being a writer, given the sheer number of books being published and one's inability to read even a fraction of them in a lifetime. 'Why go to such trouble just to add a few more, or even one more, to the heap?' he asked himself dejectedly.[13] With such negative thoughts eating away at him, Glaskin had begun to descend into a mire of despair. The very urge to write dissipated. 'I shrank from it with a dread like that of death itself', he wrote. 'Worse ... after so much pain and inertia, even death no longer held the fears for me that once it had.'[14] But his dream was telling him otherwise. He had the tools to express himself and was free from other responsibilities, so there was nothing to stop him writing. Although it may not have provided a miracle cure, the dream did at least give him the desire to write up what he had experienced in the form of a magazine article, which later became three books published over six years.[15]

The following year, 1972, Glaskin was visiting London and, having dropped off a manuscript at his agent's office, found himself with a free afternoon, so along with Leo van de Pas he decided to check out the nearby British Museum. Deterred by the long queue for the special exhibition of the Egyptian ruler Tutankhamen, Glaskin decided to try his usual tactic of doing a quick scan of the total exhibits and then hone in on those that interested him. He was so glad he did. In a small upstairs room he found a limestone tablet, or stela, of almost the same dimensions as the one at which he had seen himself working in his dream. He also came across a pair of leather sandals similar to those 'he' had worn. His interest was aroused. 'I had an uncanny feeling ... that I somehow belonged to such articles, and that they equally belonged to me', he wrote.[16] Having picked up the scent, he was eager to continue the hunt and see if he might be able to pinpoint his dream in time and place. To aid him in this task, he consulted the museum's guidebook to their Egyptian collection. To his growing excitement, descriptions of locations, people and objects Glaskin had seen

---

13 Ibid., 2.
14 GMG (1989b, 23).
15 Ironically, GMG had earlier had a natural dream in which he had envisaged himself writing three books, each beginning in the same way. He had interpreted this dream as a warning against writing too many of the same kind of books, so for the next five or six years he experimented with other kinds of writing, including screenplays and a musical. None of these was ever published or performed.
16 GMG (1989b, 25).

in his dream began to fall into place. The glittering sea he had seen could have been the large lake, Birket Qarun, near the Fayum, the vast depression south of Cairo and west of the Nile, and the escarpment may well have been the nearby Gebel Qatrani. What is more, he discovered the prevalence of cliff-face burial tombs for the elected leaders or nomarchs, copper tools with ivory handles and small white-domed houses. The pieces of the puzzle were coming together. Further sleuthing allowed Glaskin to situate his dream experience in pre-dynastic Neolithic times around 3500–4000 BC.

Such extraordinary coincidence of historical detail with his dream was almost too much for Glaskin to bear. While he still maintained that this didn't necessarily verify a past-life reincarnation, he was itching to find a way to go to Egypt and see how the dream and the museum's revelations corresponded to present-day reality. He had to wait four years for the opportunity but when it came it was so fraught with serendipity and synchronicity that Glaskin felt convinced it was meant to be. In 1976 he had received an invitation from Wildwood House, the publishers of his second Christos book, *Worlds Within*, to come to London for the book's launching. In spite of the cost of the trip and his poor health he wanted to go and inquired with his travel agent whether a stopover in Egypt might be possible. Alas, given the recent embargo on foreign tourists during the Arab-Israeli war there was now much greater demand and all tours were fully booked. The agent told him to check on tours when he arrived in London but he wasn't at all hopeful. What is more, in June Glaskin was hospitalised with another of his transient ischaemic attacks and advised by doctors not to travel. Such advice only made Glaskin more determined than ever to make the trip. But faced with full flights from Perth to London he couldn't even find a seat on an aircraft. Then his travel agent called to say there was one cancellation on the first day of the off-season. 'I'll take it,' Glaskin told the agent unhesitatingly, feeling inclined to add, 'because it was meant for me.'[17] Just before leaving Perth he attended a function at which he met the Dutch Vice-Consul, whose former posting was Cairo and who volunteered names of friends whom she thought might be helpful to Glaskin should he happen to get there. Fate seemed to be favouring him.

Well, almost. Money he was expecting to receive from publishers in England had inadvertently been sent to Australia and would be difficult to return. However, the publishers then discovered a contingency in their contract to pay an extra £500 on publication of *Worlds Within*, so his cash

17 Ibid., 42.

flow problem was solved. But he still had no luck in finding a place in a tour group to Egypt. Just when he was resigning himself to not being able to go there, he received a surprise phone call from a long-time London friend who asked if Glaskin would like to join him on a holiday ... in Egypt! Glaskin's heart soared, until he learnt the trip would not be until the following January, at which time he needed to be back in Australia. But the next morning his friend called again to tell him his travel agent had another couple who were due to travel to Egypt in October and November but wished to swap with someone for January. 'Take it', said Glaskin with almost medieval certainty. 'It was meant for us.'[18] Convinced he had a tryst with destiny, Glaskin boarded the Cairo-bound flight in London. As the plane approached its destination, the captain announced that due to weather conditions they would have to land from the southwest rather than the usual northern approach. Glaskin was nearly beside himself because this would most likely mean they would fly over the area in which he presumed his dream had been set. Armed with his camera, he finagled a good window seat and took photographs until he ran out of film – an activity the captain later announced was illegal in Egypt, given the country's obsessive concern with security.

On arrival in Cairo, Glaskin could barely contain his excitement. His hosts, Dr Wilson and Hedy Bishai, invited another guest to join Glaskin and his friend for dinner. The guest was a physician and parapsychologist with a keen interest in Egyptian history and archaeology, who not only provided useful background information to Glaskin but informed him that techniques for inducing dreams may well have originated in Egypt, where the first recorded dreams were discovered. Bishai himself proved to be more than a congenial host because his family once owned property in the region Glaskin wished to visit in the western Fayum, so he gladly took time out of his dental practice to offer Glaskin his black Mercedes and chauffeur and accompany them on a visit to the location.

Monday 25 October 1976 was the magical day. After the two-and-a-half-hour drive from Cairo and a 40-kilometre detour to repair a flat tyre, Glaskin's entourage went as far as their driver would take them without fear of damaging the car on unpaved roads. Glaskin was pleased to have come so close to his perceived site and had already taken numerous photographs, including some of white-domed houses, the shimmering Birket Qarun and the looming escarpment of Gebel Qatrani. Just as he was resigned to calling it

---

18 Ibid., 43.

a day, he and his hosts had a chance meeting with two Arab guides who were willing to take them within 20 kilometres of the place Glaskin imagined he had dreamt. The closer they went, the more positive Glaskin became that he had found the source of his dream five and a half years before. He was in ecstasy. 'The revelation was shattering, the most overwhelming I have ever experienced', he declared. 'The experience was not only so tremendously awesome, it filled me with the conviction that there is, after all, some part of us which is indeed truly immortal.'[19] Although his heart told him he had located the place of his dream, his head told him he should check out other possibilities just to be sure. In touring different parts of Egypt, he found nothing remotely approaching the place he had located in the western Fayum as the site of his dream. Furthermore, a visit to the Cairo Museum revealed a stela precisely of the style and shape as the one at which he had seen 'himself' working and a bas-relief of a royal scribe dressed in exactly the robes he had envisaged 'himself' wearing. What further confirmation could he ask for?

As satisfying as the exercise had been, it still left Glaskin with many unanswered questions. Had this induced dream actually revealed a past life? Was it precognitive of things to come? Was it a one-off experience? How did this kind of dream relate to those that occur naturally in sleep? These and other questions had persisted since his first Christos experience in 1971. Glaskin's immediate response to them was intriguing and indicative of his response to life in general. He did not head for the nearest library or university department and ferret out research done in this field; nor did he attempt to contact the writer of the original article he had read, Jacqueline Parkhurst, to discuss the subject with her. That wouldn't happen until three years later when he was about to publish his first book on the subject. Instead, Glaskin threw himself into undergoing more 'runs' himself and inviting others to try the method. On his second run he dreamt he was an early human, such as a Cro-Magnon, who, driven to leave his own hostile environment, found acceptance in a community of strangers 'with faces like Van Gogh's *The Potato Eaters*' who possessed language, which his own people did not. Glaskin took this to be a reminder of how desperate life would be for him without language. 'Did I need any other lesson ... to send me scuttling back to my typewriter?' he asked.[20] He also pondered if it were just coincidence that shortly after this dream, the mother of van de Pas offered the two of

---

19 Ibid., 54–55.
20 Ibid., 101–102.

them the use of her house in the Netherlands to continue their work. This they did for most of 1972 but then returned to Australia to face another five years that Glaskin described as 'very near disastrous'.[21]

While his own involvement with the Christos Experience continued to fascinate him, it also propelled Glaskin to share the technique with others with almost missionary zeal. At the end of *Windows of the Mind* he wrote, 'The duty, I feel, is to make so simple a procedure and its results known as soon as possible to as many as possible, for I think one does not have to give it much thought to realise the tremendous benefit it can bestow on all mankind.'[22] Some of his first converts were friends and acquaintances, many of whom were as dubious about the procedure as Glaskin himself had been at first. One of those was his friend Paul Lee. 'It's not going to work because I don't daydream', protested Lee. But Glaskin urged him to have a go, and Lee obliged. After the experiment Lee was sold. 'I was quite staggered actually', he reported. 'It took a long time for me to float but when I eventually did, it fascinated me. It gave me a different insight into the mind and the human body.'[23]

Experiences varied widely. One young man foresaw his mother's death, another found himself engaged in a highly homoerotic exchange and a middle-aged woman discovered that her long-held phobia of birds flapping their wings had diminished. Glaskin wrote up their experiences in *Windows of the Mind*, using first names and the initial of their surname to protect their privacy. However, this procedure backfired because when the book was published in 1974 critics accused him of fabricating the reports of these subjects. As a result, in his second Christos book, *Worlds Within*, published two years later, he chose to disclose full names and a little biodata to make it transparent that the subjects were real people. Presumably Glaskin had obtained permission from each subject for this but at least one of them – the member of a prominent Perth family and son of a federal government minister – was reputedly furious when he discovered that he had been written up in this way. He later obtained a copy of the book from a friend and destroyed it, much to the displeasure of the book's owner. Another person, who found out at the eleventh hour that Glaskin wanted to use transcripts of his experiences in the book threatened legal redress if he did so.

Some of those whom Glaskin included in his books weren't the only ones who were offended by his efforts to proselytise the Christos cause. One of

---

21 Ibid., 103.
22 GMG (1974b, 205).
23 Paul Lee to JB, interview by author, 12 November 2002.

those was Jacqueline Parkhurst, who wrote that *Windows of the Mind* was 'unintentionally misleading in so far as it allowed the general public to become aware of the technique without really understanding how to use it effectively. Many people gained the impression that the technique could only be used in a rigid way and for experiences of a past-life type. Prior to the release of Glaskin's book I had only used the technique in a small research group setting, and was unaware of [Glaskin's] intention to publish it until it was virtually a *fait accompli*.'[24] Parkhurst, who only came to meet Glaskin about six months before his first book was published in 1974, was surprised he had not contacted her sooner, given that he had stumbled upon her article three years before. Glaskin maintained he had tried for some time to contact Parkhurst but having returned her article to the Haabjoerns and with his year's absence in Europe, he could not remember her name on his return. In the meantime she had remarried and changed her name, which added to his difficulty. However, Glaskin did eventually find her and had a number of conversations with both Jacqueline and her husband. In contrast to Parkhurst's above statement (written in 1982), Glaskin wrote that she was 'not only pleased but enthusiastically excited at the imminent publication of my book ... for she had been trying for a number of years to have her own findings about the Christos Experiment published ... and had met with no success.'[25] In the front of *Windows of the Mind* Glaskin acknowledged Parkhurst indirectly as the 'founder' of the Christos Experiment and when he presented her with a copy in April 1974 he inscribed in it, 'To Jacqui and Nick Parkhurst, with the author's profound appreciation of your work with the Christos Experiment. With sincere gratitude for all your help. With affection, Gerry Glaskin.'

Parkhurst's concern over Glaskin's book was well founded. When he first telephoned her, she did not know anything about him. Her initial thought was, 'Is he publishing something totally inaccurate?' When it became clear he did not have any training in psychotherapy or counselling, her concerns increased. She was only too aware that when you start working with the human mind, you don't know what you will uncover and you need certain skills to deal with it. When she suggested they talk Glaskin readily agreed. In his second book, *Worlds Within*, he devoted a chapter to the Parkhursts and invited them to contribute their thoughts on the subject. Expressing their gratitude to Glaskin for bringing the Christos Experiment to the

---

24 Parkhurst (1982, 27).
25 GMG (1976, 196–197).

attention of the public, they provided references to other books dealing with altered states of consciousness and shared several lessons they had learned from their work. They emphasised that past life remembrances are real and should be taken at face value, that some form of genetic memory is involved, that all experiences are symbolic of stages of growth or emotional/mental states in a person's life, and warned that subjects often respond in ways they think will please the practitioner.

The Parkhursts were not the only ones Glaskin consulted in the course of his work with the Christos Experience. Another was a young Scotsman, Alistair McIntosh, whose family hailed from the Isle of Lewis in the Outer Hebrides. McIntosh's father was a doctor who used hypnotherapy in a medical context, so it may not have been surprising that as an undergraduate at Aberdeen University in the early 1970s McIntosh was drawn to research in altered states of consciousness. When he came across Glaskin's books, and in turn the work of the Parkhursts, he not only contacted them but undertook his own Christos experiments on 20 subjects, most of whom were university students and staff. Unlike Glaskin, he had a more solid theoretical grounding in the field of parapsychology, as well as an academic interest in it. In common with Glaskin he didn't use the Christos Technique as a therapeutic tool in the way Jacqueline Parkhurst had done. However, he did find it to be a valuable method for inducing not only lucid dreams but, with selected subjects, out-of-body experiences and sometimes 'super-conscious' states that American psychologist Abraham Maslow termed 'peak' experiences. McIntosh wrote several articles (and an unpublished book) on the results of his work, one of which Glaskin included in a 1978 reprinted edition of *Worlds Within*.[26]

As well as describing some of the more remarkable results on his own subjects' experiences, McIntosh shed light on the steps of the induction procedure itself. He was sceptical about subjects actually dreaming past lives. 'The reason why many subjects have reincarnative type dreams during Christos experiences is due to the role played by suggestion, rather than to an unearthing of past life experience lying deep within the psyche', he wrote. Nevertheless, dreams related to a previous incarnation did feature significantly among McIntosh's subjects. He concluded that given a good subject and environment, the Christos procedure and supplementary techniques could help induce even the most highly valued altered states of consciousness.

---

26 McIntosh (1978, 227–244; 1979, 377–392).

McIntosh was grateful to Glaskin and the Parkhursts for having risked, and received, ridicule in order to make the technique known. 'It is largely through people like these, who are not afraid to state what they have discovered and think, that man is able to make any progress at all towards digging himself out of the existential ruts in which ignorance and cultural taboos hold him rigidly', he stated.[27] However, when McIntosh met Glaskin on the latter's visit to Scotland in August 1976 he was not quite so impressed with the man behind the pen. 'Frankly, I was a bit disappointed', confessed McIntosh. 'It was a pleasant enough visit but I thought he was lacking in intellectual depth. He was a novelist, after all, not a great intellectual. I was full of youthful yearnings and … rather averse at that time to Gerry's somewhat camp mannerisms and style of speech. I think, equally, he was a bit surprised to meet me. He hadn't realised, I don't think, that I was only about 20. The saving grace was my parents – my father … demonstrated medical hypnosis on Gerry to help him, if I remember rightly, with biting his fingernails!'[28] While Glaskin may not have been the inspiring figure McIntosh had imagined him to be, he did do one thing for the young Scotsman that proved highly beneficial in later years. When McIntosh attended the launching of *Worlds Within* in London in August 1976, Glaskin introduced him to his agent, Sheila Watson. Years later, Watson placed one of McIntosh's books with an excellent publisher. Conscious of how beneficial his early Christos-based publications had been, McIntosh telephoned Glaskin and thanked him for his influence and help.

McIntosh, in turn, had been of service to Glaskin. His article, 'A Commentary on the "Christos" Technique', which Glaskin appended to the 1978 paperback edition of *Worlds Within*, provided a helpful and much needed contextual framework for the uninitiated reader to understand what Glaskin had been describing in his first two books. When Glaskin published the third volume in his Christos trilogy, *A Door to Eternity*,[29] the following year, in which he explored the relationship between lucid dreaming and natural dreaming, he revealed much broader and deeper reading on the subject, so much so that some parts of the book come across as obscure and esoteric. Given the amount of repetition in the three books, it would seem in retrospect that Glaskin would have been better off waiting and publishing just one book that contained both a theoretical overview of the subject and

---

27 McIntosh (1978, 243).
28 Alistair McIntosh to JB, personal communication, 11 December 2001.
29 This book was republished as *A Door to Infinity* in 1989 in the UK and Australia, and was also distributed in the USA.

the outcome of his many experiments with the Christos Technique. While such a logical and compact approach may have appealed to scholars, it was not the Glaskin way. He was not interested in a finely tuned academic treatise on the subject but in sharing with the world something that had affected him deeply and which he believed could help others. This he did and although book sales were limited he established for himself a name in yet another field of writing. More importantly, his work with the Christos Technique had afforded him an opportunity to begin to pull together some of the divergent strands in his life and try to make sense of them. It also led him to delve further into naturally occurring dreams, a subject on which he elaborates in his last Christos book, *A Door to Eternity*.

Glaskin was convinced that the subconscious was a huge and severely neglected part of the human experience, which for the creative artist in particular was a deep well waiting to be tapped. He read widely on the subject and embraced the commonly accepted wisdom that everyone dreams three or four times a night, although few people practise recall. Determined to buck the trend, he became a firm advocate for recording one's dreams. From as early as 1975 until a couple of years before his death in 2000, Glaskin faithfully kept a dream diary in which he logged and indexed dreams that came to him during sleep. Like most people, he was not always able to recall his dreams but his rate of success was impressive. In his initial sample referred to in *A Door to Eternity*, he recalled 68 dreams out of 103 nights; over an 18-month period he recalled 400. His failures he attributed to such factors as ill-health, medications – the number and variety of which he took was staggering at times – dozing in bed, getting up too hurriedly, excessive worry and interruptions to sleep. But recording was merely the first step of a longer process of extracting the meaning from one's dreams and applying it in daily life, a practice he referred to by the Greek name of 'oneirics'. Glaskin gave himself to this task with vigour and dedication, always swift in making interpretations when others may have been more wavering. Over a period of time he noted different types of dreams and certain recurring themes. Some were of an artistic or inspirational nature, some seemed precognitive, some resurfaced old grief or unsolved problems and others appeared as possible reincarnations or tapped into his ancestral memory. He usually appeared as a younger man in his late twenties and locations often reflected his own travels and residency in places like Singapore and Amsterdam.

Of particular interest were his erotic dreams, which in one sample constituted a sixth of the total number. True to Glaskin's claim to being 'trisexual' – try anything at least twice in case you don't like it the first time – his sexual dreams were inclusive in every sense of the word. He dreamt being involved with both sexes, in active and passive roles, and with a single partner and a group. As he openly acknowledged, 'I must admit to a certain degree of libidinosity in character.'[30] And in a somewhat envious tone he added, 'I very much appreciate the greater pleasure of dream-sex, if only because it was performed with such a fit and beautiful body only 26 years of age. This is a rather pleasant compensation for "frustration" indeed.'[31] The latter comment may carry more weight than it would seem at first glance. According to his long-time partner, Leo van de Pas, Glaskin did experience a sexual dysfunction for much of his adult life, due to a surgical accident in 1971 when a physician accidentally cut nerves and muscles connected to his sexual organs. Another friend with whom Glaskin had sex as a young man reported that Glaskin attributed a hole in his penis to a war injury he had suffered. Assuming there is some truth in these claims, they may partly explain why Glaskin had such frequent and vivid erotic dreams because, as some researchers have noted, the more sexual functioning deteriorates, the more rampant sexual dream imagery is likely to become, especially with a highly sexed person. Be this as it may, Glaskin himself did not address the issue of whether his erotic dreams were compensatory or not. He acknowledged that there was a substantial body of work devoted to this subject and declined to pursue it.

Glaskin's journey of discovery into the world of dreams led him down many paths. He tackled Jung and Freud, British scholars Ann Faraday and J. W. Dunne, Arthur Koestler and Miguel de Unamuno among others. Indeed, at one point he claimed to have read hundreds of books on dreams, although in the selected bibliography at the end of *A Door to Eternity* he lists only 18, with the note, 'And many others too numerous to list'. Jacqueline Parkhurst's Open Mind publication on the Christos Technique had opened a floodgate for Glaskin. This is intriguing because he was not academically inclined and in *A Door to Eternity* he confessed, 'History has never interested me a great deal, and certainly nowhere near to the extent perhaps expected of an author. It was man's present circumstances, or his future, which had concerned me.'[32] But at this point in his life, lessons from the past were speaking loudly to his present situation and his future and he was driven to bleed the meaning from them. He was fascinated to learn

---

30 GMG (1989b, 83).
31 Ibid., 84.
32 Ibid., 20.

that dream incubation or inducement had been practised in many cultures from ancient times and that its degeneration was only marked in Western societies, primarily due to suppression by the Christian church. He likened the high degree of involvement in dreams to that experienced in watching a film, the difference being that in the former, the main protagonist is oneself with a separate alter ego. In the Christos Experience, however, the self is not only the main protagonist but the audience and the projector operator as well, able to stop the 'film' at will. This distinction is important and one of several that Glaskin made between lucid and natural dreaming. But both types of dreaming shared one thing in common – the dreamer has no choice what the dream is about. For Glaskin this undeniable fact pointed to the presence of an omniscient and omnipotent suprahuman or 'overself'.[33]

It is this insight that represented the culmination of Glaskin's work with dreams. In a chapter titled 'Credo' near the end of *A Door to Eternity*, he wrote, 'I began this project six years ago with a bemused scepticism inducing me to expose what I considered a lamentable hoax. I have ended in confrontation with my maker.'[34] Such a statement smacks of religious conversion, which in a sense this was for Glaskin. Or perhaps more precisely it was a spiritual epiphany. Disparate parts of his life came together; things made sense. There was a fusion between the external world and his internal being, as he expressed when he wrote, 'There is no other "sense" to the world than in that eternity which lies beyond it, the door to which is within each and every one of us.'[35] The religious trappings of his Roman Catholic upbringing, which he struggled to relate to his real life and found obfuscating and remote, he could now finally discard or at least reinterpret with fresh meaning and symbolism. Instead, a new spiritual path had opened up for him. 'It had taken the Christos Experience to lead me to teach myself the recall and recording of natural dreams; and it was in these ... that I saw the proof of a being of such incredible superiority compared with man ...'[36]

Having been privileged to have experienced such enlightenment, Glaskin felt compelled to share it with others, not just first hand through conducting the Christos Experiment but with his wider reading public via his novels, albeit his unpublished, later novels, in particular *Do Animals Go to Heaven?* and *At the End of It All*. However, Glaskin's fascination with psychic phenomena and the machinations of the human mind did not begin with his

---

33 Ibid., 80. The scholar he quoted was Paul Brunton.
34 Ibid., 179.
35 Ibid., 178.
36 Ibid., 176.

discovery of the Christos Technique.[37] A number of his earlier novels dabble in such matters, although more by way of fantasy than spiritual probing. *A Change of Mind* is based on the imaginative concept of a switch of psyches between two close friends and *The Man Who Didn't Count* is a Cold War drama in which Russian scientists attempt to brainwash and 'mindbend' a London-based Australian journalist. But his later works, enhanced by his discovery of and excitement about lucid dreaming as well as his research into natural dreaming, take a different approach. They explicitly incorporate the Christos Technique into the stories themselves. *Do Animals Go to Heaven?* is a story about eight-year-old Paul, who lives on a farm south of Perth and who has an intense love for his pet kangaroo. Paul has been acting very strangely, spending his days and nights outside, even sleeping with his pet in the farm shed. The story opens when Paul's grandfather calls on his wartime friend, Geoff – the narrator – to come to spend time with them to see if he can help resolve what is becoming an impossible situation. Geoff, an unmarried writer, has considerable affection for and affinity with the boy that finally allows him to break through to the child and help return a sense of normalcy to this distressed household, but not before a series of bizarre and terrifying events occur that climax in a near tragedy. It is a simple yet unusual story that displays Glaskin's penchant for delineating the harsh realities of life through the eyes of a child. It touches on the universal themes of love and hate and, as one publisher's reader noted, concerns 'the unintentional insensitivities of adults to children and vice versa [that] would strike chords for possibly millions of people of all ages'.[38]

Although it did strike chords with some publishers and film and television producers, it never made it into print or on to the screen. Not only did Glaskin wish this for the story's own sake, but he was hopeful that it might enhance the sales of his Christos books as well, which had been fairly dismal.[39] This was undoubtedly in his mind when he wrote chapter 14, which is Geoff's attempt to answer Paul's question, "Do animals go to

---

37 LvdP reported that when GMG was asked if he believed in paranormal activities he would always say that he did not disbelieve in them. In the early 1970s, along with LvdP and another relative, he consulted a clairvoyant in Perth. Her predictions for each person turned out to be amazingly accurate.

38 Reader's comment for the Fremantle Arts Centre Press (now Fremantle Press), quoted by Glaskin at the front of the manuscript.

39 Hard copies of all three books were remaindered. Delacorte described the US edition of *Windows of the Mind* as a flop, despite Glaskin's report to a French literary agent of earlier predictions by Delacorte's managing director that the book would be 'one of the publishing events of the year, if not for some time'. GMG to Cécile Verdurand, 4 January 1974.

heaven?" Geoff – who, like Glaskin, has just spent six years writing three books on the subject of lucid dreaming – does this by explaining to the boy his work with the Christos Experience. 'Dreams are the one undeniable proof of [God's] existence ... We need someone far more able than we are to make them all for us', Geoff tells Paul. 'That can only be the work of our creator. And if he goes to so much trouble to communicate with us for much time in our lives, then I believe he must also care enough for us to go on to another life after this one ... For some, this other life can be heaven, though perhaps not for others.' While Paul manages to assimilate these adult ramblings he is forced to ask, 'But what's it got to do with animals?' Geoff answers by reminding Paul that most animals dream, as indicated by their rapid eye movement and noises they make while asleep.[40] Noting that Paul was of above-average intelligence, Glaskin tries to convince us that a nine-year-old boy can comprehend Geoff's adult descriptions of lucid dreaming, the subconscious mind and Freudian symbolism. It is a stretch but Glaskin manages to bring it off, even though he lapses into a pedagogical style at points. He wrote *Do Animals Go to Heaven?* in one month – after spending four months researching the habits of kangaroos – in December 1979. He then spent the next decade trying to find a buyer for it.

But this wasn't Glaskin's first attempt to incorporate the Christos Experience into fiction. His initial effort was in *At the End of It All*, in which he devotes 135 typescript pages to it in Book Three of this 210,000-word trilogy, as a denouement to the novel. Glaskin dreamt the scenario during a Christos run that he self-induced on board the Italian liner *Achille Lauro* in 1972 en route to Europe. Immediately after the experience he made notes that he later elaborated on. For him it was the ultimate mystical experience, traversing the limitless reaches of outer space through unparalleled darkness until finally glimpsing hints of light that gather momentum into a brilliant effulgence. He likened it to the transformation of matter into spirit. But as powerful as this imagery was to Glaskin, it was too taxing on the average reader's credibility and understanding, even the most avid science fiction fan, who might have been expected to resonate with it to some degree. Alas, no publisher wanted to touch it.[41]

Another reason Glaskin's neo-mystical ending to *At the End of It All* may have deterred publishers was its curious fusion of the Christos Technique with the Australian Aboriginal concept of 'the Dreamtime'. Glaskin is

---

40 GMG (1979b, 98–107).
41 As of May 1975 nine publishers had declined it.

mixing metaphors with this one and possibly offending followers of both at the same time. The protagonist, ex-electrical goods salesman Jim Bailey, arrives at the small Western Australian town of Denham near Shark Bay, after spending time in a Benedictine monastery.[42] Here he tried to cleanse his past life of booze and illicit sex and erase the guilt associated with the suicide of his wife and children, as well as his own failed attempt at the same. Bailey is taken in by an older American woman, Mrs (Polly Olga) Turner, whose husband has recently died and who needs a man to help about the house. Turner has a domestic servant, an Aboriginal woman, Mary, who introduced her to the Christos Experience, which Turner shares with Bailey. She describes three of her own 'dream-time' experiences with him, each of them pointing to events in past lives that have significance for her present. Bailey then undergoes his own Christos Experience, during which he revisits the death of his wife and children, a previous life in which his wife and children die from the plague and a future life in which he acts as a kind of planetary Noah, taking specimens of all animal species with him on an intergalactic journey away from a disintegrating Earth. To add zest to this imaginative stew is a subplot about Mrs Turner's successful efforts to thwart an attempt by the United States navy to capture visiting dolphins for use in underwater warfare, along with theories about the origins of the universe enunciated by Turner's late husband. It is quite a mouthful for most readers to swallow in one gulp.

But the complexity and fancifulness of the story didn't seem to bother Glaskin. It was all coming to one poignant conclusion, if only the reader would bear with him through the twists and turns of his imagination and endless page turning to reach it.[43] It had to do, no less, with the meaning of life and death. Through the character of Mrs Turner, Glaskin spells out such meaning. 'I believe that trying to live one's life to the utmost is the only possible preparation for – well, what most people call death, but which we, Mr Turner and I, soon learned to look upon as *passing on*. Not *merely* "passing on" though, Mr Bailey. Not *merely* at all. For I assure you, there is

---

42 GMG himself had spent time at the Benedictine monastery at New Norcia, 132 kilometres north of Perth, where he obtained material for inclusion in this novel.

43 GMG justifies the length and diversity of *At the End of It All* in a note at the end of the manuscript. 'It was originally planned for three separate volumes, a point of view that no one else appeared to appreciate, perhaps just as well if the one volume proves not too bulky. And if this one volume should seem an incredible mixture of styles and subject, of the tragic and the comic, sex and violence, satire and sentiment, fantasy and science-fiction, then my only answer to that is: So is life. Well, isn't it?'

absolutely nothing mere about it whatsoever.[44] When you understand this, Glaskin maintained, not only life but death becomes 'thrilling'. Such an understanding evolved out of Glaskin's reading from many sources but he mentions two writers in particular who influenced him a great deal – Prior Roger Schulz of the French Catholic community of Taizé and the Spanish philosopher, poet and novelist Miguel de Unamuno (1864–1936). Drawing on the insights of these two men, Glaskin wrote in a postscript to *A Door to Eternity*:

> The purpose of death is to give us the will to live for ever, for without mortality we could not comprehend and therefore appreciate immortality. Hence, without death and its apparent conviction, or illusion of finality, immortality would be without meaning and therefore unrealisable.[45]

In a separate note Glaskin stated, 'Had I written nothing else in my life, the conclusion of this project resulting in the four-and-a-half lines on p. 181 of *A Door to Eternity* (the penultimate paragraph) would have been enough ... I should like this to be the prime quote for these books, and even my epitaph.'[46]

This was Glaskin at his most profound. In his search for meaning and purpose in his life he felt he had struck gold. It probably couldn't have come at a better time. Not only did he continue to be plagued by health problems but his career as an author was in serious jeopardy. He could use a few gems of wisdom, if not entire books of them. With the publication of the last of his Christos trilogy in 1979 two lean decades would follow until his death in 2000. Only his memoirs, *One Way to Wonderland* and *A Many-Splendoured Woman*, would offer any consolation, along with the gratification that the filming of *A Waltz through the Hills* brought him in 1988. Dreams had offered him a thread of hope and with that thread he spun a fabric that covered his entire life. Dreams had always played a role in his life in different ways. He claimed that several of his published stories came to him in dreams. *The Road to Nowhere* he said he dreamt in its entirety, although his travelling companion on his northern Australia road trip, Paul Lee, says it was based on an actual experience they had in the Kimberley. Both could be true. *Turn on the Heat* was revealed to him in a dream while he was holed up in a hotel in Lebanon. *O Loneliness* and *Flight to Landfall* sprang from a dream or an image derived from a dream. This was also the case for sections of *A*

---

44 GMG (1972a, 480).
45 GMG (1989b, 181).
46 GMG (n.d.). Author's note. LvdP private collection.

Change of Mind and *Alicia*, the latter being the part told in the short story 'The Ice Yacht'.[47] Glaskin was also intrigued with the process of aging and its concomitant 'reverism' and daydreaming, which he encountered in his maternal grandmother, Nan. What was often written off as senility, Glaskin regarded instead as a way people are 'released from their material or waking existence to return to the psychic or spiritual world which soon becomes as real to them as so-called reality, and quite rapidly, even *more* real to them.' He advocated that this should be seen as something 'constructively beautiful instead of pathetically destructive'.[48]

But these encounters with dreams were only preliminary to what was to come. It wasn't until his introduction to the Christos Experience that they took a quantum leap forward and infused his life with direction and purpose. His work with the Christos Experience also opened doors for Glaskin. He began to probe different religions and philosophies, notably Taoism and Hinduism, with the help of friends steeped in these traditions.[49] His reading became more divergent and had a distinct mystical bent, ranging from Sri Aurobindo to Gurdjieff, Idries Shah to Teilhard de Chardin. Glaskin began to find comfort and strength in the teachings of such thinkers, theologians and philosophers, just as he had in the world of dreams. It was as though he sensed himself at a transition point in his life, ready to move over to a different path, one that would lead to his own passing on from this stage of life to the next. In November 1985, answering a question from the audience after addressing The Australian Society for Psychical Research, he acknowledged this. 'My brain is not a very good one, I'm afraid, and it's reached a stage of having a good deal of contentment within imagery rather than words or definitions, which I'm beginning to find more and more unsatisfactory.'[50]

---

47 GMG (1974b, 202–203).
48 GMG (1989b, 144–145).
49 Taoism and the teachings of Lao Tse were introduced to GMG by a Chinese stockbroker friend, Mr Chua, while Hinduism came from his Scottish-Indian mentor friend, Amber Rooijakkers-Watts.
50 GMG (1985b, Questions, ii).

Chapter 13

Don't Go West, Young Man

A prophet is not without honour,
save in his own country and his own home.

Gospel of St. Matthew 13:57

In an article headed 'Author lashes out at home city' that appeared in the Perth *Sunday Times* in April 1964, that *enfant terrible* of Australian writing, Xavier Herbert, wrote, 'Perth is a mean and ugly city and its people are snobs. Its buildings and streets are colourless and the city generally has an air of poverty. WA is a place that has been made out of nothing – by a lot of people without much talent. It is inferior. Having an Englishman as a lord mayor would never happen in another Australian city.'[1] This demeaning, acerbic comment plucked at Glaskin's heartstrings and he couldn't let it pass without responding. He zipped off a reply titled 'Let's have another lash', in which he decried local reviewers for disparaging local writers so viciously that they discouraged readers from delving into the works of their native sons and daughters. Acknowledging Herbert's bitterness as understandable he wrote, 'We are in great danger … of wallowing in our inferiority fixation as a "Cinderella" state … as we have done for too long. But paucity of both circumstance and population … give reasonable excuse. Yet we are emerging from that now, determined to stand on our own firm feet.'[2] Despite

---

1   Herbert (1964, 3). Among Herbert's several novels *Poor Fellow, My Country* stands out, not least for being one of the largest, longest novels ever published in English – 1463 pages and 850,000 words.
2   GMG notes, State Library of Western Australia.

Glaskin's optimism, the self-depreciation that had dogged generations of Western Australians had not yet been vanquished. Indeed, it may well have contributed to Glaskin's own struggle to gain recognition as a writer in his time and place.

The term 'Cinderella state' was not one Glaskin conjured up. It was a familiar phrase used by Western Australians – and others – to describe their place in the grander Australian scheme of things. Even from the early days of the Swan River Colony, those who struggled to carve out a settlement on Australia's west coast found themselves at a distance, geographically and metaphorically, from the nerve centres of the rest of the country. With nationhood in 1901, the state of Western Australia, while largest in area, was one of the least populated and often found itself relegated to the lower rungs of the ladder of importance in almost any field of endeavour. Although a two-thirds majority of WA electors voted to join the federation in 1900, 33 years later a similar two-thirds voted in favour of Western Australia's secession from it. Fuelled by the devastating effects of the Depression and a sense of being cut off and ignored by the more dominant eastern states, Western Australians saw secession as the only way out. They took their grievances to the British parliament, but after nearly two years of pleading their cause, failed to achieve their goal. Other calls for secession have reared their heads since then, one as recently as 2003, although these have not garnered the serious attention of most Western Australians.[3] The economic ascendancy of Western Australia in recent decades has added a new factor into this equation.[4]

While the 'Cinderella state' syndrome might be attributed partly to sour grapes or perceived slight, there is no question that Western Australia's physical isolation from the rest of the country has significantly shaped its self-image. For many years, Western Australia found itself on the fringes of the nation's cultural life, with many national and international performers bypassing the state. In a country where sport has often been regarded as a national religion, Western Australians have also found themselves on the outside looking in. It wasn't until 1956 that the state gained full status into the national cricket competition and it took another 14 years

---

3   See 'Western Australia and Federation' (2000), a website of the State Library of Western Australia.

4   Due in large part to massive mineral and natural gas projects, fuelled heavily by the increasing demand for these commodities by China and other rapidly developing Asian countries, Western Australia's economic growth has far outstripped the rest of the nation in recent years.

before the Australian cricket establishment deemed Perth suitable to host an international 'test' match. On the football field, the story was much the same. The day after the Perth-based West Coast Eagles team won the Australian Football League's grand final for the first time in 1992, *The West Australian* newspaper ran a front-page headline, 'Now football is truly Aust-ralian'. There was a collective sigh of relief that not only had the the state of Victoria's historical stranglehold on Australian Rules Football finally been broken, but no longer could Western Australia – its football and much more – be dismissed as irrelevant or second-rate.

Even as the 'tyranny of distance' was conquered with improved comm-unications and transportation, the inferiority complex and underdog men-tality that plagued Western Australians persisted and contributed to a marked sense of regional identity. It was not until the 1960s and 1970s when that state found itself in the middle of an unprecedented mineral boom and subsequent prosperity that Western Australia began to shed its old debilitating image and replace it with a more self-affirming one. In the arts the transition seems to have taken longer but according to a 2003 book, Cinderella has now been finally farewelled.[5] During Glaskin's lifetime, however, she was still very present and trying desperately to gain entrance to the ball. Glaskin frequently referred to his home city by the commonly used phrase, 'the most isolated city in the world'. In his more disparaging moments he would qualify that with 'I live on the moon … and on the wrong side of the moon at that'.[6] He also slipped references to the Cinderella state into several of his novels. In *A Waltz through the Hills*, the narrator quotes a member of the opposition raising questions in the federal parliament about the search for the missing children. 'Or was the government just standing complacently by, as usual, and letting the "Cinderella" State fend for itself?' he asked.[7] Glaskin's allusion to the term is even more pointed and sarcastic in *No End to the Way*. Referring to the vicious, scheming sugar daddy, Rob Hamilton, Glaskin writes, 'You can't imagine for the life of you Hamilton being a company manager … even for a branch in a small state like the West. But perhaps that's it; perhaps he rose up in the scale in the usual way, and then the directors found they had to make him a branch manager; but they didn't want him in any of the eastern states, so they sent him over to the West. That sort of thing happens all the time, among the big companies.

---

5   Bolton et al (2003).
6   GMG to HS and Vincent Ruthnaswamy, 2 October 1980.
7   GMG (1961a, 218).

And so the West gets all sorts of weird-looking types being sent over – Cinderellas for the Cinderella-state, you guess.'[8]

Glaskin is making a point above and beyond the call of the narrative itself, as he frequently does in this novel. His references to 'the eastern states' and their relationship to 'the West' give the impression that not only was he describing an objective reality but one that affected him personally. That he chose to set *No End to the Way* in Perth and not some other Australian or fictional city is significant in itself. It suggests that he was trying to make a point, and one that several other commentators have noted. In his doctoral exegesis *A Personal Manifesto: Why I write homonarratives*, Sydney-based scholar Jeremy Fisher wrote, 'It was both a shock and thrill to begin reading *No End to the Way* and realise it was set in Australia, *in Perth of all places* [my emphasis], though this is not immediately obvious.' He went on to add, 'The book says a great deal about Australia in the 1960s, especially life in the West.'[9] In his anthology *Australian Gay and Lesbian Writing*, Robert Dessaix remarked on Glaskin's choice of setting for this novel. 'Many readers were astonished to learn that in Perth in the mid-1960s a gay culture existed, with bars, dinner parties, "marriages" and social networks, and that many men even in Perth during that period lived more or less satisfying lives predicated on a homosexual orientation.'[10] No doubt Glaskin relished his readers' astonishment. He liked to shock and raising the national consciousness a notch or two, even on a relatively minor issue such as this, would have greatly pleased him.

As conscious as Glaskin was about being born into a part of Australia that had long been regarded as on the periphery of the country's mainstream, he didn't feel victimised by it. Although he frequently flip-flopped in his love/hate relationship with Western Australia, he evinced a certain pride in his home state nonetheless. At one point, he considered a proposal from friends in the state government to become a kind of 'ambassador-at-large' for Western Australia in Southeast Asia. Given his knowledge and experience of the region from his time spent in Singapore, as well as his business acumen, articulate manner and striking appearance, he would have seemed ideal for the job, but it never eventuated. However, in the mid-1960s the then Western Australian Minister for Industrial Development and later premier, Sir Charles Court, appointed Glaskin to act as a part-time public relations consultant-cum-advisor in the Netherlands, when Court was trying to woo

---

8   Jackson (1965, 91).
9   Fisher (2003, 21 and 22).
10 Dessaix (1993, 13).

the Dutch to build a dry dock in Cockburn Sound south of Perth. Although Court never succeeded in this endeavour, Glaskin managed to win his confidence and build a relationship with him that he tried to make use of to gain Court's support for other causes, although to little effect.[11]

In seeking to overcome the handicap, real or imagined, of being from 'the Cinderella state', Glaskin did what many young enterprising and adventurous Western Australians have done over the years. He leapfrogged over the barriers represented by the eastern states and went straight to the international arena, where domestic Australian notions of 'us' versus 'them' mean nothing. He proved himself competent as a stockbroker and a writer and returned home with an impressive reputation in both fields, which in other circumstances might have been greeted with respect and recognition. But two factors militated against this. One was Australia's 'tall poppy syndrome', whereby those who dare to rise above the rest in any field of achievement are prime targets to be lopped down to size. Although this propensity appears to have diminished in recent years, it was thriving in Glaskin's time. He was only too aware of it and denounced it strongly, while also trying to explain it. 'Most other people regard such fortunates with respect, even reverence, and sometimes perhaps with downright awe. But the Australian all too frequently regards them as an opportunity for "having a go" and even venting his spleen. I have a theory that the Australian aggressiveness is due to the suppression of a real sense of inferiority, producing only a guilt complex for not being able to regard himself with an adequate sense of humility.'[12]

The other factor Glaskin had going against him was of his own making. His forceful personality, sharp tongue and haughty style did little to attract local support for him or his work. In spite of his claims that he received little media attention in Australia, Perth newspapers featured articles about Glaskin on numerous occasions, as well as published a number of his letters to the editor.[13] In addition, he often appeared on radio and television in Perth. He intentionally courted the local media and usually succeeded in getting their attention, although when he tried to convince the Australian Broadcasting Corporation to do a television feature about one of his disputes with *The West Australian* newspaper – even going so far as nominating the

---

11 GMG tried to get Court to intervene with the Commonwealth Censor (presumably over the banning of *No End to the Way*) and to subsidise a US/UK tour of his play, *Turn on the Heat*, neither of which Court responded favourably to.
12 GMG (1978b, 59).
13 I have come across more than 100 articles about or by GMG in Western Australian newspapers.

particular program on which he thought the interview should appear – they politely, and wisely no doubt, declined his offer. When he succeeded in luring the press to his lair, Glaskin didn't always appreciate the treatment he received from them and made no bones about telling them so. In one instance, he was annoyed that neither the morning nor evening daily papers in Perth had shown any interest in his unique achievement as a Western Australian author who had three of his novels purchased for filming, one possibly on location in the state.[14] He contacted a friend at *The Daily News* who sent a reporter to interview Glaskin but the young woman had not done her homework so Glaskin refused to talk with her. He then tried *The West Australian* but their representative didn't come up to his standards either. She asked Glaskin if he would provide notes on his books but he objected, deeming this something she should have researched herself.

Personality aside, Glaskin did suffer as an author by virtue of his Western Australian roots and residence. Other local writers acknowledged this as a disadvantage. A former friend and admirer of Glaskin, Ethel Webb Bundell, was one of those. 'He lived in WA', she said, as though that said it all. 'Everything dies in the Nullabor. All of Australia's major publishers are in the eastern states. The tyranny of distance still applies.'[15] Another Glaskin acquaintance, Perth travel writer Margot Lang, echoed similar sentiments. In the 1970s Lang had been the Western Australian representative for *The Australian Women's Weekly*. 'I soon realised they didn't want anything from Perth, except the quaint, the oddball, the quirky. I wrote a story about pioneering work being done in Perth on muscular dystrophy by a research team who used family trees and traced genetic transmission of the disease. It was important work but the magazine didn't regard it that way. If it were truly important, it would have been done in Sydney or Melbourne. It's not so much despising Western Australia. It's just not recognising it exists. It's a complete lack of consciousness or belief that anything important comes out of Western Australia.'[16]

In spite of this disadvantage that Western Australian writers of his time had to contend with, not all of them were as affected by it as Glaskin seemed to be, at least in finding national publishers willing to promote their work. Henrietta Drake-Brockman, Mary Durack, Alexandra Hasluck, Xavier Herbert, Dorothy Hewett, Elizabeth Jolley, Katharine Susannah Prichard, Randolph Stow and others were all published by major Australian

---

14 GMG to the Managing Editor of *The West Australian*, 29 January 1971.
15 Ethel Webb Bundell to JB, personal communication, 23 December 2002.
16 Margot Lang to JB, interview by author, 25 November 2002.

publishing houses on the east coast. Why did Glaskin have such trouble following in their footsteps? Several answers suggest themselves. First, he spent much of his early adult life – his most productive and successful as a writer – outside Australia so wasn't as well known as some of his contemporaries. Among the above writers Stow is the only one who did this to any significant degree, when he quit Australia and settled in England in 1966. But by this time he had already published all his popular Australian-based novels, several while he was still studying at the University of Western Australia, where he had a number of faculty members championing his cause. Second, because Glaskin had succeeded in finding a British publisher who liked his work and kept on liking it to the point of publishing 13 of his 20 books,[17] he had little incentive to make a serious effort to court Australian publishers, given the nature of the publishing industry at the time.[18] Third, when he was in Australia, and especially in the latter and least productive part of his life, his lack of an Australian agent and his propensity to become combative with publishers and others were strikes against him.

But Glaskin knew that if Western Australian writers were going to gain recognition nationally they needed to do more than rant and rave at east coast publishers. Closer to home, more had to be done to encourage local writers to devote themselves to their craft. As early as 1960 Glaskin took up the cudgel on their behalf in an article that may well have been titled 'The Impossible Plight of the Western Australian Writer', but which was a call for a literary prize for WA writers.[19] It was published in the literary journal *Westerly*, which for many years was one of the few vehicles Western Australian writers had for displaying their wares and voicing their concerns. In an article well laced with statistics, Glaskin laid out the grim prospects faced by a young writer at the time. It was a doomsday scenario and one that hasn't changed significantly over time, if a 2003 report is to be believed.[20] As well as presenting the writer's dismal economic reality,

---

17 Fourteen, if *A Bird in My Hands* is included. It was published by Herbert Jenkins, who later merged with Barrie to become Barrie and Jenkins.
18 For elaboration on the state of Australian publishing, see Chapter 11, 'Tilting at Windmills'.
19 GMG (1960b, 28–30).
20 In 1985, in an open letter to all federal and state members of parliament, the then chairman of the Australian Society of Authors, Ken Methold, wrote that 'a survey conducted by the Australia Council showed that less than 5 per cent of creative writers earn more than $6000 a year from their work.' A similar survey in 2003 found that 50 per cent of all artists in Australia still earn less than $7300 a year from their work, although writers fared better than most other types of artists. Throsby and Hollister (2003).

Glaskin bemoaned the fact that short stories were no longer published in any local publication for general consumption – *Westerly* being the exception, but directed to an academic and literary audience – thereby depriving aspiring young Western Australian writers of the opportunity to learn their craft. In light of this, his first request was for local magazines and newspapers to resume the publication of short stories, something they had done quite vigorously in earlier years and which had been responsible for launching Glaskin's own literary career. He also was scathing about the high cost of books, the competition books faced by the advent of television, the rise of cheap paperbacks and the surging demand for the 'robust' novel. Finally, he noted that there were no Western Australian publishers of world repute, which forced writers to seek publishers and rely on markets elsewhere.[21]

Glaskin's solution to this dilemma was to institute a literary prize 'firstly to keep our writers writing, and secondly, to keep them writing about WA'. According to Glaskin, the only such prize in Australia at the time was the annual Miles Franklin Award worth £500. By contrast, he boasted knowing of at least 25 such prizes in Britain. He did acknowledge the Australian Commonwealth Literary Fund but then it only made three annual awards of £1000, one of which he had received in 1956.[22] Glaskin had something similar in mind for Western Australian writers, somewhat prophetically perhaps, given that he would have to wait more than 20 years to have his vision actualised.[23] He suggested a one-time sum of £25,000 to be invested to finance in perpetuity a prize of £1000 for a book, £100 for a short story and the balance to pay judges and maintain the fund. £25,000, he argued, was not much to ask, compared with £200,000 allocated for an aquatic center, £750,000 for a cathedral or the millions spent annually on sport and race tracks. Attempting to answer critics that such a prize would only parochialise Western Australian writing, Glaskin asserted that it could be

---

21 This, arguably, has changed. Both the University of Western Australia Press and Fremantle Press (formerly Fremantle Arts Centre Press) have grown significantly in stature and output since Glaskin's time.

22 In June 1962, the Commonwealth Literary Fund's committee decided to increase fellowships to £2000 ($4000) but to award no more than two in any year. Shapcott (1988, 21).

23 Annual literary awards were inaugurated by the Western Australian Government in 1982 to honour and celebrate the literary achievements of Western Australian writers. Initially known as the WA Week Literary Awards, in 1990 they became the Western Australian Premier's Book Awards. In addition, the T. A. G. Hungerford Award (named after the Western Australian writer Tom Hungerford) was established in 1998 to encourage new writers from Western Australia who have not previously been published in book form.

awarded to a Western Australian-born writer for a book set anywhere in the world or an overseas writer who used Western Australia as a locale, or even a writer temporarily residing in the state. To those who argued that *any* good book written on Western Australia *will* find public acclaim and financial reward, Glaskin replied that, 'They are talking through a hat they have no right to wear'. Only people with private financial resources or those who were the recipients of Commonwealth grants – such as Henrietta Drake-Brockman, Alexandra Hasluck and Hal Porter[24] – could claim such success, he maintained.

Many of Glaskin's points were echoed in another article in *Westerly* seven years later by Glaskin's friend and mentor John K. Ewers.[25] In 1929, at age 25, Ewers began publishing a weekly series of articles on Australian writers in *The West Australian*. Like Glaskin, Ewers found local newspapers a great outlet for his budding literary talent. But when The West Australian Newspaper Company, which had the monopoly of the daily morning and evening newspapers, ceased to publish poems and short stories, Ewers was sadly disappointed. *The West Australian*'s conversion from a broadsheet to a tabloid newspaper was partly responsible for this, but Ewers detected more than space limitations at work. 'There is an antipathy towards writers who are not journalists, and anyone living in Perth for, say, 12 months, would be unaware of the fact that there are in this State a large number of creative writers who are highly regarded both in other Australian States and overseas', he wrote.[26] Ewers' advice to young Western Australian writers of the day was to leave. It was advice reluctantly given. 'I believe sincerely', he lamented, 'that a community has need of its writers and that every one of them who goes away is the community's loss'.[27] Glaskin was one of those who took this advice and maybe paid the price for doing so.

Ewers had one other piece of advice that Glaskin may have had more trouble endorsing. The British writer H. G. Wells was the first of many well-known foreign writers to visit the Western Australian branch of the Fellowship of Australian Writers, of which Ewers was the Foundation President. At a dinner held in Wells' honour, Wells articulated the commonly espoused opinion by overseas visitors that Australian writers must learn to be international, which Ewers and others took to mean emulating British or

---

24 Although Hal Porter was a Melbourne-based writer, he wrote *A Handful of Pennies* in Western Australia on a Commonwealth grant.
25 Ewers (1967).
26 Ibid., 71.
27 Ibid.

American writers. Ewers found this hard to swallow. 'True international-ism,' he asserted, 'is achieved by writing so brilliantly about what one knows through personal experience that it overflows national boundaries and is acceptable to discerning readers in other countries *for its own sake*.' He then added, 'One reason few contemporary Australian novelists or poets are acc-epted in this way is simply that they are not good enough, and many are not good enough because they consciously copy overseas literary fashions instead of building upon the literary traditions already developed in Australia's comparatively short national history.' But not all blame for Australia's literary woes did Ewers lay at the writers' feet. 'The real trouble is, of course, and always has been that most Australian readers seem to think a book is of no consequence unless it has received the praise of overseas critics.'[28]

Although many of Glaskin's novels did receive praise from overseas critics – some of it quite lavish – and even from a few at home, this did not translate into popular acclaim and impressive book sales in Australia. Apart from his vexatious personality, his choice of contentious subject mat-ter and his propensity to dabble in multiple genres instead of mining the one in which he seemed most proficient, Glaskin faced one other hurdle that, given today's more enlightened attitudes, is easy to dismiss as of minor consequence – his homosexuality. But those who knew him during his lifetime and knew the environment in which he operated were not so prone to downplay this aspect of his life. Bundell was one of those. 'Being homosexual, he'd probably taken a lot of flak over the years. Attitudes used to be far more intolerant than they are now. He didn't try to please anyone, win them over, soften his approach. What you saw was what you got.'[29] Writer and teacher, David Hough, was another. 'Given Gerry's sexuality, this wasn't a very sympathetic environment. In the early 1960s I was involved in the theatre and the ballet company. I was also very athletic, playing football until I was 29 and in the surf club. I moved between those two worlds. Gerry was actually living here with Leo in a gay relationship. I don't know what it would have been like for him. He would have been a big fish in a small pond.' But like Bundell, Hough intimated that Glaskin had charisma and charm that more than compensated for any problems he may have encountered due to his sexuality. 'He was very international in outlook. He was urbane, sophisticated … all the things I wanted to be. I was about 20 and he must have been in his early forties. I was a kid from the country

---

28 Ewers (1983, 195).
29 Bundell to JB, personal communication, 18 April 2001.

so here was a role model for me in more ways than one. And of course with his brilliant smile and suntan and all those sort of things. I think he made himself a bit of a martyr in a way.'[30]

'Martyr' is probably too strong a word; 'role model' might be more appropriate. It was his homosexuality, coupled with his audacity and basic writing ability, which mingled to produce what may be Glaskin's most lasting legacy to a new generation of gay men and aspiring young writers. Before the chant 'gay and proud' became a mantra of the gay liberation movement Glaskin embodied it. His writing exuded it, especially *No End to the Way*. Not all gay men of his generation appreciated Glaskin's daring writing and unapologetic affirmation of his same-sex orientation because there was still so much fear and ignorance associated with it in Australia's heavily macho culture of that time. Writer and academic Graham Willett noted this in his book *Living Out Loud: A History of Gay and Lesbian Activism in Australia*, in which he refers to *No End to the Way* as 'the strongest literary representation of this fear'.[31] Willett emphasises that the book's depiction of the dangerous world in which gay men lived in 1950s Australia was not unreasonable, given the illegality of homosexual acts between men, even in private, and the persecution and harassment they faced by police and other members of the community.

While many young gay men in today's Perth and other cities may wonder why Glaskin and his novel caused such a stir, some may marvel at what they achieved. One already has. Rob Cover was a young gay man and writer who first connected with Glaskin in 1994 when he interviewed him for an article he wrote for Perth's gay newspaper, the *Westside Observer*. Contrary to Cover's usual practice, he allowed Glaskin to read a draft of the article before it went to press. Glaskin insisted on a very careful reading, made corrections to the grammar and approved the rest. In this sense, the article was authorised but, as Cover noted, this didn't necessarily imply its truth or accuracy. 'He had a slight propensity, not so much for exaggeration as for muddling his stories, or allowing his listener/reader to get a muddled impression as he tended to jump from one to another within the same sentence.'[32] Others experienced the same habit, especially later in Glaskin's life when, perhaps under the influence of heavy medication and sheer aging, he would skip from one thing to another, his mind overflowing with the abundant experiences of a

---

30 David Hough to JB, interview by author, 19 November 2002.
31 Willett (2000, 9).
32 Rob Cover to JB, personal communication, 16 December 2002.

life 'lived to the inch'.[33] While Cover found this annoying, he did appreciate Glaskin's eagle eye as a copy editor, as he discovered when he gave him the interview transcript to review and received it back riddled with Glaskin's editorial hieroglyphics. When Cover's article appeared in the newspaper, Glaskin was ecstatic. He wrote one of his more effusive letters to the paper's editor, praising him and Cover for 'easily the best recorded and written-up interview I have ever had over some fifty years in masses of newspapers and magazines pretty-well all over the world'.[34]

Such positive, if hyperbolic, language was a welcome change from that found in many of Glaskin's letters and suggested that Glaskin regarded this interview as especially significant. Here at last he was recognised and lauded for his efforts as a writer and gay man by younger gay men in his home city. He had waited nearly 30 years for such acknowledgement and deeply appreciated it. Little wonder he could hardly restrain himself when it finally happened. Cover felt its impact too. 'Gerry used to speak of my interview with him as his "first in years and last forever" … It was certainly a coup for me, but I think also for him – there was a sort of bravado in his speech at the time that he didn't have afterwards when we became friends. I used to think this had a lot to do with a certain sense of quite justified self-importance in being interviewed at that stage of his life.'[35]

Glaskin's delight with Cover went beyond this one effort. A few days before the interview, a clairvoyant had told Glaskin he would meet his potential protégé that week. Glaskin often referred to Cover in this way and did act as a mentor to him – 'both self-appointed and gratefully accepted'[36] – for a couple of years after the interview. He took a strong interest in Cover's fiction, insisting on seeing everything before it was dispatched for publication. As Cover noted, he was not alone in being a recipient of Glaskin's attention in this way. 'He used to spend a lot of time being concerned for writers who had been "semi-forgotten" or "disrespected" in some way in Australia … I always presumed this was as much a concern about himself, and I do think in his last few years he expressed this concern in a great number of his activities, from taking his archives from the State Library to his day-to-day dealings with neighbours and doctors', said Cover.[37] Glaskin's continued interest in

---

33 'Lived life to the inch' was how his cousin David Buchanan described GMG. Buchanan to JB, interview, 12 November 2002.
34 GMG to Gavin McGuren, 2 July 1994.
35 Cover to JB, personal communication, 16 December 2002.
36 Ibid.
37 Ibid.

Cover may well have had more to it than a desire to mentor an up-and-coming young gay writer. At one point the idea of Cover writing Glaskin's biography came up. Cover's recollection was that Glaskin suggested it, but it never materialised because Cover was studying heavily, working long hours and anticipating a move to Melbourne to do a doctorate. When Cover visited Glaskin's Mosman Park apartment and saw his archives occupying an entire room from floor to ceiling, his interest in the project was dealt a fatal blow.

Cover's hunch that Glaskin's concern for forgotten writers reflected his concern about his own plight may be close to the truth. For someone who was told by doctors that he couldn't expect to live much beyond 40, then survived to nearly twice that age; for a writer who dared to challenge orthodoxy and tackle taboo subjects, yet received only modest acclaim for his efforts; for a young man from the Cinderella state who lived a vibrant life in Singapore and Amsterdam with people of all backgrounds and socio-economic strata, only to return to the mundane monoculture of suburban 1970s Australia – it must have seemed that return for effort was minimal at best. To have had such rich experiences yet found few avenues to share them with those who would follow him in life must have demoralised him. One wouldn't need to be a fanatical egoist to want to pass on the legacy of such a life to the next generation, especially to writers, gay men and those of both groups who, like Glaskin, had ties with Western Australia. Yet with passing years, deteriorating health and decline as a published writer, Glaskin must have increasingly felt the urge to do this. When Cover appeared on the scene, took pains to listen patiently to Glaskin's story and present it in his article in such an articulate and acceptable fashion, Glaskin was jubilant. Perhaps here was a link to the future he had been hoping for yet unable to find. When Cover decided that a Glaskin biography was not for him, Glaskin must have felt passed over once again. Although Cover's decision did not sour their relationship, it left a hole that Glaskin needed to fill.

If any one aspect of Glaskin's abundant life was a role model for future generations, especially for young gay men, it was probably his 32-year relationship with his partner Leo van de Pas. In many ways, Glaskin and van de Pas were an unlikely couple. Apart from basic differences of nationality and age – Glaskin was 19 years older than van de Pas – they were made of different stuff. Glaskin's sophisticated urbanity and sharp tongue contrasted starkly with van de Pas's more low-key, polite, almost unctuous style. Glaskin's love of classical music and art films did not strike the same deep chord in van de Pas, who would be happy to follow more middle-of-the-road cultural pursuits. Glaskin's encounter with the Christos Experience and his continued fascination with lucid and natural dreaming led to the realisation that he and van de Pas were different in other ways, too. Glaskin was a strongly visual person who had little trouble detaching himself from the here-and-now and immersing himself in other worlds of a different time and place, which he could describe in vivid and accurate detail. Van de Pas, being more of a kineasthetic or tactile nature, experienced considerable difficulty in making such journeys into his inner consciousness.[38]

Nevertheless, from their first meeting in Amsterdam in July 1968 their attraction and adoration for each other was strong and mutual. Like any relationship, however, this one had its ups and downs. By the late 1970s van de Pas was feeling the need to assert his financial independence. Although he had been working with Ansett Airlines of Western Australia (formerly MacRobertson Miller Airlines) since 1973, he had never owned any property. Approaching 40, he decided – along with Glaskin – to purchase a flat in Mosman Park. Eleven years after arriving in Australia, van de Pas became the owner of his own home in September 1979. Van de Pas set about buying furniture and readying the place for Glaskin and himself to move in. Meanwhile, Glaskin still owned the Warnham Heights unit in Cottesloe and continued to do so for more than another decade, during which time he used it as his office and as additional guest space. Since it was close to his favourite beach and with commanding views of the Indian Ocean, he was reluctant to give up his precious 'little box by the sea'. Perhaps he, too, wanted to keep the independence that Cottesloe afforded him.

Initially, Glaskin seemed reluctant to make the shift to Mosman Park, but a letter from van de Pas may have helped him decide. In this letter van de Pas announced his resignation as Glaskin's part-time literary and personal assistant, unless Glaskin moved from Warnham Heights to Mosman Park. Van de Pas wrote it in a caring and apologetic tone, using the word 'regret' three times, including in the Glaskinesque salutation, 'Yours most regretfully'. But at the heart of the letter was a menacing reality that had been eating away at van de Pas for some time – persistent harassment tinged with threats of violence and intimidatory tactics by several neighbours in Warnham Heights. Even when he and Glaskin obtained a restraining order on their obnoxious neighbours, van de Pas still suffered. In what he later described as 'a little bit of blackmail to make sure he would come over',[39] van de Pas threw down the gauntlet to Glaskin. Whether because he couldn't

---

38 For more detail of LvdP's 'haptic' nature, see Chapter 12, 'An Egyptian Nomarch'.
39 LvdP to JB, personal communication, 21 June 2004.

manage without his partner and carer or whether he too had become fed up with torrents of abuse, Glaskin joined van de Pas to live in his Mosman Park unit and did so until several months prior to his death in March 2000.[40]

But irritating and offensive neighbours were not the only thing that began to erode the relationship between Glaskin and van de Pas. Another factor, potentially more devastating, was the entrance into their lives of a young man, Clayton Wholley. Wholley had lost a substantial amount of money in the stock market crash and needed advice on what to do, advice Glaskin was glad to dispense. However, Glaskin's role as financial advisor began to evolve into something more. Although ostensibly not gay, Wholley exercised a certain charm that Glaskin found irresistible. Gradually Wholley wormed his way into Glaskin's life and van de Pas found himself increasingly sidelined. For a time, Glaskin allowed Wholley to live in his Cottesloe flat while Glaskin and van de Pas resided at Mosman Park, but when Wholley occupied what had been his room, van de Pas felt he had been supplanted in Glaskin's life. Matters came to a head one night when, after the three of them had been drinking at Mosman Park, Glaskin locked van de Pas out of the Cottesloe apartment. Notes became a common form of communication between the two of them. One particular note stood out from the rest. Glaskin found it in his car on a cold October morning in 1988. It began 'Is Clayton the beginning of the end?' Wholley's presence in their life features heavily in the note.[41]

According to van de Pas, this *ménage à trois* could have worked if Glaskin had handled it differently. But because it seemed that Glaskin had to keep Clayton for himself, van de Pas felt excluded. '*What* is my home?' asked a confused van de Pas. 'I don't mind Clayton fitting in with us, but after 20 years I don't like being shifted around where and when it suits Clayton.'[42] His feeling that Glaskin cast him as 'the black sheep, the nasty one' in Wholley's eyes, while setting himself up as Wholley's benefactor and advisor, added fuel to the fire. In the end Wholley engineered his own downfall. When Glaskin discovered he had been using the Cottesloe apartment for making and taking drugs, he decided Wholley had to go. When Wholley finally vacated the apartment and their lives he left behind a badly damaged relationship.

Van de Pas described himself as upset and hurt and predicted he would have a nervous breakdown. But not all the blame for this state of affairs

40 LvdP to JB, personal communication, 9 October 2001.
41 LvdP to GMG, 10 October 1988.
42 Ibid.

could be laid at Wholley's feet. Things had been spoiling between Glaskin and van de Pas for some time. That Glaskin's career as a writer seemed to be over just as van de Pas's work as a genealogist was beginning to bear fruit may have had something to do with it. In his note to Glaskin, van de Pas recounted advice that one of Glaskin's friends had given him many years ago – 'Don't be too successful with genealogy, Gerry will only resent it.' The tedium of daily life was eating away at Glaskin and van de Pas found himself accused of being largely to blame for that. As van de Pas saw it, it was his own life that was tedious. 'I might as well be death [sic]. And by the sound of it, Gerry thinks so too.'[43] Apparently, the idea had crossed Glaskin's mind. He grew concerned that van de Pas's depression and their alienation might lead to suicide, so he discussed the matter with a mutual friend of theirs who dropped in on van de Pas to see how he was doing.

The deterioration in their relationship was also fed by what van de Pas called Glaskin's incessant 'picking and bitching'. 'The bile that comes out continuously, about everything and everyone, why ever do I put up with it?' he wrote. 'What Gerry gives with one hand, he busily destroys with two.'[44] On top of this, van de Pas was deeply affected by the death of his sister, something Glaskin curtly dimissed as being beyond his control. 1989 did not bring any amelioration to their decaying relationship. The pain of their separation no doubt affected the health of both men. Their relationship continued on tenterhooks for some time, but the turning point came the morning after Glaskin's lockout of van de Pas from their Cottesloe apartment. Glaskin had woken up not knowing who he was and called van de Pas. Apparently, his heavy intake of medicinal drugs mixed with excessive alcohol had taken its toll. Said van de Pas, 'Then I realised there was something not right with Gerry and when he came to me for solace we just continued where we left off. I started to become more understanding and more accommodating of Gerry's behaviour and condition.'[45]

Around this time Glaskin had other battles to fight on different fronts. During the 1990s his disputes with the state and national libraries over which should house his papers consumed much of his energy and anger, as did his physical and legal battles with neighbours, this time at Mosman Park. During such episodes van de Pas defended Glaskin to the hilt. While he had his own spats with neighbours and dealings with the law, van de Pas

---

43 Ibid.
44 Ibid.
45 LvdP to JB, personal communication, 21 June 2004.

wrote letters to authorities on Glaskin's behalf that documented the lengthy proceedings. By the mid-1990s, the bitterness and strain between Glaskin and van de Pas that had nearly split them asunder seemed to have subsided. With the need for increasing care to deal with his ever-present health problems, Glaskin came to depend on van de Pas more and more. He despised hospitals and nursing homes and thanks to van de Pas's attention to his every need Glaskin was able to avoid such institutions for much of his last two years. The Department of Veterans' Affairs, from which Glaskin received financial and practical assistance, acknowledged van de Pas as Glaskin's carer. More importantly, Glaskin himself accepted and appreciated van de Pas in that role as well. In *Never Again* he wrote, 'He was the best full-time nurse I could possibly have.'[46]

In December 1998 Glaskin was experiencing mobility problems and was taken to hospital. Shortly before Christmas Glaskin phoned van de Pas. The hospital had offered to place Glaskin in a nursing home but neither Glaskin nor van de Pas would entertain the idea. They both wanted him home and faced with their persistence the hospital agreed. Glaskin returned home on Christmas Eve and because he was only able to move with the assistance of a walking frame he was housebound. Whenever he had to go to hospital or the dentist he had to use an ambulance. Since they lived on the upper floor of their two-storey block of flats this was a complicated manoeuvre.

As if life hadn't become difficult enough, in January 1999 the ceiling of van de Pas's living room collapsed, trapping Glaskin under a pile of rubble for half an hour. Saved from serious injury by his walking frame, Glaskin attributed the accident to the weakening of the coconut fibre straps that held the plaster ceiling in place. Although this was a commonly used technology in the early 1960s when their units were constructed, it now posed a serious hazard. Glaskin decided that his misfortune was a portent of things to come for countless other unfortunates. 'Families with babies and elderly people would be unaware of the danger which hangs over their heads', he was quoted by the local newspaper that covered the story, replete with a photograph of van de Pas and himself situated beneath the remnant of a ceiling.[47] Glaskin now had another cause to add to the many he had espoused over the years, another piece of publicity to raise his waning profile and another incident that could have been much more damaging. The destruction of their printer seemed to be the main casualty of the episode.

---

46 GMG (1978b, 70).
47 No author listed. *The Post*, 16–17 January 1999, 5.

Although it did not get off to an auspicious start, 1999 was a relatively pleasant year for Glaskin and van de Pas. Circumstance had brought them back together and helped heal the rift in their relationship that had come so close to disintegrating a decade before. In hindsight, van de Pas referred to the 12 months from December 1998 to December 1999 as a happy time for both of them.[48] Their routines were regular and relatively free from stress. They would get up in the morning, have breakfast and while Glaskin digested his many pills they would sip coffee and play a game of cards. Glaskin would then return to bed until late morning, when he would move to a sunny spot on the balcony to read the paper, listen to music and talk to the birds. At times, in a reversal of former roles, he would help van de Pas by correcting his genealogical biographies. Following lunch and a siesta, Glaskin would again retire to the balcony to take in his limited world on Murray Avenue. In the evenings, he and van de Pas would play cards or watch television, and if he could muster the energy Glaskin would edit more biographies. Days merged into each other, fewer people visited and a new kind of peace and stability entered their lives. It was a situation tailor made for the title of Glaskin's first novel, *A World of Our Own*. In retrospect van de Pas wrote, 'Sometimes at night when I locked up before going to bed, I would find the chain was still on the front door from my locking up the previous night, indicating that even I had not been out of the flat.'[49]

But such calm and predictability was not to last. Early in December 1999, Glaskin became incontinent and was again taken to hospital. He found it difficult to sleep and needed constant attention. Late one evening a most distraught Glaskin called a nurse to see if she could help him. Concerned at Glaskin's state, but against his expressed wish, she called Glaskin's doctor, Dr P. M. Connor, who was at his wit's end in dealing with his obstreperous patient. 'He was probably the most impossible patient I have ever known', wrote an exasperated Connor. 'He was constantly complaining and in the most abusive manner, to everyone about everything. He gave the nurses hell. He gave the junior medical staff hell. He never cooperated with our attempts to help him. He was constantly (daily) going to report staff (medical, nursing, administrative) to someone. He told lies. I suspect he refused to wash.'[50]

Although Connor's no-nonsense attitude may have provoked Glaskin, Connor was not alone in his reaction to this unusually difficult patient. Glaskin's file at Hollywood Private Hospital is filled with comments about

---

48 LvdP to JB, personal communication, 17 October 2001.
49 Ibid.
50 P.M. Connor to JB, 9 July 2004.

his abusive and pugnacious nature. One frustrated medical attendant wrote 'total body transplant recommended'.[51] When Connor visited Glaskin the next morning, he informed Glaskin that he was no longer prepared to act as his medical adviser and was making alternative arrangements for him. Glaskin rose to the occasion and became embroiled in what one nurse politely described as 'a clash of personalities'. Distressed by the situation, Glaskin telephoned van de Pas, who tried to intervene but to no avail. However, he did succeed in having Glaskin transferred to the care of his friend and physician, Dr Alex Cohen, Clinical Professor of Medicine at the University of Western Australia. Around the same time, the Department of Veterans' Affairs installed a 'monkey bar' above Glaskin's bed at home in anticipation of his return. However, doubt began to creep into van de Pas's mind about whether this would actually happen. Preparing for the worst, he began visiting nursing homes to see what options might be should Glaskin have to face that ugly prospect, but was not impressed by what he found.

Christmas 1999 came and went and Glaskin remained in hospital. The more he discovered about hospital life, the more van de Pas joined Glaskin in revolting against it. Inefficiencies in the system, a lack of a sense of personal responsibility and what appeared to be uncaring, even aggressive, attitudes towards patients riled him. 'Patients were treated as bags of potatoes who could not think for themselves and just should do whatever and whenever a nurse wanted them to do. It seemed as though they could not absorb what patients said.'[52] He questioned and protested about such behaviour, but to little effect. Meanwhile, Glaskin continued to call on van de Pas more than ever. He would phone van de Pas several times a day. Van de Pas became Glaskin's full-time carer, visiting him daily, often multiple times for extended periods, and tried to assist the nursing staff as much as possible. If Glaskin needed shifting from his bed to a chair or taken to the shower, van de Pas often replaced one of the two nurses needed and he was always present during meal times to help Glaskin with eating. He took Glaskin for wheelchair rides around the buildings so he could admire the paintings hanging from its walls. Some days they ventured outside to explore the hospital grounds or simply sit under Glaskin's favourite tree, a mammoth lemon-scented gum.

On 8 February 2000 Glaskin phoned van de Pas at 1 am, distressed that the nurses had disconnected his bell. Glaskin's demands had become

---

51 P.M. Connor to JB, 14 August 2004.
52 LvdP to JB, personal communication, 17 October 2001.

too much. Although he maintained that he only used the bell if he had a valid reason, when nurses came he could not always recall why he had rung. When van de Pas arrived on the scene he found Glaskin stinking of urine and one leg sticking out the side of the bed. Glaskin begged him to take him out of the hospital and book him into a hotel. Van de Pas promised he would complain to the administrator the next day but Glaskin insisted that van de Pas obtain the name and number of the second person in charge, in case the administrator wasn't available. Glaskin had pushed van de Pas's seemingly limitless patience to the edge. In the middle of the night, in the presence of another patient, van de Pas found himself at loggerheads with Glaskin and stormed out the room. Concerned that visitors should not be present at this time and disturbed by the verbal altercation he had had with Glaskin, a nurse challenged van de Pas over his actions. Another argument ensued. Van de Pas was teetering on the brink of nervous exhaustion.

The next day, after fragments of sleep and three more phone calls from Glaskin before 7 am, van de Pas was alarmed when he woke up and discovered a large purple mark on the side of his face. His doctor informed him he had cellulitis, a condition he was told that could have been fatal if it hadn't been treated immediately. His doctor advised him to stay home and away from Glaskin for a few days, advice that came as a strange kind of blessing to the beleaguered van de Pas. Another small respite, although adding to his list of daily cares, came to van de Pas in the visit of his brother and sister-in-law from New South Wales. They had come to say goodbye to Glaskin, but Glaskin's death was not something van de Pas was ready to deal with at this moment. He received only vague answers from doctors when he asked about Glaskin's prospects. The best Dr Cohen could advise was 'If Gerry didn't get pneumonia, he should have about another year to live'. Quite early in his stay in hospital, Glaskin asked van de Pas whether he thought he was dying. Shocked and not knowing what to say, van de Pas told Glaskin that he didn't think so since he was looking so well. But as much as he didn't want to admit it to himself and to others, van de Pas knew that Glaskin's question had a horrible ring of truth about it. A part of him probably wished it sooner rather than later, although such a thought he would not admit to himself, let alone to others.

If van de Pas wasn't ready for the end, other friends and family members began to anticipate it. Visits from nephews and nieces, long-time acquaintances and others became more frequent. His sister, Loris, was a regular caller but other siblings were notable by their absence. Roland came at least once but Glaskin was sleeping so he missed him. His other brother,

Llew, contending with the terminal illness of his own granddaughter and concerned about infections he may contract, never made it the hospital. One such infection had been detected in the hospital and as luck would have it Glaskin contracted it. A nurse referred to it as 'golden staph'. Within a few days, Glaskin was shifted to a private room and a sign was posted on the door advising people to wash their hands if they touched him. He had one more battle to fight, in addition to the many he was already engaged in. By the end of February it was obvious that Glaskin was being affected by the increasing doses of morphine he was being given to help alleviate pain. On 6 March van de Pas arrived to find Glaskin's hands covered in blood. He lifted the sheet and discovered everything underneath saturated in red. Shocked, he raced to the nurse's station where he was told a doctor was on his way. A catheter had been inserted through Glaskin's penis to his bladder and something had gone terribly wrong. All this time Glaskin had been dozing in a morphine-induced stupor, barely conscious.

During his three and a half months in Hollywood Private Hospital, Glaskin referred to his pending death several times. He wrote a poem about it but was reluctant to share it with others. He also made a start on yet another book, titled *O My God!* It began with an anecdote about the three-year-old Glaskin asking his father to explain such unfathomable terms as 'Father, Son and Holy Ghost', 'Mother of God', and 'Son of God'. No doubt Glaskin himself was struggling to find words to put on the inexplicable experience of dying he was undergoing. It was not an experience he welcomed and it became a race against the clock. In his autobiographical notes, *Now & Then*, which he wrote in hospital, he said, 'I am 75, knocking 76. I want to live till 2001 to see the new millennium. 2000 just won't do. I'll be 77 and a bit. My three score years and ten. A 10 per cent bonus, my mother having Italian ancestry, a "mancia" – a little extra than a tip. Will I make it? Right now it hardly looks like it. But I'll try.' In another entry he added, 'Considering the hereafter. I'm quite prepared to go, but nowhere near ready to leave. Still far too much to be done.'[53] Glaskin never relinquished his attacking spirit. During the last months of his life, Dr Cohen had told him that he could not have surgery because of the danger posed to him by general anaesthetics. When other surgeons differed Glaskin took up the challenge. 'Yet the surgeons seem so determined', he commented. 'But so am I. Wonder who'll win?' Apparently he did, with help from Cohen. All surgery was delayed except that involving his left sinus, which was badly infected,

---

53 GMG (1999).

causing phlegm to pour ceaselessly from the roof of his mouth, especially after eating or drinking. This required about three weeks' treatment before surgery. However, Cohen described the delay as fortuitous and Glaskin agreed, since it gave him time to collate all the details so they could both decide whether to proceed or not. Wrote Glaskin, 'We agree that I'd rather be a live paraplegic than dead from a transient ischaemic attack turned final under a general anaesthetic.'[54]

The same day he wrote this entry was van de Pas's 57th birthday. That morning he was greeted by an expansive view of a glorious, cloudless dawn. 'I wonder, my Father-Creator, how many more I shall be privileged to see?' he asked himself. As a birthday present for van de Pas he bought two boxes of chocolates and toffees. These gifts were an attempt to express the respect and affection he felt for his partner. Perhaps he captured this more succinctly in the simple sentence, 'No words compare with the sight of a precious face.' When he had arrived home for the last time in October 1999 he wrote, 'What would home be, without Leo – to meet me and great me? How I pray we will be given much longer.'[55]

Another six months would be all he would get. But how important those months would be for both of them. Glaskin encouraged van de Pas to share with him thoughts and words held back until now. He acknowledged and regretted he had never shown more affection towards van de Pas over their three decades together. Since the early blissful days of their relationship, Glaskin had displayed a kind of dual personality in his relationship with van de Pas, one in public and another in private. Van de Pas had weathered this treatment gracefully, even if at some cost to his own well-being. 'Gerry was two different people – one with and one without an audience. With an audience he needed to sparkle and be the centre of attention. He would be challenging and outrageous. He was dreadful like that. When you got used to it, you put up with it. Although he made it clear to certain people that I was special for him, in public he was very aloof and I was just one of the crowd.'[56]

In spite of Glaskin's lack of physical affection and public acknowledgement of their relationship, mentally and emotionally the two men developed an intensely close bond. 'We got to a point of being able to finish each other's sentences', said van de Pas. But more than sentences, they shared work and interests that gave their life a common focus for many years. 'Gerry and I

---

54 Ibid.
55 Ibid.
56 LvdP to JB, personal communication, 21 June 2004.

would be days on end together in the flat without anybody else coming and neither of us were the least bored', he recollected. Moreover, with the benefit of hindsight, van de Pas came to realise that he depended on Glaskin as much as Glaskin did on him. 'I don't know what I would have done in my life if I hadn't met Gerry', he said. 'I put up a barrier around me which not many people were capable of breaking through. Gerry was one of the few who succeeded. I needed somebody like him to relate to.'[57]

On 10 March Dr Cohen announced to van de Pas that gangrene had set in but assured him that they would not amputate Glaskin's leg. Van de Pas again asked Cohen how much time he thought Glaskin now had, but Cohen could give no indication. Knowing there was nothing else he could do at the hospital, van de Pas returned home. About 2.30 am he awoke with the urge to go to the hospital. Since it seemed a strange time to visit he didn't go. Half an hour later the phone rang. The hospital told him to come but not to hurry. When he arrived at the hospital 10 minutes later he was told Glaskin had died five minutes earlier. Van de Pas was an emotional zero. He felt robbed, especially after his months and years of caring for his partner. He had so much wanted to be with him when he died. He stayed until 4.15 am and then went home.

Glaskin's funeral was held at Perth's Karrakatta Cemetery on 15 March 2000. A sizable crowd attended and several local newspapers ran stories about the man and his work. With help from his friend Rae Kean, van de Pas wrote the eulogy and organised the service. Kean also hosted a reception afterwards at her home. Family members were present but did not play a major role in either event. A year later, accompanied by two friends, van de Pas took Glaskin's ashes to the groyne at Cottesloe and scattered them in the Indian Ocean. Once more, Glaskin was reunited with the one place he loved more than any in the world, the place that gave him his bearings and his identity – his beautiful beach.

---

57 Ibid.

Chapter 14

Home, if not Hosed

So much life crammed into one body.

David Buchanan

On 22 January 2003 a remarkable exhibition opened at the Western Australian Museum in Perth. Titled 'The Gay Museum', it was billed as 'an exhibition exploring the history of lesbian and gay presence in Western Australia' and ran for two months. It was curated by a young artist, Jo Darbyshire, and was funded by Curtin University, the Museum itself and private sponsors. According to Darbyshire, 'the theme of the exhibition was chosen not only to redress the lack of representation of lesbian and gay people in West Australian history, but also because few objects had been collected by the Museum to illustrate homosexuality or to acknowledge this cultural group'.[1] The Museum decided to support the project after the Western Australian parliament passed gay law reform in February 2002, which outlawed discrimination on the basis of a person's sexual orientation and finally brought the state into line with the rest of the country in this respect, after more than three decades and four unsuccessful attempts to do so. At last, Cinderella had made it to the ball. The time had come for her to make her debut and to do it in grand style. Gay men and lesbians in Western Australia could shed their phobias and self-censorship and unapologetically take their rightful place in the annals of the state's history. No longer would some in Perth's gay community feel it necessary to destroy evidence of their

---

1   Darbyshire (2003, inside cover page).

existence, as happened when the local chapter of CAMP, Inc. closed in the late 1980s. On the contrary, it was now time to put some of that evidence on public display.

One such item on display was a blow-up of the bright yellow paperback cover of Glaskin's *No End to the Way*, with a black-and-white photograph of Glaskin and his cat and a quotation from a local gay man, in which he explained how this book had changed the course of his life.[2] It wasn't as eye-catching as some of the exhibits, nor did it have the historical intrigue of others, but it was there. Glaskin had been granted recognition by the gay community in the city and state in which he grew up and which helped mould the person he was. Like Rob Cover's article in the local gay newspaper, it honoured the role he had played as a gay man in his time and place and as one who dared go much further than most – albeit wearing the mask of a writer – to declare the way it was for so many young men, himself included. Had Glaskin been around to witness this public acknowledgement of his life and work he would no doubt have had some pithy one-liner to herald its announcement. And if his reputation for enlivening such occasions had been noted, he may have even been asked to make an opening speech.

But it wasn't only as a gay man and author of a groundbreaking gay novel that Glaskin would want to be remembered. There was, as his cousin, David Buchanan, so succinctly put it, 'so much life crammed into one body'.[3] While clear about many of Glaskin's shortcomings, Buchanan was also effusive in his praise of the man. 'He was what made the sun shine and wine taste nice … and complained of nearly everything in a way that made you want him to complain again, just so you could see him being him.' And turning Glaskin's passion for his 'beach at the end of the world' into a metaphor, Buchanan added, 'he surfed almost every wave he could and all this and more with that smile, implacable, riding life to the shore'.[4] Buchanan might well have added, 'and with a neck brace to boot'.

Another person who was able to see through his flaws and acknowledge Glaskin's strengths was Patsy Millett, daughter of Dame Mary Durack, who came to know the man through his many visits to her mother. Beyond his filmstar good looks and presence that 'was certain to lend glamour to any occasion', Millett admired Glaskin's thoughtfulness and kindness to friends, especially in times of crisis. When Millett's younger sister, Julie, died at 26, Glaskin appeared at once and with calm efficiency took charge of contacting

---

2   See Chapter 9, 'Love', for further details.
3   David Buchanan to LvdP, personal communication, 4 April 2001.
4   Ibid.

family members, answering phone calls and doing whatever was necessary. Dame Mary was extremely grateful and wondered how she would have managed without him. Said Millett, 'He was chivalrous and sympathetic, and ever willing to go forth and slay a dragon for someone if required.' While not dismissing his shortcomings, these were overridden for her by his genuine goodness. Like others who acknowledged Glaskin's propensity to express anger, suspicion and dislike, Millett claimed that he showed no malice. Moreover, despite many travails Glaskin managed to extract much more enjoyment from life than most people. Above all, she remembered him for 'just being gorgeous and brightening our dull lives'.[5]

However much one might find fault with Glaskin's writing or displeasure with aspects of his personality, it is impossible not to acknowledge a life-seeking exuberance in this man that defied the odds and was at times extraordinary. From the nine-year old boy who accepted a dare to crouch under a railway line as a train screeched overhead to his last days in hospital when he engaged in ferocious verbal battles with the medical staff, he refused to live life on the periphery. Only the centre was good enough for him, and often a painful, explosive centre at that. His litany of health problems with their heavy and overlapping dosages of medications; his wartime, surfing and automobile accidents; and his attempted suicide were all part of Glaskin's charmed life, as he was fond of referring to it. His other favourite saying – try anything at least twice in case you don't like it the first time – underscores his unrestrained zest for living.

Glaskin was essentially an experiential person, not an intellectual one. He approached life by jumping in feet first and recording the experience afterwards. His opinions on a variety of subjects were quickly formed and boldly stated, not measured and refined. Whether he may have developed more reflective capacities and a more restrained style had he gone to university or pursued the academic study of literature we will never know. Although he had dexterity with words, both spoken and written, they were basically tools to project, transfer and extrapolate experiences from his own life to others. He relied heavily on people, places and events he knew first hand as grist for his books and used them well to tell a good tale. In this sense, his agent David Bolt was accurate in identifying Glaskin's writing strength being primarily that of a first-rate storyteller.

When all is said and done, maybe that is the way Glaskin deserves to be remembered. But he was not just a good storyteller. He was one who dared

---

5   Patsy Millett to JB, 28 May 2001.

to push the boundaries of acceptability in his choice of subject matter and who experimented with diverse forms and styles of writing to communicate with his readers. To many Australians living in the 1950s, '60s and even '70s, he opened windows on their shuttered lives and provoked them to think twice about issues they had either ignored or simply not had to deal with. To many readers outside Australia, especially in Europe, he offered a glimpse of people and places they had never encountered firsthand. In so doing, his books, like his life, formed a bridge between vastly different worlds. When Glaskin died in 2000 he left a legacy worthy of scrutiny and respect. Surely the time has come to give him his due.

The Major Published Works of
Gerald Marcus Glaskin

Listed in chronological order from publication of first edition.

A World of Our Own	1955	London: James Barrie
Terug in het Paradijs	1955	The Hague: Succes (Nederlandse Boekenclub)
Vår Egen Verden	1957	Edie, Norway: Essforlagene
A World of Our Own	1961	London: Panther Books
Les Héros sans Emploi	1967	Paris: Editions Fleuve Noir
A Minor Portrait	1957	London: Barrie Books
The Mistress	1959	London: Ace Books
The Mistress	1965	London: Panther Books
A Minor Portrait	1974	Bath, UK: Cedric Chivers
A Change of Mind	1959	London: Barrie Books
A Change of Mind	1960	London: Ace Books
A Change of Mind	1960	New York: Doubleday
Billets de Logements	1961	Paris: Denoël
De Man die een Ander Werd	1963	Amsterdam: Elsevier
A Change of Mind	1968	London: Mayflower
A Lion in the Sun	1960	London: Barrie & Rockliff
Een Leeuw in de Zon	1960	The Hague: Succes (Nederlandse Boekenclub)
A Lion in the Sun	1963	London: Panther Books
A Lion in the Sun	1964	London: Four Square Books
Un Lion au Soleil	1964	Paris: Editions Fleuve Noir
En Løven I Solen	1965	Copenhagen: Bogforlaget Union
Ett Lejon I Solen	1967	Halsingborg, Sweden: Bra Böcker
A Lion in the Sun	1967	London: Barrie & Rockliff
A Lion in the Sun	1994	Singapore: Graham Brash
The Beach of Passionate Love	1961	London: Barrie & Rockliff
Der Rätselhafte Mister Lee	1962	Wiesbaden, Germany: F.A. Brockhaus

The Beach of Passionate Love	1964	London: Four Square Books
La Plage du Bout du Monde	1964	Paris: Editions Fleuve Noir
Der Rätselhafte Mister Lee	1964	Berlin: Deutsche Buch-Gemeinschaft
Het Strand van de Hartstochtelijke Liefde	1969	The Hague: Succes (Nederlandse Boekenclub)
The Beach of Passionate Love	1995	Singapore: Graham Brash
A Waltz through the Hills	1961	London: Barrie & Rockliff
Vlucht naar de Kust	1961	Haarlem: De Spaarnestad (Kennemer)
Vlucht naar de Kust	1961	The Hague: Succes (Nederlandse Boekenclub)
Fuite vers la Côte	1961	Brussels: Société d'Editions Periodiques
Im Busch verlor sich ihre Spur	1963	Berlin: Universitas Verlag
A Waltz through the Hills	1964	London: Heinemann (New Windmill Classic)
Dans Gjennom Tarer	1966	Oslo: Fredhøis Vorlag
Upplysninger kan Lamnas till …	1967	Halsingborg, Sweden: Bra Böcker
A Waltz through the Hills	1970	Harmondsworth, UK: Penguin (Peacock)
A Waltz through the Hills	1988	Perth: Barron Films (television movie)
The Land That Sleeps	1961	New York: Doubleday
The Land That Sleeps	1962	London: Barrie & Rockliff
A Small Selection	1962	London: Barrie & Rockliff
Sometimes It Wasn't So Nice	1968	London: Panther Books
Flight to Landfall	1963	London: Barrie & Rockliff
Flight to Landfall	1965	London: Panther Books
Vlucht naar Landfall	1965	The Hague: Succes (Nederlandse Boekenclub)
Vlucht naar Landfall	1965	Amsterdam: Elsevier
Oubliés de Dieu	1965	Paris: Presses de la Cité
Flight to Landfall	1974	Bath, UK: Cedric Chivers
Flight to Landfall	1977–	New York: Readers Digest Condensed books (14 editions, 10 languages)
Flight to Landfall	1980	New York: St. Martin's Press

O Love, O Loneliness	1964	London: Barrie & Rockliff
O Love, O Loneliness	1966	London: Panther Books
No End to the Way	1965	London: Barrie & Rockliff
No End to the Way	1967	London: Corgi Books
No End to the Way	1985	London: Corgi Books
The Man Who Didn't Count	1965	London: Barrie & Rockliff
The Man Who Didn't Count	1965	New York: Delacorte
Achtervolging in Amsterdam	1967	Amsterdam: Elsevier
Achtervolging in Amsterdam	1967	The Hague: Succes (Nederlandse Boekenclub)
El Hombre con quien no Contaban	1967	Barcelona: Molino
The Man Who Didn't Count	1968	London: Mayflower Books (Maypole)
The Road to Nowhere	1967	London: Barrie & Rockliff
A Bird in My Hands	1967	London: Herbert Jenkins
Windows of the Mind	1974	London: Wildwood House
Windows of the Mind	1974	New York: Delacorte
Windows of the Mind	1975	London: Arrow Books
Windows of the Mind	1986	Dorset, UK: Prism Press
Windows of the Mind	1987	Lindfield, Australia: Unity Press
Two Women	1975	Sydney: Ure Smith
Turn on the Heat [play]		
The Eaves of Night [memoir]		
Worlds Within	1976	London: Wildwood House
Worlds Within	1978	London: Arrow Books
A Door to Eternity	1979	London: Wildwood House
A Door to Infinity	1989	Dorset, UK: Prism Press
A Door to Infinity	1989	Lindfield, Australia: Unity Press
One Way to Wonderland	1984	Fremantle: Fremantle Arts Centre Press
A Many-Splendoured Woman	1995	Singapore: Graham Brash

Notes

1. *A Lion in the Sun* and *A Waltz through the Hills* were also published in Russian, but Glaskin received no income from either of them. He did, however, have the pleasure of seeing them showcased in Russian bookstores on a visit to Moscow in 1966. I have not been able to obtain publication details or sales figures for these books.

2. In addition to the above, a list of Glaskin's published short stories and poems can be found on the website www.geraldglaskin.com.

References

Unless stated otherwise, communications between two parties are letters. Telephone calls, e-mails and face-to-face exchanges are listed as 'personal communications'.

Archival Sources

Glaskin's manuscripts and personal papers reside in a number of institutions and private collections. The following have been of great assistance in my research:

AustLit website: www.austlit.edu.au

Gay and Lesbian Archives of Western Australia, Special Collections, Murdoch University, Perth, Australia.

Howard Gottlieb Archival Research Center, Boston University, Boston, USA.

National Library of Australia, Canberra, ACT, Australia.

Special Collections, Australian Defence Force Academy Library, Canberra, ACT, Australia. (Material in this collection has since been transferred to Murdoch University.)

State Library of Western Australia (formerly the Library and Information Service of Western Australia), including the J.S. Battye Library of West Australian History.

West Australian Newspapers Limited Library.

Publications

A. A. 1955. Review of *A World of Our Own. The Sun Herald.* 14 August: 79.

Anonymous. 1927. 'Special Meeting' under 'Carnamah Notes', *The Midlands Advertiser.* 19 August.

Anonymous. 1955. Review of *A World of Our Own. Times Literary Supplement.* 24 June: 345.

Anonymous. 1959. 'Lovely place'. *The West Australian.* 25 November.

Anonymous. 1960. 'Author's story is one of success'. *The West Australian.* 24 September.

Anonymous. 1961a. 'Decision reserved'. *The Daily News.* 4 January.

Anonymous. 1961b. 'Author denies nude walk on beach'. *The West Australian.* 5 January: 16.

Anonymous. 1961c. 'Author goes on bond in beach case'. *The West Australian.* 10 January: 14.

Anonymous. 1962. Review of *The Land That Sleeps. Times Literary Supplement.* 10 August: 589.

Anonymous. 1974. 'Perth cited as top homosexual city'. *The West Australian*. 7 June.

Anonymous. 1980. Review of *Flight to Landfall*. *Kirkus Reviews*. 1 October.

Anonymous. 1998. 'Youth suicide rate alarms'. *The West Australian*. 11 August.

Anonymous. 1999. 'Author escapes ceiling collapse'. *The Post*. January 16–17: 5.

Anonymous. 2001. 'Mosman writer dies at 77'. *The Subiaco Post*. [Internet]. Released 19 May. Accessed 24 May. Formerly available at www.postnewspapers.com.au/20000318/news/016.shtml.

Bannon, Barbara. 1980. Review of *Flight to Landfall*. *Publishers Weekly* 218. 22 August: 43.

Barnard, Marjorie. 1957. *Meanjin*. 16 (2) Winter: 205–206.

Benchley, Peter. 1974. *Jaws*. New York: Doubleday.

Bibby, Peter, ed. 1982. *The Ultimate Honesty: Recollections of John K. Ewers, 1904–1978: With Some Glimpses Culled from His Works*. Perth: Fellowship of Australian Writers, W.A. Branch.

Blainey, Geoffrey. 1966. *The Tyranny of Distance: How Distance Shaped Australia's History*. Melbourne: Sun Books.

Bolton, Geoffrey; Rossiter, Richard; Ryan, Jan, eds. 2003. *Farewell Cinderella: Creating Arts and Identity in Western Australia*. Crawley, Western Australia: University of Western Australia Press.

Bromby, Robin. 1989. 'Brought to book: The ills of Australian publishing'. *The Weekend Australian*. July 15–16: 25.

Buddee, Paul. 1982. In *The Ultimate Honesty: Recollections of John K. Ewers, 1904–1978: With Some Glimpses Culled from His Works*, edited by Bibby, Peter. Perth: Fellowship of Australian Writers, W.A. Branch: 25.

Burbidge, John. 1995. 'As happy as a pig in poo: Australia's young man of letters'. *Word From Down Under* 3 (12): 3.

Campbell, Michael. 1967. *Lord Dismiss Us*. Chicago and London: The University of Chicago Press.

Christian, Tina Chad. 1968. *Baby Love*. London: Jonathan Cape.

Commonwealth Literary Fund. 1967. 'Fellowships'. In *Helping Literature in Australia: The Work of the Commonwealth Literary Fund 1908–1966*. Canberra: Commonwealth Government Printer. Reproduced in Shapcott, Thomas. 1988. *The Literature Board: A Brief History*. St. Lucia, Queensland: The University of Queensland Press.

Conon, Leo. *1957*. *The Iconoclast*. Ghaziabad, India: Bharti.

Courtenay, Bryce. 1989. *The Power of One*. Richmond, Victoria: William Heinemann.

Cover, Rob. 1994a. Interview with Gerald Glaskin [typescript]. 16 May.

Cover, Rob. 1994b. 'Gerald Glaskin: No End to the Way'. *Westside Observer* (July).

Darbyshire, Jo. 2003. 'The Gay Museum: A History of Lesbian and Gay Presence in Western Australia'. Exhibition brochure, Western Australian Museum, Perth, 22 January to 16 March.

Davis, Geoffrey. 2002. 'Proudly Gay: One Man's Life'. Personal essay.

De Vreeda, Mischa. 1999. *Maak Me Mooi* [Make Me Beautiful]. Breda, the Netherlands: De Geus.

Dessaix, Robert, ed. 1993. *Australian Gay and Lesbian Writing: An Anthology*. Melbourne: Oxford University Press.

Drake-Brockman, Henrietta. 1946. *Blue North*. Sydney: Frank Johnson.

Drake-Brockman, Henrietta. 1957. *The Wicked and the Fair.* Sydney: Angus & Robertson.

Drake-Brockman, Henrietta. 1963. *Voyage to Disaster.* Sydney: Angus & Robertson.

Durack, Mary. 1968. 'A literature of loneliness'. *Westerly* 4 (December): 64–66.

Durack, Mary. 1982. In *The Ultimate Honesty: Recollections of John K. Ewers, 1904–1978: With Some Glimpses Culled from His Works,* edited by Bibby, Peter. Perth: Fellowship of Australian Writers, W.A. Branch: 21.

Eijsbouts, Geert. 1986. *Edgar Vos: De Man, De Mode.* Haarlem, the Netherlands: J.H. Gottmer.

Ewers, John K. 1955a. 'Six Perth people in new suits'. *The West Australian.* 3 September.

Ewers, John K. 1955b. 'The making of a novel'. *The West Australian.* 17 September.

Ewers, John K. 1967. 'A writer in Perth'. *Westerly* 4 (December): 63–71.

Ewers, John K. 1983. *Long Enough for a Joke: An Autobiography.* Fremantle: Fremantle Arts Centre Press.

Fiction Editor. 1956. 'Perth is the setting for our new serial'. *The Countryman.* 26 April: 8.

Fisher, Jeremy. 2003. *A personal manifesto: Why I write homonarratives.* Doctor of Creative Arts exegesis. Sydney: University of Technology, Faculty of Humanities and Social Sciences.

Forster, E. M. 1971. *Maurice.* Terminal note. New York: Signet Books.

Glaskin, Gerald. 1949a. Personal diary (January–February). Typed copy. Leo van de Pas private collection.

Glaskin, Gerald. 1949b. Glaskin papers. J. S. Battye Library of West Australian History.

Glaskin, Gerald. 1955. *A World of Our Own.* London: James Barrie.

Glaskin, Gerald. 1956. 'Birthright'. *The Countryman.* 23 August.

Glaskin, Gerald. 1957. *A Minor Portrait.* London: James Barrie Books.

Glaskin, Gerald. 1959. *A Change of Mind.* London: Barrie & Rockliff.

Glaskin, Gerald. 1960a. *A Lion in the Sun.* London: Barrie & Rockliff.

Glaskin, Gerald. 1960b. 'A literary prize for WA writers'. *Westerly* 2: 28–30.

Glaskin, Gerald. 1961a. *A Waltz through the Hills.* London: Barrie & Rockliff.

Glaskin, Gerald. 1961b. *The Beach of Passionate Love.* London: Barrie & Rockliff.

Glaskin, Gerald. 1961c. *The Land That Sleeps.* New York: Doubleday & Company.

Glaskin, Gerald. 1962a. 'Creative art Down Under: The apathy and attitudes against art in Australia'. *Eastern Horizon* 2 (1) January: 41–46.

Glaskin, Gerald. 1962b. *A Small Selection.* London: Barrie & Rockliff.

Glaskin, Gerald. 1963. *Flight to Landfall.* London: Barrie & Rockliff.

Glaskin, Gerald. 1964. *O Love, O Loneliness.* London: Barrie & Rockliff.

Glaskin, Gerald. 1965a. *The Man Who Didn't Count.* London: Barrie & Rockliff.

Glaskin, Gerald. 1965b. *No End to the Way.* London: Barrie & Rockliff. [Written under the pseudonym of Neville Jackson.]

Glaskin, Gerald. 1967a. *A Bird in My Hands.* London: Herbert Jenkins.

Glaskin, Gerald. 1967b. *The Road to Nowhere.* London: Barrie & Rockliff.

Glaskin, Gerald. 1968a. 'The asking price'. *Westerly* 1 (March): 5–11.

Glaskin, Gerald. 1968b. *Sometimes It Wasn't So Nice.* London: Panther.

Glaskin, Gerald. 1972a. *At the End of It All.* Unpublished novel.

Glaskin, Gerald. 1972b. *Any Girl Will Do: Stories Not in a Literary Style.* Unpublished short stories.

Glaskin, Gerald. 1974a. 'Why I write'. *The Australian Author* (Summer): 20–23.

Glaskin, Gerald. 1974b. *Windows of the Mind: The Christos Experience*. London: Wildwood House.

Glaskin, Gerald. 1975. *Two Women*. Sydney: Ure Smith.

Glaskin, Gerald. 1976. *Worlds Within: Probing the Christos Experience*. London: Wildwood House.

Glaskin, Gerald. 1977. 'A little verse: Five poems by G.M. Glaskin'. *Artlook* 3 (9) November: 28–29.

Glaskin, Gerald. 1978a. 'So long, Keith Ewers'. *The Australian Author* 10 (3) Winter: 30–33.

Glaskin, Gerald. 1978b. *Never Again*. Unpublished memoir.

Glaskin, Gerald. 1978c. *Worlds Within*. London: Arrow Books.

Glaskin, Gerald. 1979a. *A Door to Eternity*. London: Wildwood House.

Glaskin, Gerald. 1979b. *Do Animals Go to Heaven?* Unpublished novel.

Glaskin, Gerald. 1980. *Flight to Landfall*. New York: St. Martin's Press.

Glaskin, Gerald. 1984. *One Way to Wonderland*. Fremantle: Fremantle Arts Centre Press.

Glaskin, Gerald. 1985a. Address to a family gathering at the launch of Leo van de Pas's first book on Glaskin's ancestors. 6 May.

Glaskin, Gerald. 1985b. Address to the Australian Society for Psychical Research, 20 November; Perth, Western Australia.

Glaskin, Gerald. 1989a. *The Way You Went*. Unpublished memoir.

Glaskin, Gerald. 1989b. *A Door to Infinity*. Bridport, Dorset, UK: Prism Press and Lindfield, NSW: Unity Press.

Glaskin, Gerald. 1994. 'A vogue long gone'. Unpublished article.

Glaskin, Gerald. 1994–1999. 'My literary mama: A memoir of Henrietta Drake-Brockman'. Unpublished essay.

Glaskin, Gerald. 1995a. *A Many-Splendoured Woman: A Memoir of Han Suyin*. Singapore: Graham Brash.

Glaskin, Gerald. 1995b. 'Shells: Some notes on Professor Zhang Taijin'. Unpublished essay.

Glaskin, Gerald. 1996. Personal diary. Leo van de Pas private collection.

Glaskin, Gerald. 1998. *Autobiographical notes*. Unpublished.

Glaskin, Gerald. 1999. *Now & then: Autobiographical notes* (written in Hollywood Private Hospital, 26–29 October). Unpublished.

Graham, John. 1962. 'A riot of local color'. Review of *The Land That Sleeps*. *The Bulletin*. 1 September.

Greene, Graham. 1971. *A Sort of Life*. London: The Bodley Head.

Greenwood, Irene. 1982. In *The Ultimate Honesty*: *Recollections of John K. Ewers, 1904-1978*: *With Some Glimpses Culled from His Works*, edited by Bibby, Peter. Perth: Fellowship of Australian Writers, W.A. Branch: 46.

Harris, Max. 1965. 'The most unkindest cut'. *The Australian*. 29 March.

Herbert, Xavier. 1964. 'Author lashes out at home city'. *The Sunday Times (Perth)*. 26 April.

Hetherington, John. 1961a. 'Australian writers in profile. G.M. Glaskin: A Perth man makes his name abroad'. *The West Australian.* 14 January.

Hetherington, John. 1961b. 'Australian writers in profile. G. M. Glaskin: More satisfaction in writing than finance'. *The Age.* 14 January.

Hetherington, John. 1963. 'G. M. Glaskin: A world of his own'. *Forty-Two Faces*. London: Angus and Robertson.

Hewett, Dorothy. 1967. 'Turn on the Heat ... O Love, O Loneliness ...' interview with Gerald Glaskin, Eileen Colocott and Frank Baden-Powell. *Westerly* 2: 34–37.

H. H. & J. L. 1956. *Southerly* 17 (4): 231.

Holt, Patricia. 1978. 'Publishing in Australia'. *Publishers Weekly*. 4 September: 42–83.

Hughes, Robert. 1987. *The Fatal Shore*. New York: Alfred A. Knopf, Inc.

Hungerford, Tom. 1964. 'Blurb off the mark'. Review of *Flight to Landfall*. *The West Australian*. 21 January.

Jackson, Neville [pseudonym for G. M. Glaskin]. 1965. *No End to the Way*. London: Barrie & Rockliff.

John Curtin Prime Ministerial Library. 2002. '"School Days" in war and peace, rationing and rebuilding: 1940s life in Cottesloe, Western Australia'. [Internet]. Accessed 19 May 2004. Available from: www.john.curtin.edu.au/1940s/school/.

Juno Beach Centre: Canada in WWII. 2003. 'British Commonwealth Air Training Plan'. [Internet]. Canadian museum and cultural centre, Courseulles-sur-Mer, France. Accessed 17 May 2004. Available from: www.junobeach.org/e/4/can-tac-air-bca-e.htm.

King, Ivan. 1996a. Interview with Johan Knollema [recording]. 19 June.

King, Ivan. 1996b. Interview with Ray Mills [recording]. 11 December.

Kornweibel, A. H. 1961. 'Englishman finds fate in Malaya'. *The West Australian*. n.d.

Kotai-Ewers, Trisha. 1996. Interview with Gerald Glaskin. Perth: Fellowship of Australian Writers, W.A. Branch.

Lang, Jean. 1982. In *The Ultimate Honesty: Recollections of John K. Ewers, 1904–1978: With Some Glimpses Culled from His Works*, edited by Bibby, Peter. Perth: Fellowship of Australian Writers, W.A. Branch: 57.

Lang, Margot. 1989. 'An author looks back on life and literature'. *The West Australian*. 15 July, Big Weekend: 7.

Lauder, Stuart. 1962. *Winger's Landfall*. London: Eyre & Spottiswoode.

Lenton, Cindy. 1988. 'Long wait for classic'. *The Daily News*. 30 September: 41.

Lowerfeld, Viktor; Brittain, W. Lambert. 1947. *Creative and Mental Growth*. New York: Macmillan.

Mackenzie, Kenneth [Seaforth]. 1937. *The Young Desire It*. London: Jonathan Cape.

MacQueen, Val, 1994. 'Interesting only for the riots'. *New Straits Times*. 24 December: 29.

Marchant, Sylvia. 1995. 'Lightweight tales of Aussies abroad'. *The Canberra Times*. 27 May: C12.

Marquis Who's Who LLC. 1976. *Who's Who in the World 1976–1977*. New Providence, New Jersey: Marquis Who's Who LLC.

Martin, David. 1965. 'Victim of incest'. Review of *O Love, O Loneliness*. *The Bulletin*. 23 January: 40.

Martin, Jean. 2002. 'The great Canadian air battle: The British Commonwealth Air Training Plan and RCAF fatalities during the Second World War'. *Canadian Military Journal* (Spring): 65–69.

Masters, Robert; Houston, Jean. 1966. *The Varieties of Psychedelic Experience*. New York: Holt, Rinehart & Winston.

McCullough, Colleen. 1977. *The Thorn Birds*. New York: Harper & Row.

McIntosh, Alistair I. 1978. 'A commentary on the "Christos" technique'. In *Worlds Within*. Glaskin, G M. London: Arrow Books: 227–244.

McIntosh, Alistair, 1979. 'The "Christos" procedure: a novel ASC induction technique'. *Psychoenergetic Systems* 3: 377–392.

Moran, Rod. 1990. 'He went to die in the Swan ...' *The West Australian*. 16 June.

N. B. 1964. Review of *Flight to Landfall*. *Books and Bookmen* (January): 32.

Nabokov, Vladimir. 1958. *Lolita*. New York: Putnam.

O'Sullivan, Dan. 1961. '"Rogues and vagabonds" (and Mother Grundy) on our beaches'. *The West Australian*. 14 January.

Parkhurst, Jacqueline. 1982. The Christos Technique for inducing imagery and symbol formation. Glen Forrest, Western Australia: Self-published.

Princess Michael of Kent, HRH. 1993. *Cupid and the King: Five Royal Paramours*. London: Fontana.

Rose, John. 1961. *At the Cross*. London: Andre Deutsch Limited.

Schmidt, Mareya and Peter. 1996. 'Jackson, Neville (1923–)'. [Internet]. OzLit@ Vicnet Database of Australian Writers. Accessed 20 October 2000. Formerly available from http://home.vicnet.net.au/~ozlit.

Seymour, Alan. 1962. *The One Day of the Year*. London: Angus & Robertson.

Shapcott, Thomas. 1988. *The Literature Board: A Brief History*. St. Lucia, Queensland: The University of Queensland Press.

Smith, Eleanor. 1953. *Isle of Girls*. Perth: Paterson Brokensha.

Spurling, Hilary. 1990. *Paul Scott: A Life*. Hutchinson: London.

State Library of Western Australia. 2000. 'Western Australia and Federation: Issues 2001, Echoes of secession.' [Internet]. Accessed 25 February 2005. Available from: www.slwa.wa.gov.au/federation.

Stow, Randolph. 1958. *To the Islands*. London: MacDonald & Co.

Swygard, William. 1971. 'Multi-level awareness'. *Borderlands* 27 (2) March-April.

Tanglin Club. 2012. 'Club History'. [Internet]. Accessed 27 May 2012. Available from: www.tanglinclub.org.sg/the-club/club-history.html.

Throsby, David; Hollister, Virginia. 2003. *Don't give up your day job: An economic study of professional artists in Australia.* Surry Hills, New South Wales: Australia Council. Accessed 7 July 2004. Available online from http://hdl.handle.net/1959.14/128217.

Van de Pas, Leo. 1994. *Glaskin: Introduction to Ancestors of Gerald Marcus Glaskin.* Mosman Park, Western Australia: Self-published.

Van de Pas, Leo. 1999. *Royal Ancestor: Eight Generations of Descendants of Kind Edward III.* Mosman Park, Western Australia: Self-published.

Van de Pas, Leo. 2010. *Portraits of Ancestors.* Canberra: Self-published.

Van de Pas, Leo. n.d. *Quartiers Report.* Unpublished list of GMG's ancestors.

Van Langenberg, Carolyn. 2002. 'The compelling Mr Glaskin: A work in progress'. Pubtalk Series, Murdoch University. 5 September.

Van Niekerk, Michael. 1993. 'Heady brew of history recalled'. *The West Australian*. 26 January.

Watkins, Griffith. 1967. *The Pleasure Bird*. London: Longmans.

Willett, Graham. 1999. Interview with Gerald Glaskin [typescript]. 13 January.

Willett, Graham. 2000. *Living Out Loud: A History of Gay and Lesbian Activism in Australia*. Sydney: Allen & Unwin.

Winton, Tim. 1993. *Land's Edge*. Sydney: Macmillan.

Yee, Robin. 1996. *8 Days* (magazine), January. Singapore: MediaCorp Publishing. *8 Days* (Singapore)   130

Index